KU-009-298

# Moral Leadership in Action

This book belongs to the
University of Strathclyde

Hunter Centre for
Entrepreneurship

Please do not remove from these
premises

Date......10/06/04

NEW HORIZONS IN LEADERSHIP

**Series Editor: Joanne B. Ciulla**
Professor and Coston Family Chair in Leadership and Ethics,
Jepson School of Leadership Studies, University of Richmond, USA
and UNESCO Chair in Leadership Studies,
United Nations International Leadership Academy

This important series is designed to make a significant contribution to the development of leadership studies. This field has expanded dramatically in recent years and the series provides an invaluable forum for the publication of high quality works of scholarship and shows the diversity of leadership issues and practices around the world.

The main emphasis of the series is on the development and application of new and original ideas in leadership studies. It pays particular attention to leadership in business, economics and public policy and incorporates the wide range of disciplines which are now part of the field. Global in its approach, it includes some of the best theoretical and empirical work with contributions to fundamental principles, rigorous evaluations of existing concepts and competing theories, historical surveys and future visions.

# Moral Leadership in Action

Building and Sustaining Moral Competence in European Organizations

*Edited by*

Heidi von Weltzien Hoivik

*Norwegian School of Management*

NEW HORIZONS IN LEADERSHIP

**Edward Elgar**

Cheltenham, UK • Northampton, MA, USA

© Heidi von Weltzien Hoivik 2002

All rights reserved. No part of this publication may be reproduced, stored in a retrieval system or transmitted in any form or by any means, electronic, mechanical or photocopying, recording, or otherwise without the prior permission of the publisher.

Published by
Edward Elgar Publishing Limited
Glensanda House
Montpellier Parade
Cheltenham
Glos GL50 1UA
UK

Edward Elgar Publishing, Inc.
136 West Street
Suite 202
Northampton
Massachusetts 01060
USA

A catalogue record for this book
is available from the British Library

**Library of Congress Cataloguing in Publication Data**
Moral leadership in action : building and sustaining moral competence in European organizations / edited by Heidi von Weltzien Hoivik.
    p. cm. – (New horizons in leadership series)
    1. Business ethics–Europe. 2. Leadership–Moral and ethical aspects–Europe.
   3. Industrial management–Moral and ethical aspects–Europe. I. Høivik, Heidi von Weltzien. II. Series.

HF5387.5.E85 M67 2002
658.4'092–dc21                                          2001053219

ISBN 1 84064 746 9

Printed and bound in Great Britain by MPG Books Ltd, Bodmin, Cornwall

# Contents

# List of boxes

# List of figures

# List of tables

# List of contributors

**Manuel Becerra** holds a Ph.D. from the University of Maryland (Smith). He is Professor of Strategy and International Management at the Instituto de Empresa (Madrid, Spain) and also collaborates with the Norwegian School of Management-BI (Sandvika, Norway). His current areas of research include trust and social capital, multinational corporation management and competition in network-based industries.

**Luk Bouckaert** is Professor of Philosophy of Science, Ethics and Business Ethics at the Katholieke Universiteit of Leuven (Belgium). In 1987 he started the Centre for Economics and Ethics in the university's Faculty of Economics and is Director of the Dutch postgraduate programme in Applied Ethics. His recent publications are in the field of social responsibility in profit and non-profit organizations.

**Tomas Brytting** is Associate Professor at the Stockholm School of Economics. He is working as a lecturer, author and consultant and is presently involved in establishing ETHOS – Academy for Ethics at Work (www.ethos.nu) which is an independent foundation set up to promote the human person in all aspects of economic affairs.

**Stephan Cludts** holds degrees in business administration and philosophy. He is currently research assistant at the Centre for Economics and Ethics of the Catholic University of Leuven. His research focuses on employee participation, social capital and normative stakeholder theory.

**Jane Collier** is an economist who now teaches business ethics. She is Senior Research Associate and Director of the M.Phil. Programme in the Judge Institute of Management Studies, University of Cambridge, UK. She edits the journal *Business Ethics: A European Review*.

**Rafael Esteban** is a Roman Catholic priest, a White Father who spent ten years in Ghana teaching theology. He currently lectures on the social and economic context of mission to degree students in the Missionary Institute London, a college affiliated to Middlesex University.

**Wojciech W. Gasparski** is Professor and Director of the joint Business Ethics Centre at the Institute of Philosophy and Sociology, Polish Academy of Sciences and the L. Kozminski Academy of Entrepreneurship and Management, Warsaw, Poland. He teaches business ethics and organizational design. He also serves as Distinguished Consulting Faculty Member at the Saybrook Institute, San Francisco. He is a member of the Academy of Management and of the International Society for Business, Economics and Ethics (ISBEE). He serves as Chairman of the Programme Council of the Polish Association for Business Ethics (EBEN-Poland).

**Sonja Grabner-Kräuter** is Associate Professor of Marketing and International Management at the University of Klagenfurt, Austria. Before starting her university career she worked in the export finance department of an Austrian bank for several years. She teaches in the areas of international marketing and export finance. Her research focus is on business ethics, international marketing and risk management in international business.

**Eamonn J. Harrigan** received a Bachelor of Commerce and a teaching qualification from the National University of Ireland Galway, and an MBA from University College Dublin. He is a member of the Chartered Institute of Management Accountants, and of the Irish Institute of Corporate Treasurers. Currently, he is Financial Controller of Patrick J. Tobin & Co. Ltd. (Consulting Engineers) and Tobin Environmental Services. He has a wide range of experience in industry and public service, including Ericsson, The Dublin Institute for Advanced Studies and Hitachi.

**Heidi von Weltzien Hoivik** (Ph.D.), Associate Professor, was until August 1993 elected Executive Vice-President and Dean of Faculty of the Norwegian School of Management. She is a Fellow of the Harvard Executive Programme of the Institute of Education Management, and a Fellow of the Harvard Programme on International Negotiations. From 1995 to 1997 she was Visiting Professor of Business and Values in Society at Tel Aviv International School of Management, Israel. In 1994/5 she launched the Centre for Ethics and Leadership at the Norwegian School of Management. She is currently President of the European Business Ethics Network (EBEN), an executive member of the Caux Round Table, Transparency International Norway and the International Society for Business, Ethics and Economics (ISBEE).

**Lars Huemer** is Associate Professor of Strategic Management at the Norwegian School of Management. Dr Huemer's research interests centre around the concepts of trust and learning in organizations. His book on trust in business relations received an award in 1999 from the Swedish National Association of Master of Science in Business. He is currently Programme Director of the Master of Science Programme in Strategy and International Business. His recent publications focus on strategic change and organizational learning in the construction industry.

**Gerhard Hütter** is employed by Siemens AG, Corporate Communications – Public Relations, Munich, Germany. Since 1997 he has been responsible for the development of Corporate Principles of Siemens.

**Iordanis Kavathatzopoulos** is Associate Professor of Psychology at Uppsala University and does research in the areas of business ethics and information technology ethics. His research focuses mainly on education and development of ethical competence and on construction of test methods for the assessment of ethical skills.

**Christen Andreas Larsen** is Director of Health Administration of the Bergen Eidsvåg/Salhus municipality. His experiences as a manager date back to 1979. According to him ethics and life quality issues are even more important today when faced with major changes in public sector management.

**Henry-Benoît Loosdregt** is Director, Global Ethics and Values Programme, Suez Lyonnaise des Eaux, Paris, France. Henry-Benoît Loosdregt supervises the implementation of the 'Global Ethics and Values Programme' at the business ethics office of Suez Lyonnaise des Eaux, a French–Belgian multinational corporation dealing world-wide with energy, water, waste and communication services.

He has been with Suez Lyonnaise des Eaux since 1966, serving in various capacities in the water division, being involved in engineering, purchasing, corporate PR, lobbying and business ethics. He is now at the parent company head office, in charge of its ethics programme. He graduated in mechanical engineering and economics.

**J. Félix Lozano** is a philosophy graduate of the Valencia University, with further studies at Erlangen-Nürnberg University (Germany). He was Assistant Director of the ETNOR Foundation during the last four years. Currently, he is lecturer of Business and Professional Ethics at Valencia Polytechnic University. He has developed business ethics programmes for relevant Spanish organizations like ACERALIA S.A. and ONCE. His major research interests: philosophy foundations for business and the process of applications with special considerations of codes of ethics.

**Eleanor O'Higgins** is on the faculty of the Graduate Business School of University College Dublin, where her teaching, research and publications specialize in the areas of strategic management and business ethics. She is on the editorial board of *Business Ethics: A European Review* and *Irish Business and Administrative Research*. Dr O'Higgins is a regular contributor to the *Monday Management* column of the *Irish Times*. Her extensive experience in industry and commerce through various activities includes consulting work, her previous managerial career, and as a director of IDA Ireland, the agency for attracting and developing inward investment to Ireland. Dr O'Higgins is a director of the Well Woman Centre, a group of outpatient clinics and a member of the Enterprise Ireland Mentor Programme, where she is a mentor to Irish SMEs.

**Verner C. Petersen** (M.Sc.) 1973, D.Phil. 1985 is Research Professor at the Department of Organization and Management, the Aarhus School of Business. He is the founder and leader of CREDO (Centre for Research in Ethics and Decision-making in Organisations). Verner C. Petersen has published books and articles on ethics and value-based leadership. He teaches ethics and value-based leadership at the Aarhus School of Business and other leadership programmes and has been responsible for projects on value-based leadership in private businesses and the introduction of value-based leadership in various public institutions. Currently, he is engaged in writing extensively about the importance of self-organization and spirited leadership in value-based organizations.

**Gregory M. Reichberg** is Senior Researcher at the International Peace Research Institute, Oslo. He obtained his Ph.D in Philosophy (Emory University, 1990). He first worked as Assistant Professor at The Catholic University of America (1990–95) and then as Associate Professor at Fordham University (1995–99). Current research interests: ethics in war and peace, medieval political philosophy and international business ethics. He has published articles in, *inter alia*, *International Philosophical Quarterly*, *Journal of Peace Research* and *American Catholic Philosophical Quarterly*.

**Eberhard Schnebel** is currently employed in the corporate planning division of Württembergische Hypothekenbank AG, Germany and is working as a scientist and consultant in the field of business ethics. From 1992 to 1995 he was a member of the Interdisciplinary Ethics Institute of the University of Munich and obtained the doctoral degree (Ph.D.) in May 1995 with the topic: 'Description of specific references between economy and ethical behaviour in management'.

**Fred Seidel** is Professor of Comparative Analysis of Business and Management Systems at E.M. Lyon, France. He graduated in history and political sciences from the University of Marburg (Germany). He has business experience in advertising and management development. His present focus in consulting and training deals with how to implement business ethics in international companies, intercultural training of members of the board for a Franco-German company and business-to-business marketing.

**Bernhard Seitz** has studied Business Administration in Saarbrücken, Paris, Oxford and Berlin. After having worked for two years consulting in Eastern Germany and three years in industry for a Swiss-Franco floatglass manufacturer, he began working in 1998 on his Ph.D. with Prof. Dr. Karl Homann, then Chair of Business and Corporate Ethics at the business faculty of the Katholische Universität Eichstätt. His research focuses on the relationship between business and society. The objective of his work is to formulate from a business, profit-maximisation point of view a strategy that leads to more productive interactions with social players. Additional areas of his research are globalization, corporate governance and tertiary education.

**Alejo José G. Sison**, Ph.D., teaches Ethics and Human Resource Management at the University of Navarre, where he is also Executive Secretary of the Institute for Enterprise and Humanism. Previously, he worked at IESE (Barcelona) and at the University of Asia and the Pacific (Manila). In 1997, he was appointed Fulbright Senior Research Fellow and Visiting Scholar at Harvard University. His research deals with the issues at the juncture of ethics, economics and politics.

**Laura J. Spence** lectures and researches in business ethics at the School of Business and Management, Brunel University, UK, where she is active in the Centre for Organisational and Professional Ethics (COPE). Her Ph.D. was on Comparative European Business Ethics. Other research interests include ethics in relation to small firms, human resource management and communication. She has published articles in the *Journal of Business Ethics*, *Business Ethics: A European Review* and *Business Ethics Quarterly*. Laura has been a member of the European Business Ethics Network Executive Committee since 1998.

# 1. Moral leadership in action: building and sustaining moral competence in European organizations

## Heidi von Weltzien Hoivik

The theme of this book is moral leadership in action as it manifests itself implicitly and explicitly in business organizations. We understand leadership as interplay among people at all levels within organizations and also within the economic system by which people are bound together through particular forms of interaction. The focus on moral leadership is meant to signal that there is a need for leaders at all levels to understand the importance of building and sustaining moral competence in organization.

The original idea was to collect samples of European thinking and approaches under the sole heading: 'Building and developing moral competence in organizations'. As it turned out, the results were somehow different than anticipated. The first research workshop with this title was organized by the European Business Ethics Network (EBEN) in Oslo in June 1999. It led to the realization that various approaches in thinking and in doing research when dealing with this topic would have to be recognized. We quickly learned that we could indeed benefit from not pursuing only one single goal, but rather learn how to tolerate and even applaud our unique diversity in Europe. The chapters in this book mirror the plurality of approaches we find in the theoretical writings of academics in different European countries. The additional business cases collected from six different countries show how leaders actually have adopted and integrated working with values in their own organizations, that is how they put moral leadership into action. The selected papers are not meant to be representative of each country. However, particular economic and cultural traditions are apparent in both thinking and managing moral leadership and thus have been given special attention by the authors.

We hope that by presenting this emerging multicultural pattern of Europe we actually can contribute to a better and more knowledgeable understanding of how European leaders pursue their goals.

At the Second World Congress of the International Society of Business, Economics and Ethics in July 2000 in Sao Paulo, Brazil the chapters included in this volume were presented for discussion to an international audience. Again the underlying reasons for the existence of particular diversities in Europe was confirmed during the discussions in the workshop and group sessions. While some authors viewed moral competence from a micro-level, others felt that questions about moral competence and leadership had to be dealt with from both the macro- and mezo-level. This is more than a personal choice of the participating authors. Their choice of perspectives clearly reflected the long-standing traditions of thinking about ethics and morality in business and/or economics typical for different parts of Europe.

The contributions from Germany, Belgium and Spain stand out for their particular desire for grounding ethical principals philosophically and for a distinct understanding of ethics in economics. For that reason two chapters were selected as an introduction to what we may call the 'European scene'. Both authors have attempted to highlight what can be seen as apparent differences. Laura Spence in Chapter 2 'Is Europe distinctive from America? An overview of business ethics in Europe' rightly points out that 'business ethics' in Europe originally benefited from what in the early 1970s and 1980s had been developed in the USA. However, when considering the most recent developments she sees changes emerging in Europe that may allow us to clarify a possible European distinction in the future.

In Chapter 3 entitled '"Unternehmensethik" in German-speaking countries' Sonja Grabner-Kräuter attempts to fill a gap among non-German-speaking readers by highlighting how the German research tradition has led to a relatively clear distinction between '"Wirtschaftsethik"– ethics of the economic system' and '"Unternehmensethik" – ethics of the business firm'. This distinction is critical to understanding how German leaders of organizations understand their own role when deciding on what their 'leadership guidelines' (Unternehmensleitfäden) are to be and how these should be implemented.

In Chapter 4 Bernhard Seitz clearly follows in the tradition of Karl Homan's economic theory of morals by redefining the idea of corporate citizenship in terms of economics. In this case moral leadership in organizations also requires managers to actively participate in the building and development of political and social frameworks. He claims that only this interaction will make good corporate citizenship possible and profitable. Again, the interrelationship between the mezo- and the macro-level is emphasized and forms the basis of thinking about moral competence.

The organizational or mezo-level is the main focus of Chapter 5 by Stephan Cludts from Belgium. He attempts to argue for the need of balancing legitimate claims of multiple stakeholders and diverse stakeholder interests. After challenging the stakeholder agency theory, the social contract theory and the theory of stakeholders as investors he tries to prove that a more adequate normative core of the stakeholder theory should be based on the internal goal of an organization which is common to all stakeholders. This can be achieved by building relationships of co-operation and participation, by introducing democratic principles of governance and by showing respect for the stakeholders. In spite of the theoretical tone of the article, the practical implication of a change of attitude of leaders in organizations is evident.

Exactly how the level of trust within boss-subordinate dyads is closely associated to different aspects of their relationship effectiveness is the theme of Chapter 6 by Manuel Becerra and Lars Huemer of Spain and Norway, respectively. The results from a survey of 392 MBA students with work experience show that the perception of moral character, that is high integrity of their leaders, is likely to improve the effectiveness of their relationship. This is related to the level of communication openness, emotional conflict, decision-making speed and willingness to take risks.

Luk Bouckaert in Chapter 7 'Reducing opportunism through moral commitment' with the subtitle 'The ethical paradox of management' raises some intriguing questions about whether it is possible to reduce opportunism through moral commitment in organizations. Is ethics indeed an efficient way to overcome or at least temper the negative effect of opportunism? If the answer were yes, it would be rational to introduce ethics management in the firm. But is this rational approach to business ethics convincing and effective? Undoubtedly it sounds good, but does it work? Sometimes it does, but often it does not. And if it works why does it work? His chapter reflects a novel way of thinking about the role of moral leadership.

Chapter 8 focuses on 'Rational discourse as a foundation for ethical codes' as a means to institutionalize ethics in organizations. J. Félix Lozano from Spain claims that ethical codes as an instrument need to be legitimized through a better understanding of their rational ethical foundation. He claims that this can best be done by using Adela Cortina's interpretation of discourse ethics as erudite, 'postconventional', and based on individual autonomy. Having understood this legitimate grounding, it will be easier for leaders to develop a process of institutionalizing business ethics in organizations.

Chapters 9–11 of this book come from three different countries, Norway, France and Poland. All three 'case studies' have in common that they describe how a particular organization invested time and effort in a process of shaping, formulating and designing moral values or codes of ethics in their respective organizations.

In Chapter 9 Heidi von Weltzien Hoivik's intent was to describe how leaders of a Norwegian public sector organization implicitly applied non-normative approaches when accessing and articulating moral values as part of a strategic change process. She wants to offer a very different 'case story of business ethics' which does not follow the traditional thinking from applied ethics where concepts and techniques are taken from normative theories and then used to assess or prescribe ethical behaviour in organizations. Instead, she describes how a participative dialogue process was initiated in order to create a congruence between aspired moral values and values in action. A public sector organization offered a unique opportunity to study how public organizations are applying more and more private sector thinking when developing their visions and values as a foundation of a more customer/client-oriented service strategy. At the end her observations are being analysed with regard to existing relevant theories in applied business ethics.

Fred Seidel and Henri Benoit Loosdregt in Chapter 10 present and discuss how a rapidly expanding French firm decided to shape a rather unique ethical approach for its business while fully acknowledging its highly decentralized structure, which also included different professions and trades.

Wojciech W. Gasparski in Chapter 11 offers a first glance at how the Association of Volkswagen and Audi Dealers in Poland decided to develop its own code of ethics as part of an ethical programme in spite of or because of the ongoing transformation of the economic system.

The next group of 'cases' again is very different. Rafael Esteban and Jane Collier in Chapter 12 have called their contribution 'Building moral competence in organizations: the difficult transition from hierarchical control to participative leadership'. Behind this intriguing title is an attempt to show that the transition from hierarchy to autonomy in change organizations is fraught with conceptual, practical and moral difficulties. According to the authors much has been written about the conceptual and practical aspects of the change process, but little emphasis has been placed on the moral aspects. Their chapter tries to correct that. Esteban and Collier argue that the key to successful adaptability in the face of change is given by the degree of organizational 'moral competence'. Using metaphorical understandings drawn from complexity theory and chaos theory they characterize the 'transition' problems experienced by organizations moving into situations of organizational renewal in terms of necessary shifts in moral values. Their argument is supported by two case studies based on their experience of facilitating organizational change in one particular not-for-profit sector. Their experience of the first facilitation gave them an understanding of the pitfalls of transition from hierarchy to participative processes. The organization in this case failed to make the transition because it was not capable of letting go of the old ways of valuing and relating. The second facilitation (in another organization) happened eight months later, and here their experience was entirely different.

The other presentation of an actual event is in Chapter 13 by Alejo José G. Sison from Spain. His chapter relates how and why the BSCH–Champalimaud strategic alliance failed, due to the intervention of the Portuguese government, basically. Although the European Commission claimed victory for the outcome, its jurisdiction over such economic transactions was, in theory and in practice, far from being definitively upheld. Rather than argue in favour or against 'national champions' and 'unified markets', Sison intends to provide a basis for the discussion of the ethical issues involved. He is concerned particularly with the duplicity of actors who pay lip-service to free markets, liberalization, deregulation, privatization and fair competition, while implementing measures that are protectionist, interventionist, discriminatory, populist and perhaps, even corrupt. He asks the following questions: How could privatization be compatible with government ownership of golden shares, or free markets with state subsidies and tax-breaks? How could deregulation coexist with increased bureaucracy, or the pursuit of economic efficiency with the protection of social, cultural and political interests? Could sovereignty be shared by a nation state, the repository of our loyalties and sentiments, and an economic union, that appeals to a cosmopolitan sense of justice and reason?

Also in Chapter 14, Eleanor O' Higgins and Eamonn Harrigan from Ireland report on exploratory research to ascertain why some business actively undertake 'green' measures, and the benefits from doing so. The results of their study show that the main reasons for undertaking active environmental management were legislation, competition and catering to multinational customers or to parent companies. They found that the efforts made were generally considered successful, notably due to cost reduction from better housekeeping and to an improved reputation. The results indicate which levers are more effective first in encouraging the uptake of 'green' business practices, and then those benefits experienced that support the maintenance of that practice, for enlightened self-interest. The 'stick' is more effective than the 'carrot' to attract companies to initiate environmentally friendly practices in the first place, but positive economic, reputational and other outcomes reinforce the continuation of the practices.

In contrast to the above chapter and case studies written by academics, the following chapters have been written by people working in organizations. Gerhard Hütter in Chapter 15 presents 'Corporate ethics and social responsibility: principles and practice at Siemens AG. He first provides a short background to Siemens' mission and its traditional company culture. The following section contains an overview of the different types of norms that, in the company's view, apply to the organization. The particular German traditional thinking about a company's role is expressed when he states that as a corporate citizen Siemens has a right and a duty to participate actively and constructively in shaping its social and political environment. He illustrates in his chapter how ethical norms at Siemens are implemented in daily life by giving examples from Siemens' activities. The key message is summed up in the following statement: In Siemens' company culture, personal development based on rational insight and understanding is valued above formal controls and routine.

Cultural differences of value-based management is the theme of Chapter 16 by Eberhard Schnebel. His study compares two approaches to values-driven, or rather ethical, management in corporations by means of examples from General Electric Company (USA) and Siemens AG (Germany). According to him their differing ideas about the role of ethics and values in management are apparent in the different ways they deal with management guidelines. The prevailing characters of their values-based management systems are expressed in the different kinds of interactions that arise through the application of a more informal or a more instrumental approach. The study also deals with the related cultural differences in the application of values-driven management in multicultural organizations and leads to a deeper understanding of the particular meaning of ethics in economic organizations.

Christen Andreas Larsen's narrative in Chapter 17 is a unique contribution to our case studies. The author is the Director for Health Administration of the municipality he describes. He presents in his own words a project on ethics that was carried out under his leadership within Bergen's municipalities in 1994–1996. Individuals participating in the project were employed in the Health and Social Welfare department. This chapter describes the entire process and how the different groups participated in its completion. The goal of the project was to 'create an awareness of attitudes and ethics through education and process-oriented action'. He concluded by saying, 'If I had not had the authority that I have as Director for Health Administration in Bergen, it would have been difficult to get the acceptance necessary to carry out a project of this magnitude. That is to say that one has freedom within the given boundaries, but also has the responsibility that goes along with this'. It is not often that we can access the thinking of leaders as directly as in this case description.

Tomas Brytting, living and working in Sweden, in Chapter 18 brings us back to our common theme: moral competence. He argues for the need of a hermeneutic definition of moral competence, which involves the whole person in his or her struggle to live meaningfully in a complex but real world. According to him, the interpretations we make of the reality we meet – the theories that we use – must be able to convey relevant aspects of it. He suggests that if we talk of moral (interpretive) competence, our interpretations must be able to convey the *moral* aspects of reality, that is the ways in which the common good is challenged. In order to explore this theoretically derived conception of moral competence, especially its social and collective aspects, he interviewed loss adjusters working with people inflicted by severe physical damages. The rationale behind that choice was that he was looking for practitioners working in situations where the well-being of others was challenged, and where the practitioner's behaviour had a major impact.

The final chapters in this book contain another challenge to our theme. Verner C. Petersen from Denmark invites us in Chapter 19 entitled 'Habits of the heart: arguments for an ineffable, social grammar' to reread and reflect on Michael Kohlhaas, written by Heinrich von Kleist in 1808. The purpose is to show the tacit and ineffable foundation of our values, attitudes and behaviour. He then discusses what consequences tacit knowledge and ineffable ethics might have for our understanding of individual attitudes and responsibilities. What can we learn from this when attempting to regulate behaviour through detailed and explicit rules? He contends that once ethics becomes institutionalized, rule-based and controlled, it stifles ethical thought and imagination.

In Chapter 20 Iordanis Kavathatzopoulos, a psychologist from Sweden, believes that it is possible to assess reliably and train effectively the acquisition of all aspects of moral competence in business. According to him ethical competence in business organization is defined as: (1) high ethical awareness; (2) individual skills to handle ethical issues satisfactorily; (3) effective organizational structures and routines to handle ethical issues, create ethical rules and continuously develop and adapt the rules to new situations; (4) communication and argumentation skills to explain and convince; and (5) confidence in own ability and emotional strength to cope with controversial issues. He describes how a test and an educational programme for ethical competence were constructed and applied on professionals from different areas. The test and the training focused on psychological processes underlying the handling of moral problems, and not on normative aspects. His research showed that it is possible to assess reliably and train effectively the acquisition of all aspects of ethical competence in business.

The last chapter in the book is written by Greg Reichberg, Senior Researcher at the Norwegian Peace Research Institute. His chapter raises a set of ethical questions that business leaders can ask themselves when deciding to operate in nations with grave violations of human rights. These questions are drawn from a Western tradition of moral inquiry known as 'just war' (*bellum justum*). Codified by Thomas Aquinas in the thirteenth century, this tradition has devised a set of criteria helpful in organizing our ethical thinking about war. He begins his chapter with what may have seemed an improbable proposition: that the ethics of war can serve as a paradigm for thinking about the hard issues of business. In his opinion it is not coincidental that there is a connection between these two spheres of activity.

The entire book hopefully will satisfy the need to balance the extensive collection of thinking and business cases we can find in the USA and the UK with samples from other European countries that normally do not publish in English. Teachers of courses such as *Ethics in Management, International*

*Business Ethics* or *Business and Society* have often asked for material from and about Europe. We are glad that the project that we have undertaken can be the beginning of filling such a gap. We would like to thank the Norwegian Research Foundation (Verdinett) for giving us some support when I initiated this project with a research conference in 1999. Last but not least my personal thanks go to all my colleagues in Europe who have made this volume possible. I dedicate my work in honour of our common meeting place, the European Business Ethics Network (EBEN), which always has provided me with new inspiration when working in this demanding academic field.

# 2. Is Europe distinctive from America? An overview of business ethics in Europe[1]

## Laura J. Spence

Despite the many and varied definitions of, and perspectives and opinions on, business ethics, its current appearance on business, academic, social and policy agendas across the world suggests that, whatever it is, it is here to stay. As with business issues more generally, internationalization and the global business environment require an increasingly sophisticated understanding of business ethics. The work of the International Society of Business, Economics and Ethics is leading the way in looking at business ethics from a world-wide perspective (see Enderle, 1999).

In Europe, the identity of business ethics is not clearly formulated. The aim of this chapter is to consider recent developments in business ethics in Europe and attempt to map out the status and infrastructure of any 'European' business ethics movement in the year 2001. This will involve both the structures and activities relating to business ethics and the content of the field in Europe.

The standard against which European business ethics is commonly measured is American business ethics. The status of American (United States of America) business ethics, as perceived from Europe, is briefly outlined below, allowing for any European distinction to be clarified.

## AMERICAN BUSINESS ETHICS

A number of articles have addressed differences between American and non-American (mainly European and Japanese) business ethics as discussions centring around the idea that American business is 'more' ethical than elsewhere, demonstrating the perspective of ethics as how we ought to live (see for example Singer, 1991; Vogel, 1992, 1993; Murphy, 1994). This perspective is reflective of a distinctive character of the critical mass of members of the American business ethics field as purveying 'an unusually moralizing society' (van Luijk, 1990, p. 542), demonstrating an assumed similarity in expectations and conduct of Europeans and Americans (Enderle, 1996a, p. 36).

Nash (1994) summarizes an 'American' perspective of the content of business ethics as focusing on the individual's moral norms in the commercial context, the choices he or she faces with respect to the law, and the pre-eminence of one's own self-interest. American business ethics centres on the study of dilemmas for the individual (Frechen, 1995), and recommendation of how an upright citizen should behave; in short, it is the implementation in the business context of 'honesty, fairness and apple-pie' (Nash, 1994, p. 11). In a survey of business ethics in North America, Shaw (1996) noted a move towards a broadening of the perspectives taken, identifying three models: the standard model, which reflects the predominant position described above; the politics model focusing on business systems as a whole; and the virtue model advocating a move towards individual moral judgement and away from seeking guiding principles for business practices. McMahon suggests that virtue ethics may be the key to American business ethics in the future (1999, p. 351). In this book, Gasparski further discusses characteristics of American business ethics. While the standard model still prevails, perspectives on business ethics are widening.

Vogel (1992, p. 30) has suggested that there is an 'unusual visibility of issues of business ethics in the United States' due to the 'distinctive institutional, legal, social, and cultural context'. Certainly there is an emphasis on regulating for ethics in the United States, the Foreign Corrupt Practices Act being a clear example. Furthermore firms can be rewarded for demonstrating the artefacts of ethics: codes of conduct, ethical ombudsperson, ethics hotline, through the Federal Sentencing Guidelines (Nagel and Swenson, 1993). Hence in American business there is a requirement that business acknowledge ethics. This is reflected in business schools, where 'almost all colleges and universities now offer a course (on business ethics)' (Shaw, 1996, p. 489). There is also a plethora of American textbooks on ethics teaching (Sassower, 1988, p. 279) and many business ethics research centres. Vogel concludes that the American approach to business ethics is unique. He says that it is more 'individualistic, legalistic and universalistic than in other capitalist societies' (1992, p. 30).

This chapter considers business and government initiatives and a focus on academic advancements in business ethics in Europe. The academic perspectives cover business ethics teaching, networks, literature and business ethics research. What is of interest is not activities in European countries *per se*, but activities among European countries, where there is some kind of international co-operation and collaboration within the countries of Europe (not restricted to the European Union – EU).

## EUROPEAN BUSINESS ETHICS

Europe was the home of the Western philosophers. It is Europeans who first laid the foundations of Western ethics. The principles and approaches for assessing right from wrong which have been adopted by American business ethics are derived from Europe. Europe was the home of the Ancient Greeks, the developers of early Western theology, natural law, rights and duty, the social contract, utilitarianism and existentialism. These developments in philosophy are inextricably linked with the historical, political, economic and cultural situations of their time. In looking at the history of business philosophy, Davies (1997) argues that 'what has gone before in large measure shapes our current understanding in the world of ideas, as well as shaping the physical world'. In a region with such a rich history in ethics, combined with an equally rich history in commerce and economics, the roots of business and ethics run deep in contemporary Europe (van Luijk, 1996; Enderle, 1996a).

Important roots also exist in the religious heritage of Europe (see Gasparski in Chapter 11, this volume). European countries, and regions within them, are often defined by the dominant influence of Catholic, Protestant, Islam and other religions. Citing Adam Smith's 'invisible hand', Verstraeten (1998, p. 121) argues that apparently academic perspectives are actually often based on a belief in a deistic god mediating between 'private vices' and 'public virtues'. Argandoña (1999) suggests that the teachings of the Catholic Church in Spain, and the rise of its social doctrine laid the foundations of modern economic and business ethics. Many universities teaching business and business ethics have religious affiliations as do individual business practitioners. Verstraeten (1998, p. 120) believes that 'creation of a moral community always goes together with the construction of a religious identity'. The influence of religion on European business ethics is not insignificant and, Argandoña (1999) suggests, is one of the reasons why continental Europeans may be unlikely to give equal status to different theoretical approaches, preferring the philosophical or theological perspective of their own tradition.

Keeping these philosophical, historical and religious influences in mind, the status of business ethics in Europe can be considered. Here we will be talking primarily about the emergence of an academic field and practical business approach called 'business ethics' which appeared in that form on the European scene in the 1980s.

The subject has been mapped previously by van Luijk (1990, 1996, 1999) and Enderle (1996a). Developments are occurring rapidly, and this chapter is part of an attempt to help understand a European perspective of business ethics to Europeans and non-Europeans alike. It is important to acknowledge that the development of the subject is a dynamic process, and studies such as this can only represent one person's perspective on business ethics activities in Europe at a moment in time.

Van Luijk (1996) has suggested six parameters with which to describe and analyse business ethics as what he calls a 'social institution'. These are: style of philosophical reflection; weight of ideological forces; state of economic development; distribution of social power; academic institutions and business education; open or closed culture. Enderle (1996a) acknowledges the difficulty of suggesting a homogenous grouping in either 'American' or 'European' approaches to business ethics, but presents a summary of possible dissimilarities. In his article he argues that distinctions in continental Europe from North America are: multiple languages and reluctant talk about business ethics; focus on macro-level; more international; constraints on actors; economic arguments for business ethics; weak practical focus; social science paradigm; no general acceptance and integration of teaching; few but increasing corporate initiatives; role of business ethicists as teachers; limited consultancy (p. 37). Enderle's defining perspectives will be referred to later in the chapter.

## BUSINESS AND GOVERNMENT INITIATIVES

Business initiatives relating to business ethics are evident at a variety of levels. Here European cross-national initiatives are presented, which disregards some excellent nationally based initiatives and individual company efforts that may well have cross-cultural perspectives.

The Social Ventures Network Europe (SVN Europe) was launched in Amsterdam in 1993 as a daughter group of the American Social Ventures Network founded in 1987. SVN Europe is 'an association of companies and individual business leaders who believe they can – and must – make a significant contribution to solve social and environmental problems locally and globally' (SVN Europe, 2001). Funded in part by the European Commission, one initiative of SVN Europe from 1998–2000 demonstrated a distinctively European focus. The project aims to activate dialogue between networks and organizations working towards sustainability. After an initial perspective heavily influenced by the American SVN model, it seems that SVN Europe now works towards integrating with European partners and within the European political and economic frameworks.

A clear European basis was the impetus from the start for a further business network, the European Business Network for Social Cohesion (EBNSC), suitably based in Brussels, and renamed CSR Europe (Corporate Social Responsibility Europe) in 2000. The network formed in 1995 in response to the European Declaration of Businesses Against Social Exclusion and the network continues to work closely with both business and EU institutions (CSR Europe, 2001).

SVN Europe and CSR Europe draw on EU funding to support their work. In this respect they sustain political as well as business and social agendas.

Transparency International (TI) has a particular focus on tackling corruption and bribery in politics and business. TI is a world-wide network, originated in Germany, with national chapters as well as an international perspective. It aims to combat corruption in a sustainable manner by involving 'all of the stakeholders which include the state, civil society and the private sector' in partnership (TI, 2001).

The Caux Round Table (CRT) was founded in Switzerland in 1986 by 28 senior business leaders from Europe, Japan and North America. They aim to stimulate business leaders to create a better world for all peoples by extending the opportunities and addressing the challenges of globalization. They operate at a high level, working with governments and non-governmental organizations alike. CRT see priority areas as: trade, investment and the employment dilemma; trust and transparency; wider environmental issues (CRT, 2001)

Enderle (1996a) is correct in noting the increasing use of codes by individual companies in Europe but reticence to have ethics officers and training programmes. The rise of consultancy in the field may change this in the future. There are, however, joint codes as statements of values in Europe, for example the CRT Principles for Business (see de Bettignies et al., 1999) and the International Business Ethics Code for Christians, Moslems and Jews (see Webley, 1999).

Enderle (1996a) also notes that talk about business ethics is more reluctant in Europe than in North America. Certainly the avoidance of the term 'business ethics' in the business initiatives discussed above supports this. Enderle's point that in Europe other rhetoric and terminology such as good practice and benchmarking, social responsibility, social and ethical auditing arc at least as prevalent, and indeed relevant, as talk of ethics is a fair one. Business ethics initiatives by European firms are increasing. The business approach to ethics tends to be normative and prescriptive. There is an emphasis on presentation of case studies that demonstrate profit and reputation gains as outcomes of social responsibility. Business initiatives in Europe have not on the whole developed far beyond the perspective of encouraging enlightened self-interest.

CSR Europe, TI and CRT demonstrate active co-operation and collaboration between business and government. In continental Europe this is not unusual in contrast to the antagonism common in Anglo-American business-governmental relations. The collaborative approach, privileging consensus over prescription, is also evident in the inclusion in this group of the trade unions, which in Europe can have influential roles on company boards.

While there seems to be a tendency for business and academic initiatives to remain broadly separate, there is evidence of some convergence. There are certainly academic members in primarily business networks and business members in academic networks. It could be that it is only appropriate for business and the academy to join forces in business ethics as each has begun to establish its own position, networks and resources. Cummins (1999, p. 8) argues that business is creating the demand for business ethics to be raised on the academic agenda and taught more in business schools. Whatever the impetus, business ethics education is growing in Europe.

## ACADEMIC ACTIVITY

### Teaching

Business education as a part of economics, the humanities and social science is common within Europe, influencing the way in which business ethics is taught. Drawing from the social science tradition at least as much as philosophical ones, European approaches tend to focus on consideration of what business ethics is, as much as what is ethical in business.

Information on what business ethics teaching is going on within Europe is somewhat incomplete. As part of an EU-funded programme, initial work identifying university courses on 'Corporate Social Responsibility, Citizenship and Business Ethics' is underway by CSR Europe. In a draft report they acknowledge that their review had 'touched only a fraction of those teaching in the field' (EBNSC/Copenhagen Centre, 1998, p. 9). Identifying business ethics in the courses of related names, such as 'business in society' is problematic, making an overview of teaching difficult. The EBNSC/ Copenhagen Centre presents 60 cases of relevant degree courses in Europe, which are divided roughly in half between 'Corporate Social Responsibility and Citizenship' and 'Business Ethics' and includes business ethics courses at the Catholic University of Leuven, Witten-Herdecke University, IESE University of Navarra, Nijenrode University and Manchester University. There are many other universities throughout Europe (including beyond the EU) which offer established business ethics courses. A handful of missing examples are University of Erlangen-Nuernberg, University of Eichstaett, Tilburg University, Brunel University, Estonian Business School, Norwegian School of Management and there are many, many more. New research is needed to identify the full range of business ethics and related teaching.

In his edited book *The European Difference: Business Ethics in the Community of European Management Schools*, Zsolnai (1998) offers more depth by concentrating on business ethics teaching in eight European countries[2]. In most cases cited, teaching of the subject started in the early 1990s, with the exception of ESADE. Approaches to teaching business ethics fall into three groups:

1. the sociology of business (ESADE);
2. applied ethics (Copenhagen, Rotterdam, Paris and St Gallen);
3. ethics as a business/social issue (Stockholm, Prague, Budapest).

The most singular perspective is that taken at ESADE where: 'Since the very outset (1958), one of the distinctive features of an ESADE education has been the inclusion of studies aimed at fostering a critical analysis of society' (Lozano, 1998, p. 50). The approach taken to teaching business ethics is often one of teaching it as an instance of applied ethics, much like medical ethics, but with a focus on business. This requires understanding and then application of normative ethical theories to examples of business in order to determine right from wrong. This is also the approach most common in the UK (Cummins, 1999).

In Stockholm, Prague and Budapest business ethics has been added to the business studies curriculum as an issue with which business people must deal. In addition the work at the Copenhagen Business School has taken a practical turn in developing social and ethical accounting as a tool of ethics management. It is particularly interesting here that the Central and Eastern European countries take this approach in developing their understanding of 'business' in the post-communist economies. It seems that they have been better able to treat business ethics as a relevant business issue than some of their Western European counterparts.

In terms of theory building the most significant steps in this small sample have been taken at St Gallen. This is reflective of the state of business ethics in Europe as a whole where the German-speaking countries tend to be developing theories of the ethic of business at a macro level (Preuss, 1999). Seidel et al. (1998) argue that the theoretical conceptualization of business ethics in German-speaking countries is a requirement for establishing business ethics as a fully acknowledged academic discipline in those countries.

At the most fundamental level, the medium of communication about business ethics in different European countries will most likely be through the national language. Enderle (1996a, p. 36) notes that: 'talk about morality and business is deeply culture-bound and "language"-dependent, in spite of the fact that business is becoming increasingly international and English is the dominant international business language'. The linguistic barriers to understanding subtle variations in the concept of business ethics are not necessarily surmountable by the common adoption of (American) English (Löhr, 1995). The growing body of German language literature, for example, is missed by those reliant only on English translations. Sterling efforts such as that by Preuss (1999) and Grabner-Kräuter (Chapter 3, this volume) ensure at least some wider awareness of German language business ethics. In some countries there is a battle to get away from the American texts, for example in the Netherlands the use of existing American texts means that some students learn an imported version of business ethics rather than developing understanding rooted in their own language and culture (de Leeuw, 1995). Löhr (1995) further notes that access to understanding national interpretations of business ethics is bound to be difficult without language skills and a good understanding of the philosophical traditions of different cultures. It might transpire that even good linguistic translations of nation-specific texts would remain culturally indecipherable for the foreign reader.

In terms of the international orientation of business ethics in Europe (Enderle, 1996a) since the Management Schools represented in 'The European Difference' are almost all part of the Community of European Management Schools network we can expect them to be predisposed to an international perspective in all their teaching, including business ethics. Whether this is the case in other universities which teach business ethics is unconfirmed. However the ease of travelling between European countries, the mobility of labour and free trade agreements mean that international competition, even for those who stay in domestic markets, is an everyday part of business.

The paradigm of business ethics being connected with social sciences (Enderle, 1996a) is supported by the various approaches to teaching business ethics presented above. This is where the departure from the American approach becomes most clear. The European examples support the perspective of business, and business ethics, as a science of the social world, fundamentally of human interaction and social structures. Importantly, a number of the authors in 'The European Difference' place the development of business ethics in an economic-political-historical context. Some examples of this are shown in the cases of Spain and the Czech Republic with their shifts between different macroeconomic systems. Changing economic structures are common in the history of Europe, and are bound to influence ideas of how business should be done.

While the academic movement of business ethics is taking hold, the progress cannot be said to be consistent across Europe. Opinion varies as to the stage of development. Van Luijk (1996) argues on the one hand that there are sufficient clusters of effort to justify the recognition of the area as having a firm and permanent status in Western European society. Enderle (1996b, p. 60) on the other hand takes a more conservative stance, saying that 'the task of developing business ethics as an academic discipline is very demanding and by no means completed'. Implied in both perspectives, however, is the acceptance that the academic field of business ethics in Europe exists and is continuing to grow in credibility and strength. This growth is supported strongly by the networks to which the teachers and lecturers of business ethics belong.

## NETWORKS

There are two main cross-European academic networks working in the area of business ethics. The European Ethics Network has a broader remit than just business ethics and concentrates on all areas of applied ethics. The second, the European Business Ethics Network, is the only predominantly academic group with a focus on business ethics.

The European Ethics Network (EEN) was set up in 1996 sponsored by EU funding under the Thematic Network Socrates/Erasmus Programme. EEN has about 500 members. The network aims to: support pedagogic development of teaching applied ethics; encourage transversality – transfer across different applications of ethics; promote ethics in society. EEN's membership was originally rooted in Catholic EU universities. Projects include: writing of core texts for teaching applied ethics, including one on business ethics; setting up Applied Masters degrees with cross-European validity and modular exchange; a directory of members each year; a regular conference; a refereed Journal 'Ethical Perspectives'; the European Centre for Ethics in Leuven. In response to the need for pedagogic development in the area, 'The primary aim of the network … is the realization of integrated co-operation between university centers for ethics with a view to improving the quality of education in ethics at graduate and post-graduate level' (EEN, 1999). The EEN is in a transitional phase, and since 2000 continues on a membership fee basis.

The 'European Business Ethics Network' (EBEN) is perhaps the most sustained European body of people interested in business ethics. EBEN, founded in 1987 as a result of an initiative taken by the first Chair in Business Ethics in Europe Henk van Luijk, is a pan-European business and academic network. In the mid-1990s national networks within EBEN became partners rather than subsidiary groups, reflecting the different cultural perspectives within Europe. This focused acknowledgement of the importance of the plurality of Europe with respect to values and practices in business, prevailing over a unitary, normative approach, is a significant moment in European business ethics. The EBEN 1996 conference reflected the celebration of national differences in business ethics, focusing particularly on the theme of 'Working across cultures'. In an article about the conference, the organizers state that 'Since differing norms and values are at the heart of differing cultures, the ethical, or values based, approach is an inevitable concept for corporations acting in cultural diversity' (Löhr and Steinmann, 1996, p. 126).

In recent years EBEN's sphere of influence has stretched to embrace Central and Eastern European countries with members from Bulgaria, Czech Republic, Estonia, Hungary, Lithuania, Poland, Russia, Slovak Republic, Slovenia. By 2001 there were Czech and Polish national EBEN networks, in addition to Spain, the Netherlands, Germany and the UK. The research conference at the Norwegian School of Management in 1999 helped galvanize the efforts in Europe, leading to this text. Research centres associated with EBEN at various stages of development include the European Institute for Business Ethics at Nyenrode University and the Zentrum für Wirtschaftsethik at the University of Constance.

In September 2001 EBEN had over 750 members from more than 30 different countries. Key goals for the future are to improve the network further into: a respected European voice on business ethics; a network for information and co-ordination; an agora for building bridges; a supporter of academic research and knowledge gathering.

The networks bring together individual members and representatives from the many small but active business ethics research centres across Europe, and act as facilitators for the dissemination of business ethics literature.

## LITERATURE

In 1990 it was considered that 'There is as yet no specific bibliography available on business ethics in Europe. The practical use of such a bibliography would be limited anyhow, given the language differences' (van Luijk, 1990, p. 538). The language issue continues to be a handicap in assessing business ethics literature across Europe (van Luijk, 1996) and is a problem which is growing as bodies of literature become more sophisticated and developed within language groups. There have nevertheless been publications in many of the European languages.

A few teaching texts have been aimed at addressing business ethics from the European rather than the national level, and notably published in the English language, for example those by Donaldson (1992), Koslowski (1992), Harvey (1994), de Geer (1994), Harvey *et al.* (1994). These texts are primarily aimed at the academic sector, particularly for use in teaching business ethics. A further relevant book with an eye on business application particularly is by Nino Kumar and Steinmann (1998). Misleadingly, these early 'European' texts sometimes do not reflect the diversity of interest in Europe, and have tended to follow an American style.

Given the differing national approaches to business ethics it is hardly surprising that the tendency is for nation-specific publications (Löhr, 1995). In contrast, the one language and basically unified approach in the American field of business ethics supports a more coherently developed business ethics literature base. With the exception of the EBEN conference publications, the European texts do not include much reference to business ethics research, which tends to be published in different spheres.

## EUROPEAN BUSINESS ETHICS RESEARCH

Disseminators of research findings include *Business Ethics: A European Review*, the EBEN conference publications (through the Kluwer 'Issues in Business Ethics' series or in special issues of the *Journal of Business Ethics*) the *Journal of the European Ethics Network*, *Ethical Perspectives* and the newsletters of EBEN.

Some of the European work published consists of country-specific discursive tours around the state of business ethics (van Luijk, 1996), occasionally incorporating empirical research. There is also evidence of the American-style normative discussion of elements of business and how they should be carried out. Murphy's (1994) work is an example of an attempt at accessing European managers' views on corporate ethics. Comparative business ethics work presented at the EBEN 1996 conference, made significant inroads into the barren landscape that had existed before (Lange et al., 1998). Brioschi (1998) compared the main self-regulatory codes relating to advertising in 15 European countries. While the work is mainly descriptive, it shows in an instant the diversity of approaches and, inherently, attitudes to self-regulation across Europe. French and Mühlfriedel (1998) applied the German discourse ethics approach to negotiations between individuals of different cultures. At least two papers, those by Métivier (1996) and Seidel *et al.* (1998), specifically tackled the different approaches within Europe to business ethics, the first at a theoretical level, and second drawing widely on publications from Germany, France and the UK specifically.

The paucity of comparative business ethics research has been commented on by Robertson (1993) and Enderle (1996a). As Enderle remarks, and as the preceding discussion supports, 'Intercultural comparisons call for particular sensitivity to semantic issues and differences, and require extraordinary caution in evaluating actual ethical conduct in comparative terms' (p. 44).

In 1987, Richard de George from the United States said:

> Business ethics has become an established field. The work already done shows only how much more there is to do. Yet the number of people doing original work in the field is still relatively small. The field will stand or fall on the quality of research done in it (sic). The higher the quality, the easier it will be to distinguish business ethics from the polemics, self-serving articles, and moralizing with which it is still too often confused (1987, p. 209). '

Eight years later, Collier (1995) notes that quality research in business ethics is still greatly needed: it seems to be underway in Europe where academics of business ethics are working in a wide variety of areas, including, but by far not limited to, those held to be relevant in the American literature. The 'polemic, self-serving' articles can certainly be found in the European literature, but there is a strong undercurrent of feverish research activity which must soon surface into the wider arena. Much of this work is empirical in nature. Verstraeten argues that empirical research must be a precursor to normative ethics (1998, p. 113).

In a summary of research interest of some EBEN members at the end of 1998, Hummels (1998) suggests the following groupings of interest: values; stakeholder approach; ethical accounting; working in different cultures. This perhaps points us to a distinction between American and European approaches to business ethics research. The American business ethics research was dominated in the early years by normative, philosophically based contributions. In Europe, empirical traditions and sensitivity to our local cultural and contextual differences lead to a reticence to take the normative approach without a thorough empirical basis.

## CONCLUSION: THE STORY SO FAR

This chapter has set out some of the infrastructure and approaches to business ethics in Europe. When comparing with the American business ethics approach briefly outlined at the beginning, there are some important distinctions. These relate in particular to:

1. the theological and philosophical traditions in Europe;
2. the collaborative approach of business, trade unions, government and non-governmental organizations;
3. experience of diverse macroeconomic systems;
4. multiple linguistic, legal and social perspectives;
5. business studies located as a social science with an empirical basis.

The varied religious and philosophical traditions in Europe are the source of great educational strength and local conflict. These traditions will continue to inform the actions of individuals and groups in their private and business lives. Schools of thought will and do argue for the superiority of their view on how one ought to behave. In a Europe becoming more culturally diverse through the settling of people from non-Western traditions, these powerful influences on everyday life become still more complex. The long recorded history of Europe leaves an ancestry full of lives dedicated and lost to particular schools of belief which communities are unlikely to give up lightly after centuries, even millennia, of convention.

In many countries of Europe there is a tradition of consensus building and inclusion in decision making such that business, government, trade unions and non-governmental organizations work together to set goals and achieve targets. We see this where business networks support European political initiatives with regard to improved social inclusion and employability. To date, business developments remain largely within the profit maximization paradigm, keen to emphasize the profit and public relations advantages of ethical behaviour. The inclusion of trade unions and others with legitimate claims on business in stakeholder dialogues and open discourse bodes well for an inclusive approach to business ethics.

The social history of Europe includes major changes in how society, business and politics are organized which are still commonplace in the living memory of Europe's citizens. This contributes to the plurality of approaches to business ethics. In a collection of people who have seen so much change in their own time, one would not expect the search for universalistic solutions, but rather the acceptance of temporal, geographical and social locations of complex processes. Furthermore, the European awareness of different macroeconomic systems, and experience of changes in Central and Eastern European economies, allows for the reconsideration of the ethics of economics and business as an obvious element of business ethics. This in part helps explain the macro-perspective on business ethics in Europe.

As with European life, culture and history, what we see in European business ethics is a pluralistic, inclusive collection of approaches. This is in keeping with what van Luijk (1999, p. 361) calls 'a miracle of discord' wherein 'distinct groups and cultures are fiercely unwilling to coagulate and equally stubbornly refuse to fall apart'. Linguistic barriers continue to impede the dissemination of research and teaching materials across Europe. These difficulties are significant, for example translating 'business ethics' is problematic in languages such as French and Polish, and are barriers to developing debate or an accessible European body of literature on business ethics. We as business ethicists must learn to be more proactive in properly translating and communicating our work across linguistic boundaries in order that we have the possibility to develop our field more coherently. Perhaps the best technique, however, is to foster joint work which allows for disciplinary, linguistic and cultural differences to be dealt with early in research processes (Spence, 1998). The building of cross-European links in research and teaching is likely to be the strongest single contribution to the future of European business ethics.

There is evidence of business ethics being taught in a scholarly, scientific manner in universities in Europe, with an emphasis on social context. This is also apparent in European business ethics research which is often empirical. The social science perspective, and acknowledgement of economic, cultural and linguistic contexts of business are important in European business ethics, and distinctive from standard American approaches. There remains, however, the influence of institutions in Europe with declared theological and philosophical biases which take a more normative approach to teaching and researching business ethics.

What we see is a multi-tiered, sometimes contradictory field. On the one hand, theological and philosophical traditions mean that consideration of morals and ethics is well established. On the other hand, 'business ethics' as a discipline in business schools is a subject which is still developing and slowly coming of age. It would be premature to say that business ethics is fully established in Europe, it is not. Neither is there a homogeneous approach to the subject. We should not be surprised or discouraged by this. A wide foundation for future development is likely to be a strength of European business ethics. Returning to Vogel's definition of American business ethics as 'individualist, legalistic and universalistic', we could suggest a European view as social, historical and pluralistic. If American business ethics were actually a business ethics of the Americas, a similar plurality may exist.

The evidence in this chapter, and indeed this text, indicates that there is a level of competence in European business ethics. What is lacking to date is confidence in European business ethics and among European business ethicists to celebrate and embrace our differences as part of the rich set of cultures we have inherited. The development of business ethics in Europe can be characterized as a dynamic process. The evidence presented has been selective, but enables the broad mapping of the European business ethics terrain. In doing this, the discussion regarding the distinctiveness of European business ethics can be embarked upon with an understanding of contemporary institutions, interests and perspectives on business ethics in Europe. This volume, in turn, contributes to the field and its developing strength.

## NOTES

1.  Comments and extensive feedback by participants at the EBEN Research Conference, Sandvika Norway (19–20 June 1999) have resulted in significant improvements in the study for which I am extremely grateful. Omissions remain the responsibility of the author.
2.  Eight chapters are presented from: Copenhagen Business School, Denmark; Stockholm School of Economics, Sweden; Rotterdam School of Management, the Netherlands; HEC School of Management, France; ESADE Spain; University St. Gallen, Switzerland; University of Economics, the Czech Republic; and Budapest University of Economic Sciences, Hungary. For a review from which some of the perspectives presented here draws see Spence (2000).

# REFERENCES

Argandoña , A. (1999), 'Business ethics in Spain', *Journal of Business Ethics*, **22**(3), 155–174.

Brioschi, E. (1998), 'The principles of the advertising self-regulation in Europe', in Lange, H., Löhr, A. and Steinmann, H. (eds), *Working Across Cultures: Ethical Perspectives in Intercultural Management*, Issues in Business Ethics, Volume 9, London: Kluwer, pp. 321–339.

Collier, J. (1995), 'Business ethics research: shaping the agenda', *Business Ethics: A European Review*, **4**(1), 6–12.

CRT (2001), *History and Meetings*, www.cauxroundtable.org, 23/01/01.

CSR Europe (2001), *Our Mission*, www.csreurope.org, 23/01/01.

Cummins, J. (1999), *The Teaching of Business Ethics at Undergraduate, Postgraduate and Professional Levels in the UK*, London: Institute of Business Ethics.

Davies, P.W.F. (ed.) (1997), *Current Issues in Business Ethics*, London: Routledge.

de Bettignies, H-C., Goodpaster, K. and Matsuoka, T. (1999), 'The Caux Roundtable Principles for Business: presentation and discussion', in Enderle, G. (ed.), *International Business Ethics: Challenges and Approaches*, Indiana: University of Notre Dame Press, pp. 131–142.

de Geer, H. (ed.) (1994), *Business Ethics in Progress?*, Berlin: Springer-Verlag.

de George, R. (1987), 'The status of business ethics: past and future', *Journal of Business Ethics*, **6**, 201–211.

de Leeuw, J. (1995), 'Twee Bijeenkomsten Over Bedrijfsethiek', *Dilemma*, 5, October, p.16.

Donaldson, J. (1992), *Business Ethics: A European Casebook*, London: Academic Press.

EBNSC/Copenhagen Center (1998), '*Business in society*', *in European Universities and Business Schools: An initial review of courses on Corporate Social Responsibility, Citizenship and Business Ethics*, Draft Paper, EBNSC, Brussels.

EEN (1999), *European Ethics Network: Objectives*, www.kuleuven.ac.be/oce/, 11/06/99.

Enderle, G. (1996a), 'A comparison of business ethics in North America and Continental Europe', *Business Ethics: A European Review*, **5**(1), 33–46.

Enderle, G. (1996b), 'Towards business ethics as an academic discipline', *Business Ethics Quarterly*, **6**(1), 43–65.

Enderle, G. (ed.) (1999), *International Business Ethics: Challenges and Approaches*, Indiana: University of Notre Dame Press.

Frechen, M. (1995), 'Wirtschafts- und Unternehmensethik in den USA – ein Einblick in die Amerikanische Business Ethics-Bewegung', *Forum Wirtschaftsethik*, 3 (März, Sonderheft Literatur 1, ed.: Müller, E.), 19–21.

French, W. and Mühlfriedel, B. (1998), 'Discourse instead of recourse: is it worth using a guided approach to negotiation when working across cultures?', in Lange, H., Löhr, A. and Steinmann, H. (eds), *Working Across Cultures: Ethical Perspectives in Intercultural Management*, Issues in Business Ethics, Volume 9, London: Kluwer, pp. 263–285.

Harvey, B. (ed.) (1994), *Business Ethics: A European Approach*, Hemel Hempstead: Prentice Hall International.

Harvey, B., van Luijk, H. and Steinmann, H. (1994), *European Casebook on Business Ethics* (European Casebook Series), London: Prentice Hall.

Hummels, H. (1998), 'Business ethics research by EBEN members', *European Business Ethics Newsletter*, December (3), 8–9.

Koslowski, P. (ed.) (1992), *Ethics in Economics, Business and Economic Policy* (Series ed.: Koslowski, P., Studies in Economic Ethics and Philosophy), Berlin: Springer-Verlag.

Lange, H., Löhr, A. and Steinmann, H. (eds) (1998), *Working Across Cultures: Ethical Perspectives in Intercultural Management*, Issues in Business Ethics, Volume 9, London: Kluwer.

Löhr, A. (1995), 'Die Europäische Diskussion um Wirtschafts- und Unternehmensethik', *Forum Wirtschaftsethik*, 3 (März, Sonderheft Literatur 1, ed. Müller, E.), 15–19.

Löhr, A. and Steinmann, H. (1996), 'Working across cultures in the Europe of tomorrow: the EBEN 1996 annual conference', *Business Ethics: A European Review*, **5**(2), 126–128.

Lozano, J.M. (1998), 'From teaching to learning of business ethics in Barcelona', in Zsolnai, L. (ed.), *The European Difference: Business Ethics in the Community of European Management Schools*, Dordrecht: Kluwer, pp. 47–58.

McMahon, T. (1999), 'A brief history of American business ethics', in Frederick, R. (ed.) (1999), *A Companion to Business Ethics*, Oxford, UK and Massachusetts, USA: Blackwell, pp. 342–352.

Métivier, F. (1996), 'Cultural Difference and Methodological Unity: The Organization of the Multitude as the European Foundation of a Business Ethics', presented at the European Business Ethics Network's 9th annual conference: *Working Across Cultures*, 18–20 September, Frankfurt.

Murphy, P. (1994), 'European managers' views on corporate ethics', *Business Ethics: A European Review*, **3**(3), 137–144.

Nagel, I. and Swenson, W. (1993), 'The Federal Sentencing Guidelines for Corporations: Their development, theoretical underpinnings, and some thoughts about their future', *Washington University Law Quarterly*, **71**, 205–259.

Nash, L. (1994), 'Why business ethics now?', in Drummond, J. and Bain, B. (eds), *Managing Business Ethics*, Oxford: Butterworth-Heinemann, pp. 7–24.

Nino Kumar, B. and Steinmann, H. (1998), *Ethics in International Management*, Berlin: de Gruyter.

Preuss, L. (1999), 'Ethical theory in German business ethics research', *Journal of Business Ethics*, **18**, 407–419.

Robertson, D. (1993), 'Empiricism in business ethics: suggested research directions', *Journal of Business Ethics*, **12**, 585–599.

Sassower, R. (1988), 'The business of ethics', *Journal of Business Ethics*, **7**, 279–282.

Seidel, F., Schlierer, Hans-J. and Tovey, I. (1998), 'Business ethics in three European countries: a comparative approach', in Lange, H., Löhr, A. and Steinmann, H. (eds), *Working Across Cultures: Ethical Perspectives in Intercultural Management*, Issues in Business Ethics, Volume 9, London: Kluwer, pp. 235–261.

Shaw, W. (1996), 'Business ethics: a survey', *Journal of Business Ethics*, **15**(5), 489–500.

Singer, A. (1991), 'Ethics: are standards lower overseas?', *Across the Board*, September, 31–34.

Spence, L.J. (1998), 'On effective interdisciplinary alliances in European business ethics research: discussion and illustration', *Journal of Business Ethics*, **17**, 1029–1044.

Spence, L.J. (2000), 'Teaching business ethics: are there differences within Europe and is there a European difference?', review of 'The European Difference: Business Ethics in the Community of European Management Schools', L. Zsolnai (ed.) (1998), Dordrecht: Kluwer, *Business Ethics: A European Review*, January.

SVN Europe (2001), *Social Venture Network Europe*, www.svneurope.com/, 23/01/01.

TI (2001), *Welcome to Transparency International*, www.transparency.de/, 23/01/01.

van Luijk, H. (1990), 'Recent developments in European business ethics', *Journal of Business Ethics*, **9**, 537-544.

van Luijk, H. (1996), 'Business Ethics as a Social Institution in Europe: A Search for Effective Alliances', Report prepared for the *First World Congress of Business, Economics and Ethics*, 25-28 July, Tokyo, Japan.

van Luijk, H. (1999), 'Business ethics in Europe: a tale of two efforts', in Frederick R. (ed.), *A Companion to Business Ethics*, Oxford, UK and Massachusetts, USA: Blackwell, pp. 353-365.

Verstraeten, J. (1998), 'From business ethics to the vocation of business leaders to humanize the world of business', *Business Ethics: A European Review*, **7**(2), 111-241.

Vogel, D. (1992), 'The globalization of business ethics: why America remains distinctive', *California Management Review*, Fall, 30-49.

Vogel, D. (1993), 'Differing national approaches to business ethics', *Business Ethics: A European Review*, **2**(3), 164-171.

Webley, S. (1999), 'Values inherent in the Interfaith Declaration of International Business Ethics', in Enderle, G. (ed.), *International Business Ethics: Challenges and Approaches*, Indiana: University of Notre Dame Press, pp. 96-108.

Zsolnai, L. (ed.) (1998), *The European Difference: Business Ethics in the Community of European Management Schools*, Dordrecht: Kluwer.

# 3. *'Unternehmensethik'* in German-speaking countries: economic rules versus moral argumentation?

## Sonja Grabner-Kräuter

For years German-language business and corporate ethics has focused on the theoretical task of elaborating and justifying normative obligations of business firms. Only recently a growing concern for bridging the gap between theoretical research and its practical applicability can be observed. By now business ethics research in German-speaking countries is done from an array of different perspectives (Preuss, 1999, p. 407). German research tradition has led to a relatively clear distinction between *'Wirtschaftsethik'*, the 'ethics of the economic system' that focuses on the economic order with its multiple institutions (the macro-level) and *'Unternehmensethik'*, the 'ethics of the business firm' which focuses on the decision-making and actions of and within the company (the meso-level of the organization and the micro-level of the individual person).

This chapter outlines three concepts that can be considered as major works in the present-day German-language *'Unternehmensethik'* discussion: Steinmann's and Löhr's conception of corporate ethics, Ulrich's approach to transform economic rationality and Homann's economic theory of morality. These approaches argue ethically reflected positions and have a discernible foundation in ethical theory. Discourse ethics and contractarian theories can be seen as the most elaborated theoretical foundations in German-language *'Unternehmensethik'* research. The discussed approaches are more comprehensive than concepts of corporate ethics in the United States. Although the focus is on the organizational level neither the macro-level of the economic order nor the micro-level of the individual are completely neglected (the different levels of acting have been developed for example in Enderle, 1993, p. 20).

Defenders of contractarian and discourse ethical approaches argue for different strategies and means on how to improve the ethical quality of corporate decisions and actions. Whereas discourse ethical approaches suggest for example ethics committees or corporate dialogues with all concerned stakeholders, contractarian approaches require to set up adequate rules that are competitively neutral and generally binding. It can be said that the different proposals have their roots in two different ethical paradigms: the principled moral reasoning view (to which discourse ethics belong) focuses on the decisions, actions and moral duties of the individual or small group under certain conditions. On the other hand the regulatory, compliance-based approach to ethics (established in contractarian theories) starts from a system's perspective and interprets moral norms as voluntarily and collectively agreed upon behavioural constraints that guarantee the freedom of the individual – moral behaviour of individuals is discussed and legitimated in its social functions. I will argue that the common goal of improving the ethical quality of corporate decisions and actions can only be achieved if both perspectives are considered. Beyond that, the importance of soft, emotional factors such as an ethical sensitivity to the situation and an awareness of the feelings, expectations, and concerns of the other involved individuals have to be recognized.

## 1   STEINMANN'S AND LÖHR'S CONCEPTION OF CORPORATE ETHICS: MANAGEMENT SUBJECT TO THE MORAL PROVISO FOR PEACE

Steinmann and Löhr were amongst the first German researchers who systematically developed a conception of corporate ethics based on a sophisticated theoretical foundation. To sum up one may say that this approach intends to distinguish the general, free consensus reached in practical discourses as the only adequate alternative for a reasonable foundation of ethical norms as well as for the solution of ethical conflicts (see for example Steinmann and Löhr, 1994a). The theoretical foundations are discourse ethics (see for example Habermas, 1983), Apel's communication community (see for example Apel, 1988) and the constructive philosophy of the Erlangen School.

Discourse ethics conceives of moral theory as a theory of moral argumentation. Mutual understanding or agreement reached by autonomous citizens in a process of unconstrained exchange of opinion that is free from domination ('herrschaftsfreier Diskurs') is seen as the best way of coordinating actions. The basis of this procedural approach is concisely expressed in the principle of discourse ethics, which states that 'only those norms may claim validity with which all possibly affected persons agree or could agree as participants in a practical discourse' (Principle 'D', Habermas, 1991, p. 12, translated by the author). Beyond that, any valid norm has to be submitted to all others for purposes of discoursively testing its claim to universality. (Principle 'U': 'Any valid norm has to meet the condition that the consequences and side effects which probably result from its general observance can be accepted by all affected persons without any constraint') (Habermas, 1991, p. 12, translated by the author). The aim of practical discourses is to generate a rationally motivated consensus on controversial claims.

Discourse ethical approaches stress the right of self-determination and take the view that management has the obligation to recognize and acknowledge the legitimate interests of the corporation's stakeholders or those affected by its decisions (see also Reed, 1999). The discourse principle provides procedural rules for testing the validity of norms and for reaching rational, consensual decisions. It requires that controversies over the validity of norms be settled through a dialogic process in which the consensus of all stakeholders decides upon the legitimacy of the controversial norm. In everyday business decision-making discourses with all concerned individuals usually cannot be realized. In such cases a discourse ethics calls for consideration of the interests of those affected by the results of the discourse who do not or cannot participate in the discourse for any reason. That means that instead of a real dialogue or discourse the decision-maker has either to integrate advocates or to imagine a fictitious dialogue in which he or she takes into consideration the anticipatory arguments of all persons affected by the consequences of the decision in question.

Steinmann and his co-authors argue that private corporations should be held responsible to contribute to peace as the highest ethical principle of modern societies in so far as conflicts with corporate stakeholders are – or may be – caused by corporate strategy (for example Steinmann and Scherer, 1998, p. 12). Therefore all corporate decisions have to be reviewed if they are 'apt for consensus or peace'. Corporate ethics is understood as a restriction, because it reduces the set of feasible means available to management for making profits. In striving for profits, management has to design and implement strategies in such a way that they contribute to a peaceful relationship with the stakeholders of the firm. A peaceful and successful conflict resolution can only be reached by a discourse or a dialogue between the company and its external and internal stakeholders that results in self-imposed rules which supplement the existing law as a basis to legitimate corporate action.

## 2    ULRICH'S INTEGRATIVE APPROACH TO BUSINESS ETHICS

Ulrich does basic work by methodologically mediating between morality and rationality and systemetically discussing issues in philosophy, economics and business administration. His goal is to overcome the disciplinary border between ethics and economics and to reunite the disciplines. Ulrich's approach starts from the insight that economic thinking or economic rationality itself is a normative logic that needs ethical reflection. It intends an ethical critique of the economic logic of the free enterprise and aims at broadening the concept of economic rationality from its normative basis. Ulrich's programme of communicative-ethical rationality is built on a comprehensive critique of utilitarianism and a discourse-ethical broadening of contractarian approaches (Ulrich, 1993, p. 173). He develops a discourse-ethical concept of responsibility that explicitly requires to acknowledge all those affected by business activities as responsible persons who are capable of arguing reasonably. Ulrich's approach focuses on the mediation and reunion of ethical reason and economic rationality. To this end he transforms the concept of economic rationality into the concept of socio-economic rationality. Ulrich specifies his regulative idea of socio-economic rationality for the economic system as a whole (Ulrich, 1989) as well as for the management system (Ulrich, 1991). For the latter he proposes to systematically integrate ethical questions into management rationality by classifying different management duties in three levels of normative, strategic and operative management, each requiring a different type of rationality (see Figure 3.1). For management duties at the operative level, where the company is seen as a combination of factors of production, instrumental rationality is adequate. According to Ulrich, duties at the level of strategic management, where the company is seen as a socio-technical system, require socio-technical rationality. At the level of normative management the company is seen as a quasi-public institution. The concept of a quasi-public institution acknowledges that a company has a variety of internal and external stakeholders. Individual preferences are not necessarily served best by a formal corporate goal (such as profit maximization), nor can they be aggregated into consistent collective preferences. A collective order of preferences can only be established by consensus of all stakeholders. Thus normative management requires communicative-ethical rationality to achieve non-persuasive, uncoerced and unbiased understanding.

Corporate ethics is seen as the constitutive groundwork of any socio-economically rational business firm. It aims at clarifying and safeguarding all normative preconditions for a life-conducive 'value-creation' in the corporation (Ulrich, 1998). This has to be done on two levels of corporate morality. First, management has to pursue a life-conducive corporate mission, that means, that a business firm should only make money with products and/or services that have a real value for the 'good life' of the customers and do not impose negative externalities on other people or the community as a whole. Secondly, a corporation and its managers must recognize a republican co-responsibility for the life-conduciveness of the economic order. Thus Ulrich

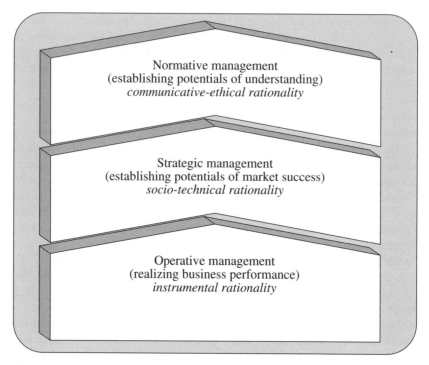

*Figure 3.1    Adequate types of rationality in the business firm*

holds business firms and managers as corporate citizens responsible to initiate
and to support ethically sound reforms of the economic order.

## 3    HOMANN'S ECONOMIC THEORY OF MORALS

Homann's approach is distinguished by its strictly institutional perspective
and its focus on the economic order. Homann presents a two-stage model
of business ethics, where the economic order lays down the rules for business
decisions and actions. He stresses the importance to distinguish between the
level of the regulations of the economy and the level of activities within these
regulations, or as he puts it in the language of sports 'between rules of the
games and moves' (Homann and Blome-Drees, 1992, p. 20). Within the
framework of the economic order – which is seen as the 'methodic place of
morality' – business acting can exclusively be oriented by efficiency. Hence it
is of crucial importance to formulate the rules for business behaviour in such
a way that they represent positive incentives for morally desirable behaviour
and negative incentives for morally undesirable behaviour.

Homann uses the well-known prisoner's dilemma as a general heuristic for the analysis of social decisions and actions. The central notion of this concept is that in each interaction the involved individual actors have common as well as conflicting interests. As all individual actors are locked into a situation of living together, their common interest is to establish a social order. The conflicting interests are the result of sharing the contributions and social gains. In a dilemma structure, the common interests do not necessarily result in the individual actions that are necessary to realize them. Just the opposite is true – individual actions lead into a 'social trap', which is often referred to as 'collective irrationality'. As each actor must be prepared that his cooperative behaviour could be exploited by the other actor(s), mutual defection is the dominant strategy for the individual. This is also true with decision problems in business life: moral actions of managers or companies will be exploited by their competitors. Therefore morally acting companies will be punished financially and finally driven out of the market. Homann and his co-authors argue that the only way out of this situation of mutual defection is the design of different rules of the game. Moral problems in business can only be solved collectively: adequate moral norms have to be made compulsory for all competitors, thus providing a competitively neutral solution. As it is impossible to construct perfect economic rules there always exist deficits in the economic order that have to be compensated by individuals or companies. When the economic order does not fulfil its function the moral responsibility temporarily falls back to the individual manager or to the company (Homann, 1994, p. 115). However, the final aim always is to enforce morality by means of collective, competitively neutral economic rules.

Homann's approach is based on the assumption that doing good depends much more on the institutional regulations than on individual motives. From that point of view moral attitudes, individual dispositions and personal preferences are only secondary factors in business ethics. Homann argues that because of the functional logic of the free enterprise it is a moral duty for companies to make profits. In case of conflicting demands between morality and economic efficiency the only thing a responsible company or manager has to do is to voice concern about given rules or practices and work towards an improvement of the collective incentive structure. From an economic point of view moral norms can only achieve lasting effectiveness if they are beneficial to individuals, otherwise they will be eroded. Relying on Buchanan and Gauthier, Homann argues that the decisive reason for the individual to accept and to obey moral norms is their productivity. The most important advantages resulting from voluntarily agreed upon morals are the reliability of mutual expectations of behaviour and the increase of individual freedom of action. Homann's concept makes clear that morality can only counterbalance isolated incentives to immoral action; in the long run morals need the institutional support of incentives and advantages to 'survive'. Thus the focus is shifted to the conditions of business behaviour, which are often neglected in US-American approaches to business ethics.

At the level of the business firm, Homann and Blome-Drees propose two different types of strategies that companies should realize to deal with the strained relations between morals and profit: a competitive or a regulatory strategy (Homann and Blome-Drees, 1992, p. 133). The reference point to characterize the different types of strategy is the institutional framework. Within a given economic order, due to the logic of the free enterprise, a corporation can only pursue a competitive strategy that is profit-oriented. Firms should try to 'functionalize' morals in order to earn more money. A regulatory strategy aims at changing existing rules and comprises political activities of the company. This type of strategy can either be realized through participation of the company or its managers in political decision-making or through collective self-enforcement of companies in the form of ethical codes for a whole industry.

It depends on contextual factors which strategy should be realized. To characterize the situation for business firms that want to integrate moral aspects in their strategy formulation Homann and Blome-Drees propose a scheme with four quadrants based on the two dimensions – moral acceptance and profitability (see Figure 3.2). A situation which allows actions that are profitable as well as morally acceptable calls for a competitive strategy – in the *case of positive compatibility* in quadrant I a firm should try to gain a competitive advantage by emphasizing the ethical quality of its action. In *cases of negative compatibility* possible alternatives are morally unacceptable and not profitable at the same time. The best option is to withdraw from the market. Quadrants II and III describe situations that present a moral dilemma for the firm. Quadrant III shows a situation in which a morally acting firm has an economic disadvantage. However, in the long run the firm will not be able to give away profits and act against the logic of the free enterprise. Thus the only recommendable alternative in *cases of economic conflict* is a regulatory strategy that aims at changing prevailing rules. It can be realized either with industry-wide self-regulation or political activities to change existing laws. A situation in which highly profitable decisions are morally unacceptable can be described as a *case of a moral conflict* – economically efficient, legal actions would not consider the legitimated claims of one or more stakeholders. Companies either can improve the ethical quality of their own behaviour and thus realize a competitive strategy or they can try to influence the behaviour of all competitors towards higher moral acceptance, implementing a regulatory strategy.

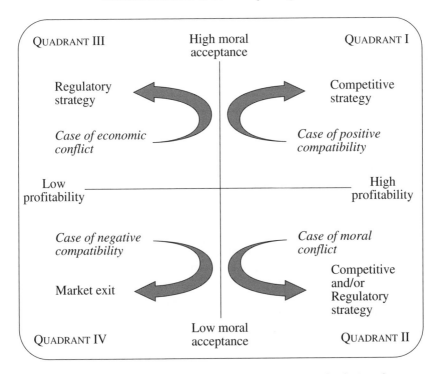

*Figure 3.2 Strategic alternatives to deal with the strained relations between morals and profit*

*Source*: Adapted from Homann/Blome-Drees 1992, 133 and 141.

## 4 ASSESSING THE CONTRIBUTION OF DISCOURSE ETHICAL AND CONTRACTARIAN APPROACHES TO IMPROVE THE ETHICAL QUALITY OF BUSINESS DECISIONS AND ACTIONS

### 4.1 Contribution of Discourse Ethical Approaches

#### 4.1.1 Theoretical considerations

Discourse ethical approaches stress the right of self-determination and take the view that management has the obligation to recognize and acknowledge the legitimate interests of the corporation's stakeholders or those affected by its decisions. Recently Reed has developed a normative stakeholder management theory that heavily draws upon the works of Habermas (Reed, 1999). In focusing on normative theory, Reed has demonstrated how a discourse ethical approach brings two important advantages to the analysis of stakeholder management theory: first, its theoretical rigour provides a firm basis for establishing both the validity and the scope of responsibilities that management owes to stakeholders. Second, its conceptual clarity concerning the distinction of three different normative realms (namely, legitimacy, morality and ethics) provides 'the basis for clearly establishing who is a stakeholder, the nature of the responsibilities owed to stakeholders, the circumstances that can influence these responsibilities, and how disputes involving conflicting stakes can be resolved' (Reed, 1999, p. 480).

A critical assumption of discourse ethical approaches is that individuals are already capable as well as motivated to resolve moral conflicts in a discoursive procedure in which all participants transcend their subjectivity to reach a common consensus. Thus a high level of individual competence in moral thought and moral judgement emerges as an essential prerequisite without which the implementation of practical discourses becomes illusionary. In other words, the moral result the discourse is to produce is already presupposed in the discourse participants (Rebstock, 1993, p. 811). It is relatively easy to instruct a person in his or her cognitive moral competence and much more difficult or even impossible to teach empathy, caring and sense of responsibility. However, these emotionally oriented constructs are precon-ditions for acquiring and realizing cognitive moral competence.

### 4.1.2  General questions of implementation

Focusing on concerns of application, it can be said that discourse ethical approaches foster the emergence of true dialogic processes in business firms. The ideal of genuine communication can serve as a ground against which typical organizational communication patterns and business goals and strategies are analysed. Even if the ideal of a *'herrschaftsfreier Diskurs'* can never be realized in business practice it makes sense to stress the discourse principle's character as a regulative idea. Discourse ethics spells out the elements and requirements of a process for 'right' decision-taking. In the reality of business decision-making the dialogic process aims at identifying stakeholder views and moral claims more effectively, discussing these claims in a relatively open forum, uncovering social and ethical challenges and trying to work out acceptable solutions. What is important in the context of business decision-making is the *procedure of discoursive argumentation* that serves to orient and regulate the decision-making process or even the process of leadership as a whole.

Discourse ethical approaches require a structure of the management process which is itself open to and promotes dialogues between organization members, managers as well as employees. Thus an important managerial task is to create a framework or a climate that encourages open discussion of moral questions in practical situations. It can be said that the implementation of a corporate ethics as discourse ethics calls for a paradigmatic change in management from a monologue-oriented to a dialogue-oriented rationality. Discourse ethical approaches encourage managers to take into account different points of view in their decisions and to engage in critical reflections on their stated positions. To implement discoursive processes does not imply that personal moral understandings are subsumed in some greater 'group norm'. It implies that managers as decision-makers respect difference and see it as something which brings richness to the decision-making process rather than as something negative or destructive. In a climate of value diversity processes of ethical decision-making require altruistic and charismatic leadership that strengthens people's perception of their own efficacy and worth and thus supports an effective organizational community of dialogue (Collier, 1998, p. 645). What is needed is a non-coercive participatory and democratic relationship between leaders and followers that recognizes individual autonomy. Managers have to create transparency, work towards consensus, consult as widely as possible and ensure that the needs and interests of those not represented at the point of decision-making also are taken into account.

To realize practical discourses corporate dialogues can be established, where companies discuss various public interest issues with their external and internal stakeholders searching for understanding and consensus when assessing the consequences of alternative corporate actions (Zöller, 1999, p. 197). Depending on who is potentially concerned, dialogue participants come either from the local or a wider environment. A corporate dialogue that obeys certain principles such as interactivity, openness, inclusiveness and neutrality should result in more and better information for the company and its stakeholders, more transparency, room for new arguments, clear differentiation between consensual and contentious arguments, an improved problem-solving capacity and more adequate risk assessment.

### 4.1.3   A practical case: environmental protection

The following short discussion of concrete strategy recommendations based on discourse ethical approaches focuses on the practical moral issue of environmental protection. Discourse ethical approaches propose to establish *corporate dialogues* as a potential means to project the values of different stakeholders so as to be recognized by organizational governance. Corporate dialogues can focus on different questions and issues with more or less ethical content, searching for mutual understanding and – if possible – consensus or agreement on controversial points. Hansen et al. recently have identified 25 dialogical procedures in German enterprises (for example Unilever Deutschland, Kraft-Jacobs-Suchard, Henkel, Procter & Gamble Germany), indicating a growing importance of corporate dialogues (Hansen, et al., 1997).

Confronted with critical voices concerning the water-polluting effects of a new detergent Procter & Gamble Germany was amongst the first companies that realized corporate dialogues. In the WAGE dialogue (WAschen und GEwaesserschutz: washing and protection of rivers and seas) they established a 'discourse arena' in the firm, where different stakeholders were talking about laundry and water pollution. Representatives of the industry, universities, trade unions, churches, environmentalists, consumers and housewives were participants in the dialogue, but there were no politicians or journalists.

According to Hans Merkle, communication director at Procter & Gamble Germany, the dialogue helped to objectivize the discussion and initiated the search for consensual solutions (Merkle, 1991, p. 430). Another example of a company that has successfully established a corporate dialogue is Hoechst, a conglomerate of chemical companies producing pharmaceuticals, agricultural products and commodities for industrial chemistry (Zöller, 1999, p. 202). The headquarters are in Germany at the biggest site, Frankfurt am Main. Several years ago Hoechst suffered some severe accidents where toxic emissions escaped, a worker was killed and some people were injured. Reacting to the accidents (and the following very bad press coverage), the board of management established a corporate dialogue with affected neighbours of the Frankfurt site, known as the 'Hoechst Neighbourhood Circle'. The circle meets about four times a year. The general manager of the site, other managers and staff members listen to the concerns of citizens' groups, environmental groups, clergy, children and youth groups, local sports clubs and the local ex-pats' association and offer feedback. Discussed topics include air pollution and emissions, transport of hazardous material, energy supply and the environmental auditing system. Hoechst managers confirm that through dialogue, a new forum for discussing different perspectives and asking critical questions has been created. As a result of the corporate dialogue some long-standing conflicts could be solved: the company has begun to publish detailed emissions data of its Frankfurt site and has finally installed early-warning sirens in case of an accident.

The institutionalization of practical discourses as proposed in discourse ethical approaches can be regarded as an ideal procedural method for resolving conflicts between a corporation and ecological pressure groups. Carefully constructed discourse forums can serve as a new form of management control that could also foster greater managerial awareness, for example the ecological impacts of products and production processes. Establishing corporate dialogues requires that managers not only are able to justify rationally the positions they hold, but that they also engage in the effort to understand the reasons advanced by others to the point of being able to put themselves in the other's shoes (Collier, 1998, p. 643). Managers have to be aware of their own interests in the issue as well as of the interests of others and they also have to take into account how these interests will be affected by the outcome of the decision in question.

## 4.2 Contribution of Homann's Economic Theory of Morals

### 4.2.1 Focus on the economic order

Homann provides a sophisticated economic analysis of the chances of and the conditions for the implementation of moral norms and ideals. His economic theory of morals explains if and how the compliance with moral norms and ideals can be made profitable (Homann, 1994, p. 123). It offers a rational defence of basic moral constraints by way of appeal to the maximized self-interest of the individual. Homann argues that the decisive reason for the individual to accept and to obey certain moral norms is the productivity of these morals. The practical implementation of moral norms requires that they are advantageous for every individual. Morality is thus given a sure grounding in a weak and widely accepted conception of practical rationality. Homann's concept makes clear that morality can only counterbalance isolated incentives to immoral action; in the long run morals need the institutional support of incentives and advantages to survive.

Homann stresses the importance of the economic order that systematically can create incentives for companies and managers to act morally. Because of the globalization of business relations and transactions the rules for business behaviour would have to be formulated on a global basis, thus making the monitoring extremely difficult and expensive (Grabner-Kräuter, 1998, p. 79). The result is a dilemma between either strictly binding regulations inducing extremely high costs of control or rather 'soft' rules that would not produce unaffordable costs of control. Homann argues that within the rules of the game maximizing profits is not only legitimate but also essential for preserving the corporation's competitiveness and thus ensuring social welfare. However, rules at the macro-level can only help to assure proper corporate behaviour in appropriate situations. They cannot completely determine actions at the individual or the organizational level in any case. The remaining ethical gap can only be filled with individual and/or corporate responsibility.

### 4.2.2 A practical case: environmental protection

Following Homann's line of reasoning questions of environmental protection have to be analysed as an economic problem. From an economic point of view environmental protection will only be realized when it is beneficial or profitable for the firm. Although there certainly are non-economic aspects of pollution, they must not dominate the business ethics discussion. Understanding environmental pollution in *economic terms* implies that adequate economic incentives have to be given that encourage companies to make investments in environmental protection. For a company that wants to consider ecological aspects in its business policies Homann and Blome-Drees (1992, p. 135) recommend two different types of strategy to deal with the strained relations between morals and profit: a competitive or a regulatory strategy. Within a given economic order, due to the logic of the free enterprise a corporation can only pursue a *competitive strategy* that is profit-oriented. Firms should try to functionalize morals in order to earn more money. Hence it is necessary that a firm takes a competitive advantage out of ecologically beneficial products or non-polluting methods of production. This can be done for example by differentiating a product via an ecological dimension and thus gaining an argument for higher margins. A firm in the detergent industry could reach a competitive advantage by developing an effective detergent with only biodegradable components and by convincingly communicating the ecological positioning to its target groups. This strategy was successfully realized for example by the German company Erdal that introduced a complete line of relatively high-priced green detergents with the brand name 'frog' (the original German brand name is 'Frosch') several years ago and thus was able to aquire distinctiveness in the highly competitive detergent market. In this case, the morally right way to act simultaneously is financially rewarded. A regulatory strategy aims at changing existing rules and comprises political activities of the company. This type of strategy can either be realized through participation of the company or its managers in political decision processes or through collective self-enforcement of companies in the form of ethical codes for a whole industry (for example a collective agreement of all firms in the detergent industry to produce detergents that are biodegradable up to a certain amount). With the formulation of ethical codes for an industry corporations substitute government regulations and possibly enhance the moral acceptance of a whole industry. Collective agreements are more flexible than state laws, but because they are public goods they are subject to the problem of free-riding. Thus it is necessary to develop effective control mechanisms to ensure the compliance with industry-wide ethical codes.

## 5  CONCLUSION

This chapter has set out prominent, theoretically based approaches to 'Unternehmensethik' in Germany and Switzerland. The integrity-based approach to ethics (to which discourse ethics belongs) focuses on the decisions and actions of the individual under certain conditions and is very important in business ethics. In this context the discourse principle can be seen as a regulative idea to orient individual as well as organizational decision-making. But the individual, action-oriented perspective dominating the business ethics discussion has to be complemented by a social, institution-oriented perspective. Individual ethics will have only a limited effect if it is not accompanied by a change in structures and processes in the firm as well as in the economic order with its multiple institutions. With its focus on the systemic macro-level of the economic order Homann's contractarian approach provides an appropriate institutional perspective.

A corporate ethics cannot prescribe certain generally binding norms and specific actions as a final remedy for moral problems. 'Connecting' management and ethics rather means to look at problems from a new or unusual perspective, to ask critical questions and to contribute alternative aspects to the discussion. Adequate economic rules and procedural methods to resolve moral conflicts are not sufficient to improve the ethical quality of corporate decisions and actions. The 'ethicality' of business organizations or their managers is something more than compliance with externally imposed regulations or standards. The discussed approaches rather neglect that moral decisions require not only rationality but also affective and intuitive skills. In concrete circumstances ethical decision-making always requires a sensitivity to the situation, as well as an awareness of the beliefs, feelings, attitudes, and concerns of each involved individual and of the relationships between those individuals.

In order to improve the ethical quality of corporate decisions and actions all levels of acting must be considered – the macro-level of the economic order, the meso-level of the organization and the micro-level of the individual. At the level of the individual, the capability to consider abstract ethical principles in moral decision-making usually is not sufficient to result in moral behaviour in a particular situation. Soft, emotional aspects such as a sense of responsibility, caring, human warmth and friendliness often play a crucial role in making ethically sound judgements and decisions in corporate practice and therefore must not be neglected. Here the contributions of studies of ethical issues related to leadership and the ethics of leadership can add considerably to our understanding of what ethical decision-making in managerial relationships means (see for example Ciulla, 1995).

## REFERENCES

Apel, K.-O. (1988), *Diskurs und Verantwortung. Das Problem des Übergangs zur postkonventionellen Moral*, Frankfurt a.M.: Suhrkamp.

Benhabib, S. (1986), *Critique, Norm, and Utopia. A Study of the Foundations of Critical Theory*, New York: Columbia University Press.

Bowen, M.G. and Power, F.C. (1993), 'The Moral Manager: Communicative Ethics and the Exxon Valdez Disaster', *Business Ethics Quarterly*, **3**(1), 97–115.

Ciulla, J.B. (1995), 'Leadership Ethics: Mapping the Territory', *Business Ethics Quarterly*, **5**(1), 5–28.

Collier, J. (1998), 'Theorising the Ethical Organization', *Business Ethics Quarterly*, **8** (4), 621–654.

Dierkes, M. and Zimmermann, K. (1994), 'The Institutional Dimension of Business Ethics: An Agenda for Reflection Research and Action', *Journal of Business Ethics*, **13**, 533–541.

Enderle, G. (1993), *Handlungsorientierte Wirtschaftsethik. Grundlagen und Anwendungen*, Bern et al.: Haupt.

Grabner-Kräuter, S. (1998), *Die Ethisierung des Unternehmens. Ein Beitrag zum wirtschaftsethischen Diskurs*, Wiesbaden: Gabler.

Habermas, J. (1992), *Faktizität und Geltung. Beiträge zur Diskurstheorie des Rechts und des demokratischen Rechtsstaats*, Frankfurt a.M.: Suhrkamp.

Habermas, J. (1991), *Erläuterungen zur Diskursethik*, Frankfurt a.M.: Suhrkamp.

Habermas, J. (1983), 'Diskursethik – Notizen zu einem Begründungsprogramm', in: Habermas, J. (ed.), *Moralbewußtsein und kommunikatives Handeln*, Frankfurt a.M.: Suhrkamp, pp. 53–125.

Habermas, J. (1981), *Theorie des kommunikativen Handelns*, Band 1 und Band 2, Frankfurt a.M.: Suhrkamp.

Hansen, U., Niedergesäß, U. and Rettberg, B. (1997), 'Erscheinungsformen von Unternehmensdialogen', *PR-Forum für Wissenschaft und Praxis*, **3**, 32–36.

Homann, K. (1998), 'Normativität angesichts systemischer Sozial- und Denk-strukturen', in Gaertner, W. (ed.), *Wirtschaftsethische Perspektiven IV*, Berlin: Duncker & Humblot, pp. 17-50.

Homann, K. (1994), 'Marktwirtschaft und Unternehmensethik', in Forum für Philosophie Bad Homburg (ed.), *Markt und Moral. Die Diskussion um die Unternehmensethik*, Bern et al.: Haupt, pp. 109-130.

Homann, K. (1989), 'Die Rolle ökonomischer Überlegungen in der Grundlegung der Ethik', in Hesse, H. (ed.), *Wirtschaftswissenschaft und Ethik*, 2nd edn, Berlin: Duncker & Humblot, pp. 215-240.

Homann, K. and Blome-Drees, F. (1992), *Wirtschafts- und Unternehmensethik*, Göttingen: Vandenhoeck & Ruprecht.

Merkle, H. (1991), 'Ökologische Lernprozesse in einem Markenartikelunternehmen', in Steinmann, H. and Löhr, A. (eds.), *Unternehmensethik*, 2nd edn, Stuttgart: Poeschel, pp. 427-436.

Preuss, L. (1999), 'Ethical Theory in German Business Ethics Research', *Journal of Business Ethics*, **18**, 407-419.

Rebstock, M. (1993), 'Moralische Entwicklung in Organisationen. Zur Ergänzung der unternehmensethischen Diskussion', *Die Betriebswirtschaft*, **53**(6), 807-818.

Reed, D. (1999), 'Stakeholder Management Theory: A Critical Theory Perspective', *Business Ethics Quarterly*, **9**(3), 453-483.

Steinmann, H. and Kustermann, B. (1996), 'Current Developments in German Business Ethics', *Business Ethics - A European Review*, **5**, 12-18.

Steinmann, H. and Löhr, A. (1994a), *Grundlagen der Unternehmensethik*, 2nd edn, Stuttgart: Schäffer-Poeschel.

Steinmann, H. and Löhr, A. (1994b), 'Unternehmensethik – Ein republikanisches Programm in der Kritik', in Forum für Philosophie Bad Homburg (ed.), *Markt und Moral. Die Diskussion um die Unternehmensethik*, Bern et al.: Haupt, pp. 145-180.

Steinmann, H. and Scherer, A. (1998), *Corporate Ethics and Management Theory*, Working Paper No. 93, University of Erlangen-Nürnberg.

Ulrich, P. (1989), 'Diskursethik und Politische Ökonomie', in Biervert, B. and Held, M. (eds.), *Ethische Grundlagen der ökonomischen Theorie. Eigentum, Verträge, Institutionen*, Frankfurt a.m./New York: Campus, pp. 70–99.

Ulrich, P. (1998), *Integrative Economic Ethics. Towards a Conception of Socio-Economic Rationality*, Working Paper No. 82, University of St Gallen.

Ulrich, P. (1993), *Transformation der ökonomischen Vernunft. Fortschrittsperspektiven der modernen Industriegesellschaft*, 3rd edn, Bern et al.: Haupt.

Ulrich, P. (1991), 'Unternehmensethik – Führungsinstrument oder Grundlagen reflexion?', in Steinmann, H. and Löhr, A. (eds.), *Unternehmensethik*, 2nd edn, Stuttgart: Poeschel, pp. 189–212.

Zöller, K. (1999), 'Growing Credibility through Dialogue. Experiences in Germany and the USA', in Charter, M. and Polonsky, M.J. (eds.), *Greener Marketing. A Global Perspective on Greening Marketing Practice*, Greenleaf Publishing, 196–206.

# 4. The economic approach to corporate citizenship: the main argument

## Bernhard Seitz

## 1 INTRODUCTION

The purpose of this chapter is to present the basic fundamentals of the economic approach to corporate citizenship. Two arguments are central to this endeavour. The first fundamental assertion is that *good* corporate citizenship is only possible if the conditions under which corporations operate allow it. The second assertion is that corporations have an interest in the development of such conditions.

What comes to mind when we think about citizenship? Most of us probably think of a society in which adults create and maintain a political and social order, and of the rights and duties of individuals in their relationships with others.

Social rights and duties are anything but natural. They emerge from rules that encourage specific behaviour in specific situations. But who determines these rules? How are they made? Rules may be informal or formal and we must ask these questions with respect to legal regulations as well as social expectations or even regulative ideas.[1]

The concept of good corporate citizenship – which in itself is a specific definition of rights and duties, of rules – has been receiving a great deal of attention lately. But again, in a pluralistic society, who decides what the 'good' stands for? Should we accept Milton Friedman's (Friedman [1962], 1982, p. 133) classical liberal statement that 'there is only one social responsibility of business – to use its resources and engage in activities designed to increase its profits so long as it stays within the rules of the game'? Or should we go along with researchers who argue for a primacy of ethics (Ulrich, 1998) or for corporate social responsibilities (Wood, 1994), where primacy or responsibility are synonyms for the use of corporate resources without a measurable competitive return on investment, and thus go against economic logic?

This chapter proposes an answer to these questions by taking economic logic one step further. On the basis of an economic theory of morals (Homann,

1999; Homann and Suchanek, 2000) we can redefine the idea of citizenship in terms of economics. In the logic of an economic theory of morals, institutions and rules – and thus the idea of citizenship – are the result of the behaviour and reflections of self-interested individuals.

With this as the starting point, we can construct the idea of corporate citizenship along the same lines as personal citizenship, as a means to improve the individual's situation. This approach goes further than Milton Friedman, who ultimately underestimates the implications of medium-term corporate profit maximization in a world of systematically incomplete contracts. It also resolves the problems of Peter Ulrich's or Donna Wood's oversimplified approaches which ultimately ask business to maximize something other than its profits, thus going against the economic logic on which the efficiency of a sophisticated and functional economic system depends.

## 2  THEORETICAL FUNDAMENTALS

### 2.1  The Purpose of Rules and of the Idea of Citizenship

Rules encourage specific behaviour in specific situations. Rules create restrictions and impose duties on the individual. Rules generate costs. The concept of citizenship requires the individual's involvement. Involvement as a citizen implies costs, measured in time and resources.

Both rules and the concept of citizenship are thus basically disadvantageous, because they entail costs and restrictions. So why should an individual or a company agree to rules or become involved as a citizen?

From an economic point of view the answer is clear. Individuals will only agree to a specific rule or become involved as citizens if doing so improves their situations in comparison to the relevant alternatives. Such behaviour must be advantageous – not all the time but on the whole. The consequences of a rule may be advantageous or disadvantageous for an individual in a particular instance. But if the rules that govern an interaction are evaluated by an individual, then the rules as rules must be generally advantageous: I may find it difficult in a specific situation to respect somebody else's property rights. But I support the rule that property rights ought to be respected, even though maybe in some situations I would prefer not to have to respect them.

As rules are disadvantageous in principle, they must create some additional value in order to become advantageous. Therefore, rules must increase security and improve the conditions for investment and/or exchange.

### 2.1.1  Conclusion
The purpose of both rules and the idea of citizenship is to improve the

individual's situation in comparison to the relevant alternatives by increasing security and encouraging exchange and longer-term investment.

## 2.2 The Making of Legitimate Rules

In the prisoners' dilemma, which in our approach theoretically represents the mechanics of interaction, rules can only be agreed upon individually and collectively by both players (Kant [1786], 1984). Neither player, regardless of the individual's moral disposition, can arrive at the Pareto-superior solution alone. Unequal power of the parties does not alter this fundamental principle (Buchanan, 1995).

In modern society with multiple layers of rule-making bodies, the principle that rules are made individually and collectively by the parties concerned is much less obvious. One of the major problems with modern states may be that rules are made by players who do not or do not adequately represent those who are actually affected, which may lead to rules which are neither advantageous nor enforceable.

One of the most exciting aspects of corporate citizenship is its function as the cornerstone of a more sophisticated political system – extending the power to make rules to those affected by them.

### 2.2.1 Conclusion
The parties subject to a rule individually and collectively determine that rule.

## 2.3 Individuals and Corporations

With regard to citizenship and the making and enforcement of social rules, we should examine the differences and similarities between the individual as a single human being and the individual as a corporation. The two are similar in so far as they are both identifiable entities that can be held accountable – although in different ways – and both have specific interests which they express and pursue. It is only because of these similarities, and because the content of the individual's interests is secondary for economic theory, that an economic concept of citizenship which embraces both individuals and corporations can be developed.

The most important difference between individual and corporate citizenship here is that the corporation as a theoretical system is in itself a specific set of rules, created directly or indirectly by human beings for their own advantage on the basis of their wants. The owner- (profit-) oriented corporation is a social tool designed to improve everybody's situation in the long term. Its success in fulfilling that task has been confirmed by two hundred years of capitalism which have brought a higher standard of living than ever to a greater number of individuals.

To assure that the complex interactions among the different systems of society efficiently fulfil their ultimate objective, individuals, in their roles as citizens, must remain the ultimate guardians of society's overall development.

Corporate citizenship neither replaces personal citizenship, nor for example governments, churches or NGOs as citizens. Through their conflicts and their cooperation, they all work together in order to further improve individual welfare. The rule of their relationship is that according to each players own interests they will succeed or fail together.

### 2.3.1 Conclusion

The owner-oriented corporation is in itself a tool to improve individual situations in the long term.

### 2.4 The Objective of the Corporation

According to the rules that constitute and govern a corporation, the owners' interests are the residual variable. Because the success of a corporation is increasingly measured on the financial markets in terms of the corporation's profitability, profit maximization or shareholder value become more and more the owner's predominant interests.

The typical corporation must maximize its profits or shareholder value. It can satisfy any restriction which is imposed on it but it cannot maximize anything else. Any restriction or duty imposed on the corporation will be measured against its longer-term positive impact on this variable.

Profit maximization usually has a negative connotation with its emphasis on short-term success. But this understanding is oversimplified, because profit maximization is also the sole objective of investment. Short-term profit realization (not maximization!) is only possible through medium-term investment.

In a competitive environment, the company with the best investment strategy, which is always a medium-term strategy, will be successful. The logic of a market economy forces corporations to calculate the future as accurately as possible. If the calculation is too short or oversimplified, thus overemphasizing profit realization, it will disregard important investment opportunities. If a corporation's calculation is too long or too complex, uncertainty will invalidate the projection and the estimation of investment risks.

### 2.4.1   Conclusion
Profit maximization is the residual variable of listed corporations. The objective of profit maximization leads to a medium-term investment strategy.

## 2.5   Collective Goods and the Profit-oriented Corporation

The fundamental question here is: does the profit-oriented corporation have an interest in the availability and further development of collective goods such as education, a functioning legal and political system, an intact environment and a wealthy society in general?

The general answer to that question is clearly 'yes'. Education increases human productivity. Educated people tend to have more sophisticated needs. Corporations can satisfy these needs while making better profits. The same logic applies for the legal or political system, the environment and so on.

If there is one general condition for long-term business success, it is a prosperous society. The optimal business environment is a society which is growing in many ways, be it in size, income, knowledge or opportunities. Business makes profits on growth and with new, innovative products. It loses money in shrinking markets and with outdated products. However, in our own interest, we cannot and should not expect corporations to let their decision process become less economical for the sake of providing collective goods. The logic of the prisoner's dilemma, in which an unprotected investment is ultimately as unproductive as no investment at all, has to be addressed carefully.

The problem is not that corporations have no interest in collective goods. It is rather that complex dilemmas must be resolved in order to provide these goods. In this respect, human citizenship and corporate citizenship are similar. They differ in that in a period of a few thousand years human beings have developed institutions of human citizenship which resolve these dilemmas. We are accustomed to the idea that the existing institutions can continue to efficiently supply collective goods. But globalization and increased social differentiation make this impossible. The challenge ahead is to develop new institutions that resolve the complex dilemmas existing within and between corporations and other organizations such as nation states, churches and non-governmental organizations. The purpose of these new institutions from a corporation's point of view is to create opportunities for economically profitable investments in collective goods.

### 2.5.1   Conclusion
Corporations have an interest in the availability of collective goods. They will be prepared to invest in providing those goods as long as institutions can be

created to resolve complex dilemmas. Business itself has an interest in the creation of such institutions.

## 3 THE ECONOMIC DEFINITION OF CITIZENSHIP AND CORPORATE CITIZENSHIP

Based on economic theory as it has been developed in Ingolstadt and München, and of which some main elements have just been outlined, the following comprehensive normative definition of citizenship and corporate citizenship can be proposed:

> A citizen should discover his or her own interests, identify the conditions which support the medium-term maximization of these interests and integrate this set of conditions into the social rule development process.[2]
> It is a citizen's right to pursue his or her interests. It is a citizen's duty to strive for the maximization of his or her interests by means of calculation and investment.[3]

Citizenship becomes corporate citizenship with the following addition:

> Systematically, the residual self-interest of a corporation is medium-term profit maximization.

Other types of corporations may pursue different residual self-interests. From these definitions a descriptive version can be derived:

> Corporate Citizenship designates a business strategy in whose centre stands the idea of the corporation as a self-responsible player, that demands rights in its relationships with others, that is in exchange prepared to carry duties and that invests out of well-understood self-interest into the development of its society. Corporate Citizenship builds on the logic of the economic system and comprises immediately economic interactions. Its distinct task are complex social investments, including the response to social requests or problems.

The leitmotiv of shareholder value maximization must not be confused with profit realization or short-term shareholder orientation. Maximum shareholder value is never a state, always an idea for the future – that requests investment today.[4] The social profitability derives from the investment requirement, because to invest means to give first (with the intention to receive, which is as a rule as well in the interest of the giver, as of the recipient).

One advantage of the above definition is that it becomes immediately clear that 'I' for my self-interest need others: the baker's bread as well as nature's oxygen. Sustainable improvements of my position are only possible through mutual employment: I want the baker to supply good bread continuously.

Therefore I have an interest in the baker making a profit, because otherwise he will not supply good bread continuously. Adam Smith's invisible hand (Smith [1776], 1990) is then simply the expectation and greater profitability of further interactions.

From a corporation's point of view the main advantage of this definition is its comprehensiveness. There is only one normative strategy for a corporation's interactions[5] with economic, political and social players.[6]

Another advantage of the proposed definition is that it links rules with interests. Immediate and longer-term interests collide in many cases. In order to realize more valuable, longer-term objectives it is necessary to impose restrictions on immediate behaviour. Modern economic theory offers tools on how we can deal with these conflicts in a productive and sustainable way. Therefore it can guide corporations to become successful rule makers: good corporate citizens.

# 4   INVOLVEMENT AS A CORPORATE CITIZEN

## 4.1   Stakeholder Thinking as a Business Tool

The stakeholder model is often considered as an opposite to shareholder value orientation. From the perspective developed here however, a stakeholder understanding is a useful tool in order to implement a profit-oriented strategy. The reason for that is that none of the interaction partners of a corporation will interact with the corporation for the corporation's interest,[7] but only for its own interests. To pursue its interests successfully, the corporation has to take into account systematically the interests of its interaction partners. The corporation must prove that it is profitable for the interaction partners to interact with the corporation, because only if they experience that the interaction is profitable for them according to their interests will they contribute (so to say non-intentionally) to the corporation's residual objective.

Using the stakeholder model, and taking a specific problem as the starting point, a corporation can map its environment as an ensemble of interdependent players, each pursuing its own interests. The stakeholder map informs about the conditions under which the corporation operates. A social player like Greenpeace, the Catholic Church or the demonstrators on the streets of Seattle may become relevant for business simply because the player starts having an interest in business. The simple fact that players like these voice their interests creates conditions with which business has to deal. The other way around, for example, a university may become relevant for a corporation, because the corporation starts having an interest in this player. Either way the social technique to make an interaction sustainably advantageous remains the same:

Mutual employment for individual benefit. That mutual employment may not be feasible or mutually profitable in a specific situation does not change its systematic individual preferability.

Seen in this way shareholder value maximization can embrace and promote stakeholder thinking.

## 4.2 The Central Role of Frameworks

Modern society is characterized by large and complex systems of formal rules. If we accept that human beings as such have not changed much over the last few thousand years, then the wealth and freedom of modern society is mainly due to the social systems we live and work with – corporations and the economy being parts of these systems.

Considering that the welfare of each player relies at least as much on the productivity of these systems as on its individual performance, it is an essential task for corporate and personal citizens to develop these systems. This now leads to an extended vision of corporate citizenship.

In business practice corporate citizenship is mainly associated with corporate giving, foundations, volunteering and the like. With the concept of strategic social investment (Smith, 1994; Logan et al., 1997) these activities have been aligned closer to business objectives. However, these concepts do not seem to take into account sufficiently the logic of the prisoner's dilemma. The critique is that these approaches focus on profitability and feasibility without a sufficient conceptual base. The consequences are a rationalization of corporate citizenship and corporate social investment that loses out of sight the more difficult but most important issues: the formal rules and institutions through which a society develops and the publicly shared ideas that determine where a society is going to.

Just because it is very difficult to invest in these assets does not mean that they are not very important for long-term business success. Even in the most modern concepts of corporate citizenship, the political aspect of making the formal socio-political framework under which corporations operate, do not play the role which it should. Corporate investments in a public spirit that embraces key factors for long-term business success like ambition, a fundamental readiness to cooperate, creativity or trust (Rippberger, 1998) hardly play any role at all.

To understand the fundamental economic relevance of formal and informal social rules one may look at the competitive advantages of American companies because of the well-developed American capital markets and a social spirit of innovation. The strength of American pharmaceutical or software companies has little to do with the individual companies' efforts. That Microsoft has become the leading company in PC-software is accidental. That an American company had to become this force was a necessity, just as it is today with Internet companies or many other high-tech industries.

The question that corporations must ask today is: Which national and global, functional and inter-functional, formal and informal institutions will generate the competitive advantages of the next 30 years? With which players do we need to cooperate in order to build the supportive formal and informal institutions and frameworks?

Due to the social macro-phenomenon of increasing functional differentiation and mutual penetration, the importance of complex institutions involving non-traditional and non-economic players will grow. Due to globalization and regionalization as two other social macro-developments, new global and local frameworks and institutions will also play a greater role.

As a concept corporate citizenship so far has not engaged sufficiently in its main field of action: the development of the socio-political order of a given society. Strategic management theory seems to be more aware of the problem, but has not yet – at least to my knowledge – produced comprehensive strategies for social and economic investment (Porter, 1999; Brandenburger and Nalebuff, 1996). As modern economic theory offers a bridge for the gap between self-interested lobbyism and 'public interest', it can help corporate citizenship and strategic management theory to move on. Corporate citizenship and social investment are not only about the use of 1 or 2 per cent of profits for corporate giving or about a non-governmental organization (NGO) staging a campaign. The stakes involved are somewhere between 30 to 60 or more per cent of turnover.[8] The business question is: How can we increase in a sustainable – and therefore socially profitable – way the payback of our contributions to social institutions in forms of taxes, social security payments or corporate contributions? In order to construct possible answers to this question, corporations need to understand the mechanics of social cooperation and the implications of an economic theory of morals, or they will act as one-sided lobbyists that will ultimately fail in the socio-political sphere.

Practical problems with regard to the implementation of such a strategy result from the fact that investments in socio-political frameworks are generally long term, complex and require special knowledge. Whereas a sales or line manager should focus more on immediate success, a socio-political manager needs to think in much larger dimensions. Building a society is by nature a strategic task that needs specialized people and structures. Furthermore, traditional methodologies of calculation seem unable to deal with the degrees of complexity and uncertainty involved at reasonable cost. A solution to this question may come from a rule-oriented approach, working with qualitative categories.

## 5   SUMMARY AND A VIEW ON GLOBALIZATION

An economic approach to corporate citizenship leads to a comprehensive business strategy proposal for economic and social investment. Corporations have no other residual responsibility than to strive for profit maximization. The leitmotiv of profit maximization however leads to social investment, because as all players are self-interested, only those players will succeed that manage to build up networks of mutual employment. To invest in society and to involve as a corporate citizen are therefore necessary expressions of a rational corporate strategy. The success of such a strategy depends on the reciprocity among the relevant players. The corporation alone can only make its own investment decision.

As our economies and societies become ever more complex, business and society have an interest in building up new frameworks and institutions that can deal effectively with the new dilemmas of the new world. Corporations and other players should involve themselves through their roles as citizens in the creation and development of these institutions and frameworks.

In today's complex economy to produce no longer means to nail or to screw something together, but to organize a great variety of players – the equivalent of attracting other players and developing and implementing a system of rules: *to produce means to build a society!*

With globalization the need for a corporate policy capability to produce proposals which can reach genuine consent from a large variety of players has grown enormously. There is no (and should not be) a global superstate. Global corporations for their own interest and together with other players need to build socio-political global frameworks as functional equivalents to traditional states that resolve the most urgent economic *and* socio-political problems. Economic globalization cannot progress unless together with other systems. The essential task for a good global corporate citizen is to support directly and indirectly the creation of profitable global frameworks that other players can live with.

Corporations have to take on this role of managing change because the inefficiency of the (non-) existing global structures threatens their longer-term interests. The essential business strategy can be described in two words: corporate citizenship. The goal of this inter-systematic role as a corporate citizen is the development of rules, which frame short-term-oriented actions and guarantee medium-term profitability. In other words: The development of a political framework that makes *good* corporate citizenship profitable is the most important step of good corporate citizenship.

## NOTES

1. The latter two represent informal rules insofar as they guide (set incentives for) individual behaviour in social situations. Values, visions or ideas like freedom or honesty can be considered as having a character as informal rules.
2. In an appropriate way, which means to accept conflicting interests and to search for common interests.
3. In a less economic terminology one may use the term self-regulation instead of investment.
4. Theoretically, every expenditure of the corporation should be an investment that serves profit maximization. Even dividend payments of the corporation are from that perspective investments of the corporation under the leitmotiv of profit maximization: the corporation offers a payment today, so that shareholders support the longer-term business strategy, which must promise an additional value.
5. From the perspective developed here, there is only one strategic approach for all investments. The economic system is also socially constructed. Social investment therefore is the generic term, including investment in economic, political, educational, scientific, juridical or other social systems.
6. Including those representing nature.
7. Employees, customers, universities, ... even the actual shareholder of a company will not have interests that are identical with those of the corporation as a rule system.
8. Considering economic investment as being separate from social investment. As described earlier, economic investment is a part of social investment. If a corporation increases the wealth of its shareholders or purchases goods from a supplier, then that is obviously also a contribution to social wealth.

## REFERENCES

Brandenburger, Adam and Nalebuff, Barry (1996), *Co-opetition*, New York: Doubleday.

Buchanan, James M. (1995), 'Individual Rights, Emergent Social States, and Behavioral Feasibility', *Rationality and Society*, Vol. 7, No. 2, April, pp. 141–150.

Friedman, Milton [1962] (1982), *Capitalism and Freedom*, Chicago/London: University of Chicago Press.

Homann, Karl (1999), 'Konzept II der Wirtschaftsethik: Ethik mit ökonomischer Methode', in Wilhelm Korff (ed.), *Handbuch der Wirtschaftsethik*, Band 1, Gütersloh: Güterloher Verlagshaus, pp. 332–343.

Homann, Karl and Suchanek, Andreas (2000), *Ökonomik - Eine Einführung*, Tübingen: Mohr Siebeck.

Kant, Immanuel [1786] (1984), *Grundlegung zur Metaphysik der Sitten*, 2. Aufl., Riga, Stuttgart: Reclam.

Logan, David, Roy, Delwin and Regelbrugge, Laurie (1997), *Global Corporate Citizenship - Rationale and Strategies*, Washington, DC: The Hitachi Foundation.

Porter, Michael E. (1999), 'Unternehmen können von regionaler Vernetzung profitieren', *Harvard Business Manager*, **3**, pp. 51–63.

Rippberger, Tanja (1998), *Ökonomik des Vertrauens: Analyse eines Organisationsprinzips*, Tübingen: Mohr Siebeck.

Smith, Adam [1776] (1990), *Der Wohlstand der Nationen*, 5. Aufl., München.

Smith, Craig (1994), 'Der neue Hang zu wohltätigem Handeln', *Harvard Business Manager*, **4**, p. 104 f.

Ulrich, Peter (1998), *Integrative Wirtschaftsethik: Grundlagen einer lebensdienlichen Ökonomie*, 2. Aufl., Bern/Stuttgart/Wien: Haupt.

Wood, Donna J. (1994), *Business and Society*, 2nd edn, Harper Collins: New York.

# 5. Normative stakeholder management: balancing legitimate claims[1]

**Stephan Cludts**

## INTRODUCTION

Who is entitled to the profits of a corporation? In the neoclassical tradition, the answer is straightforward: the corporation should be managed in order to maximize *shareholder* value (Friedman, 1970). The shareholders are said to occupy a *prima facie* privileged position (Goodpaster, 1991). They alone have a legitimate claim on the corporation's profits. This legitimacy rests on the neoclassical belief in individual and systemic rationality, supported by a welfaristic utilitarian meta-norm (Van de Ven, 1998). This utilitarian meta-norm converges with the standard economic assumption that in a world of scarcity, more is better than less, and therefore corporate resources should be used in the most efficient way. Several scholars of the firm have argued that productive efficiency would be enhanced if the shareholders had full control rights over the corporation (Williamson, 1984; Alchian and Demsetz, 1972; Jensen and Meckling, 1983). But since the emergence of institutional investors on global capital markets, the concentration of share-ownership and the power of shareholders have increased to such an extent that this race for efficiency is run not to the benefit, but to the expense of other constituencies (Van de Ven, 1998; Ellerman, 1992). Therefore, an increasing number of scholars recognize an urgent need to design new protection devices for the other stakeholders (Leader, 1999).

These scholars question the supremacy of the shareholders mainly because they question the underlying utilitarian meta-norm. They argue that the race for efficiency is at odds with important human values, including justice and a more egalitarian distribution of wealth. Caillé claims more specifically (1) that the typically utilitarian insistence on individual freedom cannot guarantee the respect due to each human person, (2) as a corollary, that social welfare cannot be reduced to economic wealth, and (3) as a consequence, that these utilitarian principles have to be complemented by basic individual rights and rules of fair distribution of the created welfare (Caillé, 1991). In addition, decisions about this trade-off should not be confined to the political realm, but included within the scope of responsibility of corporate managers (Kuhn and Shriver, 1991). Stakeholder theory, being an attempt to map all the stakeholders to which the corporation has to pay attention, has appeared during the last decade as a particularly adequate theoretical instrument to support this evolution.

There tends currently to be a consensus on the fact that normative stakeholder theory involves two basic ideas: (1) morally legitimate stakeholders of a corporation are identified by their interests in the corporation, whether the corporation has any functional interest in them or not; (2) the interests of these stakeholders are of intrinsic value and should be taken into account by the management of the corporation, both when they make strategic decisions *and* in the day-to-day running of the corporation (Donaldson and Preston, 1995: 67). Unfortunately, this consensus is limited, because at least two questions are left unanswered (Ambler and Wilson, 1995): whose interests should be considered morally legitimate? And how should one balance equally legitimate but nonetheless conflicting claims?

Normative stakeholder theory attempts to answer these two basic questions. Unfortunately, there does not yet exist a 'standard' consensual normative stakeholder theory. On the contrary, a bewildering variety of normative theories have been suggested as normative cores of stakeholder legitimacy (Mitchell et al., 1997). A – not exhaustive – list of theories suggested would include at least Kantian ethics (Evan and Freeman, 1988), the (feminist) ethics of care (Wicks et al., 1994; Burton and Dunn, 1996), the ethics of fiduciary relationships (Goodpaster, 1991; Boatright, 1998a), social contract theory (Donaldson and Dunfee, 1999; Freeman, 1994), the theory of property rights (Donaldson and Preston, 1995), a principle of fairness (Phillips, 1997), a theory of the stakeholders as investors (Blair, 1995; Etzioni, 1998), communitarian ethics (Argandoña, 1998) and critical theory (Reed, 1999).

Freeman (1994) has suggested that stakeholder theory is really nothing but a *genre* of stories, or narratives that help us 'understand the human process of joint value creation'. These narratives help people to structure their experience, and their benefit is just 'how they allow us to live'. From his pragmatist and pluralistic perspective, Freeman encourages the development of a multiplicity of normative cores, or 'stakeholder narratives', and he views that diversity as intrinsically valuable. However, contrary to Freeman, we experience this multiplicity of the theories suggested as normative core for stakeholder theory as a weakness of stakeholder theory in its current state, for two distinct reasons. First of all, on a practical level, if academics or business consultants want to use stakeholder theory to develop behavioural advice or prescriptions for managers, and if the range of influence of stakeholder theory is to be extended beyond the limits of academia, we should isolate 'clearly practicable' and unambiguous approaches to managing corporations (Marens and Wicks, 1999). This means that stakeholder theory should become more specific – or convergent (Jones and Wicks, 1999) – instead of increasingly diverse.

Secondly, on a theoretical level, if the stakeholder concept is to be a meaningful concept, then the stakeholder theory of the corporation should be markedly different from other theories of the corporation. Normative *stakeholder* theory should also be markedly different from other normative theories of the corporation. We submit that this is true even if stakeholder theory is nothing but a genre of narratives: the stakeholder genre must be markedly different from other genres of stories about the corporation, otherwise there is simply no point in using stakeholder theory when trying to develop normative guidelines for corporate constituencies. This begs immediately the following question: what is the distinct and specific contribution of the stakeholder concept? What is the additional insight provided by stakeholder theory? In this chapter, we attempt to answer this question. The answer will allow us to find a criterion to distinguish between more and less adequate normative cores, though all of them obviously have both strengths and weaknesses. A normative stakeholder theory should indeed at least be consistent with the distinct contribution, or the specific intuition of the stakeholder concept in order to be valid. This criterion will form the basis of a critical review of different normative cores of stakeholder theory.

## THE DISTINCT CONTRIBUTION OF THE STAKEHOLDER CONCEPT

What is the distinct contribution of the stakeholder concept? Following the distinction made by Donaldson and Preston (1995) between normative, instrumental and descriptive stakeholder theory, we should first investigate on which level this distinct contribution would lie. We have seen *supra* that most *normative* theories that have been suggested as normative cores for the stakeholder theory have a record going back in time long before the stakeholder concept was born. Hardly any new normative theory, specifically geared towards the stakeholder concept, has been developed yet. In the current state of its development, normative stakeholder theory looks rather like a hollow shell that can be filled with any existing normative theory.

On the instrumental level, the picture is very similar: well-known concepts of social science have been labelled and used as 'stakeholder' concepts, but hardly any new concept has been developed yet. The latest and most developed instrumental stakeholder theories rely on mechanisms involving, for example, trust (Jones, 1995), power, urgency, (Mitchell et al., 1997) and resource dependency (Frooman, 1999). There is no doubt that those mechanisms can be applied to stakeholders, but they were already applied before the term 'stakeholder' was invented, for example in political models and in two-party settings.

Nevertheless, the stakeholder concept has, according to us, delivered a significant and distinct contribution on the descriptive level, by raising an awareness of the existence of multiple stakeholders and of diverse stakeholder interests. This is the essence of the first principle of the Consensus Statement on stakeholder management:

> The first requirement of stakeholder management is an awareness of the existence of multiple and diverse stakeholders, and an understanding of their involvement and interest in the corporation. (Preston et al., 1999: 5)

This principle is specific to the stakeholder stream of research, and stands in sharp contrast with one of the basic premises of the (competing) descriptive utilitarian paradigm underlying some of the now most prominent descriptive theories of the corporation, for example the agency theory developed by Alchian and Demsetz (1972) and the transaction cost theory developed by Williamson (1984). This basic premise of neoclassical economics is mono-utilitarianism, which means that the stakes of all stakeholders can be calculated solely in terms of one abstract measure called utility, which often boils down to material welfare. Within that paradigm, all the stakeholders are conceptualized as identical rational economic agents, whereby 'rationality' involves maximization of one's welfare in the most efficient way.

Despite the appearances, these neoclassical assumptions do not leave much room for diverse stakeholder interests, because many of these, in particular value-driven interests, cannot be expressed in terms of the core concept of welfarist utilitarianism, namely 'efficiency'. These value-driven interests include for example the identification with one's company, the need to develop personal relationships, the need to be able to influence one's future, the desire of justice and so on. Descriptive stakeholder theory is more realistic, because it is more encompassing: it allows us to draw a richer picture of the stakeholders of a corporation, which would come closer to the picture drawn by behavioural scientists, psychologists or anthropologists. Descriptive stakeholder theory, because it is more encompassing, is also more complex. However, a more complex theory may be of use to corporations that evolve in an increasingly complex world, where the management does not only have to take shareholders' claims into account, but also customers', environmentalists', employees', competitors' and so on.

When one acknowledges that the language reached out by the neoclassical paradigm is inadequate to account for the concerns of all legitimate stakeholders, one should realize that the consequences of a paradigm shift will reach beyond the descriptive level. Indeed, we claim that these consequences are *crucial* for normative stakeholder theory too. Normative theories are never independent from our descriptive accounts of human behaviour (Bowie, 1998: 48), and stakeholder theory is no exception to this rule. More specifically, stakeholder theory is often described as the challenger of 'stockholder theory'. However, the neoclassical stockholder paradigm is very difficult to overthrow, because within this paradigm descriptive and normative utilitarianism are intimately intertwined with each other (Caillé, 1991). Though descriptive utilitarianism has already been shown to have poor descriptive value years ago, it has not yet been abandoned, precisely because of the unique appeal of normative utilitarianism. Consequently, anyone wanting to overthrow the dominance of the neoclassical stockholder paradigm with an alternative normative theory also needs an alternative descriptive account of human behaviour. Descriptive stakeholder theory provides us with such an account.

Accordingly, our first claim is that if we want to develop a normative theory of the corporation that would really be a normative stakeholder theory of the corporation, then we must reject descriptive utilitarianism and ground our normative theory in the descriptive stakeholder principles.[2] This means rejecting mono-utilitarianism and recognizing that the diversity of interests, needs, values and expectations of the various stakeholders is not compatible with an overarching principle of economic efficiency. As a corollary to the recognition of that diversity, a normative theory of stakeholder management must rely on problem-solving methods involving an ongoing (moral) dialogue between the stakeholders (Preston et al., 1999), because this is the only way management could keep up with the evolution of the different claims of all the stakeholders. These considerations provide us with a clear criterion that we can use to reject some kinds of normative stakeholder theory that would be less adequate. These considerations imply indeed a clear preference for normative stakeholder theories that acknowledge and tolerate diversity, at the very least the maximal amount of diversity that will fit with the pursuit of the particular goal of the organization under consideration.[3]

Our second claim is that most normative stakeholder theories are based either on behavioural assumptions that neglect or contradict the distinct contribution of the stakeholder concept, that is its richer descriptive value, or on assumptions that are so vague that they do not allow one to reject claims incompatible with the recognition of the fact that stakeholders are multiple and that their interests are of diverse natures. As a result, they cannot serve to develop valid stakeholder management norms. We will show in the next sections that this second claim holds at least for the stakeholder agency theory, the social contract stakeholder theory and the theory viewing stakeholders as investors.

## STAKEHOLDER AGENCY THEORY

Boatright (1998a) provides the most developed argument to show that agency theory can provide a foundation to normative stakeholder theory. His argument is based on the claim that 'the standard principles of fair contracting, which underlie an agency theory approach of the firm, require managers to consider the rights and interests of each constituency' (Boatright, 1998a: 5). He further claims that in the 'nexus-of-contracts firm ... every constituency is able to advance its interests by exercising a right to contract with the firm'. The current corporate governance arrangements would according to that theory result from a fair bargaining process between all the stakeholders, because it would best serve the interests of all stakeholders. The argument is based on 'standard economic assumptions of self-interested individuals ... who seek to maximize their own utility under conditions of scarcity' (Boatright, 1998a: 4). It goes as follows[4]: each party which brings transaction-specific assets to a contract will charge a lower price for his assets when adequate *bilateral safeguards* can be devised, that is when that party has enough guarantees that he or she will recover the cost of his investment. If parties cannot devise such bilateral safeguards through contracting, then the owner of the asset will charge a higher price for his or her asset. This higher price may be thought of as being the base price augmented with a risk premium, which compensates the asset owner for the risk that his or her investment won't be repaid fully. Another, cheaper solution, may be to grant the owner of the asset *generalized safeguards* through voting rights. Since one cannot be protected adequately against residual risk by transaction-specific bilateral safeguards, voting rights may therefore be given to the bearer of the residual risk. Moreover, transaction cost theory assumes that stockholders are in a better position than other stakeholders to diversify efficiently their holdings across a number of assets, hence to reduce their exposure to risk. Therefore, additional *efficiency gains* are realized when they bear the residual risk. Therefore, allocating the residual risk – and voting rights – to stockholders is supposed to be beneficial to all parties involved because it minimizes transaction costs. Hence, the stockholders alone, as the bearers of this residual risk, should have the right to elect the board of directors. In other words, corporations ought to be run for the benefit of shareholders, because as a result, *all constituencies would be better off.*

The fundamental problem with this reasoning is that the assumed efficiency gain has no value in itself in the stakeholder paradigm, neither from a normative nor from a descriptive point of view. Efficiency can help to increase pleasure, happiness, justice or whatever is good for persons, but of itself it has no moral worth. What has moral worth is to be determined by the stakeholders, and we should expect that they would claim *various* things to have moral worth, including values which cannot easily be reconciled with efficiency, like for example the quality of human relationships, the respect for the environment or a just distribution of corporate profits.

A second point linked to this first one is that, since the stakeholders are assumed to be driven primarily by economic efficiency, the *moral* responsibility of the 'nexus-of-contracts' corporations is *externalized* onto the government. However, just as it is impossible to write complete contracts, it is plainly impossible to write complete laws; consequently, 'mere compliance with the law can be unduly limited and even unjust' (Goodpaster, 1991: 70). Therefore, externalized responsibility is not sufficient; the duty towards the stakeholders has to be carried out at least in part by the management. Though the stakeholder agency theory raises important issues about the distribution of risk among the stakeholders, we think, because of the two points just discussed, that it is not adequate as a normative stakeholder theory.

## STAKEHOLDERS AND THE SOCIAL CONTRACT

We want to argue that the social contract stakeholder theory is fundamentally ambiguous, because there exist as many social contract theories as there are different sets of assumptions about the social contractants. Freeman (1994) has provided one of the best developed accounts of a stakeholder theory based on the social contract, inspired by the pragmatic liberalism articulated by John Rawls, Richard Rorty and others. His 'redesigned contractual theory' attempts to capture the liberal ideas of *autonomy*, by realizing that each stakeholder must be free to enter agreements that create value for themselves, *solidarity*, by recognizing the mutuality of stakeholder interests, and *fairness*, by claiming *à la* Rawls that a contract is fair if the parties to the contract (that is the corporate stakeholders) would agree to it in ignorance of their actual stakes. Among the principles on which the stakeholders would according to him agree, the most significant are:

1. The *principle of externalities*: 'if a contract between A and B imposes a cost on C, then C has the option to become a party to the contract, and the terms are renegotiated'.
2. The *agency principle*: 'any agent must serve the interests of all stakeholders'. (Freeman, 1994: 416–417)

Those principles are 'virtually equivalent to [Evan and Freeman's (1988)] assumption that all parties affected by a business have a right to participate in the business's decision-making process' (Hasnas, 1998: 28). A first objection to that assumption is that there is no obvious practical sense in which everyone bearing the cost of externalities could 're-negotiate' the terms of the contract. In addition, such principles are useless without any guideline for balancing the conflicting interests of the stakeholders, which Freeman does not provide. A second objection to this social contract approach is that Freeman assumes, like Rawls, that all stakeholders are moved by the same desire to achieve an identical conception of fairness. This assumption is not only idealistic and naïve, but also in contradiction with the assumption that stakeholders have 'plural interests'.[5] Though Freeman can legitimately assume that all the stakeholders would agree on some common principle, he commits the same error as Rawls and other contract theorists who 'by basing [their] position on an hypothetical discourse (...) seek to establish norms monologically, not intersubjectively' (Reed, 1999: 465).

Generally speaking, the social contract approach contains a fundamental ambiguity, because there exist as many social contract theories as there are different sets of assumptions about the social contractants. This ambiguity is very well illustrated by the social contract that would emerge if social contract theorists would hypothesize that the common principle on which all the stakeholders would agree would not be a Rawlsian principle of fairness, but an economic principle of efficiency. Indeed, a 'social' contract written by people exclusively interested in the economic efficiency of the corporation would not be essentially different from the governance rules developed from the perspective of agency theory and transaction cost theory. Indeed, rational social contractors willing to benefit everyone in the community, by creating and distributing goods and services, and by providing opportunities for meaningful (that is productively efficient) work, or in short, by increasing the *economic efficiency* of their society (making more out of less), could also think of the classical privileged relationship between managers and stockholders as the organization principle of private firms. There is nothing that prohibits social contract theorists from adopting such a narrow utilitarian view of the individual and societal good.

In short, the adoption of social contract methodology does not necessarily lead to the rejection of the conclusions reached within an agency framework, which form the essence of the stockholder theory. It is quite unfortunate that an identical set of *procedural* hypotheses, which could be named the social contract methodology, when it is associated with different *behavioural* hypotheses, leads to two radically conflicting doctrines: one privileging the stockholders above all other stakeholders, and the other giving to all those claiming to be affected by the right to renegotiate contracts. This fundamental ambiguity casts serious doubts upon the ambition of social contract theory and all the versions of stakeholder theory that rely on these contracts to provide us with normatively valid guidelines concerning the various stakeholders of the corporation, unless everyone could agree on one particular set of behavioural assumptions. However, descriptive stakeholder theory allows too much complexity to ever reach such an agreement. This is not a reason for despair, but a stimulus to look for alternative normative accounts that can handle that complexity.

In addition to the problems just mentioned, because of the monological nature of social contract theory, it is very difficult to predict what would result from a real fair bargaining process among all the constituencies, even if we were able to agree on one particular set of behavioural assumptions, because there exists a fundamental gap between rational contractors bargaining in ideal conditions of fairness on the one hand, and actual parties to a bargain on the other hand. In the next paragraph, we illustrate this shortly with the stakeholder agency theory sketched above.

Agency theory characterizes the stockholders as contracting to assume a substantial part of the risk associated with the business venture – the entrepreneurial risk, or residual risk. They guarantee the performance of the other contracts, accepting the risk of net loss in return for the entitlement to any net profit. Given the peculiar nature of the risk they agree to bear, they need a special protecting device, something like a legally binding fiduciary contract with management. But though it is beyond doubt that the investment of the shareholders should be protected through adequate means, one could claim that the shareholders are already adequately protected without giving them the control over the firm's management. They have a series of statutory rights to elect the board of administrators, to vote on general assemblies, and so on; they can get rid of their shares swiftly and almost without cost on stock markets; they are entitled to any superior return the firm would produce, and finally, they have limited liability, which shifts part of the residual risk onto other stakeholders (creditors, suppliers and so on.). For all these reasons, it is definitely possible to argue that managers should not necessarily act for the *exclusive* benefit of the stockholders in order to spread risks and benefits *fairly* among the stakeholders. Freeman and Evan (1990) indeed argue that if the stakeholders were engaged in a fair bargaining process, it would be irrational for *any* stakeholder to give up the ability to participate in monitoring the firm and the right to make changes in the contractual mechanism.

Though, the contractualistic approach to stakeholder theory may seem to be intrinsically fair, because it rests on basic egalitarian assumptions; but within the contractualistic tradition, the constituencies are also assumed to be fully informed, fully rational and free individuals, though the very notions of free and informed consent, and rationality, which lie at the basis of contractualistic ethics (Scanlon, 1982), have been debated about during the whole history of Western philosophy (Jaggar, 1993). Moreover, the ideal of free, rational and fully informed subjects conflicts with the basic insight of stakeholder theory, which we interpret as the recognition of the fact that stakeholders pursue different goals, are neither fully informed nor absolutely free – because actual human relations always emerge in a context of unequal power; the stakeholders may even have different conceptions of rationality. Therefore, though the social contract methodology has proven very valuable in other contexts, we think that it is not adequate as a normative core for stakeholder theory.

## STAKEHOLDER THEORY AND PROPERTY RIGHTS: THE STAKEHOLDERS AS INVESTORS

The theory of stakeholders as investors (Donaldson and Preston, 1995; Blair, 1995; Etzioni, 1998) rests according to us on a similar reduction of the stakeholder concept: the stake of the stakeholders is limited to their investment. Blair (1995) defines the stakeholders as 'all parties who have contributed to the enterprise and who, as a result, have at risk investments that are highly specialized to the enterprise' (Blair, 1995: 239). She emphasizes the importance of human capital, which she considers to be as important as financial capital. Hence the investors of financial capital should according to her not be given any priority over the investors of any other kind of capital in relation to the company's profit. This implies for example that the employees, as investors of human capital, gain the right to have a seat on the board, in order to defend their claim to their share of the company's residual. However, Blair does not address a basic question: what constitutes a fair return on 'capital'?

Etzioni (1998) goes a step further and provides a rationale for distributing the corporation's returns. Since investors give up some immediate benefits and voice in order to seek a better return for the future, Etzioni claims that they may legitimately expect to participate to some extent (1) in the decisions that affect what their return may be in the future and (2) in the decisions concerning the social usages of the resources they invest. This applies to all stakeholders who invest some resources in the corporation in expectation of a future return. Regarding the respective stakes of the various stakeholders, Etzioni notes that the scope of the representation of each group should parallel the scope of its investment. Hence, one should give more weight to employees who have worked for many years in the company than to those who were hired more recently, because long-time employees have invested more in the company in terms of what workers invest, whose measure is approximated by counting years at work. Employees could for example receive a specific number of votes according to the years they served in the corporation.

Unfortunately, Etzioni does not address the trade-off between different kinds of investment, for example human and financial. Moreover, his claim that 'the scope of the representation of particular stakeholders should parallel the scope of their investment' is almost equivalent to saying that 'the more one can affect the firm's activities, the more one should be allowed to participate to the decisions affecting the firm'. However, it seems to us that an *exclusive* consideration of the extent to which the stakeholders can *affect* the firm is characteristic of a *strategic* stakeholder theory, based on the 'might makes right' principle (Dobson, 1999; Cludts, 1999), while stakeholder theory cannot claim to have ethical normative strength unless it takes those *affected* into consideration, as initially suggested by Evan and Freeman (1988): '[The stakeholders] are the parties that can significantly affect, *or are significantly affected by* the firm's activities' (emphasis added).

When each stakeholder's voice is proportionate to the size of his investment, more powerful stakeholders will be allowed to neglect the various interests of the multiple weaker stakeholders. Nonetheless, we feel intuitively that *normative* stakeholder theory is meant precisely to give a voice to *all* the stakeholders of the corporation, and especially to protect the weaker stakeholders from the more powerful. Such care for the weaker stakeholders must be driven by an inherently moral sense of stakeholders' responsibility.

## TOWARDS A PROCEDURAL SOLUTION FOR BALANCING CONFLICTING CLAIMS

Though the three normative stakeholder theories discussed above have provided numerous valuable insights and marked important steps in the development of stakeholder thinking, we hope by now to have made clear why we think they are inadequate as normative cores for stakeholder theory. Numerous other theories have been suggested as normative cores for stakeholder theory, but it is beyond the scope of this study to discuss them all in detail. Instead, we will rather show the way forward in the rest of this chapter, and that way leads to a procedural solution. Indeed, we claim that a procedural solution involving an ongoing (moral) dialogue between the stakeholders is the only way management could keep up with the diversity of the claims of the different stakeholders, and consequently arbitrate conflicts in ways that are acceptable to all parties.

We do not want to promote the ideal moral dialogue envisioned by Habermas, because his approach suffers from a number of weaknesses that have sufficiently been documented by other authors. We can only point to a couple of those. Firstly, Habermas calls for all those affected to take part to the dialogue, though this will most often be materially impossible because of the lack of time and resources (Benhabib, 1986; Grabner-Kraeuter, 2000).[6] The concept of rationality used by Habermas has also been questioned (Jaggar,

1993; Elster, 1982). Habermas further demands that the participants to the discourse attain a level of reflection that can only be achieved by highly educated people – still a vast minority in this world. Finally, as soon as real-life dialogical processes deviate from the ideal value-free dialogue, critical theory cannot help us to evaluate whether that real-life dialogue comes more or less close to the ideal.

Hence, instead of an ideal dialogue, we think that managers would be better served by a fair procedure that could lead real-life stakeholders towards achieving a consensus about the legitimacy of their various claims, and about the way management should prioritize these.

Donaldson and Dunfee (1994, 1999) have moved in that direction with their *Integrative Social Contract Theory* (ISCT). They view the corporation as a particular kind of community, as a 'self-defined, self-circumscribed group of people who interact in the context of shared tasks, values, or goals and who are capable of establishing norms of ethical behavior for themselves' (Donaldson and Dunfee, 1994: 262). They claim that local communities may formulate 'authentic' ethical norms for their members within their own moral free space, while 'hypernorms' place limits on these authentic norms. Hypernorms may for example mandate the recognition of certain fundamental stakeholder claims.[7] Moreover, they claim that adherence to local norms can be assumed as part of the membership to the community. Consequently, the norms delineating stakeholder rights and obligations will vary among communities to reflect local customs, moral and cultural preferences, legal systems and economic goals. The core values of the corporation will be particularly critical in guiding decision-making about stakeholder obligations.

Donaldson's and Dunfee' articulation of the macro-social and micro-social contracts has been subject to criticism (Velasquez, 2000). Though, their ISCT represents an important step towards the recognition of the moral validity of particular and contingent stakeholder claims, provided that all stakeholders would internalize the values of trust, co-operation and reciprocity; which are indeed basic conditions to the development of ethical negotiation processes (Van Es, 1996). But they do not provide clear guidelines for setting the boundaries of the 'communities', nor for arbitrating conflicts between the parties involved to the negotiation. This is a crucial point: in some sense, it is the whole point of stakeholder theory. Therefore, we want to support a solution that could be called a 'product-centered approach to moderating stakeholder claims' (Koslowski, 2000). This approach amounts to a focus on the 'common good' of the corporation, where this common good is conceptualized as the corporation's survival and growth, in order to achieve its mission. This mission has essentially an economic nature: not to enhance shareholder value, but to deliver products or services, as laid down in the corporation's by-laws. Though the particular interests of the different stakeholders are infinitely varied, and sometimes conflicting, firm growth and survival through the delivery product or services are nonetheless desired by all stakeholders, and in this sense, a truly *common* good. That common good may be conceptualized as the intersection between the interests of all stakeholders (Leader, 1999).

This approach calls for a definition of the stakeholders based on what they do in common. Since virtually any economic transaction may be interpreted as a co-operative scheme (this idea is as old as Adam Smith), we can quite obviously think of the different stakeholders of a corporation as the members of a co-operative venture for mutual advantage. In order to distinguish those groups from other stakeholders who are not members of this co-operative venture for mutual advantage, we will call them the primary stakeholders. All primary stakeholders are, to varying degrees, involved in the same economic co-operative scheme, and the success of each is intertwined with the success of all others. All primary stakeholders thus have duties of fairness towards the corporation (Phillips, 1997), but fairness also commands that they share the benefits generated by the firm's activities.

We submit that the *common good* of the participants to a co-operative venture can help us solve the issue of the distribution of the benefits earned within the co-operative venture involving the different primary stakeholders, given that all their contributions are different in nature but necessary. In addition, we submit that a normative core for stakeholder theory based on the common good is more in harmony with the stakeholder intuition than the previously examined normative theories, provided that the common good is defined in the less restrictive possible way.

The concept of common good has indeed a long history in political philosophy, where it is often seen as conflicting with 'individual' goods, as if the pursuit of a personal objective was incompatible with the good of society, as if the good of society was a burden to its members. Fortunately, this is not the case if the common good is defined as: 'the overall conditions of life in society that allow the different groups and their members to achieve their own perfection more fully and more easily' (Argandoña, 1998: 1095). The primacy of this kind of common good does not exclude the pursuit of private ends as such; on the contrary, it creates the conditions that will enable the primary stakeholders to achieve a variety of personal goods. This common good is perfectly compatible with the pursuit of private interests; only private ends detrimental to the common good are precluded.

Of course, the management will have to give the primacy to the common goal of the primary stakeholders, over their individual interests. While the common interests of the primary stakeholders will appear to be dominant on the corporate agenda, their particular interests will appear to be secondary in nature (Leader, 1999). Hence, when the management sets the corporate agenda, it does not need to strike a fair balance between the various interests of the primary stakeholders. Rather, it should identify the best means to help the company to prosper according to its own objectives, and only in a second phase ask about the fairest way in which to distribute the resulting costs and benefits among the stakeholders. The functionality of the corporation should be the dominant objective, tempered by objectives of personal justice, but not overruled by them.

## ONE PRACTICAL IMPLICATION AND POSSIBLE OBJECTION

A delicate issue within the stakeholder debate concerns the list of stakeholders. The rather narrow definition of primary stakeholders adopted in this chapter – those who make direct contributions to the corporation's mission – implies a rather short list, that would probably include employees, customers, suppliers, shareholders, creditors and the local community. All of them would have, *qua* stakeholders, identical rights: low-skilled workers and high-skilled employees, suppliers and creditors, because all are equally necessary to the corporation.[8]

One objection to this definition might be that many other – secondary – stakeholders are themselves significantly affected by the corporation, though they do not contribute anything. Low-skilled unemployed are for example not members of any co-operative game, but nevertheless, many people feel that corporations have a positive responsibility to provide jobs to those people (Schokkaert and Sweeney, 1998). We acknowledge this responsibility, but though every corporation can be argued to have a moral duty to provide jobs to low-skilled unemployed, we would not grant these people legitimate claims over *one particular* company. While the claims of primary stakeholders are *particular*, the claims of low-skilled unemployed are *general*, precisely because they are not stakeholders of *a particular* corporation in the sense of the corporation having particular duties towards these people in virtue of its unique relationship with them. We think that it is necessary at this point to make a distinction between duties towards stakeholders *qua* stakeholders, and other moral duties.

However, it is also the moral duty of the primary stakeholders, and this is an important one, to listen to the claims of those other stakeholders, whether they be low-skilled unemployed, environmentalists, representatives of future generations, competitors or any other third party. But notice that if the local community is treated as a primary stakeholder, obviously, this local community will itself be a heterogeneous mix of different pressure groups and stakeholders, among which we are likely to find environmentalists and representatives of low-skilled unemployed. More generally, models of stakeholder salience (Mitchell et al., 1997) can help the primary stakeholders to listen to other stakeholders and to distinguish legitimate claims. Independent board members, as advised in the corporate governance literature, may also be useful in this respect.

## CONCLUSION

We have shown in this chapter that some theories suggested as normative cores of stakeholder theory are inadequate, because they jeopardize the internal consistency between descriptive and normative stakeholder theory. The three theories which we have challenged in this chapter – the stakeholder agency theory, the social contract theory and the theory of stakeholders as investors, share a common universalistic and monological approach which proves unable to accommodate the inescapable and fundamental differences between the various stakeholders' interests. In contrast, we have suggested at the end of this chapter that stakeholder theory could be provided with a more adequate normative core based on the internal goal of an organization, which is common to all the stakeholders of that particular organization, but clearly not universalistic. Such particularism provides us with better opportunities to recognize the wide variety of values that may guide decision-making in corporations. These values should nonetheless be effectively constrained by societal rules of acceptance. However, we believe that a decentralized approach to business ethics is the only viable way to transforming stakeholder relationships characterized by power asymmetries into relationships of co-operation and participation, through democratic governance and respect for the stakeholders.

## NOTES

1. We gratefully acknowledge the support of Luk Bouckaert and Heidi von Weltzien Hoivik. This study has also benefited from valuable comments by two anonymous reviewers and by the participants to workshops at the 1999 SBE meeting in Chicago and at the 2000 ISBEE meeting in São Paulo.
2. This is not an invitation to commit a naturalistic fallacy: a good normative theory should guide our moral behaviour in the real world, not only in textbooks; therefore, it has to be based on a realistic descriptive account of the world, even though it does not infer an 'ought' from an 'is'.
3. To the goal of private corporations we will come back *infra*.
4. Cf. Williamson (1984); Alchian and Demsetz (1972).
5. Ironically, Freeman himself argues in favour of a pluralistic approach in the same article where he sketches his 'new social contract'.
6. Ironically, such a fictitious dialogue would come close to the hypothetical discourse envisioned by social contract theorists.

7. Donaldson and Dunfee suggest the use of presumption as a means for identifying relevant hypernorms. One of these hypernorms should for example require that the norm-generating microsocial contracts should be grounded in informed consent buttressed by rights of exit and voice.
8. This equality is characteristic of a *normative* stakeholder theory. Even if strategic stakeholder theorists admit that all the 'primary' stakeholders are necessary, and consequently deserve being taken care of, they will insist on differentiated treatments according to each stakeholder's contribution. Indeed, as Adam Smith already noted two centuries ago, 'in the long run the workman may be as necessary to his master as his master to him; but the necessity is not so immediate' (Smith, 1776, I, viii, 5).

# REFERENCES

Alchian, A. and H. Demsetz (1972), 'Production, information costs, and economic organization', *American Economic Review*, **62**, 777–795.

Ambler, Tim and Andrea Wilson (1995), 'Problems of stakeholder theory', *Business Ethics: a European Review*, **4**(1), 30–35.

Argandoña, Antonio (1998), 'The stakeholder theory and the common good', *Journal of Business Ethics*, **17**(9–10), 1093–1102.

Benhabib, Sheila (1986), *Critique, Norm and Utopia. A Study of the Foundations of Critical Theory*, New York: Columbia University Press.

Blair, Margaret (1995), *Ownership and Control: Rethinking Corporate Governance for the Twenty-first Century*, Washington: Brookings Institution.

Boatright, John R. (1998a), 'The search for the normative core: normative stakeholder theory and the agency theory of the firm', *Proceedings of the IABS annual conference*.

Boatright, John R. (1998b), Staking claims: the role of stakeholders in the contractual theory of the firm, unpublished manuscript.

Boatright, John R. (1994), 'What's so special about shareholders?', *Business Ethics Quarterly*, **4**(4), 393–407.

Bowie, Norman (1998), 'A Kantian theory of capitalism', *Business Ethics Quarterly*, Special Issue 1, 37–60.

Burton, Brian K. and Craig P. Dunn (1996), 'Feminist ethics as a moral grounding for stakeholder theory', *Business Ethics Quarterly* **6**(2), 133–147.

Caillé, Alain (1991), 'Rationalisme, utilitarisme et anti-utilitarisme', *Proceedings of the Bentham Colloquium*, Geneva.

Carson, Thomas L. (1993), 'Does the stakeholder theory constitute a new kind of theory of social responsibility?', *Business Ethics Quarterly*, **3**(2), 171–176.

Cludts, Stephan (1999), 'The stakeholders as investors: a response to Etzioni', *Business Ethics Quarterly*, **9**(4), 673–676.

Dobson, John (1999), 'Defending the stockholder model: a comment on Hasnas, and on Dunfee's MOM', *Business Ethics Quarterly*, **9**(2), 337–345.

Donaldson, Thomas and Lee E. Preston (1995), 'The stakeholder theory of the corporation: concepts, evidence, and implications', *Academy of Management Review*, **20**(1), 65-91.

Donaldson, Thomas and Thomas W. Dunfee (1994), 'Toward a unified conception of business ethics: integrative social contracts theory', *Academy of Management Review*, **19**(2), 252–284.

Donaldson, Thomas and Thomas W. Dunfee (1999), *Ties that Bind: A Social Contracts Approach to Business Ethics*, Cambridge: Harvard Business School Press.

Ellerman, David P. (1992), *Property and Contracts in Economics*, Cambridge: Blackwell.

Elster, John (1982), 'Sour grapes – utilitarianism and the genesis of wants', in Sen, Amartya and Williams, Bernard (eds), *Utilitarianism and Beyond*, Cambridge: Cambridge University Press, pp. 219–238.

Etzioni, Amitai (1998), 'A communitarian note on stakeholder theory', *Business Ethics Quarterly*, **8**(4), 679–691.

Evan, William M. and R. Edward Freeman (1988), 'A stakeholder theory of the modern corporation: Kantian capitalism', in Beauchamp, Tom and Bowie, Norman (eds), *Ethical Theory and Business*, 3rd edn, Englewood Cliffs: Prentice-Hall, pp. 101–105.

Fama, E.F. and M.C. Jensen (1983), 'Agency problems and residual claims', *Journal of Law and Economics*, **26**, 327-349.

Freeman, R.E. (1984), *Strategic Management: A Stakeholder Approach*, Boston: Pitman.

Freeman, R.E. (1994), 'The politics of stakeholder theory: some future directions', *Business Ethics Quarterly*, **4**(4), 409–421.

Freeman, R.E. and William Evan (1990), 'Corporate governance: a stakeholder interpretation', *Journal of Behavioral Economics*, **19**, 337–359.

Friedman, Milton (1970), 'The social responsibility of business is to increase its profits', *New York Times Magazine*, 13 September, 32–33, 122–126.

Frooman, Jeff (1999), 'Stakeholder influence strategies', *Academy of Management Review*, **24**(2), 191–205.

Goodpaster, Kenneth E. (1991), 'Business ethics and stakeholder analysis', *Business Ethics Quarterly*, **1**(1), 53–73.

Grabner-Kraeuter, Sonja (2000) '"Unternehmensethik" in German-speaking countries', Paper presented at the ISBEE World Congress, São Paulo, 22 July.

Hasnas, John (1998), 'A guide for the perplexed', *Business Ethics Quarterly*, **8**(1), 19–42.

Jaggar, Alison (1993), 'Taking consent seriously: feminist practical ethics and actual moral dialogue', in Winkler, E.R. and Coombs, J.R. (eds), *Applied Ethics. A Reader*, Cambridge: Blackwell, pp. 69–86.

Jensen, M.C. and W.H. Meckling (1983), 'Theory of the firm: managerial behavior, agency costs, and ownership structure', *Journal of Financial Economics*, **3**, 301–325.

Jones, Thomas M. (1995), 'Instrumental stakeholder theory: a synthesis of ethics and economics', *Academy of Management Review*, **20**(2), 404–437.

Jones, Thomas M. and Andrew C. Wicks (1999), 'Convergent stakeholder theory', *Academy of Management Review*, **24**(2), 206–221.

Koslowski, Peter (2000), 'The limits of shareholder value', *Journal of Business Ethics*, **27**(1–2), 137–148.

Kuhn, James W. and Donald W. Shriver, Jr. (1991), *Beyond success: corporations and their Critics in the 1990s*, Oxford: Oxford University Press.

Leader, Sheldon (1999), 'Participation and property rights', *Journal of Business Ethics*, **21**(2–3), 97–109.

Marens, Richard and Andrew Wicks (1999), 'Getting real: stakeholder theory, managerial practice, and the general irrelevance of fiduciary duties owed to shareholders', *Business Ethics Quarterly*, **9**(2), 273–293.

Mitchell, Ronald K., Bradley R. Agle and Donna J. Wood (1997), 'Toward a theory of stakeholder identification and salience: defining the principle of who and what really counts', *Academy of Management Review*, **22**(4), 853–886.

Phillips, Robert A. (1997), 'Stakeholder theory and a principle of fairness', *Business Ethics Quarterly*, **7**(1), 51–66.

Preston, Lee E., Leonard J. Brooks and Tom Donaldson (1999), *Principles of Stakeholder Management*, Toronto: Clarkson Centre for Business Ethics.

Rawls, John (1964), 'Legal obligation and the duty of fair play', in Hook, S. (ed.), *Law and Philosophy*, New York: New York University Press pp. 3–18

Reed, Darryl (1999), 'Stakeholder management theory: a critical theory perspective', *Business Ethics Quarterly*, **9**(3), 453–483.

Scanlon, Thomas (1982), 'A contractualist alternative', in DeMarco, J.P. and R.M. Fox (eds), *New Directions in Ethics*, New York: Routledge, pp. 42–57.

Schokkaert, Erik and John Sweeney (1998), 'Social exclusion and ethical responsibility: solidarity with the least skilled', *Journal of Business Ethics*, **21**(2–3), 251–267.

Smith, Adam, (1776), 'An inquiry into the nature and causes of the wealth of nations', reprinted in Skinner, A.S. and Campbell, R.H. (eds) (1976), Oxford: Clarendon Press, p. 543.

Van de Ven, Bert-Willem (1998), 'Rationaliteit en ethiek in de onderneming. Grondslagen van bedrijfsethiek', Tilburg: Tilburg University Press.

Van Es, Robert (1996), *Negotiation Ethics. On Ethics in Negotiation and Negotiating in Ethics*, Delft: Eburon.

Velasquez, Manuel (2000), 'Globalization and the failure of ethics', *Business Ethics Quarterly*, **10**(1), 343–352.

Wicks, Andrew C., Daniel. R. Gilbert, Jr. and R. Edward Freeman (1994), 'A feminist reinterpretation of the stakeholder concept', *Business Ethics Quarterly*, **4**(4), 475–497.

Williamson, Oliver (1984), 'Corporate governance', *Yale Law Journal*, **93**, 1197–1230.

# 6. Moral character and relationship effectiveness: an empirical investigation of trust within organizations

## Manuel Becerra and Lars Huemer

Based on the current management literature, trust is associated with a number of advantages for those able to establish, maintain and utilize it. Some of the many examples of these advantages include the reduction of complexity and need for constant surveillance; the constraint of opportunism; the decrease of transaction costs; and the production of positive attitudes and commitment (Zand, 1972; Barber, 1983; Luhmann, 1979; John, 1984; Morgan, 1991; Ring and Van de Ven, 1994; Jarillo, 1990; Rousseau, Sitkin, Burt and Camerer, 1998). Despite this acknowledged importance of trust within business settings, there is still scarce empirical research on how trust actually affects relationships, particularly on its value-creation effects.

The focus of this study is on the effects of trust. We will concentrate particularly in the perceptions about moral character in business settings, as one critical dimension of trust. We expect trust to affect business relationships by influencing how people actually behave and, ultimately, having a significant impact on relationship effectiveness. This presumed positive effect of trust on the effectiveness of business relationships constitutes the main goal of our study.

As far as empirical analysis is concerned, the role of trust in cooperative relationships is still not well known. Noorderhaven (1999), for instance, calls for more data and less need for more theory. The scarce existing empirical research, mostly on interorganizational relationships, indicates that trust in such exchange relations matters for performance and relationship effectiveness (Zaheer, McEvily and Perrone, 1998; Moore, 1998). In contrast, intra-organizational relationships provide the empirical setting of this study, and more specifically, manager-subordinate dyads. We study how subordinates' perceptions about the trustworthiness of their managers, particularly their integrity, are closely associated with the characteristics of their dyadic relationship, such as the degree of communication openness, conflict level, decision-making speed and the willingness to take risks.

## TRUST AND RELATIONSHIP EFFECTIVENESS

Despite the lack of a unified conceptualization of trust, most scholars agree that the expectations that one holds about another's intentions and behaviour towards us constitutes the essence of trust (Rousseau et al., 1998; Mayer, Davis and Schoorman, 1995). Many dimensions of the expectations about another's trustworthiness have been suggested to date in the social sciences. Mayer, Davis and Schoorman (1995), in their model of trust that builds on an extensive review of the earlier literature, suggest that there are three main evaluations that one person (the trustor) may make about another person (the trustee) in business settings: (i) integrity, that is, a matter of the trustee's overall ethical attitude such as his perceived lying and cheating to others; (ii) benevolence, which refers to the trustee's goodwill or positive intentions toward the trustor from the latter's viewpoint, that is, the intention to harm or do good to the trustor; and (iii) competence, that is, the trustee's ability or competence in doing his or her job. There is some empirical evidence that these three separate, though highly correlated, dimensions of trust load on one common latent construct of trust (Becerra, 1998). On occasions, it may be thus worth while to distinguish among the specific dimensions of trust under investigation, though most frequently we can consider trust as one concept that measures our overall positive or negative expectations or 'psychological state'with regard to another party (Rousseau et al., 1998).

In this study, we are interested in the characteristics of high-trust relationships. We argue that relationships with greater trust not only enjoy lower monitoring and other transaction costs, but also take advantage of a more positive value-enhancing environment that improves relationship effectiveness. This occurs through the effect of trust on four aspects of a relationship, namely the level of open communication, emotional conflict, decision-making speed and willingness to take risks. Though trust may also be closely associated with other aspects of relationships, in our opinion these are the critical ones that may be considered as representative of the effectiveness of the relationship. How each one relates to trust is discussed below.

### Communication Openness

Trust research focusing on antecedents of trust suggest that interpersonal communication is necessary to build trust (Hallowell, 1999; cf. Granovetter, 1985), that companies must communicate with employees to develop trust

(McCune, 1998), and that effective communications between buyer and suppliers creates a base for trust and cooperation (Langfield-Smith and Greenwood, 1998). Managerial trustworthy behaviour seems to be related to how interpersonal communication takes place (Whitener, Brodt, Korsgaard and Werner, 1998).

Zaheer, McEvily and Perrone (1998) suggest that interorganizational trust mitigates the information asymmetries inherent in relational exchange by allowing more open and honest sharing of information. Trust makes possible open communication, since nobody is afraid to speak his or her mind (Kets de Vries, 1999). Hence, a positive relationship between trust and information flows may be expected (Fisman and Khanna, 1999). Dooley and Fryxell (1999) found that loyalty (regarded as a key dimension of trust) facilitates the constructive processing of dissenting opinions during the course of a strategic decision-making process. It promotes an open communication and sharing of information. In summary, accurate and open communication would be expected when trust is high (O'Reilly, Chatman and Anderson 1987; Ellram and Hendrick, 1995).

*Hypothesis 1    There is a positive relationship between trust and the degree of communication openness.*

**Emotional Conflict**

The connection between trust and the level of conflict in business relationships is a complex one. Organizational members' objectives and motivations are seldom identical; their goals may diverge to some extent and disagreements may reduce the effectiveness of their relationships. On one hand, it is plausible to argue that trust actually may promote higher levels of interpersonal conflict. For instance, Rao and Schmidt (1998) initially predicted that trust would lead negotiators to behave less opportunistically and more cooperatively, using less hard tactics and more soft tactics in negotiations. However, trust was in fact negatively associated with negotiators using soft tactics. The authors suggest that once trust is established, soft tactics become unnecessary because negotiators withstand 'frank' talk. Similarly, Zaheer, McEvily and Perrone (1998) argue that rather than reducing conflict, high levels of trust may actually promote conflict. The existing trust gives the different parties the confidence to be open with each other, knowing that shared information will not be used against them.

On the contrary, we believe that a negative relationship between trust and conflict can be expected once the effect of open communication has been controlled for. The level of open sincere communication associated with greater trust should not be confused with emotional conflict. Trust can be expected to reduce affective and emotional conflict beyond the degree of task conflict that arises from interdependence, where open communication is also expected (Porter and Lilly, 1996; Jehn, 1995). Partners in relational exchange working under conditions of high trust are more likely to give each other the benefit of the doubt and the leeway in mutual dealings. Such leeway will tend to reduce the scope, intensity, and frequency of dysfunctional conflict, even if 'hard-talk' about operational problems is also taking place (Zaheer, McEvily and Perrone, 1998).

*Hypothesis 2    There is a negative relationship between trust and the level of emotional conflict.*

### Decision-making Speed

The level of trust has also been related to the decision-making process by earlier research. Kim and Mauborgne (1998) study different aspects of the decision-making process as antecedents of trust. They argue that when people feel their strategic decision-making processes are fair, they display a high level of voluntary cooperation, closely associated with their level of trust and commitment. Loyalty and competence, as dimensions of trust, can be expected to have an impact in building decision commitment and decision quality. The level of shared trustworthiness among team members is a key element in synthesizing dissent and consensus arguments (Dooley and Fryxell, 1999). Not-trusted personnel may even be completely left out of decision-making processes (Bashein and Markus, 1997).

The presence of trust affects the general working atmosphere, since matters are accomplished faster without too much haggling. It promotes decision-making speed since deals can be solved on the 'right level', within a department or division, everything does not have to be sent to top management. Trust also affects the level of formality and due diligence between the parties, reducing the need for writing and checking documents, which slows down the decision-making process. Agreements made over the phone can be expected to be as good as written documents. Mutually beneficial agreements can be expected to be reached more quickly when trust is high (cf. Zaheer, McEvily and Perrone, 1998).

*Hypothesis 3    There is a positive relationship between trust and the speed of decision making.*

### Willingness to Take Risks

Situations of vulnerability can be expected to be common since self-sufficiency is rare in the interdependent activities characterizing most business relationships. Despite the intimate connection between risk and trust, scholars still debate about the limits and causality between these two concepts. Deutsch's (1958) basic suggestion is that risk taking and trusting are different sides of the same coin. Similarly, risk is what trust is all about according to Meyerson, Weick and Kramer (1996). Many organizational scientists see trust as a mechanism that mitigates against the risk of opportunistic behaviour. Contemporary research discusses from different perspectives whether trust is caused by risk, actually is risk, or reduces risk (Luhmann, 1979, 1988; Lewis and Weigert, 1985; Coleman, 1990; Mayer, Davis and Schoorman, 1995). In contrast, Williamson (1993) suggests that the idea of trust in business settings is not useful and he argues instead in favour of the analysis of the more precise notion of risk.

In our opinion, we should distinguish between trust and willingness to take risk. It is our positive expectations about others that drives our willingness to accept vulnerability in dealing with them, but they are not the same. Other factors besides trust affect our willingness to take risks, as studied for instance in prospect theory. Thus, willingness to take risks is but one of the consequences of trust, just like open communication also results from the positive expectations (that is, trust) that we may hold about the trustee. Consequently, where trust is higher, the willingness to accept risks should be greater, whereas a trustor can be expected to require more backup and be more protected when dealing with those who are less trusted.

*Hypothesis 4    There is a positive relationship between trust and the willingness to accept risks.*

## METHODOLOGY

### Questionnaire

To study the connection between relationship effectiveness and trust, a questionnaire was designed and administered to a group of undergraduate students in their senior year of Business Administration at a major American university. A total of 392 students provided valid usable answers to a set of Likert-type questions on a 1–7 scale in the survey (Strongly Disagree – Neutral – Strongly Agree). The items referred to their most recent job and their relationships with their bosses. These questions were part of a larger research project to investigate individual attitudes in a work context.

Data were collected on the hypothesized variables about each boss-subordinate dyad (that is, manager–student). These variables measure the four key aspects of relationship effectiveness under investigation as well as the existing level of trust, all of them always assessed from the subordinate's perspective. The instruments are described below and their Cronbach's alpha is reported in parenthesis:

### Communication openness ($\alpha = .92$)
Three items were obtained from the instrument designed by O'Reilly and Roberts (1976) to assess the degree of openness in the communication with another individual: 'It is easy to talk openly to this person'; 'Communication with this person is very open'; and 'When I talk to this person, there is a great deal of understanding'.

### Emotional conflict ($\alpha = .91$)
The four-item scale developed by Jehn (1995) to measure relationship conflict within a group (as opposed to task conflict) was adapted to the dyadic context of this research: 'I feel substantial friction with this person'; 'I sense personality conflicts with this individual'; 'I can perceive tension with this individual'; and 'I feel I have some emotional conflict with this individual'.

### Decision-making speed ($\alpha = .64$)
Three items were developed to measure the speed with which boss and subordinate could agree on a joint decision: 'We can reach agreements very quickly'; 'I need a lot of analysis and persuasion to agree with this person on anything' (reverse coded); and 'We never seem to be able to reach a joint decision' (reverse coded).

### Willingness to take risks ($\alpha = .71$)
Three items were developed to assess the degree of risk that the subordinate is willing to accept with regard to his or her boss in particular, following earlier research that suggests that risk is situation-specific, rather than a generic risk propensity (Slovic, 1972). The items, all reverse coded, were: 'I try to minimize risk when dealing with this individual'; 'I try to protect myself from the influence of this person'; and 'I try to avoid sharing a risky project with this person'.

### Trust
The three critical dimensions of trust (benevolence, competence, and integrity) were estimated from the subordinate's perspective with regard to his or her boss. Four items for each dimension of trust were obtained from an instrument designed by Mayer, Davis and Schoorman (1997) to estimate interpersonal trust in business settings.

a.  Trust – benevolence ($\alpha = .79$) measured the boss's goodwill or positive intentions toward the subordinate from the latter's viewpoint: 'This manager really looks out for what is important for me'; 'This manager is very concerned about my welfare'; 'My needs and desires are very important to this manager'; and 'This manager will go out of his way to help me'.

b.  Trust – integrity ($\alpha = .86$) measured the boss's moral character or ethical attitude (that is, fairness, lying) towards other individuals: 'This manager has a strong sense of justice'; 'I never have to worry about whether this manager will stick to his word'; 'This manager tries hard to be fair in dealings with others'; and 'Sound principles seem to guide this manager's behaviour'.

c.  Trust – competence ($\alpha = .91$) measured the boss's apparent competence in doing his or her job: 'This manager is very capable of performing his job'; 'I feel very confident about this manager's skills'; 'This manager has much knowledge about the work that he needs to do'; and 'This manager is known to be successful at the things he tries to do'.

**Statistical Analysis**

Structural equation modelling (EQS) was used to estimate the validity of the four aspects of relationship effectiveness under investigation as well as the three dimensions of trust. Both the convergent and the discriminant validity of the two second-order constructs, relationship effectiveness and trust were assessed. After studying the association between trust and relationship effectiveness, we also estimated a structural model to probe at a lower level of analysis which of the dimensions of trust has a greater impact on the different aspects of relationship effectiveness under study.

# RESULTS

First, let us analyse the construct validity of trust and relationship effectiveness based on the models presented in Table 6.1. The results offer clear confirmation for the validity of the multidimensional nature of trust as well as relationship effectiveness. In Model A, the items load into their appropriate first-order latent variable (the three dimensions of trust plus the four aspects of relationship effectiveness under study), which then load on only one second-order latent variable. Model A shows a relatively low fit of .884 CFI.

In contrast, Model B offers a significantly better CFI of .913 (significant decrease in ($\chi^2$ of 208 with 1 degree of freedom). In this model, the three

*Table 6.1  Structural equations models*

| Trust and relationship effectiveness | CFI | $\chi^2$ | df |
|---|---|---|---|
| A. Seven first-order dimensions and one second-order latents | .884 | 1087 | 268 |
| B. Seven first-order dimensions and two second-order correlated latents | .913 | 879 | 267 |
| C. Model F plus path Benevolence → Openness | .949 | 627 | 266 |
| D. Full Model: seven first-order correlated dimensions | .950 | 605 | 254 |
| E. Structural model Trust → Effectiveness | .950 | 614 | 264 |

dimensions of trust load on one second-order latent variable and the four aspects of relationship effectiveness load on another second-order latent. Both second-order latent variables, trust and relationship effectiveness are allowed to correlate freely. The good fit of Model B provides evidence of the discriminant validity of trust and relationship effectiveness; it is more accurate to consider trust and relationship effectiveness as two separate constructs, though very closely related ($\rho = .59$ significant at .01 confidence level).

Individuals assess whether their relationships with others are more or less effective. Different aspects of those relationships can, thus, be conceived as indicators of their overall positive or negative assessment of the relationship. The second-order latent variable extracts such an underlying assessment so that later we can investigate how it is related to the existing level of trust. As we have defined these concepts in our study, trust represents the subordinate's evaluation of his or her boss as an individual (including moral character), whereas relationship effectiveness indicates the subordinate's assessment of the relationship. Though intimately related, these two constructs are conceptually distinct and they are also empirically distinguishable.

To identify possible improvements in the model, we conducted the usual Lagrange Multiplier tests in Model B. These tests indicated that releasing one determined path would increase substantially the fit, reducing $\chi^2$ by 186 while any additional change would reduce $\chi^2$ by less than 17 in all cases. This important path goes from Benevolence to Open Communication, which makes clear sense. Beyond the general observed association between any dimension of trust and any aspect of relationship effectiveness taking place through the correlation of the second-level constructs, greater trust in benevolence generates more open communication. In other words, when subordinates believe that their boss has good intentions with respect to them, then they also consider the relationship with their bosses as more open. Model C shown in

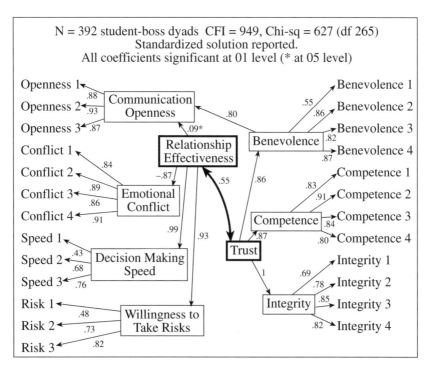

*Figure 6.1   Trust and relationship effectiveness (Model C)*

Figure 6.1 includes this closer link between benevolence and open communication, which increases the fit to a CFI of .949.

The model in Figure 6.1 is clearly consistent with our main arguments. How much we trust others in a business setting, such as our boss, depends to a large extent on how effective our relationship is with them. More interestingly, on the other hand, our level of trust in others also affects our behaviour, which ultimately can be expected to have an impact on the relationship's effectiveness as well. Consequently, trust and relationship effectiveness are likely to be mutually driven and, thus, intimately related. The high correlation between these two distinct constructs supports this idea ($\rho$ = .55 significant at .01 confidence level).

The model not only offers clear evidence in favour of the general positive association between trust and relationship effectiveness, but also confirms the expected characteristics of high-trust relationships. Relationships with greater trust are characterized by greater communication openness, lower emotional conflict, faster decision making, and greater willingness to take risks. Thus, the four hypotheses receive clear support. The results are consistent with the role that the existing literature gives to the presence of trust in business relationships. Trust not only may allow lower monitoring and transaction costs, but it is likely to also generate value by facilitating how the relationship works. Subordinates have a different more positive attitude when they have high trust in their bosses. In our opinion, it is through the positive attitude and behaviour of the individuals in these relationships that trust may improve effectiveness.

The results are particularly interesting for the students of moral character within the organization. Integrity appears to be the fundamental dimension of trust, whose loading achieved the highest possible value of 1. In other words, when we make an assessment about how much we trust others, we seem to be basically assessing their integrity, along with other evaluations less representative of the construct of trust (benevolence and competence). Earlier research has not probed into which of the dimensions of trust is more central and these results, though tentative, indicate that integrity may be the key.

To explore this point further and investigate the direct connections between the dimensions of trust and the four aspects of relationship effectiveness, we fitted a fully saturated model of the seven first-order latent variables (Model D) and, using modification indexes, obtained the best-fitting model of trust driving relationship effectiveness. The final model produced a very high fit of CFI = .963 and it is shown in Figure 6.2. This Model E clearly shows that

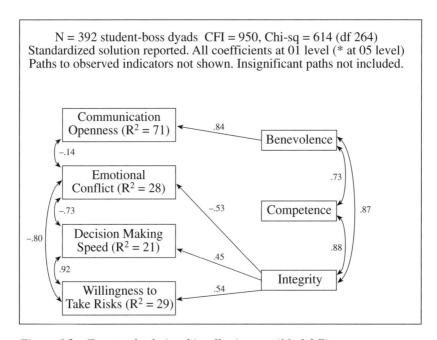

*Figure 6.2    Trust and relationship effectiveness (Model E)*

integrity can be considered the essential dimension of trust that drives the amount of emotional conflict, decision-making speed, and willingness to take risks in boss-subordinate dyads.

## CONCLUSIONS

To summarize the main ideas, our perceptions about our bosses (possibly generalizable to others within an organization) are likely to affect our relationship with them. High trust is associated with greater communication openness, lower emotional conflict, faster decision-making, and greater willingness to take risks. The results are particularly interesting with respect to the integrity dimension of trust. Perceptions about the moral character of others seem to be an essential element of trust, which ultimately affects several aspects of relationship effectiveness. These results provide further evidence for the positive effects of high integrity.

Consistent with social cognitive theory, perceptions influence behaviour, which ultimately determines relationship performance. In organizations, it is not sufficient to have high integrity, but it is also important to be perceived as doing so. This may be particularly relevant at higher levels within the hierarchy. Possibly true in lateral relationships as well, when our peers within an organization do not have high trust in our integrity, they will not be as cooperative and creative in our relationship with them.

This study has several limitations that should be identified. First, we cannot be sure of the causality direction. There is a clear correlation between overall trust and relationship effectiveness, but the causality is likely to run both ways. The final model shown in Figure 6.1 is not the only good-fitting model and alternative causal models may also be reasonable. Second, though it is more accurate to think of trust as a construct distinct from relationship effectiveness based on conceptual grounds, we could consider it another aspect of effectiveness, as the relatively high fit of .884 in Model A shows. In any case, it seems clear that high-trust relationships have greater levels of effectiveness. We cannot disregard our beliefs about others' integrity: moral character is closely associated with relationship effectiveness.

## REFERENCES

Barber, B. (1983), *The Logic and Limits of Trust*, New Brunswick, NJ, Rutgers University Press.
Bashein, B. and M.L. Markus (1997), 'A credibility solution for IT specialists', *Sloan Management Review*, **38**(4), pp. 35–44.
Becerra, M. (1998), 'Nature, antecedents, and consequences of trust within

organizations: a multilevel analysis within the multinational corporation', unpublished doctoral dissertation, University of Maryland, College Park.

Coleman, J.C. (1990), *Foundations of Social Theory*, Cambridge, MA, The Belknap Press of Harvard University Press.

Deutsch, M. (1958), 'Trust and Suspicion', *Journal of Conflict Resolution*, **2**(4), pp. 265–279.

Dooley, R.S. and G.E. Fryxell (1999), 'Attaining decision quality and commitment from dissent: the moderating effects of loyalty and competence in strategic decision teams', *Academy of Management Journal*, **42**(4), pp 389–402.

Ellram, L.M. and T.E. Hendrick (1995), 'Partnering characteristics: a dyadic perspective', *Journal of Business Logistics*, **1**, pp. 41–59.

Fisman, R. and T. Khanna (1999), 'Is trust a historical residue? Information flows and trust levels', *Journal of Economic Behavior and Organization*, **38**(1), pp. 79–92.

Granovetter, M. (1985), 'Economic action and social structure: the problem of embeddedness', *American Journal of Sociology*, Vol. 91, pp. 481–510.

Hallowell, E.M. (1999), 'The human moment at work', *Harvard Business Review*, **77**(1), pp. 58–66.

Jarillo, J.C. (1990), 'Comments on "transaction costs and networks"', *Strategic Management Journal*, Research Notes and Communications, **11**, pp. 497–499.

Jehn, K.A. (1995), 'A multilevel examination of benefits and determinants of intragroup conflict', *Administrative Science Quarterly*, Vol. 40 Iss. 2, pp. 256–283.

John, G. (1984), 'An empirical investigation of some antecedents of opportunism in a marketing channel', *Journal of Marketing Research*, **21** (August), pp. 278–289.

Kets de Vries, M. (1999), 'High-performance teams: lessons from the pygmies', *Organizational Dynamics*, **27**(3), pp. 66–77.

Kim, W.C. and R. Mauborgne (1998), 'Procedural justice, strategic decision making, and the knowledge economy', *Strategic Management Journal*, **19**(4), pp. 323–338.

Langfield-Smith, K. and M.R. Greenwood (1998), 'Developing co-operative buyer–supplier relationships: A case study of Toyota', *Journal of Management Studies*, **35**(3), pp. 331–353.

Lewis, J.D. and A. Weigert (1985), 'Trust as a social reality', *Social Forces*, **63**(4), pp. 967–985.

Luhmann, N. (1979), *Trust and Power*, Chichester, Wiley.

Luhmann, N. (1988), 'Familiarity, Confidence, Trust: Problems and Alternatives', in D. Ganbetta (ed.), *Trust: Making and Breaking Cooperative Relations*, Basil Blackwell, New York, pp. 94–107.

Mayer, R.C., J.H. Davis and F.D. Schoorman (1995), 'An Integrative Model of Organizational Trust', *Academy of Management Review*, **20**(3), pp. 709–734.

Mayer, R.C., J.H. Davis and F.D. Schoorman (1997), Instrument to measure interpersonal trust. Personal communication.

McCune, J.C. (1998), 'That elusive thing called trust', *Management Review*, **87**(7), pp. 10–12.

Meyerson, D., K.E. Weick and R.M. Kramer (1996), 'Swift Trust and Temporary Groups', in R.M. Kramer and T.R. Tyler (eds), *Trust in Organisations*, London, Sage, pp. 166–195.

Moore, K.R. (1998), 'Trust and relationship commitment in logistics alliances: a buyer perspective', *Journal of Supply Chain Management*, **34**(1), pp. 24–37.

Morgan, R.M. (1991), *Relationship Commitment and Trust in Marketing*, Doctoral thesis, Texas Tech University, Order No. 9129401.

Noorderhaven, N. (1999), 'National culture and the development of trust: the need for more data and less theory', *Academy of Management Review*, **24**(1), pp. 9-10.

O'Reilly, C.A., J.A. Chatman and J.C. Anderson (1987), 'Message flow and decision making', in F.M. Jablin, L.L. Putman, K.H. Roberts and L.W. Porter (eds), *Handbook of Organizational Communication: An Interdisciplinary Perspective*, Newbury Park, CA, Sage.

O'Reilly, C.A. and K. Roberts (1976), 'Relationships among components of credibility and communication behaviors in work units', *Journal of Applied Psychology*, **61**, pp. 99-102.

Porter, T.W. and B.S. Lilly (1996), 'The effects of conflict, trust, and task commitment on project team performance', *International Journal of Conflict Management*, **7**(4), pp. 361-376.

Rao, A. and S. Schmidt (1998), 'A behavioral perspective on negotiating international alliance', *Journal of International Business Studies*, **29**(4), pp. 665-693.

Ring, P.S. and A.H. Van de Ven (1994), 'Developmental processes of cooperative interorganizational relationships', *Academy of Management Review*, **19**(1), pp. 90-118.

Rousseau, D.M., S.B. Sitkin, R.S. Burt and C. Camerer (1998), 'Not so different after all: a cross discipline view of trust', *Academy of Management Review*, **23**(3), pp. 393-404.

Slovic, P. (1972), 'Information processing, situation specificity, and the generality of risk-taking behavior', *Journal of Personality and Social Psychology*, **22**, pp. 128-134.

Whitener, E.M., S.E. Brodt, M.A. Korsgaard and J.M. Werner (1998), 'Managers as initiators of trust: An exchange relationship framework for understanding managerial trustworthy behavior', *Academy of Management Review*, **23**(3), pp. 513-530.

Williamson, O.E. (1993), 'Calculativeness, trust, and economic organization', *Journal of Law and Economics*, **36** (April), pp. 453-486.

Zaheer, A., B. McEvily and V. Perrone (1998), 'Does trust matter? Exploring the effects of interorganizational and interpersonal trust on performance', *Organization Science*, **9**(2), pp. 141-159.

Zand, D.E. (1972), 'Trust and managerial problem solving', *Administrative Science Quarterly* (March), pp. 229-239.

# 7. Reducing opportunism through moral commitment: the ethical paradox of management

## Luk Bouckaert

Opportunism made its appearance in economic literature under different expressive names: tragedy of the commons, prisoner's dilemma, free-riding, moral hazard, agency problems and so on. Behind all this types of reasoning and behaviour, we may find a common 'rational actor' behaviour by which someone tries to turn every opportunity to its own advantage (or to the advantage of his or her own group), even if this may be costly to other people or harm the common interest. Economists have developed many strategies to cope with opportunistic behaviour in order to bridge the gap between individual rationality and the general interest. Generally speaking we may consider three types of regulation: economic incentives (for example a *bonus malus* insurance premium); regulation by a third party (for example government prohibiting some activity by law); and moral self-regulation (for example professional codes, sector covenants). In the case of self-regulation, people freely engage themselves in a shared commitment to act in a responsible way. We call this type of commitment *moral* if the underlying motive is not (only) an economic advantage or a fear of legal punishment, but if the engagement is freely inspired by a sense of social responsibility. If ethics is indeed an efficient way to overcome or at least to temper the negative effect of opportunism, it is rational to introduce ethics management in the firm. But is this rational approach to business ethics convincing and effective? Sometimes it is, but often it is not. And if it works why does it work?

The starting point of my study was the following question: does the normative stakeholder theory of the firm (in its Kantian, utilitarian, social contract or other rational version) explain and solve the problem of opportunism in a convincing way? In the first section I demonstrate that this is not the case. But are there alternative or complementary ways to cope with the problem? I found an attractive answer by reading the classical book of the French philosopher Henry Bergson, *Les deux sources de la morale et de la religion* (1932 first edition, 1941), written at the end of his life. Bergson like

David Hume and Adam Smith is sceptical about the capacity of rational theory and rational ethics to overcome opportunism. But his scepticism of rationalism led him to the discovery of two non-rational sources of ethics: social pressure and mysticism. The second section outlines the main intuitions of Bergson's moral philosophy. The challenge however was to apply the Bergsonian analysis to the field of business ethics. In the third section, I explore the idea of entrepreneurship as a key notion to build up moral commitment in order to overcome opportunism in business. For this section I make use of the excellent book of Spinosa, Flores and Dreyfus, *Disclosing New Worlds* (1997). My conclusion is a plea for a stronger hermeneutic approach to business ethics, inspired by the European tradition of hermeneutic philosophy.

## THE PROBLEM OF OPPORTUNISM IN BUSINESS ETHICS

Opportunism, as a basic human attitude, has its origin in the capacity of reasoning. Human intelligence creates a distance from reality and the possibility to change the natural flow of things. Hence to define and implement a new event structure, we need a consensus and rational co-ordination.[1] The bees in a hive or the ants in a hill do not need this kind of rational co-ordination. Their mix of egoism and altruism is well balanced by a fixed *social instinct* in function of the common good. But suppose that one of the bees one day got the capacity of reasoning. She could ask herself why she does the same job every day without bettering her condition? Why not take a day of rest while others will continue to do her job? Why not just simulate working instead of doing it? Why not leave the hive and move to another place and so on? Undoubtedly, the intelligent bee must be very careful not to be killed or isolated by the other bees reacting instinctively to the social danger of disintegration. The intelligent bee must display at least some minimal social behaviour but her driving force seems to be rational egoism and opportunism. Is there a kind of *rational* argument that could seduce the bee to a more genuine moral commitment and to behave as a loyal member of the hive without any opportunistic hidden agenda? Is business ethics, as a rational discipline or as a rational management practice, able to solve the problem of opportunism?

I consider the paper of T.M. Jones on 'Instrumental stakeholder theory: a synthesis of economics and ethics' (1995), one of the best texts to explore our question. Instrumental stakeholder theory must be distinguished from descriptive and normative versions of stakeholder theory. Its focus is on the prospective impact of ethically driven stakeholding on the economic performance of the firm. Are there some rational arguments to accept a positive relation between ethics (interpreted as co-operative stakeholding) and economics? The theory of efficient contracting indeed give us convincing arguments: good stakeholding may reduce opportunism in a much more cost efficient way than other regulations (external monitoring and control and/or economic incentives) and create a positive climate for co-operation and trust. Hence ethical stakeholding generates *coeteris paribus* a competitive advantage which means that ethics pays. If this would be true, every businessperson would be an ethical champion or at least, every rational business leader. But as a matter of fact, things are not going this way and seem to be more complicated.

As the argument of efficient contracting goes, it presupposes that there is *already* a genuine moral commitment to fair stakeholding, which we can use as a resource to reduce transaction costs. So the rational argument does not create the moral commitment but may at most reinforce it by stressing its good economic consequences. By saying that ethics pays, we just put aside the more difficult question of how to build up that pre-existent moral competence. This may explain why some businesspeople, having an economic or rational interest in ethics, do not succeed in being ethical entrepreneurs or creating a social responsible corporation. But the argument could be developed further. If the economic rational argument would be the *source* of ethical commitment, it would lead us into the complete instrumentalization of ethics, which is according to Kant's categorical imperative morally unacceptable. Instrumentalization of persons and moral values is only acceptable as a secondary motive but never as the prime mover. Reversing the order (and giving priority to the instrumental side of ethics) is the essence of opportunistic behaviour. The danger of the economic rational argument, used in the theory of efficient contracting but also in game theory, transaction cost theory, human resource management and a lot of business ethics, lies precisely in its power to cure the symptoms of opportunism while reinforcing its roots. The ultimate result will be that opportunism will reappear in a more sophisticated form, disguised as ethics, operating *sub specie boni*. This is the ethical paradox of management: instead of awaking trust and stability, ethical behaviour will raise even more suspicion and distrust. When the fox preaches, guard your geese.

The paradox may be explained in yet another way. The economic rational argument makes managers more sensitive to use ethics as a *managerial tool* instead of considering it as a *moral commitment*. As a managerial tool ethics become easily an instrument of manipulating and co-ordinating the emotions of other people as a means in the function of the objectives of the firm (Sejersted, 1996), while a moral commitment is internal to the relation between oneself and other people. In the latter case, ethics is operative on a deeper *relational* level prior to its use on the *rational* level. While rational intelligence refers to reasoning in terms of means and objectives or in terms of causes and effects, relational ethics implies a more intuitive and empathic form of commitment to values and persons including oneself.

T. Jones (1995) is well aware of these problems posed by opportunistic ethical behavior and the manipulative use of ethics. Actually, his point is that in order to realize an effective synthesis between economics and ethics, we need genuine ethics and must be able to make a distinction between genuine and pseudo-ethics. In *Passions within Reason* (1988), Frank R.H. gives us two pragmatic criteria to identify non-opportunistic ethical behaviour: honesty in communication and good reputation. By repetitive personal communication, verbal and especially non-verbal expression can give us a feeling of the trustworthiness and the honesty of another person. The second indicator is a long-term good reputation because it is difficult to feign ethics over a long period. I agree that this may be good indicators of moral commitment but they do not answer our question about the source of moral commitment. By just pointing out the indicators, managers will be inclined to identify moral commitment with a good style of communication or with reputation management. These may be helpful instruments but they do not disclose the *inner source* of moral commitment.

**Bergson's Two Sources of Ethics**

Let us turn to Bergson. One of his main convictions is that we cannot find the origin of moral obligation in rational argument,[2] although rational theory may represent moral behaviour *as if* it is the result of a process of reasoning. With this illusion rationality tries to countervail its own tendency to opportunism and egoism by opening a wider horizon of universal principles in order to explain and justify a coherent social system. There seems to be another paradox here. On the one hand Bergson takes a sceptical attitude towards rationalism which is considered from an epistemological point of view as an illusion. On the other hand, Bergson underlines the social necessity of this illusion. Why do we need this illusion? Moreover, is it possible, once we realize that it is an illusion, that it would still be able to fulfil its social function?

Let us follow Bergson's argument step by step. Reasoning breaks the natural social cohesion co-coordinated by instinct. But to build up a new and this time a rational and reasonable social order is a difficult and risky task because reasoning will first of all manifest itself as a rational concern for one's own advantage and betterment.[3] While reasoning implies resisting to the natural life of instincts, we need also resisting to the resistance.[4] We need a second-order resistance as a countervailing power to the opportunistic rationality. Reasoning tries to organize this second-order resistance by developing rational and encompassing ethical systems of rules and principles, which *imitate* the stability of the social instinct regulation of nature. But this rational order misses the mark because we can always dispute arguments and question the already accepted ones. Reasoning is a too flexible and too cognitive ground in order to commit deeply enough our will and to countervail the opportunistic tendencies of our rational nature. So the following question arises: where do we find a human substitute for the natural social instinct of the bees and the ants if we cannot take rational intelligence as a sufficient guarantee for social cohesion and commitment? According to Bergson, pre-rational feelings of moral obligation (common-sense morality) and religion do fulfil this function: they are the real source of resistance against social disintegration and opportunism. They create a *virtual instinct* in society to control the self-interested and egoistic tendencies of rationality. On this ground, rational theories and discussions may flourish and create the illusion of being the real source of our actions.

But the most interesting point of Bergson's analysis is not his sceptical attitude towards intellectualism and rationalism; it is his theory of the *two* (non-rational) sources of ethics. Moral order and moral obligation are constituted by two different ways: primarily by a system of *orders* dictated by *impersonal* social needs, and secondly by a set of *appeals* directed to our consciousness by *persons* who bring the best of humanity to the fore.[5] Both ways of constituting morality are very different in their nature and manifestation. The first kind of moral competence is built up by the pressure of society. Society strives to maintain and develop itself through a system of habits, rules, representations, symbols and institutions which constrains the free space of the individuals and socialize them towards the general interest and the collective. Although each habit or rule can change and may be considered as contingent, the whole body of obligations has a necessity, which substitutes the necessity of the instinctive order. In a society of rational actors this sense of the collective is rationalized in terms of mutual advantage or other principles. But in times of crisis and insecurity the *infra-rational* remains of social instinct seem to reappear impudently and push aside rational principles of morality (for example by using torture and murder in times of war). By a sudden pressure of social instinct and collective hallucination, the thin layer of civilization and reason can be discarded.

Bergson wrote his book in the 1930s (1932) and, as a Jew, he was well aware of the unstable situation of Europe after the First World War.

Throughout history there has been another force at work which tends towards a more *open* society and overcomes the closeness of social instinct and the weakness of rationality. This other force is *supra-rational*, taking its rise in the aspirations of exceptional men and women, who, similar to innovative artists, scientists and entrepreneurs, display creative moral and religious leadership. These privileged persons are not primarily driven by the social *pressure* to maintain society as a functioning system but by the *aspiration* to transgress existing boundaries, to disclose new horizons and to invent new practices of spiritual and social life. This aspiration is not the result of rational discourse but springs from an inner *emotion,* which creates its own representations and transforms old ideas, values and institutions. The Greek philosophers, the Buddhist monks, the Jewish prophets, the Christian saints and many others invented new practices, which were appealing to large numbers of people. In his chapter on dynamic religion, Bergson links this creative emotion to *mysticism,*[6] which brings our mind through an immediate intuitive feeling into contact with the *élan vital,* the creative force of life. This partial coincidence with life is a source of creativity, joy and relatedness and gives man an *inner experience* of the transcendental and evolutionary character of life and history. Reality is not immobile but mobile. Time is not the repetition of identical moments but the emergence of something new, openness for what is unsaid, unknown, unforeseen. Time is duration, a divine manifestation of life.

This mystical emotion to which Bergson refers cannot be reduced to a mere psychological excitement. It has an ontological meaning, relating us to the inner side of reality. While science explores reality from without, from an outside point of view, metaphysics tries to understand reality from within by intuition and imagination. It is the same mystical emotion, which, according to Bergson, discloses the universal 'love for mankind'. He insists strongly on the point that this universal love cannot be interpreted as a quantitative broadening of our sympathy from more particular to more universal contexts, say from family to nation to mankind. The transition to universality is the result of a process of inner and qualitative breaks, introduced as aspirations by enlightened philosophers, Christian saints, Buddhist monks and a diversity of other human beings. They awake through moments of individual and collective crisis the idea of infinity[7] in our consciousness. With the spiritual force of this idea, we transgress the existing oppositions between insiders and outsiders, friends and enemies and create a new and more universal form of society.[8]

It is important to realize that the second source of ethics is not religion as such but mysticism (defined in a broad sense) operative in persons. Religion is a much more ambiguous socio-cultural phenomenon, taking its form from the same non-rational sources as morality: the infra-rational pressure towards social cohesion and the supra-rational aspiration towards universal love. If social pressure is the dominant force, religion will take a static form and sustain a closed society. Bergson explores very extensively how static religion tries to sanctify social order through rituals, totems, taboos and mythology. These representations of life make it possible in a human society to give meaning to death, sacrifice and altruism (which are regulated by pure instinct or ignorance in the case of animals). They form a conservative defense of social nature against the disintegrating effects of rationality.[9] They protect the common-sense morality. Combined with the system of moral habits, they incorporate individuals deeply in a social system (a family, city or nation), which gives them an identity and an orientation but also an inclination to defend strongly their community against external enemies. Static forms of religion have often been used and misused to cultivate patriotism and to sustain war.

Bergson's sharp distinction between the closed and the open religion and society cannot be found *à l'état pur*. There are transition forms and conflicts between both tendencies. New ways of life will be incorporated in the habits and rules of the social system and become part of the static system of morality. But at the same time, gifted and unselfish persons will give voice to their inner experience of time as a creative evolution and find out new ways towards a more open society.

What may be the conclusion for a business ethicist from this Bergsonian story? I hold on two conclusions. Firstly, Bergson's analysis confirms the idea that rational theory and practice is not able to root moral commitment. On a practical level, this implies that, if business ethics wants to introduce moral commitment in the sphere of business, we must be rather sceptical about our own efforts to develop rational theories and management tools to improve ethical behaviour in business. Secondly, the dynamic source of moral commitment lies, according to Bergson, in a metaphysical experience of time. This is not a conceptual construction but an inner and emotional intelligence of how we (as ethicist or business leaders) are involved in a process of ongoing creative evolution, opening itself towards greater diversity and relatedness. If this is true, it means that business ethics must first of all be helpful in understanding this inner experience of time, not only in general terms but in the field of business itself. How can this be done? I believe that the practice of entrepreneurship is a key to understand this inner experience of time and to find an inspiring source for moral commitment.

## MORAL COMMITMENT AND ENTREPRENEURSHIP

In their book *Disclosing New Worlds* (1997), C. Spinosa, F. Flores and H.L. Dreyfus develop a 'common-sense approach' to entrepreneurship, which is inspired by a Heideggerian vision on history. By common sense they mean the way entrepreneurs do experience their effort and ambitions in concrete practices. They define entrepreneurship as *the ontological skill of disclosing new ways of being or as the art of history-making*. That skill is not restricted to the context of business. It is also of great importance for citizen actions and for the cultivation of solidarity. *Disclosing new worlds* explores the ways entrepreneurs initiate such processes of cultural innovation. The most important skill required for this capacity of disclosing new meaning in life is, first of all, the ability to sense and hold on to disharmonies or anomalies in our current way of doing things and secondly, to find a new way to handle the anomaly. The authors describe three methods which entrepreneurs use to realize the change – reconfiguration, cross-appropriation and articulation. I will not elaborate on these methods but stick to the idea of history-making as the essence of entrepreneurship.

Let us take one example, given by the authors, the invention of a new type of razor by King C. Gillette (Spinosa et al., 1997, pp. 42–43). An analysis of this case reveals that there was more at stake than just a technological innovation. The man did not only create a better crafted straight-edge razor that kept its edge longer, but he was very sensitive to the cultural change he was initiating. I quote:

> The art of learning to shave was one of the glories of coming of age. Gillette sensed that he and other men were willing to give up their masculine rituals not only for the sake of convenience in the domain of removing facial hair but also for the sake of having a different relation to things in general. Gillette sensed that masculinity could – and would, thanks in part to him – be understood as commanding things and getting rid of them when they ceased to serve rather than as caring for and cherishing useful and well-engineered things. Gillette's entrepreneurial conviction did not rest on a skillful balancing of technical know-how and needs; he sensed the dullness of the blade as unusual, *as something to be changed in the way he dealt with things generally* (Spinosa et al., 1997, p. 42).

The invention of the new product was embedded in the intuition of changing cultural habits.

Defining entrepreneurship as a history-making activity goes against the post-modern obsession of flexibility and change for the sake of change. Post-modern authors define entrepreneurship – against rational management – as an art of *surfing on chaos*, on waves of continuous change generated by turbulent markets. The entrepreneur as a surfer is always adapting him or herself to the chaotic fluctuations of the environment. This is not the art of history-making. Historicity implies a sense of continuity, a sense of making progress by introducing a new idea, product or service. History-making is more than just adaptation to market preferences; it is creatively responding to a historical anomaly or disharmony which moves from a marginal position into the centre of our consciousness and challenges the imagination of the entrepreneur. This process is analogous to T. Kuhn's description of scientific anomalies and paradigm change (Spinosa et al., 1997, pp. 45–46, p. 193).

But most of all do standard views of business eliminate the meaning of history and substitute it by the idea of controlled time processing. By giving a central place to the view that entrepreneurial activity is the optimization of profit-making activities through competitive success, the meaning of entrepreneurship as the creation of new meanings and practices disappears. Innovation is reduced to a problem of rational allocation of means and incentives in the function of profit-making. Although profit-making is an effect and a condition for entrepreneurial activity, it is not its core meaning and impetus. Ex post the activity can be restructured in this more abstract way but this will eliminate the intrinsic and subjective meaning of being an entrepreneur. As a result, the difference between a rational manager and a genuine entrepreneur gets obscured.

Rational managers try to find out the new market preferences in order to meet them by technical and commercial re-engineering of activities. They are most of all concerned about finding more cost-effective methods than the competitors in order to gain the price competition in the market. How important this may be, this is not what we mean by entrepreneurship. Entrepreneurs change the markets by creating a new style, new preferences and new cultural identities. According to our authors, the first mass-produced cars were not competing with other mass-produced cars but with another way of life. The first personal computers were not competing with other personal computers but with our pastoral habits. The first meaning of competition lies in the sphere of cultural innovation and the creation of value, defined in a much broader sense than in quantitative monetary terms. I quote:

> We compete because we enjoy the ongoing exercise of our skills in a context where those skills make sense as components of a meaningful way of life. That is, we compete to make things and ourselves more worthy. We compete to make the qualities of products that we care about or qualities of ourselves that we care about stand out. In short, we compete to develop identities within communities (Spinosa et al., 1997, p. 56).

This may sound rather idealistic but I think it is true if we consider cases of genuine entrepreneurship. A lot of businesses may not correspond to this model but they miss indeed the drive of entrepreneurial activity and are led by strategies of risk calculation and better control of existing systems. For a genuine entrepreneur profit-making is a measure of his or her success and is a possibility to develop and implement fully his or her creative capacity. People are at their best when they are involved in such processes of creating a new market or segment of a market and in transforming the quality of life of their fellow human beings. Leadership means the capacity of co-coordinating such a concrete process of collective creativity.

Is there a link between this notion of entrepreneurship and Bergson's idea of mysticism? Let us remember that for Bergson mysticism has a broad meaning and refers to an inner experience of time as creative evolution. It seems to me that the interpretation of entrepreneurship as history-making and cultural innovation fits very well within the Bergsonian approach to ethics. At least three points can be mentioned:

1.  Entrepreneurship as a process of collective creativity makes people aware of time as *élan vital*. This awareness as an inner source of spiritual energy stimulates business life through intrinsic motivation beyond external incentives and allocations.
2.  Competition is driven by a movement to overcome historical anomalies by disclosing new meanings and markets. Intuition and imagination are central to this movement. This idea of competition correlates with Bergson's idea of human progress through historical crises, which open the way for new religious and socio-cultural meaning and practices.
3.  Bergson's idea of an open society may be an inspiring model to formulate some conditions of a creative enterprise, especially the conditions of equilibrium between social pressure and personal creativity, ethical codes and moral imagination, rational management and intuitive leadership.

## CONCLUSION

Opportunism is one of the most challenging problems in the field of economics today. Tackling this problem, more and more economists and managers discover the role of ethics and virtues (trust, loyalty and commitment). As business ethicists we are supposed to provide them with instruments and tools to enhance the quality of moral competence. But here lies our ethical paradox. Ethics is supposed to solve the problem of opportunism but at the same time, as a practical instrument of ethics management, it creates new opportunities for disguised opportunism.

We tried to solve the paradox by making a distinction between two different but complementary forms of business ethics: business ethics as *ethics management* and business ethics as *a moral commitment*. In the first case ethics is seen as a system of regulations and tools to implement the values and mission of the firm (social audit, ethical codes, value management, and so on). Ethics management may be seen as a part of human resource management practice or other more global organization theories and policies. Its aim is to develop a new and more intelligent system of control and co-ordination.

The problem, however, was the crowding out of intrinsic moral commitment by external regulations and rational management. The result of this crowding out effect is the reintroduction of rational opportunism and as a result, distrust in human relations. Trust needs a non-instrumental commitment and therefore a non-instrumental analysis. I believe that the

Bergsonian philosophy gives us a key to restore the link between intrinsic moral commitment and business life by reinterpreting the dynamics and motivations of entrepreneurial activities. Take for instance the case of sustainability. The idea of sustainable growth implies an intuitive sense of time as duration. To make the concept of the triple bottom line operational presupposes already an inner motivation of solidarity with the planet and with future generations.

A lot of businesspeople will prefer the ethics management approach to the more philosophical one because they expect that this philosophical reflection will lead to the construction of abstract and rational moral theories and difficult discussions between Kantian, utilitarian or other systems deduced from some general principles. My conclusion is that we need, not as a substitute but as a complement to ethics management, a hermeneutic business ethics. Its task is to elucidate the *metaphysical core* in the moral experiences of businesspeople. This metaphysical core is not a theory but an intuition of time. Bergson has been one of the first philosophers to develop such a dynamic metaphysics of time. He anticipated the Heideggerian philosophy of 'Sein und Zeit' (Time and Being) and the post-modern philosophies of time as a creative process of deconstruction. At the same time, his philosophy has influenced a European continental stream of personalistic philosophy: Maritain, Mounier, Levinas. He inspired poets as Péguy, scientists as T. de Chardin and Prigogine, just to name a few. He is one of the rare philosophers to get the Nobel price. My point is not to promote Bergson, although he is a good companion for our task, but to indicate the richness of the hermeneutic tradition as a philosophical resource to discover and to activate moral commitment in business and leadership.

## NOTES

1. I think much of what is going on in business ethics and in political philosophy has to do with this balance between individual claims and social cohesion. The discovery of social capital and corporate culture, the communitarian criticism of liberalism, the search for national and corporate identities can be interpreted as deep-rooted reactions against social disintegration generated by global capitalism, deregulation and post-modern relativism. This social defence is needed to restore the balance between economy and society. But this social defence may be very incomplete and unable to counter the anarchism and hypercompetition generated by the globalization of the markets. To overcome the disintegration process we need an inspiring entrepreneurial ethics. The second source of ethics which Bergson calls the manifestation of the *élan vital* (creative evolution, duration) and which frees *l'energie spirituelle* (spiritual energy) in the human person, may be a good instance for the development of such a committed entrepreneurial ethics.

2. 'L'essence de l'obligation est autre chose qu'une exigence de la raison' DS p. 18. 'Jamais, aux heures de tentation, on ne sacrifierait au seul besoin de cohérence logique son intérêt, sa passion, sa vanité. Parce que la raison intervient en effet comme régulatrice, chez un être raisonnable, pour assurer cette cohérence entre des règles ou maximes obligatoires, la

philosophie a pu voir en elle un principe d'obligation. Autant vaudrait croire que c'est le volant qui fait tourner la machine' DS p. 2.

3. 'La vérité est que l'intelligence conseillera d'abord l'égoisme', DS p. 126.

4. 'La résistance à la résistance', DS p. 96.

5. 'Il reste la formule générale de la moralité qu'accepte aujourd'hui l'humanité civilisée: cette formule englobe deux choses, un système *d'ordres* dictés par des exigences sociales *impersonnelles*, et un ensemble *d'appels* lancés à la conscience de chacun de nous par des *personnes* qui représentent ce qu'il y eut de meilleur dans l'humanité. L'obligation qui s'attache à l'ordre est, dans ce qu'elle a d'original et de fondamental, infra-intellectuelle. L'efficacité de l'appel tient à la puissance de l'émotion ...; elle est supra-intellectuelle. Les deux forces, s'exerçant dans des régions différentes de l'âme, se projettent sur le plan intermédiaire, qui est celui de l'intelligence. Elles seront désormais remplacées par leurs projections' (DS pp. 85–86).

6. 'A nos yeux, l'aboutissement du mysticisme est une prise de contact, et par conséquent une coïncidence partielle, avec l'effort créateur que manifeste la vie. Cet effort est de Dieu, si ce n'est pas Dieu lui-même. Le grand mystique serait une individualité qui franchirait les limites assignées à l'espèce par sa matérialité, qui continuerait et prolongerait ainsi l'action divine. Telle est notre définition' DS p. 233.

7. It is interesting to compare Bergson's idea of infinity with the analysis of E. Levinas. The latter locates the origin of the idea of infinity in the confrontation with a metaphysical exteriority revealed by the Other (the face-to-face experience), while Bergson stresses the intuition of the inner dynamics of life (life as duration).

8. In the view of Bergson Christian mysticism differs from Buddhism not by the universality of its content but by the fact that it combines its mystical aspiration with a sense for action and incarnation in history.

9. 'La religion est donc une réaction défensive de la nature contre le pouvoir dissolvant de l'intelligence' DS p. 127.

# REFERENCES

Bergson H. (1941), *Les deux sources de la morale et de la religion*, Paris: P.U.F. (abbreviated as DS).

Frank R.H. (1988), *Passions within Reason: the Strategic Role of Emotions*, New York: Norton & Company.

Jones T.M. (1995), 'Instrumental stakeholder theory: a synthesis of ethics and economics', *Academy of Management Review*, 20 (2), 404–437.

Sejersted F. (1996), 'Managers and consultants as manipulators. Reflections on the suspension of ethics', *Business Ethics Quarterly*, 6 (1), 67–86.

Spinosa C., F. Flores and H.L. Dreyfus (1997), *Disclosing New Worlds: Entrepreneurship, Democratic Action and the Cultivation of Solidarity*, Cambridge, US: MIT Press.

# 8. Rational discourse as a foundation for ethical codes

## J. Félix Lozano

## 1  INTRODUCTION

The development of ethical codes in recent years has without doubt been spectacular, but more spectacular, to my mind, is their lack of credibility among employees, consumers and society in general. The process of elaboration, and the rational foundations, of ethical codes, and self-regulation, or self-definition, documents are the aspects which most clearly determine their legitimacy and effectiveness.

Here I wish to present the advantages of rational argumentation based on Cortina's interpretation of discourse ethics as a foundation for ethical codes. The characteristics of this type of rationality derive from its Kantian origins, but go a step further. It was Kant who discovered the practical and the theoretical uses of reason, and he demonstrated the need for an autonomous reason which derives its own laws in the moral world.

## 2  THE PROGRAMME OF COMMUNICATIVE ETHICAL REASON

The programme of communicative ethical reason is rooted in Kantian moral philosophy and its concept of rationality.[1] This critical reason accepts that it cannot be based on any sure foundation except itself. Working from this premise, Kant overcomes the heteronomy both of the utilitarian and of previous moral traditions, and derives the moral concept of autonomy.

This 'Copernican' shift gives rise to a qualitative advance in the development of the bases for human action: a basis for human action which is expressed in the maxim of universal action laid out in the categorical imperative: 'Act in such a way that you treat your humanity, as much as that of any other person, always as an end, and never as simply a means' (Kant [1785], 1974, p. 61). This imperative undoubtedly remains completely valid in our modern societies and it would be extremely desirable for it to be recognized, adopted and promoted in economic and business environments.

This imperative, despite its undoubted importance, has been the object of critiques which have transformed it considerably. The Kantian imperative shows an uncommon confidence in autonomous and individual reason which leads inevitably to an ethics of solipsistic conviction. The step from Kantian transcendental philosophy – of the private subject – to the a priori of the communicative community – intersubjectivity – was made by K.O. Apel in the transcendental-pragmatic approach.

Instead of formal logical foundations – along the lines of H. Albert (1973) and critical rationalism – transcendental pragmatism is based on strict reflection on the normative conditions for the possibility and validity of a rational argumentation. Every individual, on initiating argument, has implicitly accepted these conditions, because otherwise complete argumentation is not possible.[2]

The normative conditions for the possibility and validity of a rational argumentation are based on the double a priori of the communicative community:

### a. The argumentative a priori *of the communicative community*

It means the reciprocal recognition of individuals as subjects of argumentation, which presupposes the implicit desire to be considered a mature adult (mündig). Out of this comes an ethical minimum which should be – implicitly – considered as a presupposition of understanding in rational relations between individuals. To quote Apel himself: 'Whoever argues, is already implicitly recognizing all the possible desires of the participants in the communicative community that can be based on rational arguments and is obliging his or herself at the same time to justify with arguments his or her own desires to others' (Apel, 1973, II, p. 425).

From this arises the principle of universalization as the moral criterion of discourse ethics. The idea of an unlimited communicative community of all rational beings ('alle denkenden Wesen' Apel, 1973, II, p. 425) is the regulative idea which should guide concrete action. Discourse ethics does not attempt to establish value content-based premises, rather it *simply* attempts to determine the communicative rationality of the consensus-seeking process. That is to say it deals with the practical rationality of argumentation.

It is necessary to make a brief commentary here with regard to the question of the ethical codes that are the subject of this study. This a priori of the communicative community in which we find the regulative idea and the ethical criterion of communication is not an ideal – that is to say, distanced from reality – rather it should, and can, be integrated into concrete action. Though it is true that the search for consensus by means of ideal dialogue conditions should neither be confused with the negotiation of interests nor with factual consensus, rational communication criteria should – and can – be made operational in each real communicative community.

The *a priori* of the communicative community should be understood as ideal in the sense that it cannot be fully realized, but it is pursuable, and serves as a guide and compass in the development of factual communication. In this sense business ethics codes should take into account this desire for a consensus achieved by means of the establishment of rational dialogues in which the force of the better argument prevails, rather than the arguments of interests.

*b.   The experiential* a priori *of the real communicative community*
The *a priori* of the ideal communicative community is not a 'pure idea' distanced from reality. It is rather made explicit through the real experience of the possibilities of rational communication in practice; these possibilities of rational communication are a fundamental condition for the development of the personal identity of every human being.

We live in and are socialized by a particular communicative community, this is an anthropological fact common to all cultures: reciprocity of understanding between individuals is the necessary condition for the development of any communication. This anthropological fact is subject to both phylogenetic and ontogenetic analyses, that is, an evolution takes place both at individual and species level. This evolution can be seen as the education of the communicative reason.

At the level of the individual subject, it was Laurenz Kohlberg (1974)[3] who demonstrated the development of the moral conscience and the process of formation of the identity of the subject. Kohlberg established three qualitatively distinct levels of evolution of the individual moral reason:[4]

- *The preconventional level:* the child's actions are oriented towards pleasure and displeasure (hedonist morals) and reward and punishment. Justice is understood in terms of blind obedience to rules and authority; avoiding punishment and not causing material damage. In the second stage of this first level justice is understood as what is impartial in an instrumental exchange in which each pursues personal interests.
- *The conventional level:* the motivation for an action depends on the concrete consequences of that action in accordance with certain knowledge or a personal social authority. In this case justice is understood in terms of contribution to the maintenance of social order and welfare. At this level there is no critical conscience with regard to norms and values.
- *The postconventional level, of principles:* the final stage of this

development in which an important level of critical conscience has been reached. Here norms and social roles are not considered given by nature, rather they are critically examined from the point of view of a fully developed communicative competence in which the critical factor is universalizability. This is the ethical level of adulthood, where the individual can distinguish what is fair from what suits, and from what he or she feels like.

These levels of development of the individual conscience have their correlation in the phylogenetic evolution of the species and the development of social integration. On the basis of this evolution Habermas (1981, 1983) elaborated a model of the development of societies.

- archaic society, which contains a series of elements of conventional morals, but the dominant moral principle is utilitarian strategic equity reciprocity;
- advanced traditional society, in which society is organized in accordance with functional criteria and a conventional morality of obedience;
- modern society supersedes the previous stages; institutions have to comply with the objective of communicative legitimization.

Taking this model into account the applied ethics we propose should be appropriate to this level. The nature of the society in which we find ourselves conditions our approach to business ethics. If we consider the company a social institution, interdependent – though autonomous up to a point – with the global social system, we can attempt to propose a similar model of evolutionary development for organizations:

- *Classical companies (preconventional level)*: these would be the companies from the start of the industrial revolution in which the motives for action were the need to satisfy basic human needs, and in which the reward–punishment structure was the catalyst for action.
- *Modern companies (conventional level)*: in this case the human factor is taken into account but from a strategic point of view. The desire is for the company to function as well as possible and this gives rise to authority structures and cultures of myths and ideal images which motivate the workers.
- *Companies as stakeholders (postconventional level)*: these would be those companies which have adopted the dignity and autonomy of human beings as part of their organization. Here the need to respond communicatively to the desire for legitimization of those involved in

company activity is a constant. Socialization is no longer affected by means of external norms, or imposed symbolism, but rather by means of a commitment to minimum shared values generated by the participants in the organizational project; participants who are considered autonomous individuals.

These two *a priori* provide a solid base which legitimizes argumentative discourse, as much as a *means* for the foundation of concrete norms, as for the foundation of the principle of ethics. Nowadays the full cooperation of individuals in the *foundation* of those judicial and moral norms which are susceptible of consensus, as well as in the political *institutionalization* of practical discourse, is an indispensable requirement.

## 3    THE INSTITUTIONALIZATION OF DISCOURSE ETHICS

The point which especially interests us is the question of the institutionalization of practical discourse, to which Apel (1991) refers to in Part B of discourse ethics.

If we take practical discourse seriously we have to act as individuals who argue seriously, and we have therefore already recognized – in the real communicative community – a series of universally valid presuppositions and norms. We presuppose co-responsibility with regard to decisions (1), equal rights of all the participants in communication (2), and we recognize our capacity to achieve consensus regarding solutions to problems, which is the objective of the discourse (3).

The guiding principle of real discourse is the capacity to reach a consensus between those affected regarding solutions to problems. Discourse ethics offers a pragmatic-transcendental foundation for the principle of the foundation of norms, but it also provides a model for the foundation of situational norms of practical discourse, which is what particularly interests us here.

As Apel explains (1987) in *Fallibilismus. Konsenstheorie der Warheit und Letzbegründung,* discourse ethics is made up of two fundamental parts. Part A deals with foundations in abstract terms and Part B with foundations in the context of history.

- *Part A* is divided into two aspects, that of the ultimate pragmatic transcendental foundation for the principle for the foundation of norms, and that of the foundation of situational norms in practical discourse. In the latter is included the requirement that there be – or the necessary conditions be created for – real discourse that can lead to the formation of a consensus between those affected. That is to say that, already at the abstract, the discourse of ethics delegates to the participants the responsibility for the concrete foundation of norms, thus guaranteeing that those norms be appropriate to the situation, and furthermore giving rise to responsibility for the consequences; at the same time maximum attention to the principle of universalizability in the context of the discourse is guaranteed.

- *Part B.* Here the fundamental norm of responsibility for the conservation of the natural environment and the cultural and historical achievements of the real existing community has to be taken into account. In this part the ontogenetic is dependent on the phylogenetic on two levels:

  - moral judgement competence depends on the process of socialization;
  - the dependence of the conditions of application and of post-conventional moral competence on the collective ethical level.

Discourse ethics is not irresponsible. Apel himself (1991, pp. 171, 172) quotes an example that considerably clarifies this aspect. He asks himself 'Should I pay tax honestly when others do not?' or to put it in a more abstract manner: 'Can I and should I renounce negotiation, and the instrumental strategic rationality of interests, if the objective is to transform the conversation in the sense of discourse ethics?' His reply is clear: 'No, the individual *cannot* do something like this without failing as the subject of action, neither *should* this be done if it is supposed that he/she should be responsible not only for his/herself but also for a self-affirming system which has been entrusted to him/her: family, interest groups, state …' to which we would add company, organization and profession.

Those who have managed to understand the universal validity of the ethical principle of discourse are obliged to (1) mediate between the possibilities of resolving conflicts of interest by means of consensus in accordance with an evaluation of the situation, and the possibilities of strategic action and (2) collaborate in the long term in what could be described as a suppression of the differences between real and ideal conditions of discourse.

## 4  CORTINA'S NOTES ON DISCOURSE ETHICS

Part B of Apel's ethics of discourse provides a more direct link to the real contexts of application of discourse ethics, which allows us to speak of a responsible ethics based on principles. While Part A of the discourse ethics is guided by the idea of *foundation*, Part B is guided by the idea of *responsibility*.

Although this represents an important advance and a decisive argument against pragmatist and idealist positions, Cortina (1993) points out that Part B does not appropriately represent the development of events. According to Cortina, 'social life from its diverse perspectives has looked to ethics for improvement in moral quality and has creatively generated specific values and principles for each environment' (Cortina, 1993, p. 167).

Arguing from the assumption that ethics deals with the design and critical judgement of areas of application rather than concrete applications in themselves, Cortina is not in agreement with Habermas with respect to the idea that the only mission of ethics is to clarify the meaning of the term 'correct' when a norm is put into practice. Cortina agrees more with Apel in that communicative rationality has to be mediated in the environment of application by strategic rationality, always assuming that the intention is to achieve the following two goals:

1.  The preservation of the subject and his or her dependants,
2.  The foundation of cultural and material bases that may one day make it possible to act communicatively without endangering the preservation of oneself and others.

But Cortina (1993), while accepting Parts A and B of discourse ethics, proposes a *Part C* which would represent a further step towards the application of the ethical approach we are proposing. The application is understood not as a deductive or inductive process, but rather as a *hermeneutic critique* which reveals the particular modulations of the common principle depending on the environment in which we find ourselves.

The aim of Part C is to explore decision-making procedures in concrete reality, and in this sense it implies a further level of concretion with respect to the conditions of application: the assumptions made in this third part would be:

1.  *The activity* in which we are involved and the *goal* which gives meaning and legitimacy to this activity (its internal assets).
2.  *The values, principles and attitudes* that need to be developed in order to achieve the goal of this activity.
3.  *The values and particular principles* that arise out of the modulation of the dialogic ethical principle in this activity.
4.  *The data of the situation* which should be described as completely as possible.

This level of concretion does not mean that we forget the ideal principles that guide discourse. Other moral traditions must be taken into account 'although the coordinating element will be discourse ethics because it is legitimized in the communicative action and the subsequent argumentation, which is the coordinating medium for the rest of human activity. It is precisely the idea of the subject as a valid interlocutor which configures the common melodic background of all the spheres, and, in all of these, it is in the end the individual affected who can legitimately express his/her interests and have those that are universalizables taken into account' (Cortina, 1993, p. 176).

I believe that this interpretation of discourse ethics clearly shows the implications for the institutionalization of ethics in organizational situations, and furthermore makes this step inevitable.

## 5   THE IMPLICATIONS OF RATIONAL DISCOURSE FOR THE ELABORATION OF CODES

A synthesis of the contents of the previous sections shows the essential characteristics of discourse ethics to be as follows:

- *Communicative competence*: a human being remains worthy of undoubted respect because he or she is valuable in his or herself. The Kantian idea of the person as an autonomous being capable of using his or her own reason is transformed into *the valid interlocutor* who can defend his or her arguments in discourse.
- *Consideration of those affected*: in discourse ethics the consequences of actions are taken into account, and are the core of the validity of moral norms. If all those affected by the norms are in agreement with them, they will be moral.
- *Universalisibility*: this characteristic is fundamental if we are to speak of the morality of a norm; it is the unconditional factor which mediates in the calculation of consequences.

The formulation of these norms in the categorical imperative of discourse ethics would, in the words of Cortina, be as follows: 'Act in such a way as to direct your action as far as possible towards a basis for an ideal communicative community!' (Cortina, 1993, p.172).

Almost all the exponents of this ethical approach have defended the idea that this principle of discourse ethics can be applied to the business environment (Ulrich, 1993; Cortina, 1993; Apel, 1988). In the words of Apel (1998):

the principle of discourse ethics should be valid for the businessman, not just because he or she is an individual, but also insofar as it should provide the regulative principle for a new determination of the rationality of communicative action. A businessman should not be choosing between the imperative of the strategic maximization of strategic use in terms of the interests of the firm and the ethical imperative of the principle of discourse, instead he/she should be able to guide the principle of rationality of action – insofar as he/she is a businessman – on the basis of the principle of the rationality of discourse. (1988: 291).

If we hold to the characteristics of discourse ethics which I have presented so far, it can be seen that there are basically three implications for the development of ethical codes:

*1.   Codes should be understood more as a process than a result*
Codes should be living documents that respond to the needs and aspirations of the community they are to govern. Codes are a good system for the institutionalization of ethics in companies as long as they are understood as an authentic integration (hermeneutic critique). Furthermore one can only speak of an authentic ethics if it is in tune with the make-up of society and its level of postconventional conscience.

*2.   The processes of dialogue should be guided by the norms of rational dialogue*
This aspect is fundamental, understanding codes as process implies understanding them *fundamentally* as dialogue. 'Discourse ethics should not deal simply with the mediation of the interests of those affected, but also it should aim at a permanent improvement in the knowledge (both for those affected and their representatives) of the expected consequences and collateral effects that could follow from the norms' (Apel, 1988, p. 273).

However this is not a dialogue of the negotiation of interests, but rather a rational dialogue aimed at consensus in which certain conditions are fulfilled (or the intention is to fulfil them):

a.   All those affected keep to the agreed norms. This should be the ideal of participation in dialogue. This is impossible in the real communicative community, but it is a parameter – a compass – that should guide the conditions of dialogue. In the application of this aspect to business dialogues, the dialogue should involve the participation of the largest number of stakeholders possible.

b.   Design the internal functioning processes of the dialogue. This dialogue, in which the different groups affected participate, should have a series of internal norms which guarantee rational dialogue. The fundamental norm of this dialogue should be the primacy of the best argument ahead of factual conditions of power or interests. Norms such as active listening, the possibility of free expression for all, and trust in the truth of affirmations are essential conditions which make the primacy of the best argument possible.

c. Symmetry of conditions should be achieved in order to give rise to an authentic rational dialogue. The need for all the participants to have the same access to information is not sufficient. This is a necessary formal condition but it requires effort if access to information is to be properly facilitated. Favouring the development of the autonomy and communicative competence of each actor in the dialogue is a first-order ethical requirement. The autonomy of each subject must be supported, as well as the development of the will and a post-conventional morality which will help to avoid the dangers of paternalism.

In the business environment this is fundamental, given that the asymmetry of information and communicative competence between the different groups affected is enormous, and can affect the result of the discourse, changing it from a search for consensus to a mere negotiation of interests.

*3. The requirement of universalizability as an unconditional moral parameter*

If the dialogue is not to become a mere negotiation of particular interests it is vital to defend universalizables interests. If this is done the resulting norms of the dialogue will be authentically moral and autonomous individuals who make full use of their reason will have little difficulty in following them.

If these three conditions are held to, ethical codes can be an effective mechanism for the institutionalization and integration of an enlightened ethics in business reality. In this way, codes will respond on the one hand to the moral requirements of respecting and supporting the dignity of the individual (unconditional) while on the other they will respond to the strategic requirement of responsibility for consequences.

## NOTES

1. One of the most interesting suggestions along these lines on the subject of business ethics is Peter Ulrich's in *Transformation der ökonomischen Vernunft* (1986/1993).
2. A more detailed exploration of this controversy with critical rationalism can be found in Cortina (1986) (especially chapter 2).
3. A more detailed presentation along the interpretative lines we are following can be found in Habermas J. (1983).

# REFERENCES

Albert, H. (1973), *Traktat über kritische Vernunft*, Tübingen; Mohr Siebeck.

Apel, K.O. (1988), *Diskurs und Verantwortung Das Problem des übergangs zur postkoventionellen Moral*, Frankfurt am Main, Suhrkamp.

Apel, K.O. (1973), *Transformation der Philosophie*, Frankfurt am Main, Suhrkamp.

Apel, K.O. (1991), *Teoría de la verdad y ética del discurso*, Barcelona, Paidós.

Conill, J. (1991), *El enigma del animal fantástico*, Madrid, Tecnos.

Cortina, A. (1993), *Ética aplicada y democracia radical*, Madrid, Tecnos

Cortina, A. (1986), *Ética mínima*, Madrid, Tecnos.

Cortina, A. (1995), 'The general public as the locus of ethics in modern society', in Ulrich, P. and Sarasin, Ch., *Facing Public Interest*, Dordrech, Kluwer. pp. 43-58

Habermas, J. (1981*), Theorie des kommunikatives Handelns*, Frankfurt am Main, Suhrkamp.

Habermas, J. (1983*), Moralbewusstsein und kommunikatives Handeln*, Frankfurt am Main, Suhrkamp.

Habermas, J. (1992), *Faktizität und Geltung. Beiträge zur Diskurstheorie des Rechts und des demokratischen Rechtstaats*, Suhrkamp, Frankfurt am Main.

Jamal, K. and Bowie, N.E. (1995), 'Theoretical considerations for a meaningful code of professional ethics', *Journal of Business Ethics*, **14**, pp. 703-74

Kant, I. (1781), *Kritik der reinen Vernunft.*

Kant, I. (1785), (1974), *Grundlegung zur Metaphysik der Sitten*, Frankfurt am Main, Suhrkamp.

Kant, I. (1788), *Kritik der praktische Vernunft.*

Kolhberg, L. (1984), *Zur kognitive Entwicklung des Kindes*, Frankfurt am Main, Suhrkamp.

L'Etang, J. (1992), 'A Kantian approach to codes of ethics', *Journal of Business Ethics*, **11**, pp. 737-744

Lozano, J.Mª. (1997), *Ètica i empresa*, Barcelona, Proa.

Steinmann, H. and Löhr, A. (1994), *Grundlegung des Unternehmensethik*, Stuttgart, Schaffer Poeschel, 2 Auflage.

Ulrich, P. (1993), *Transformation der ökonomischen Vernunft,* Bern/Stuttgart/Wien, Haupt Verlag.

Weaver, G.R. (1995), 'Does ethics code design matter?, Effects of ethics code rationales and sanctions on recipients justice perceptions and content recall', *Journal of Business Ethics*, **14**, pp. 367-385

# 9. Accessing, managing and sustaining moral values in organizations: a case study

## Heidi von Weltzien Hoivik

The very first challenge any leader of an organization is facing is to acknowledge the fact that moral values are integral intangible assets that influence the organization's core activities. Moral values are present when setting goals, developing strategies and in everyday decision-making. (Enderle; 1987, Korten, 1999). According to Petrick and Quinn (2000) business leaders today often are held accountable for the costs incurred by multiple stakeholders because they neglect managing integrity capacity as an intangible, strategic key asset. The second challenge is to build consensus around the basic assumption that individuals in organizations are carriers of ethical values. Their values are implicitly and explicitly part of what constitutes an organization, namely people, processes, purposes and systems (Kohlberg, 1984; Moberg, 1997; Petrick and Quinn, 1997, 2000). Only after having fully accepted these basic assumptions is it possible for leaders of organizations to submit their organization to a process aiming at greater clarification and articulation of its existing ethical core values. The focus of such a process is to access, develop and sustain moral competence or capacity. While competence refers to levels of cognitive skills, capacity in this context denotes the collective sum of knowledge and character development (Petrick and Quinn, 2000).

This line of reasoning in our research approach is based on the understanding that business ethics is not another branch of moral theory, an abstract theory, but a theory of practice (Solomon, 1993, p. 99). For that reason any further development of business ethics as theory of practice is dependent on a matter-of-fact account of the values that actually govern business enterprises and organizations and how these are to be managed and sustained. Whether such moral values can then or ought to be understood normatively is a different question. Our main research argument rests on the fundamental understanding that business as a human endeavour is in the service of humans (Solomon, 1993). This is essentially an understanding that is in line with both

Aristotle's and Adam Smith's notion that a person's self-interest is not to be confused with 'selfishness' because as 'enlightened self-interest' it is tied to that system which we call society. Human beings when acting are always seeking approval and respect from others and thus want to be seen as contributing to the general good of society. There is, as Paul Ricouer (1991) has pointed out, after all a continuum from ethics to politics.

Having adopted this fundamental view about organizations and its people, this then leads us to review the present conception of work and the role of the employee. If we perceive the individual as a carrier of moral values and as moral agent, we must seek to solve an existing paradox in organizations. On the one hand, present-day management literature promotes giving individuals full autonomy. Yet, on the other hand, existing practices still reject giving them some sharing of power, involving them in decision-making or providing them with their share of the profits (Aktouf, 1992). The instrumental view of workers as 'human resources', as carriers of skills or lately of 'competencies' which organizations must utilize or even exploit is still prevalent. And there is a danger that viewing employees as carriers of moral competencies can not only perpetuate this instrumental view but even lead to an instrumentalization of ethics in business unless we can link these competencies to a more human-istic understanding of the *'raison d'être'* of human actions in organizations.

According to Aktouf (1992) it will be a vain endeavour to permit develop-ment of an employee's desire to belong and to use his or her intelligence to serve the firm as long as management has this one major mental model of employees. This mental model is a stumbling block because it not only views but treats the worker or employee as an instrument of production, as part of a 'needs-driven mechanism', for the rational purpose of maximizing profits. In a world where this attitude is the representative framework for thinking about employees and ethics in organizations, two different approaches to building and sustaining ethical capacity in organizations can be distinguished. Nielsen (1996, p. 160) has characterized the first as the legalistic, adversarial, labour-relations-based grievance arbitration framework and the other as the behavioural science- and philosophy-based developmental action-learning framework. The former, according to Nielsen, emphasizes guilt–innocence judgement, punishment and control. In such an environment, ethical codes of practice communicated top down are standard. The other framework stresses individual and organizational learning and development and we find an approach focusing on integrity rather than compliancy (Paine, 1997).

## THE SCANDINAVIAN ENVIRONMENT

Since our research focuses solely on a Norwegian organization, a brief survey of changes of perceptions about organizations and its employees may be called for. Worth mentioning here is Einar Thorsrud's influence and research in Norway which at its core strongly promoted the idea of democracy in the workplace. Whether this was also the result of the strong influence of political ideologies formed by a Nordic version of socialism together with the impact of its politicized labour unions can only be inferred but will not be answered within the scope of this study.

This focus nevertheless has led to major changes in some Norwegian companies and also public sector organizations (Rudeng, 1987). Norwegian research into the efficiency and productivity of organizations that were willing to adopt Thorsrud's model showed a positive development (Thorsrud and Emery, 1969). Their proposed organizational models had the following three characteristics (Nilssen, 1989):

- Cooperation and dialogue between union representatives and management about the development of organizations and problem solving.
- Participation of employees at different levels: organized work groups, project teams, representation on decision-making boards and so on.
- Cooperation with research institutions to investigate further models of participative management.

It has been pointed out (Reve, 1994 as quoted in Nilssen) that this early form of a 'stakeholder model' which allows for cooperation between owners, management, employees, unions, customers, suppliers and government authorities was particularly in line with characteristic traits of Norwegian culture that emphasizes 'working together for the common good (society)'. It allowed organizations to develop competitiveness as long as cooperation and co-decision-making remained focused on business objectives and the overall societal benefits were not neglected. In spite of some apparent weaknesses these early efforts to rethink organizations, the role of employees and the role of leadership have eased the way for experimenting with innovative organizational structures, integrated project teams and other forms of cooperation and participation in the workplace (Hoivik, 1997). Quite often a particular form of Norwegian team spirit, called *'dugnad'*, promotes flexibility and willingness to 'stick-it-out together in tough times'. The catch phrase in management literature for businesses became *empowerment*. However, we found evidence through our case study that the original roots of thinking of empowerment based on humanistic, social and democratic arguments are very much alive also in a public sector organization, such as a municipality. This heritage seemed to be very useful when greater clarity about vision and values was required.

## Why this Case?

The following case study was selected as an example of how managers can develop the organizational framework necessary for an organizational learning process by focusing on vision and ethical values. Interestingly enough, this was taking place at a time when a structural change process was to be launched that should lead to a less hierarchical structure of the entire organizations. The goal was to remove one layer of management by placing more responsibility and accountability on a larger number of subdivisions. As it turned out, even though it is difficult to know whether this was intentional or not, the initial phases of the restructuring process benefited from a prior process articulating vision and values.

## The Research Method

The fieldwork conducted spans over a period of 18 months. Thanks to the fact that the 'case' organization was close by, it was possible to observe not only snapshots of the processes in action, but to be personally present at all major group and management sessions. The mode of research was primarily observations. It included some interviews and an in-depth study of minutes, documents and surveys carried out by professional firms such as Gallup. The many dialogue and feedback sessions with different groups of employees provided the most valuable insight. As a researcher I was in contact with more than 20 per cent of all employees. My 'partners' in this observation process were the human resource manager, the training manager and at times, the facilitator of the group sessions. They provided me with the information necessary to understand the setting. The drawback when using such 'action-research-in-action' is the danger that the researcher is being influenced or biased, thus losing some objectivity. Unfortunately this cannot be avoided entirely. There is no doubt that looking for the negative as well as positive sides of such a process will colour the perception and thus the narrative aspects of the case study.

The municipality studied is of medium size. It is located on the outskirts of Oslo, the capital of Norway, and had as of 1 January 1999, 48 404 inhabitants. The local administration consists of 2874 employees who serve a total of five sectors: central administration, public schools, health and social affairs, culture, church and recreation, and technical support. As a typical public sector organization its culture was still dominated by a traditional bureaucratic management style. There is no profit motive, rather the dominating motive is to serve and satisfy the community in line with the public requirement to use financial resources effectively and prudently. The total budget in 1998 showed an encouraging surplus of 21 million NOK in extra income while cost of administration since 1995 had been reduced by 7.7 per cent. In other words, the entire administration could be proud of its budgetary discipline and financial health. However, there were signs that the future would bring challenges that could not be met without threatening the financial situation.

**The Situation in 1998/99: New Trends and Pressures on Public Sector Administration and Local Government**

Since 1990 public sector organizations, such as city and county municipalities or local governments, saw a need to undergo major administrative change processes. Viewed from an external perspective, public scrutiny of the performance of public administration and government had increased in recent times.

The news media were quick to report on matters of public interest, particularly those involving poor management and misuse of resources that have been appropriated or entrusted to local administration. A demand for more 'transparency' had definitely reached every corner of public administration. Internally the 'import' of new management approaches, the introduction of many private sector 'business approaches' such as devolution of decision-making, greater emphasis on results than processes, less control from the centre, and more engagement and personal identification with the development of departmental 'cultures' had affected municipal management's thinking. This in turn led to a renewed interest into how to redefine the role of leadership. The demands on being more budget-minded, more cost efficient and effective, were the most quoted ones. In a cultural sense, public government organizations were rapidly shedding the characteristics of a relatively 'closed firm' to being more like an 'open firm'. This was confusing to many. Most often the mental models of what once was understood as administrating a public sector organization had not necessarily internalized the new perspectives with respect to how to 'lead' such changing organizations in the future.

In this regard it was not surprising that an initiative coming from the Central Association of Local Governments (Kommunenes Sentralforbund, KS) singled out as primary focus the implementation of a 'a new employer policy'. The initiative was given a rather leading and illustrative title 'Offensive employer policy with the purpose of liberating human energy' (my translation). This signalled a clear statement of goal and means. KS launched this initiative by first developing a model for a 'top leadership programme' and offered it to management in all local governments. As stated, their intent was 'not to suggest a general model for leadership training but to focus on the new role as employer'. According to KS documents the ultimate purpose of this initiative was to support and 'inspire top management teams – and therewith the entire administration – jointly to develop an offensive policy for

all employees which recognizes their inherent human resource potential'
(freely translated from KS documents). It is interesting to observe that the
entire focus of this KS initiative had several dimensions. It was to be
comprehensive (including all managers at all levels), action-oriented
(delegation of responsibility, personal development and development of
assessment tools) and result-oriented including cost efficiency. At the same
time there was strong emphasis that KS would not want this initiative to be
seen as another 'training programme' or an 'order from the top'. Neither
should it become only a 'forum for debating abstract theories of leadership'.
The 'programme' contained first and foremost a set of suggestions that each
municipality was free to follow or modify according to own needs. One of the
suggestions was to focus on ethical values in order to develop a 'values
foundation or ethical platform'. No advice as to how to do this was given. Yet,
when analysing the rationale underlying the KS document one cannot help but
notice a set of implicit assumptions as expressed in the following statements:

- human beings understand better political and administrative decisions
  when they see which values underpin them;
- human beings no longer want to be guided ('like a donkey') in their
  work but be given responsibilities and opportunities for development;
- human beings who are given trust, challenges and responsibilities will
  make it possible to achieve results in organizations ('a spiral of
  results').

According to the KS document 'results are being driven by inert energy
which: liberates human energy and creates joy and pride at work, which again
is leading to higher service quality, more efficient use of resources, a better
work climate and less sick-leave' (my translation).

From an ethical point of view we easily recognize the utilitarian logic in
these arguments. Some might even view this as a rather instrumental approach
and thus may even conclude that the focus on ethics is used primarily as a
means to an end. What seemed to be lacking is a rights- and justice-
perspective; and there is little understanding of a virtues perspective apparent.
One may suspect that the traditional bureaucratic mental model with its tacit
understanding of managers as authorities still 'coloured' the thrust and the
language of the initiative and its texts. However, each local government was
encouraged to develop its own formulation process for its employment
policies.

**The Beginning of the Process**

In our case top management had realized that employees were constantly facing ethical issues, whatever the size and setup of their sector organizations. Top managers raised the question of whether it was now the right time to address the basic questions 'who are we' and 'who do we seek to be'; in other words 'what is our vision' and 'what do we stand for', which 'values' are important to us?

This is essentially a moral perspective. It inevitably had to lead to a process in which the 'moral basis' of the organization had to be clarified and articulated. When raising the question in the above manner, top management signalled from the start a long-term perspective for the organizations. They basically questioned the duty-based issues of responsibility, loyalty, and accountability together with their relationship with stakeholders. Similar to a financial investment organization this organization has to manage large financial resources invested and entrusted to them. Therefore the interest-based questions, well known from utilitarianism as to how this is done, must be answered as well. This then implied that the 'moral common sense of the employees of the entire organization needed to be tested against a dominant objective: maximizing a community's interests by satisfying and promoting the welfare of the prime stakeholders, the tax-paying citizens. Deserving special attention is the fact that every employee in the present organization is both an internal and, as tax payer, an external stakeholder. In other words, this may mean that the stewardship role as administrator and the role of recipient of a community's goods and services have to be distinguished carefully. Therefore, when setting a process in motion that is looking at each individual's ethical instincts it will, in this particular case, also occur through the lens of social cost and benefits' (Goodpaster, 1990).

The most common or traditional approach when developing vision and values begins with top management. At specially arranged seminars, at times facilitated by consultants, management usually starts by discussing in depth what their organization stands for and what its perceived values are. The second step is to decide how to proceed with the results. Should one communicate the values by way of statements of beliefs, called 'credos', corporate value statements, or even develop codes of ethics for the entire organization? Or should one initiate and manage a process of articulation and dialogue throughout the subsequent layers of the entire organization?

It is our hypothesis that what management decides at this juncture will have a significant impact on how an organization is able to live and act in accordance with stated values. We propose reviewing the following model. Figure 9.1 illustrates what actually occurs, if management allows an organizational process to take place.

Given that time is a constraint in more than one way, and processes do require both time and money, this decision in itself should already be viewed

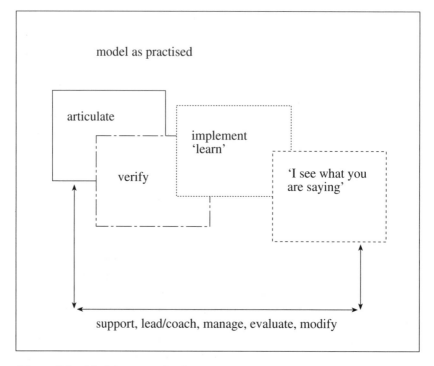

*Figure 9.1   Model as practised*

and discussed from an ethical point of view. Can one really believe that by issuing an 'order' to behave and act ethically correct by stipulating important values, one is obtaining adherence? We view this decision essentially to be a moral one as it questions and then manifests managers' basic understanding of employees as human beings. It signals whether managers take respect for persons seriously, their rights to be asked and to be heard. Ethical values can mean different things to different people. How is one to view and deal with cultural and religious differences? Should these not be part of a process? Or should one refrain from articulating ethical values because ethics is a matter of one's private conscience, and therefore is beyond the realm of management and manipulation? In the process we were allowed to observe and monitor, these issues were seriously debated at the initial meetings of top managers. Several differing opinions were voiced and were given proper consideration. We witnessed a high level of reflection with which such matters were discussed.

One important claim was that employees' ethical values could not be changed because they are formed at an earlier age than that at which people enter into employment. As it turned out, this claim correctly understood lends support to the idea of developing an organizational process that is both top-down and bottom-up before settling on a value statement. Precisely, it was argued, because people when entering employment already have acquired a personal set of values, it is of the utmost importance not to violate or even overrule these with company-defined value statements. Experience shows that competing claims will and must surface when a dialogical process about values is allowed to occur in the organization. Even conflicts between personal values and an organization's aspired values may and will surface. There might also be conflicts between basic principles and an organization's need to achieve its desired outcomes (a means/ends conflict). Quite often this is wrongly perceived and interpreted as a conflict between ethical values and the financial motives. The latter aspect, however, was never mentioned as such in the meetings, even though everyone tacitly agreed that 'meeting the budget' was the goal. In addition there was concern that there may be conflicts between values held by individuals and by those of groups of professionals in organizations, due to perceived different forms of professional obligations and demands. It was anticipated that professional differences were frequently heard of those who had 'care of people' or 'education' as a primary goal compared to other less people-oriented municipal 'service' functions.

After several meetings the management of this municipality decided to use for the most part a bottom-up approach. The conviction was that it would make little sense for a manager to talk about his trust in the abilities of employees and not give them a chance to get involved in the formulation process dealing with the vision and values for the municipality. A value-driven philosophy of leadership respecting the autonomy of followers was perceived as the basis on which to *initiate* motivation, creativity and purpose among employees. The original focus on 'employment policy' yielded in this particular case a realization that in order to develop and sustain a sense of serving a worth while purpose the employees had to become actively involved in defining both the vision and the values for their work and their environment. The meetings with top management concluded with the following statement: 'For employees to be able to effectively coordinate their goals and interests in line with an organization's aspired values and ambitions these values have to be both articulated and internalized. They have to become part of every day life and decision-making'. The instrument was to be a specially designed learning process, which allows for active involvement throughout the entire organization.

Since management was convinced that a bottom-up approach was appropriate, it was natural to initiate a 'dialogue and dissent' process. By dialogue one meant employing the capacity of members of a team to suspend assumptions and enter into a genuine 'thinking together' (Senge, 1990). In more than one way the dialogue sessions became a way of acting together in which the method was as important as the outcome. According to Gadamer, dialogue is

> the art of questioning and seeking truth ... To conduct a dialog means to allow oneself to be conducted by the subject matter to which the partners in the dialog are oriented. It requires that one does not try to argue the other person down but that one really considers the weight of the other's opinion. Hence it is an art of testing. But the art of testing is the art of questioning (Gadamer, 1989, pp. 366–367).

## Initial Reservations

The employees' reactions to the proposed processes were characterized by an initial reluctance. Most of the people interviewed admitted privately that to deal with ethical values did not require more than application of 'pure common-sense moral judgement'. Only when asked to describe concrete moral dilemmas as a basis for a more in-depth dialogue conducted in group sessions, people realized that they could not agree on issues as easily. What seemed to be simple and straightforward at first sight turned out to be much more complex. However, they found that such dialogue in fact 'brings to the surface the full depth of people's experience and thought, and yet can move beyond their individual views' (Senge, 1990, p. 41). Often the ultimate goal is not to reach agreement and consensus but an awareness of the complexity. Furthermore, participants realized that ethical considerations are constantly evolving in new settings, and can never be fully determined in advance. This became apparent when attempting, for example, to clearly define what being open and honest means? What is openness and honesty with regard to servicing clients and customers? Does this apply in all cases? What does one do when others do not act in the same way? Also, is there an obligation to report lack of openness and honesty exercised by others? What is a conflict of interest? What is meant by favoritism? What is good judgement versus abiding by rules and instructions given by the political system? In various group sessions it became evident that this style of questioning in dialogue sessions forced the participants into a different mode of thinking. It yielded a reflection about the meaning and relevance of ethical values. Concrete examples from everyday life were used to illustrate that answers to the above questions required more than gut feeling. Critical and reflective thinking was practiced.

We also observed a growing sense of realization that surrounding factors – work environment, organizational barriers, personal belief systems, other colleagues – not only influence people's personal perception of values in conflict but in some cases clearly can steer decision-making in unwanted directions. Such discussions in small groups generated a deeper understanding of the ethical values at stake in all organizations. Furthermore, these discussions strengthened the conviction that continuous evaluation and re-evaluation is necessary and that speaking out among colleagues can further this. The latter requires from management a clear commitment to continuously providing opportunities for dialogue to occur and not only when there is a need. Once an organization has started to support 'dialogue and dissent' processes as part of its culture it will find ways of integrating ethics as inseparable elements into everyday work and decision-making.

## Designing the Process

The first phase of the process consisted of developing a joint project between the five sector managers under the leadership of the administrative director of the municipality, aided by a reference group with representatives of employees of all sectors. The first kick-off meeting took place on 15 April, 1998. The reference group's mandate was to serve as a sounding board for management, to provide suggestions and function as devil's advocate if need be. The reference group's members were furthermore encouraged to discuss the issues with as many as possible in their own organizations.

The following three suggestions, developed and formulated by the above-mentioned leadership group were presented to this reference group for comments at a second meeting 27 May, 1999:

1.  Long-term vision for the municipality:
    This municipality is serious about its inhabitants and regards them and businesses as partners for cooperation that will contribute in making the municipality:
    - a good place to grow up;
    - a pleasant place to live and work;
    - a safe place to become old;
    - an attractive place to establish and run a business.
2.  Vision for our organization's culture:
    We who are working in this municipality:
    - experience pleasure about being of use;
    - accept responsibility, are effective and show care for each other and for those who live and work in this municipality;
    - are proud of our place of work.
3.  Values for our own work culture are:
    - loyalty;
    - honesty;
    - effectiveness;
    - openness;
    - care;
    - equality;

- safety;
- respect;
- creativity;
- trustworthiness.

The plan was to proceed with further bottom-up processes with the help from the reference group after the summer. The entire process was structured as shown in Figure 9.2:

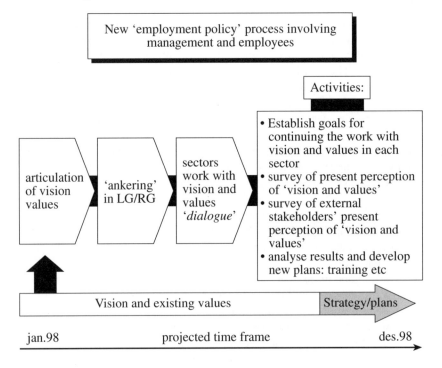

*Figure 9.2 New 'employment policy': process involving management and employees*

Thanks to a very constructive dialogue process with both the reference group (RG) together with the leadership group (LG), phase 2 clearly resulted, in a simpler and more articulate version of the initial suggestions by LG: 'Vision: A municipality of opportunities. Values: We stand for: trustworthiness, openness and mutual respect'. Phase 3 brought the entire process in form of dialogue sessions into each sector of the organization under the leadership of each sector manager. The purpose was to discuss the content and the relevance of both vision and values in the respective units and suggest necessary changes. The particular local consequences of such a commitment with respect to the daily challenges should be discussed in depth and internalized through these dialogue-driven processes among all employees. It was up to sector managers to decide which approach suited their form of management style best. While some adopted a consensus-oriented approach in small groups, others felt it more appropriate to discuss the issues in a 'questioning and learning mode'. Some group manager meetings focused on their roles as leaders and questioned both style and content.

At the same time a rather large survey was initiated among all employees. The survey was designed to resemble a 'work-climate study' with the proposed 'vision and values' integrated.[1] Top management wanted this first survey of the organization to take place before formulating a new 'employment policy' and new organizational plans for 2000. The results from this first survey lead to the conclusion: We are in good health but still have a long way to go before we are 'the municipality of opportunities' (Til Tjeneste 4, 99). The survey focused on the following areas in their questions:

- your own work environment;
- your immediate colleagues;
- your boss;
- administrative top management;
- collegiality and cooperation (your work environment);
- you yourself;
- relationship to users of services (stakeholders).

The results showed that 65 per cent agreed when asked whether they 'normally enjoyed going to work', while 14 per cent did not. 'Good humour is typical for our work atmosphere' was positively agreed to by 70 per cent. Evaluation of one's own place of work received a total of 83 per cent positive response, security of employment scored 77 per cent and influence at work 72 per cent satisfaction. A much lower score was obtained in areas such as on-the-job training and advancement, 60 per cent. Lowest score of 10 per cent satisfaction was obtained for salary levels. Only 21 per cent agreed totally that their municipality can be called 'municipality of opportunities', while another 30 per cent agreed moderately.

A much more differentiated set of scores can be found with regard to each individual's evaluation of his or her superiors. Seventy-seven per cent agree to the claim that their superiors 'live' the chosen values with 86 per cent positively stating 'credibility' and 'keeping promises' as the most prominent values. Seventy-seven per cent and 76 per cent consent positively to the claims of 'mutual respect' and 'openness', respectively. Superiors received lowest scores for giving 'feedback' and 'flow of information'. Surprisingly low scores, 40 per cent, were given when judging the administrating director's ability to be 'visible' in the organization. Noticeable, however, is that of the over 2000 employees asked only about 1100 responded to this question at all. No explanation for this was given. When ranking themselves in comparison to colleagues' ability to work together 89 per cent were satisfied with others while believing in their own efforts scored 95 per cent (!) The service they provide for the users of municipal services scored a self-satisfaction rate of 86 per cent.

After the survey, the executive director of administration and his management team concluded that the survey proved the municipality to be a good place to work. However, a closer look at the results revealed plenty of room for improvement. It became obvious that management in total and in particular the director of administration were not visible enough. This feedback can be interpreted in at least two ways: as relevant criticism or as an expression of 'an invisible style of leadership' which certainly did not affect job satisfaction. It does not come as a surprise that the managers of sectors were more visible than their own top manager. In many ways this can be seen as a positive form of leadership which 'leads by leading others', particularly in a public sector institution which prefers to use a rather democratic form of leadership style. However, in this particular case the administrative manager promised to improve his 'visibility' and presence throughout the entire organization. The fact that the survey included an evaluation of top management in itself should be seen as a positive signal towards working for a more transparent organizational culture. The results were made available to all, including the media. The decision to go public with the results was discussed at length in meetings but the fact that the municipality had stated the value 'openness' meant that withholding results of such a survey would be wrong.

The second survey was directed towards external stakeholders, such as business partners, clients and customers. It was important that the internal survey was matched by what the external stakeholders think of the organization, its values and the quality of the services rendered in order to be given full validity. Once again Norsk Gallup was engaged to handle the practical aspect of this survey. The survey was carried out by phone in early 1999. The total number of interviews was 350. Each sector was asked to select a number of external stakeholders, users and partners to be interviewed by telephone. The sole criteria were that each unit should decide which group of users/partners it would like to have a feedback from. The choice of this method does not allow comparing the results from the different units. Any generalization of the results thus must acknowledge this. Central administration, for example, chose to interview persons who had had contact with the units as part of their jobs. Most of these are members of businesses. The unit responsible for primary and secondary education only selected private individuals with whom they had had contact with recently, such as students, parents, educational authorities, medical professionals and so on. Technical support and the sector dealing with 'church, culture and sport' decided on a mixture of professional and private users of their services.

It was nevertheless possible to compare the results with those of the previous survey, which focused on the units' evaluation of themselves. As it turned out there was not much discrepancy if we disregard dealing with complaints, where the external evaluation was clearly more critical. Only in some cases the users of services gave a more positive evaluation than the employees themselves.

A further follow-up included organizing two meetings with all managers of various sub-groups to discuss how the results could be integrated into their proposals for an action programme as part of the annual budgeting process.

## DISCUSSION AND CONCLUSION

The growing public awareness that there is a need to make the fundamental meaning and relevance of moral values in organizations and society explicit has not only brought about a heightened awareness in the business sector, but has also reached the public sector. In our case it was indicative that the pressure came from three strategic foci: (1) focus on employees (motivation, retention); (2) focus on more efficient management of financial resources (tighter budgets but greater needs in the community); and (3) a focus on creating and structuring a change process leading to more delegated responsibility and accountability. The second was originally conceived, as a mode of working with employees which was 'foreign' in the public sector as it was introduced with the means and the language of 'private sector management'. It was seen as too 'money'- (profit-) oriented. This was perceived as a threat in a sector that prided itself for rendering services to the public at large. They had never been questioned or 'managed' like this before, and they had never had to question seriously how to 'save' costly resources by establishing cost-reducing measures, including outsourcing of manpower. Their politico-economic co-responsibility (Ulrich and Maak, 1997) as an organization was being targeted. Because of the particular tradition of public sector organizations, which has as its primary goal to optimize public goals (rather than economic growth and profit), the process adopted for 'creating' a new vision based on articulated moral values' was unexpected and unusual for such an organization.

Being a bureaucratic organization one would have expected a top-down approach, similar to what the organization itself experiences as a mode of working when decisions are coming from their own political decision-making body.

Yet, this did not happen. Why? We have in our introduction referred to a particular Norwegian tradition of democracy and decision-making in the workplace. However, that cannot be the only answer. Our study of how the process was structured and carried out revealed another underlying assumption. The core of services rendered by the public sector administration is essentially one that cannot be sustained unless there is a continuous dialogue process with both internal and external stakeholders. After all, citizen sovereignty both can give and can withdraw the administration its power base through the electoral system, which after all determines the use of the financial resources. That is not the case in private corporations, which must respect the divisible rights of private ownership. Applying an organizational dialogue and dissent process among employees and external users was a natural choice. This choice was strengthened by the conviction that retention of trustworthiness and credibility is one of the main pillars of public sector administration. And finally, because the third focus was on how to turn more people into 'leaders' with more delegated responsibility and authority, the process in fact turned the hierarchical pyramid upside down to discuss vision and values. People understood that they had become more autonomous, more capable of acting effectively and efficiently at all levels once the first part of the learning process was over. The glue that is holding them together consisted of the moral values they had accessed jointly and turned into 'their values' through a dialogue process. They had become more self-conscious about the meaning of their workplace, their own roles and purposes.

The process as observed reflects on a series of theories about ethics and leadership in action. One particular ethics approach comes to mind, the discourse ethics approach as proposed by Steinmann and Löhr (1991) which can foster the emergence of true dialogic process outcomes. Steinman and Löhr based their thinking on the constructive philosophy of the Erlangen School and systematically developed a conception of corporate ethics based on two sophisticated theoretical foundations. One is Jürgen Habermas' (1983) model for discourse ethics. The other refers to Georg Apel's theory of a communicative community (1988). Discourse ethics conceives of moral theory as a theory of moral argumentation. The best way of coordinating actions is based on mutual understanding or agreement reached by autonomous citizens in a process of unconstrained exchange of opinion that is free from domination (Grabner-Kräuter, 1999). According to Grabner-Kräuter the discourse ethical approach stresses the right of self-determination and takes the view that management has the obligation to recognize and acknowledge the legitimate interests of the corporation's stakeholders or those affected by its decisions. The discourse method provides procedural rules for testing the validity of norms and for reaching rational, consensual decisions. It requires that controversies over the validity of norms be settled through a dialogic process in which the consensus of all stakeholders calls into question and then decides the legitimacy of the controversial norm. In everyday business decision-making discourses with all concerned individuals can only rarely be realized. However, the principle of discourse ethics demands considering the interests of those affected by the results of the discourse who do not or cannot participate in the discourse for any reason. It is the *procedure of discoursive argumentation,* not the consensus, which serves to orient and regulate the decision-making process. Managers should always try to behave in ways that do not conflict with the principles of fair and open dialogue (Grabner-Kräuter, 1999).

To realize practical discourses in business firms Steinmann and Löhr propose to institutionalize 'discourse arenas' or ethics committees, where all those affected by business decisions can actively participate in the decision-making process, either themselves or via advocates (Steinmann and Löhr, 1991). We believe our case study shows how such an arena was staged. However, the goal of the process we observed was not to create a compromise or a consensus, but rather a congruence (Esteban and Collier, 2000) based on mutual understanding and agreement about differences as well as common values. I noticed that at the end of the process, all employees who had been involved seemed to share not only a particular plan of action in order to realize the vision, but also a framework for justifying or legitimizing both values and goals. As said before, designing such a dialogue process became part of management's present strategy. It also became the foundation for implementing a major administrative change process during the next eight months. It was important to use the moral capacity developed through the dialogue process in order to restructure the organization in a manner that would sustain motivation and joy.

The process yielded a plurality of insights. One was a renewed understanding that both harmony and conflict can exist between aspired values and managerial goals. Secondly, self-critical reflection carried out in a dialogue-driven process, strengthened self-awareness, personal professionalism and team spirit. It helped to restore a somewhat fuzzy self-image as a public sector administration and revitalized personal and organizational pride. Thirdly, the experiences dealing with issues like openness – 'we are ready to talk about tacit issues' – readdressed the fundamental question of purpose in a public sector organization. How much transparency is both necessary and wise? No precise answers were given; yet the need to keep this and other values-related questions on the agenda, to be open for dialogue, was agreed upon. This is not a small achievement by itself. Fourthly, there was some agreement achieved about further developing and sustaining a balance between financial, social and moral obligations. Finally, the process stimulated the creation of a climate in which opinions can be expressed freely. This means also that the new administrative layers of the municipality and their respective leaders can demand and expect critical moral loyalty from employees. Because the municipality early on had agreed to make public both phases of the learning process and the results of surveys, they also can expect more critical users of their services. This will add to the moral pressure to live up to the vision and values expressed. At the same time, there was renewed understanding that a continuous dialogue process with external stakeholders, especially the users of services, will be expected and required.

The same will be true internally in the organization. The initiative originally launched as *arbeidsgiverpolitikk* (employer policy) now had to include showing respect to the expectations which employees had voiced. To name a few: employees want and expect to be heard and listened to with regard to their professional and personal needs, they want to be part of setting internal criteria for personal evaluation processes and hiring policies. All new policies must reflect clearly the vision and values agreed upon. Employees expect to be involved in decision-making processes where their professional opinions matter. Lastly, this form of participation should not be seen as abandoning the need for leadership as such. Leadership in such an environment is the most demanding form of enabling others to become leaders in their own right (Bowie, 2000) This form of 'empowerment' not only honours and respects the dignity of human beings, it also secures the sustainability of the organizations. Vision and values, dialogue processes and structures are merely the means necessary to access, develop and sustain the moral capacity of people in organizations.

## NOTES

1.  Norsk Gallup Institutt, A.S. was hired to carry out the survey. The content of the survey was jointly developed by the human resource manager and myself.

## REFERENCES

Apel, K-O. (1988), *Diskurs und Verantwortung: Das Problem des Übergangs zur post-konventionellen Moral*, Frankfurt a.M.: Diesterweg.

Aktouf, Omar (1992), 'Management and Theories of Organizations in the 1990s: Towards a Critical Radical Humanism?' *Academy of Management Review*, **17**(3), 407–25.

Bowie, N. (2000), 'A Kantian theory of leadership', *The Leadership and Organization Development Journal*, **21**(4), 185–194.

Brytting, Thomas (1999), 'Moral Competence – A Non-Relativistic Definition', (unpublished paper presented at EBEN Research Conference 1999, also see Chapter 18, this volume).

Enderle, Georges (1987), 'Some Perspectives of Managerial Ethical Leadership', *Journal of Business Ethics*, **6**(8), 667–663.

Esteban, Rafael and Collier, Jane (2000), 'Building moral competence in organizations: the difficult transition from hierarchical control to participative leadership' (see Chapter 12, this volume).

Gadamer, Hans-Georg (1989), *Truth and Method*, New York: Crossroad.

Goodpaster, K.G. 'Ethical Imperatives and Corporate Leadership', in Freeman, R. (1990) (ed.), *Business Ethics. The State of the Art*. Oxford University Press, 89-110.

Grabner-Kräuter, Sonja (1999), '"*Unternehmensethik*" in German-speaking Countries' (unpublished paper presented at EBEN Research Conference 1999, also see Chapter 3, this volume).

Habermas, J. (1993), *Moralbewusstsein und kommunikatives Handeln*. Frankfurt: Suhrkamp.

Kohlberg, Lawrence (1984), *The Psychology of Moral Development: The Nature and Validity of Moral Stages*, New York: Harper & Row.

Korten, David (1999), *The Post Corporate World: Life after Capitalization*, San Francisco: Berrett-Koehler.

Moberg, D. (1997), 'Virtuous Peers in Work Organizations', *Business Ethics Quarterly*, **7**(1), 67–85.

Morgan, Garret (1986), *Images of Organizations*, Beverly Hills: Sage.

Nielsen, Richard P. (1996), *The Politics of Ethics*, New York: Oxford University Press.

Nilssen, Tore (ed.) (1989), *Mot et bedre Arbeidsliv*, IFIM antologi Oslo: Fagbokforlag.

Paine, L. (1997), *Leadership, Ethics and Organizational Integrity*, Chicago: Irwin.

Payne, S.L. (1991), 'A Proposal for Corporate Ethical Reform: The Ethical Dialogue Group', *Business and Professional Ethics Journal*, **10**(1), 67–88.

Petrick, J.A. and Quinn, J. (1997*), Management Ethics, Integrity at Work*, New Dehli: Sage Series of Business Ethics Response Books.

Petrick, J.A. and Quinn, J. (2000), 'The Integrity Capacity Construct and Moral Progress in Business', *Journal of Business Ethics*, **23**, 3–18.

Rawls, John (1971), *A Theory of Justice*, Cambridge, MA: Harvard University Press.

Rawls, John (1996), *Political Liberalism*, New York: Columbia University Press.

Ricouer, P. (1990), Soi-même, come un autre: Paris, Seuil.

Rudeng, Erik (1987), *Skjokoladekongen*, Oslo: Universitetsforlag.

Senge, P.M. (1990), *The Fifth Discipline: The Art and Practice of the Learning Organization*, New York, NY: Doubleday Currency.

Sievers, B. (1986), 'Beyond the Surrogate of Motivation', *Organizations Studies*, **7**, 335–51.

Solomon, Robert C. (1993), *Ethics and Excellence: Cooperation and Integrity in Business,* New York: Oxford University Press.

Steinmann, H. and A. Löhr (1991), 'Einleitung: Grundfragen und Problembestände einer Unternehmensethik', in Steinmann, H. and A. Löhr (eds), *Unternehmensethik*, 2nd edn, Stuttgart: C.E. Poeschel, pp. 3–34.

Thompson, D.F. (1987), *Political Ethics and Public Office*, Cambridge, MA: Harvard University Press.

Thorsrud, E. and Emery, F.E. (1969), *Mot en ny bedriftsorganisasjon*, Johan Grundt Tanun Gorlag, Oslo.

Ulrich, P. and T. Maak (1997), 'Integrative Business Ethics - A Critical Approach', *CEMS Business Review* **2**, 27–36.

von Weltzien Hoivik, Heidi   (1997), 'A Joint Stakeholder Learning Process in Participatory Environmental Ethics: A Case Study', *International Journal of Value-based Management* **10**, 147–172.

Walzer, Michael (1987), *Interpretation and Social Criticism*, Cambridge, MA: Harvard University Press.

Warnke, Georgia (1993), *Justice and Interpretation*, Cambridge, MA: The MIT Press.

Wicks, Andrew (1996), 'Overcoming the Separation Thesis: The Need for a Reconsideration of Business and Society Research', *Business and Society*, **35**(1), 89–119.

# 10. How to implement business ethics in a French multinational: a case study

## Fred Seidel and Henry-Benoît Loosdregt

Among the literature devoted to business ethics, very little has been written about such 'contextual' factors as the nature of the business activity, the goals and the history of the firm, the specific features of the home country and so on and yet they can have a strong impact on the elaboration, implementation and 'monitoring ' of a code of ethical conduct.

Other contributions concentrate on a discussion on the intrinsic value and validity of theoretical perspectives drawn from the field of philosophy. Their aim is to find norms that are universal or that can lay claim to a fairly high level of general acceptance. As for the various 'guides' designed to facilitate the drawing-up of a company code of ethical conduct, they have a strong propensity, at least in the Anglo-Saxon world, to provide rules that are supposedly universal. It goes without saying that such guides nevertheless remain coloured by the specific features of the home country.[1]

Our hypothesis is the following: over and above the debate about the possibility, or, indeed, the interest of defining 'hyper-norms' which can claim to be more or less universally acknowledged, experience shows that the extent to which a code of ethical conduct can be taken on board by the members of a company, that is to say, its degree of effectiveness, largely depends on the contextual factors which regulate the functioning of the firm being taken into account. The various 'cultural differences'[2] between the countries in which the firm conducts its business are only one of these factors.

The legal framework of a country will also determine the room for manoeuvre that firms enjoy, just as the particular orientation of public opinion will influence their decisions and corporate communication in ethical matters. Apart from the regulatory or ideological framework, the nature of a firm's business and its markets will also determine what kind of ethical problems it will be confronted with.

A firm that sells a wide range of convenience goods through a number of different brands and whose real identity is often unfamiliar for most consumers, who, moreover, can easily switch to other brands, will not face the same problems as a company that provides what amounts to a public service.

In the case of the latter, the decision to purchase is in the hands of political institutions rather than in those of the individual. The final consumer, who always has a role to play as a voter, has little influence over the choice of a service provider.

The organizational structures and the management principles which are implemented within the firm also play an important part. For an ethical approach to be widely accepted, the kind of leverage required in a highly centralized and hierarchical structure may be quite different from that required in a highly decentralized structure containing a large number of different professions and trades.

It is from this point of view that we should like to present and discuss the case of a rapidly expanding European firm[3] which shows a number of specific features linked to its activities and its home country and which has invested a considerable amount of time and effort in the formalization and shaping of an ethical approach to its business.


## THE CONTEXT

### The Situation in France

In the field of business ethics, in particular, as far as the efforts by firms to establish their business on a clearly formalized ethical footing are concerned, France distinguishes itself from most Anglo-Saxon countries on a number of points. Two aspects in particular, in our opinion, merit attention:

1.  a clear inability to establish norms which are acceptable both to firms and to society;
2.  the highly political dimension of the 'origins and causes' of ethical problems.

Contrary to what can be observed in Anglo-Saxon countries, France does not possess any common point of reference that could help define behavioural norms for the business environment.

In the United States, several factors go into creating this central point of reference. The legal framework is a major factor here. Furthermore, firms can easily obtain any one of a number of widely distributed specialized guides providing various acknowledged and well-tried approaches and solutions. Lastly, the teaching of business ethics has been a staple in business-school curricula for some time now.

In Great Britain, it is the 'business community' which has taken upon itself to define standards and control structures within firms. The Cadbury

Committee and its successors have published reports on 'best practice' in the field of corporate governance, while another organization closely linked to employers' associations, 'The Institute of Business Ethics', has been working on the drafting, introduction and adaptation of ethics codes.[4]

There is nothing resembling this in France. Here, it is common practice not to communicate on corporate actions in the field of business ethics. Thus, while the large majority of firms in the CAC 40 (an index of France's top 40 listed firms) run a web site in which they present their activities and some basic financial information, there is, on the other hand, only one which provides an explicit description of its outlook on business ethics and which makes its internal conventions available for consultation. Another alludes to the ethical dimension within a presentation of the firm's values but without giving access to the founding texts on which this approach is based. This blackout is all the more curious as many of the firms which do not communicate on this issue do indeed possess a code of ethics or guidelines on business conduct.

This confirms Georges Enderle's analysis[5] when he writes that one of the main differences between the North-American and European approaches to business ethics lies in the fact that Americans talk easily about these issues while Europeans are rather reticent. It is quite clear that the lack of public debate on business ethics and on the means needed to make business life more 'ethical' is creating a number of problems for firms (and certainly for the whole of French society, as well). A public debate would indeed allow different positions to be expressed and probably lead to some form of minimal consensus on the aims to be pursued and the means to which priority is to be given, thus contributing to the creation of a common point of reference as to the values and principles of actions that need to be supported. Since this common point of reference is still lacking, those companies that wish to establish a charter or ethics codes, which would clarify and guide their approach, are confronted with a number of problems.[6]

Any official stance on an ethical issue would be viewed with suspicion. This would be considered either as a smokescreen designed to dissimulate various shameful practices or as an attempt to indoctrinate the staff. The lack of an explicit national reference leads to a painful paradox: the lack of a reference in itself bars the route to any system of reference being introduced. The firm which, for lack of anything better, would have to look for its references, its modes of operation and its organizational structures abroad could easily be accused of betraying national values or, at least, of being opportunist and submitting to the 'moral imperialism' of another culture.

In such a climate, it, of course, becomes extremely difficult to encourage the internal dialogue which is necessary in order to get managers and employees to adhere in any real sense to the values and norms that go to make up the firm's ethics. There is a risk of a conflict emerging between formalized rules and other behaviours which correspond to an implicit 'internal culture'.

Yvon Pesqueux[7] cites two traditional attitudes that are specifically French in order to explain this reticence regarding business and company ethics. In addition to a Catholic tradition 'which rejects the idea that company rules may deal with problems of one's conscience', he mentions the technocratic and Jacobinic tradition 'which refuses the firm any active role as far as values are concerned'.

Such a tradition points in the direction of the State and the field of politics in general. It is not surprising that public opinion should predominantly stigmatize the morally questionable actions and behaviour of politicians. The political class has come in for a great deal of scrutiny from magistrates firmly supported by a public opinion that is sensitive to issues of 'abuse of power and position'. These *affaires* have caused a profound malaise in French society, and yet, they have not led the French public to overhaul their representation of capitalism, firmly rooted in an ideological model which rather schematically opposes the individual desire for profit and the disinterested stance of the State in ensuring social progress. Thus, French society does not seem inclined to call for a public debate or any legal initiatives that would provide a framework for the business environment and trace a route towards greater ethical awareness.[8]

In the present 'moral crisis' of political life, the preservation of this Jacobinic tradition results in the situation being blocked: those whose traditional role it is to provide and construct social values have lost much of their legitimacy after so many corruption scandals, while those who could possibly take their place, in particular, firms and managers, are still not accepted as valid participants in the debate.

## The Characteristics of the Firm and its Business

Nevertheless, it is not enough simply to proclaim principles for them to govern the actions and behaviour of a firm and its employers. In concrete terms, organizational structures and cultural norms have to be aligned with ethical principles for the latter to have any effect on an operational level.[9] Consequently, if the drawing-up of a code of conduct is to be effective and its existence to be felt in the firm, the specific characteristics of its business have to be taken into account. We shall limit ourselves to three essential factors within the firm: the nature of its business, which will enable us to consider the specific features of its market(s), its mode of operations, which derives from the structures and norms of the organization, and, lastly, its pattern of growth.

**The Nature of its Business**

Our initial hypothesis is that the 'ethical risk' that any firm runs by virtue of the nature of its business depends essentially on:

- the extent to which it controls the operations that put it in contact with its customers;
- the extent to which it sells its products or services to individual consumers or organizations.

By 'ethical risk', we mean that a firm risks being destabilized by public outrage at the legitimacy of its actions, on the basis of a moral judgement. We are only referring to the type of risk related to the everyday operation of the firm. It is obvious that, above and beyond the legal aspects of any situation, a firm's licence to operate also depends on the legitimacy which is accorded to its particular field of business in a given context, and that this legitimacy can be called into question.[10] As in the case of legal risk and economic risk, ethical risk can jeopardize the very existence of a firm. And yet it is very different from legal risk in as much as the latter can be defined more clearly. In principle, its only tangible basis is the diverging interpretations of familiar legal texts. Breaking the law poses the problems of the legality of a firm's actions, whereas running counter to moral conventions poses the problem of the legitimacy of its actions and behaviour. As a result, ethical risk cannot be reduced to its purely legal aspects.

The extent to which firms control operations will lead us to distinguish between services companies and firms which produced manufactured goods. The latter only rarely enjoy direct contact with their customers, who are often totally unfamiliar with the organization behind the products they buy. The completion of a service, on the contrary, supposes direct contact between the staff of the service company and the clients. As a service is generally 'intangible',[11] its real value and its material essence are sometimes difficult to control.

For the firm, the risk here is twofold: there is the possibility that one of the (often numerous) members of staff might behave 'improperly'; the actual completion of the service or its price could be contested.

The dimension concerning the type of purchaser will allow us to distinguish between those firms which operate on mass consumer markets and those which sell their goods or services to private or public organizations.

In the former case, the purchasing act is motivated by individual desire, while in the latter case, it is motivated by organizational and strategic considerations. The individual consumer generally represents a fairly small volume of sales, relatively speaking, and has few means at his or her disposal in order to bring pressure to bear on the firm if some form of ethical conflict emerges. Indeed, such pressure only becomes perceptible and effective if amplified on the social level by a consumers' association or any other form of organized pressure group.

The professional buyer, on the other hand, can often bring a certain amount of weight to bear, either because he or she represents a relatively substantial volume of sales, or because his or her firm is the ultimate reference (in terms of quality or innovation) on the market concerned. Here we can single out the case of the buyer from the political realm who, because he or she represents a public body and often buys on behalf of the citizens on whom his or her political career depends, is able to whip up a great deal of potential support in the eventuality of an ethical conflict.

Contrary to the individual consumer, the professional buyer enjoys a good deal of direct power over a supplier. He or she can often impose the 'rules of the game' and thus a more or less demanding level of ethical standards.

According to the position of the firm *vis-à-vis* the dimensions which we have just exposed, the ethical risk will be variable in different sectors of activity. If it may appear relatively weak in the case of consumer goods manufacturers, it is likely to be considerably higher in the case of services directed at public bodies and organizations. The latter case accumulates the risk which is specific to the services sector with that which comes from selling to 'political' buyers. A study of the *affaires* which have hit the headlines over the last ten years or so in France, at least, will confirm this observation.

## The Mode of Operations

The specific features of a firm's mode of operations can also increase or reduce the ethical risk it runs. Among the many dimensions we could use to define a firm's mode of operations we shall select two which seem particularly appropriate in this context: first of all, the internal organization of the firm and, secondly, its specific mode of market access.

In simple terms, first of all, we can distinguish between structures according to their degree of centralization/decentralization. A firm that is highly decentralized can be characterized by the extent to which the different units can autonomously decide on strategies and organizational forms. Such autonomy, even if it brings clear advantages on the managerial level, can increase the ethical risk.

A centralized structure will be able to maintain some form of ethical control through the lines of command and will thus rely less on members of the firm adhering consciously and voluntarily to common rules and norms. On the other hand, a decentralized structure will often experience a certain amount of difficulty in defining such common values and norms and, above all, in having rules coming from possibly distant headquarters actually respected.

The difficulty here is proportional to the number of units which enjoy a high level of autonomy and the number of core businesses within the firm. The attempt to establish core values and common principles of action faces some resistance from a desire to favour the specific features of each core business or the characteristics of each unit.

As far as a firm's mode of access to a market is concerned, we can distinguish two approaches which variously affect the ethical risk. The case of the individual firm facing the market all alone and fighting it out with all its rival firms only really prevails in micro-economic theory. More often than not, a number of competing firms have to co-operate in providing the products or the services required by the customer.[12]

This co-operation can also be required by the public authorities who wish to give a boost to a particular sector; the need to increase efficiency also makes such co-operation advisable, such as in the case where an international company which does not possess the relevant experience wants or needs to adapt its offering to local conditions with the help of a local partner. The notion of 'single source supply', which is becoming more and more common in firms' purchasing policies, is based on the main supplier co-operating with other suppliers who provide the competencies and know-how that are lacking.

The need to co-operate increases ethical risk for the simple reason that the various firms do not automatically possess the same values and norms. A tendency to relativize, and thus weaken, the behavioural norms governing each firm can thus be observed. Experience shows that this relativization as a rule favours the lowest common level of norms.

**The Pattern of Growth**

The pattern of growth has no little impact on ethical risk. Without going very far in our analysis, we can identify two essential aspects linked to the growth of a firm, which, beside profitability, is without doubt the main strategic goal of a firm. First of all, we must consider the form of growth selected. Unlike internal growth, external growth through the buying-up of other firms or by merger often increases the risk of ethical standards in each firm being weakened. Coming from different cultural backgrounds, the power stakes can once again strive to bring about a relativization of the original norms and values, at least during an initial period in which acceptable procedures and norms for all have not yet emerged.

If the firm's growth strategy includes international expansion, a lack of understanding of the norms and values of 'foreign' cultures will certainly create a major ethical risk.

# THE APPROACH ADOPTED BY SUEZ-LYONNAISE DES EAUX

Lyonnaise des Eaux merged with Compagnie de Suez in 1997. From 1994 onwards Lyonnaise des Eaux[13] had set up a formal ethics programme; this, however, was not the case at Compagnie de Suez. Suez-Lyonnaise des Eaux is a 'two-tier' company, in as much as, unlike the majority of French firms which are governed by a single board of directors, it has a separate management board and supervisory board. The chairman of the supervisory board is the former chief executive officer (CEO) of Lyonnaise des Eaux, while the management board is presided by the former CEO of Compagnie de Suez.

It is worthy of note that in the first letter that he addressed to the management of the new firm the CEO of the management board emphasized the fact that ethical values would be a reference for the future actions of the firm. At the same time, the Charter of Ethics of Lyonnaise des Eaux became the Charter of Ethics of Suez-Lyonnaise des Eaux, while work began on its reformulation and a round of consultation was initiated with the staff in order to identify what the 'values' of the new structure were to be.

Those in charge of these two projects were to bear in mind the cultures of the two initial firms and their structures. It soon became evident that the cultures were close and the structures complex.

## The Aims Pursued

It is significant to notice that the Charter of Ethics of Lyonnaise des Eaux was adopted by the new structure without any major textual modification, the only major changes being the new corporate name and logo. This easy assimilation process, together with the work on reformulating the charter, was to reveal that a common culture existed before the merger. This phenomenon was particularly noticeable at the level of the parent company, but it was less evident once one started to observe what was going on in the subsidiaries and in the smaller subsidiaries further down the line. This was not particularly surprising since the autonomy of the different firms within the group was promoted and seen as ensuring efficiency.

At its foundation, the new firm was practically a conglomerate of firms spread out across some 120 countries and active in very different areas: public services (electricity, water, waste disposal, telecommunications), infrastructure and building industries, and financial services; certain firms engaged in the same activities belong to different holding companies. Even if the new group has clearly stated its policy to refocus its activities around the public services sector in the near future, the complexity of its structure is an essential element in the elaboration of an ethical approach at Suez Lyonnaise des Eaux.

## The Values Espoused

Determining the 'values' of the group implied a methodology which solicited the efforts of the whole staff. In the autumn of 1997, the board launched the reflection process by announcing consultations with members of staff from the different activities of the group and in different parts of the world.

Unlike certain firms where the values are defined by top managers, if not by the chairperson, Suez-Lyonnaise des Eaux preferred to adopt a participative approach. This approach not only allowed management of the firm to demonstrate its commitment to the process, it also had the advantage of sounding out the perceptions and the expectations of the staff. Top management was perfectly aware of the pitfalls and was prepared to carry out a synthesis of all the information gathered at the end of the consultation process.

The staff was asked to indicate what values they perceived and hoped for within the firm, and this made it possible to give the reflection a more dynamic dimension and by the same token clarify the significance and the interest of the approach. Of the 80 000 people to whom questionnaires were sent, a little over 2000 of them gave their view; about ten discussion groups were then set up across Europe, Asia and the Americas, and interviews were held with a team of sociologists.

On the whole, there were a great deal of points which were common to all the countries and all the activities, with, however, a clear division between the Latin and the Anglo-Saxon countries on the subject of profit, which was mentioned as a value by the latter only. In the end, this notion of profit was retained by top management, the term 'value creation' being preferred, however.

Finally, on 5 January 1999, the chairman of the management board presented and commented on the values of the group: professionalism, partnership, team spirit, concern for the environment, value creation and ethical behaviour. The presentation was reproduced in a brochure which was published in four languages and widely diffused throughout the group. A certain number of people considered that too many values had been selected and that three would have sufficed. A shorter text would have given the message more impact and made it easier to retain.

The approach adopted produced a large number of values and the selection process was a difficult exercise. The values chosen have, it seems, been widely accepted by the staff. In fact, even if only a minority of members within the group are able to cite its values, they all know that they exist and that the chairman often refers to them. And this is the most important thing, finally, for the values of Suez-Lyonnaise des Eaux are not just a slogan; they are the foundation of a whole programme which concerns all the firms and all the members of the group, whatever their country or the business concerned.

## Reference Texts[14]

With the merger an entity emerged whose size and complexity posed many a problem for the implementation of an ethics code: how could one make each employee in each subsidiary feel concerned by the principles expressed in the code? The group's response was to make it possible for each person to perceive his or her own culture in the document. As it was clearly not possible to adopt the same approach as for the definition of the values, it was decided to have the codes of conduct drafted in each firm, and then to 'federate' the codes of all the firms in the same business while completing this with an 'ethics charter' which would convey a number of universal principles regulating behaviour *vis-à-vis* various stakeholders as well as a few guidelines concerning the implementation of a policy on the conformity of the arrangements.

This specific articulation of the reference texts made it possible to respect the organizational chart of the group and to display the adhesion of the various units to the general principles of conduct. The appropriation of the message was directly linked to the involvement of management at each level of the firm. The whole system may seem complex, but its advantage is that it corresponds to the functioning of a large decentralized group.

In point of fact, the group's ethics charter was drafted in the course of 1998 and presented at the same time as the group's values at the beginning of 1999. The chairman of the management board then asked the top managers of the main firms to write a *professional statement of ethics* with a view to bringing out the ethical stakes and constraints of their business. In turn, top management asked the subsidiary managers to continue in this way by drawing up codes of conduct which were concrete and pragmatic and which spoke directly to the staff of their firms.

As well as this three-tier structure, a number of complementary documents exist which clarify the behaviour of the companies and their members. At the level of the group, for example, there is an *international social charter* which presents the major principles of staffing policy as applied by the firms within the group; there are also a number of guides devoted to certain precise aspects of the ethics policy to be implemented.

## Control and Adjustment Structures

The reference texts were closely examined by management at each level and were then revised by lawyers and heads of the staff and communications departments.

Although the texts had been completely overhauled, it was generally felt that the texts of the group and the main business activities had merely been updated, probably in as much as they harked back to structures that had already been set up previous to the merger within the former Lyonnaise des Eaux.

There is an *Ethics Committee* which assists the supervisory board and a *Conference of ethical advisors* which gathers the different ethical advisors from the main firms. The ethical advisor from Suez Lyonnaise des Eaux was the main person in charge of producing the various documents, but he also involved the heads of other departments in the task to a large extent, so as to end up with texts that were easily comprehensible by a wide range of readers. The *Conference of ethical advisors* finalized the text which was then submitted to the management board, the latter made a few modifications and the *Ethics Committee* gave its approval. The same process was adopted within each firm.

A noteworthy aspect of this case is the concern for pragmatism: the documents were not written as an end in themselves, but with a view to being credible and comprehensible for those for whom they were drawn up. They appeared to be an essential precondition to the group's ethical programme, the only justification for the reference texts being their application. Ethical reflection is not an aim in its own right but a means in order to ensure the long-term success of the firm.

## Implementation

What was valid for the drafting of the documents was all the more so for their implementation. It soon became clear that the involvement of the ethical advisors and the chairmen alone was not sufficient and it became necessary to bring other structures within the firm into play, notably the corporate communications departments and the human resources departments.

It was decided to give responsibility for distributing the main documents within the firm to the department which customarily carried out this task, making it the ethical advisors' task to assist those departments for which distribution represented a new additional responsibility.

The whole was presented as *the Group's Values and Ethics Programme* the co-ordination of which was carried out by the *Conference of ethical advisors* while implementation was the responsibility of all the departments within the firms of the group. An identical organization and co-ordination structure was adopted on the level of the parent firm, the leading subsidiaries and the smaller subsidiaries further down the line.

## DISCUSSION

There is no doubt that Suez-Lyonnaise des Eaux has to cope with a high level of ethical risk. One of the constraints of its sector of business, public services, is the need to co-operate regularly with other firms as well as the buyer or the contracting principal. The business is highly visible and de facto in the public domain. The final consumer of the services provided is affected both as a consumer and as a citizen. The firm's organizational structure is complex and highly decentralized, a number of mergers have marked its recent history and it is engaged in a rapid process of internationalization.

Since it is inconceivable that a firm abandon a sector in which it has a proven track record and on which it relies for its future growth, it must, in order to pre-empt ethical risk, establish a clear strategy aimed at integrating ethical principles into its structures and operations. If the national environment is not particularly conducive to such an initiative, then this requires a high degree of involvement on the part of top management. Nevertheless, such determination is unlikely to be sufficient to anchor the principles selected and espoused in the everyday practices and behaviour of a firm which is highly decentralized, comprises a number of core businesses, and conducts its business in a wide range of cultural and political environments.

The first tangible problem to be solved consists in reconciling the autonomy of the operating units and the internal coherence of the values and principles espoused at each level of the organization with orientations that are deemed to be globally valid. Another dimension of the same problem lies in the difficulty of accepting and integrating cultural differences without giving way to more relativism.

In the present case, a 'sequential' method of elaboration, starting at the holding level before passing through the major firms and reaching the operating units, was adopted in order to create the ethical reference texts. However, this should not be confused with the traditional 'top-down' method. Instead of simply implementing decisions taken by headquarters within the subsidiaries and the operating units, the process implied 'co-drafting' of the reference texts. The reflection and the drafting of the documents was the work and responsibility of those who would have to live and work according to the rules agreed upon. They nevertheless had to abide totally by the norms established at the higher level and designed to federate rather than centralize.

The organization and the operating methods of the network of ethical advisors at Suez-Lyonnaise des Eaux reveals the same concern to reconcile local responsibility and overall coherence. It is not so much the existence of an ethics committee or ethical advisors that is interesting here but rather the organization of their actions within a network. They will perhaps manage more easily to avoid the isolation that often hangs over such an 'exotic' position, the actual usefulness of which is not obvious for all members of the firm.

Finally, if we consider the nature of the norms stated by the parent firm, we can see that they virtually limit themselves to general principles. They are not a list of recommended or forbidden behaviours. They function rather as 'procedural' norms which indicate how and in what spirit a set of rules prescribing or banning specific types of tangible behaviour should be elaborated on the operational level.

Let us, at the end of this discussion, mention two other problems which still remain to be solved if the firm wishes to develop a long-lasting response to the ethical risk which it is exposed to. The first problem concerns the continuing respect of the ethical rules within the group and in a context of expansion and internationalization, which can only be achieved if the firm's competitiveness can be maintained and even increased on its markets. The second is linked to the second fact that, in the public services market, it is the customer – the state and local government – which predominantly call the shots.

In a service firm, the real involvement of staff that is in contact with the customer is crucial for the success of an ethics policy. This involvement cannot simply be called into existence by decree. This explains why it is essential to ensure exemplary behaviour on the part of top managers and management staff in this area. Employee suspicion regarding the sincerity of the declared intentions, which is perhaps stronger in France than elsewhere, can only be combated by the observable application of the rules in everyday operations and in all critical situations.

The state, including local government, is very different from other customers. Being invested with its supreme powers, it largely determines the economic rules of the game and, what is perhaps even more important, its role is to ensure that these rules are complied with. The recent Brittany water affair shows how a firm can be damaged by incoherent aspects of state policy. The Lyonnaise des Eaux, which distributes water throughout a large part of the region, was publicly criticized for the poor quality of its water, which was shown to contain an excessively high level of nitrates. The problem is that the presence of nitrates is essentially due to extensive large-scale pig breeding in the region. It is true that regulations designed to reduce nitrate pollution exist, but they are not complied with. The firm that distributes the water is caught in a dilemma: should it assume responsibility for a dangerous level of water pollution or denounce the public authorities, which are also its customers?

Reducing the ethical risk, in the public services sector at least, depends on the concerted action of firms and public authorities. The firms within this sector should support any initiative which seeks to have this market governed by codes of conduct that are clear and abided by. The concerted action of the Organization for Economic Co-operation and Development (OECD) countries to stamp out the corruption of civil servants and public figures is one such initiative, which should contribute to facilitating the task of firms that are anxious to run their activities within a framework, which respects clear ethical rules.

## NOTES

1. The following guide provides one good example: Ethics Resource Center (1990), 'Creating a Workable Company Code of Ethics', Washington, DC.
2. If the earliest ethics codes coming from American firms generally contain few references to non-American cultures, the intercultural dimension and its implications for an ethics policy are increasingly being integrated. Motorola, for example, clearly poses the question of the compatibility of Motorola's core values born in the American Midwest with the values coming from various cultures that the firm employs today. Cf. R.S. Moorthy et al. (1998), Uncompromising Integrity: Motorola's Global Challenge, Motorola University Press, Schaumburg, Il.
3. Although officially presented as 'Franco-Belgian', the firm studied here is still dominated by its French cultural origins. If the supervisory board is made up of different nationals, the members of the management board, on the other hand, are entirely French.
4. The institute has just published a report on the use of codes of business conduct of by British firms. Cf. Martin Le Jeune and Simon Webley (1999), Company Use of Codes of Business Conduct, London, Institute of Business Ethics.
5. Georges Enderle (1996), 'A comparison of business ethics in North America and Continental Europe', *Business Ethics*, Vol. 5, pp. 33–46.
6. The description of these problems is based on our own experience of French firms. The fact that a public stance is practically impossible means that those concerned will generally only express their thoughts in private or in very restricted circumstances.
   Nevertheless, one can also consult the doctoral thesis of Samuel Mercier which is based on an analysis of a sample of France's top 50 firms. Cf. Samuel Mercier (1997), Une contribution à la pratique de formalisation de l'éthique dans les grandes entreprises, Thèse de doctorat en sciences de gestion, Université Paris IX Dauphine.
7. During a workshop organized by ANVIE, 17 March 1999 in Paris, and devoted to an evaluation of company charters in France.
8. Michael Walzer (1996), *Spheres of Justice*, Blackwell Publishers, Oxford.
9. Organizational and cultural blocking factors were first analysed along time ago by J.A. Waters. Cf. J.A. Waters (1978), 'Catch 20.5': Corporate morality as an organizational phenomenon', in *Organizational Dynamics*, Vol. 6, Spring, pp. 3–19.
10. In certain countries, the very existence of the tobacco and alcohol industry is today threatened, while other countries allow this sector to flourish without restrictions.
11. This technical term refers to one of the main characteristics of a service: unlike a (manufactured) product, it can neither be stocked nor 'tried out' before being purchased. A product can be controlled in the factory and its quality can be guaranteed before the sale, while the quality of a service can only be observed at the very moment it is 'consumed'. For a precise analysis and description of the specific features of services, cf. Ch. Lovelock (1988), *Managing Services: Marketing, Operations and Human Resources*, London, Prentice Hall.

12. It goes without saying that we only consider legal forms of co-operation here, thus ignoring cartels and other illegal forms of agreement.
13. For an evaluation of the activities of Lyonnaise des Eaux, cf Fred Seidel (1997), 'Integration der ethischen Dimension in Unternehmenspolitik und -praxis. Lyonnaise des Eaux', *Forum Wirtschaftsethik*, Vol. 5, No. 3, pp. 14–16.
14. All the documents we refer to here can be consulted on the following internet site: http://www.suez-lyonnaise-eaux.fr

# 11. Codes of ethics, their design, introduction and implementation: a Polish case

## Wojciech W. Gasparski

Many papers have been written about codes of ethics, much space has been devoted to them in books and many lectures given, but codes of ethics as the subject of conference proceedings still arouse the interest of conference organizers and, hopefully, participants. This is not surprising given that only a few companies or professional organizations in Poland have their own code of ethics.

It was estimated in the early 1990s that 22 per cent of the largest Dutch companies had a code of ethics, while the figure for France, Germany and the United Kingdom was 30–35 per cent, and as high as 85 per cent in the United States. The number has grown over this decade and continues to increase. In 1995, 45 per cent of large British companies had a code of ethics. In Hong Kong in 1997, with a population of 6.5 million, the number of organizations, companies and businesses with their own codes stood at 1000, according to the local Ethics Development Centre.[1] This means that 40-million Poland should have over 6000 units with codes of ethics. And the reality? Very poor, as very few companies and organizations have such codes, which are often introduced with difficulty, sometimes meeting resistance from the higher rungs of corporate governance, and most often without due care for their everyday enforcement. Transformations of the economic system provide an excuse for this. This is probably the case because a still small though admittedly slowly growing number of people in managerial positions realize how important ethics is for a company's reputation.

An exception in the overall bleak situation is the Association of Volkswagen and Audi Dealers in Poland (AVADP). At its very first congress, held in March 1997, this association decided to develop its own code of ethics. The code was prepared by the Association's Council and introduced for a trial period at the next congress, in December 1998. The experience gained at the code's design stage will help other organizations and companies intending to introduce codes of ethics, and may encourage further institutions and corporations to develop their own codes as well.

## THE BEGINNINGS

As in every organization, also in the association – a network of car dealers – the basic considerations include members' loyalty as well as complying with the statutes and resolutions of bodies authorized to make decisions. In other words, responsible conduct, or conduct that increases the capacity of the association as a whole, limiting any conduct on the part of some members that could be detrimental to others and thus to the association. Documents defining the organization's internal rules are insufficient for this aim, and there is a need for separate codification of what is considered the norm of conduct. 'Professional ethics, namely such codes or their elements', writes Ija Lazari-Pawlowska[3], 'are usually designed with the aim of adjusting the existing status, of bringing it on a par with a chosen model. The desired effect is for the target group to internalize the defined norms and for this to be reflected in their actions'.[2]

The decision to draw up a code is preceded by numerous talks held in larger and smaller groups of the organization's members, at statutory-body meetings and, when necessary, with an outside consultant participating. This was also the case here. The consultant's role has three aspects. First of all, they act as an adviser offering knowledge and skills. Secondly, the consultant plays the role of a facilitator, or a person who does not intervene in the direction of the dialogue between organization members, but is a supporter assisting in the discussions by encouraging members to undertake topics on which they themselves are the experts. Thirdly, the consultant helps find the proper form for the norms defined in the code. The role of a consultant is closely related to members' confidence in that person, which is a condition for the existence of an open communication process. This confidence also conditions the successful completion of the long process of designing the code of ethics – the basic element of the organization's ethics programme.

Having been invited to act as a consultant, I deemed it important to emphasize the role of the organization's members and the association's unique role in setting a precedent – the development of the AVADP code of ethics. In this way the association has become a promoter in Poland of standards characteristic of developed European business (Box 11.1).

### Stages of Work on the Code

The source of the organizational norms defined by a code of ethics lies in the

## BOX 11.1 FROM A LETTER TO ASSOCIATION MEMBERS

[. . .] A lot is being said in Poland at present about "entering Europe," we read about this in the papers, hear it on the radio and see it on television. Some support the idea, others are afraid. Meanwhile, our presence in Europe and Europe's presence here is achieved not through words but through the kind of activity that you and your colleagues are involved in, enabling Polish buyers to purchase a renowned European brand-name car. In this way, Polish residents get to know the values practiced in Europe and around the world. These are technical values, utility values and – equally important – aesthetic values. By encouraging customers to buy a car, advertising the cars on offer, selling them and ensuring service maintenance after purchase, you also promote other values. These are certainly the values that you would want to propagate in Polish commerce. They are the European values of merchant culture.

However, it is not only customers that you work with in your Volkswagen/Audi dealership. You also have employees in your showroom and service station. I have no doubt that it is your ambition for your employees to be proud to be working in your showroom and to treat the company not only as being yours but also in a sense – theirs. Then, meeting their friends over coffee, ice cream or beer, they will say about your company, 'you know, things are really great at <u>our showroom</u>'. Thus, without any great words, it becomes clear that the values of the European work culture are something natural at your company.

By complying with the norms characteristic of developed European business, you show your concern for the reputation of the dealer who is first and foremost a member of the Association of Volkswagen and Audi Dealers in Poland. You make sure to implement, I am certain, the values involved in honest competition also in relation to current and potential rivals, ensuring – to use soccer terminology – that there are no red cards, the fewest possible yellow cards, and the greatest possible number of fair play awards.

It is thanks to this kind of operation – actions, not words – that you and we, your customers, employees, rivals, inhabitants of the town where you have your showroom, and Poles in general can be perceived as competent and reliable partners of a uniting

> Europe and representatives of its standards embodied in European products and the culture in which they are offered on the Polish market [...]

values shared by the organization's members, especially those values that form the core; we can call them the *core values* of an institution, company or association. How does one find these values? In fact, we perceive an organization through the components (objects) that form it, namely the people, the tools they work with, the premises where they stay, the language they use, the methods they use to communicate with the outside world, the products they manufacture, and so on. These objects are what they are due to the specific values that the members of an organization or a company's employees share.

Someone who hates a mess will always have a tidy work station (this could be a technological neatness, not necessarily an aesthetic one, though the two can go hand in hand). Someone who does not worry about untidiness will always have a mess at their work station. 'Without [...] a group of values, a person's behavior is inexplicable', writes Boulding. 'Even if this is chaotic and irrational, it's probably because they [that person] assign great value to chaos and irrationality'.[3] Thus one has to find not only what the organization's members value highly, but what they value the most. This can be done in a variety of ways, and the choice of method depends on the type of organization, on whether it operates in a focused or scattered structure, on the members' readiness to answer questions, and so on.

In the case under consideration, a *Questions, Answers and Suggestions Form* was used. This form contained a (small) number of questions of key importance for identifying and understanding the situation (as perceived by the organization's members) in which the code was being designed. The questions touched on several issues:

- the company's mission;
- using the definition of the mission in advertising materials;
- the reasons why the association should have a code of ethics;
- membership in other organizations with their own code of ethics;
- suggestions related to the preparation of the code.

Of great interest were the responses pointing to: (a) the organization's size; (b) the aim of identifying the values shared by its members including values considered fundamental; (c) the necessity to prevent negative situations, including examples of such situations; and (d) the organization's prestige. These values were later included in the mission statement and operational goals of dealer companies.

The following reasons why members believed the association should have a code of ethics were given: (a) showing one's support for a high standard of commercial ethics; (b) gaining customers' trust; (c) ensuring that the brand name is perceived uniformly; (d) defining the values shared by the association's members; and (e) formalizing the ethical rules for members' conduct.

Not all the association's members answered the questions contained in the form. It became necessary to review the responses received, treat them as preliminary proposals and subject the resultant list to evaluation by the greatest possible number of members. An extensive questionnaire was drawn up as a result, covering the following issues:

1.  The goal (mission) of a dealer company (Box 11.2):
    - 'I', the respondent, a member of the organization;
    - 'my company' – the dealer company operated by the respondent;
    - brand name;
    - customers;
    - employees;
    - quality.

---

### BOX 11.2   DEALER COMPANY MISSION STATEMENT

a)  Enabling customers to purchase a renowned brand-name car and facilitating the purchase.
b)  Promoting high technical, utility, aesthetic and ethical values.
c)  Promoting the professional standards of developed European business.
d)  Practicing the standards of merchant culture and conscientiousness.
e)  Employing highly qualified employees with high moral standards.
f)  Complying with the rules of honest competition.
g)  Representing world standards of business ethics.

---

2.  Including elements defining the goal/mission in advertising materials.
3.  Justifying the need for the association to have its own code of ethics:
    - values shared by the organization's members (Box 11.3);
    - employees;

---

## BOX 11.3   SHARED VALUES

a) improving efficiency
b) professional honour
c) positive cooperation (fair play)
d) good manners
e) loyalty
f) responsibility
g) professionalism
h) merchant conscientiousness
i) reliability
j) natural environment
k) promptness
l) honesty
m) high quality of service
n) customer satisfaction

---

- the company's good name;
- customers;
- partnership between dealers;
- concern for the brand name;
- situations that should be prevented (for example in dealer–dealer, dealer–customer, dealer–employee relations);
- displaying the importance attached to ethical standards;
- the company image.
4. Membership in organizations with their own code of ethics.
5. The code's usefulness.
6. The code's content and form:
   - general standards;
   - conduct;
   - prohibitions;
   - the code's form.

The responses allowed to define the importance of the items contained in the questionnaire, which were written in the language of responses previously sent in to the *Questions Form*. The high importance given to codes of ethics is worth noting. Here are some examples of responses: a code of ethics 'dispels ethical vagueness in management and planning', 'unifies positive rules of conduct', 'has an impact on the conscience and honesty of the organization's members', 'eliminates bypassing of the law', 'creates a sense of satisfaction and being in the élite due to the fact of its implementation', 'is conducive to eliminating drastic violations that could harm the whole community'.

Critics of business activity as allegedly being egotistical in its very essence should be disappointed at the attitude displayed by the Association's members, who stated that creating a very good company and brand-name image is not the effect of embellishing measures, but 'requires strict compliance with very strictly defined rules that give a sense of security and comfort to the customer'. Note: the customer! Could this mean that the warning *caveat emptor* has become invalid, at least in this case?

As for the code's form (Box 11.4), respondents pointed out that it should be concise and realistic, be written in clear and comprehensible language, should provide a model of reference and be cause for pride for the Association's members.

---

### BOX 11.4   CONTENT AND FORM OF THE CODE

- Introduction
- General Principles
- Customer Service
- Cooperation of Dealers
- Relations with Employees
- Disciplinary Punishment and Resolving Disputes and Complaints
- Final Regulations

---

All this led to the development of the Association's *Code of Ethics* (Appendix 1), a document codifying the shared values of its members, defining the conduct that the Association considers proper, pointing out what is inappropriate and defining the sanctions that can be ruled when the Code is not complied with. The Code has been approved by the Association Congress for a trial period during which the consequences of its introduction into everyday practice will be observed. The necessary support measures have been set, such as consultations, meetings and discussions as well as monitoring. The Association has provided for the possibility of making changes and amendments to the Code, and for the development of a Dealer Standards Book. Such books, sometimes called guidelines, already exist in some dealerships of other car makers (for example Opel and Fiat).

## FINAL COMMENTS

Codes of ethics are the fundamental component of ethics programmes or form their beginning. It should be noted at this point that these codes go by different names. There are codes of values, codes of practice – some add 'good practice', codes of conduct, codes of compliance – meaning compliance with standards and rules of conduct, and so on. Some of these codes have names that are slogans defining their image. The best codes of ethics are thought to be those that combine a code of values, code of conduct and code of compliance with standards (for example with legal standards, for instance on honest competition).

In most cases codes of ethics are designed without the aim of developing the ethics programme further, which weakens their effectiveness. Organizations should be encouraged to create ethics programmes that also include: (a) developing a book of professional standards; (b) preparing a programme of ethics education; (c) creating a position (unit) for ethics (business ethics officer, business ethics office); (d) promoting ethical behaviour (awards, publications, seminars); (e) continuous monitoring of compliance with ethical and professional standards; (f) creating an ethics info-line (consulting, whistle-blowing); (g) systematic ethics audits; (h) adjusting the code of ethics and professional standards book as the need arises; and (i) regular updating of the ethics programme.

In Poland, organizations that have a code of ethics include ABB, Amway, Business Centre Club, small business guilds, Centre of Leaders Creation (Code of Ethics), journalists (International Rules of Ethics in Journalism, Journalists' Code of Conduct, Polish Press Agency Journalists' Code of Ethics, Ethical Principles for Television Journalists, Media Charter of Ethics), the National Chamber of Chartered Accountants (Code of Professional Ethics for Chartered Accountants), the Polish Chamber of Commerce, the International Advertising Association in Poland, PepsiCo, veterinary surgeons (Veterinary Code of Ethics and Deontology), the National Chamber of Physicians (Medical Code of Ethics), the Polish Federation of Real Estate Agents (Code of Ethics and Professional Standards), the Polish Federation of Property Valuation Associations (Code of Professional Ethics), the Polish Olympic Committee (Principles of Ethical Conduct in Sports), the Polish Association of Bank Dealers (Dealer's Code), Polish Association of Direct Sales, Prószyński and Co. (Our Rules), Association of Volkswagen and Audi Dealers in Poland (Code of Ethics), the Association of Polish Banks (Principles of Good Banking Practice), the Union of Stockbrokers and Advisors in Public Trading of Securities (Collected Principles of Professional Ethics for Stockbrokers), the Union of Legal Counsellors (Principles of Professional Ethics for Legal Counsellors).

Tobacco companies operating in Poland have agreed on a 'Voluntary Code of Conduct in Marketing'. Some hotels include elements of professional ethics in their employee handbooks (Marriott, Sheraton) or job regulations (Sobieski Hotel). The regulations of other organizations and companies operating in Poland also include elements of professional ethics (for example Medical Data Management). Some organizations or their federations make use of international codes of ethics (engineer organizations using the code of FEANI).[4]

There are most probably more organizations, associations, companies and institutions in Poland that have their codes of ethics and which are unknown to the author of this study. Unfortunately some of these organizations do not disseminate this information or treat their codes and other ethics regulations as documents not meant for a broader audience, or even for researchers and lecturers on business ethics. It seems that business ethics can also be an element of competition. Ethics is becoming increasingly important, as mentioned at the beginning of this chapter, ever since a company's reputation has begun to play a significant role. Codes of ethics are not only and not mainly part of a company's image, they are a first and foremost part of its assets.

# Appendix 1

Apply the Code!
Only a cohesive
and healthy network
can withstand threats
and be a match
for the competition.
*The Dealer's Council*

**Code of ethics of the Dealers Association of Volkswagen and Audi in Poland**[5]

## Introduction

The Dealers Association of Volkswagen and Audi in Poland promotes and disseminates the business standards characteristic of advanced European businesses. By working together, the dealer-members of the Association enable customers to buy cars of a renowned European trademark. In this way, residents of Poland learn about the values that are appreciated in Europe and world-wide. These are the technical values, utility values and aesthetic values of the offered product as well as the ethical values of honest service.

When encouraging people to buy a car, advertising the cars on offer, selling them and ensuring service maintenance after the customer purchases a car, the dealer-members of the Association also present European standards of merchant culture and conscientiousness. These are standards that they themselves comply with and which they want to promote in Polish trade.

The Association's dealer-members employ highly qualified personnel with strong moral standards in their showrooms and associated service stations. It is the ambition of the Association's dealer-members for employees to be proud to be working in a showroom or service station operated by a dealer-member of the Association and to identify themselves with their company.

The Association's dealer-members, individually and in association with all the other dealer-members of the Association, observe the standards characteristic of advanced European businesses, take care to preserve the dealer's good name, to act in accordance with the rules of honest competition, and show consideration for the region in which they operate as well as for the natural environment.

Thanks to these actions, the Association's dealer-members and the people employed in the companies they run are perceived as competent and reliable partners for all customers, and as representatives of world standards of business ethics as reflected in European products and the culture of offering them in the Polish market.

## General Principles

### §1

The present Code of Ethics, subsequently referred to as the Code, defines the ethical norms and business standards for dealer-members of the Dealers' Association of Volkswagen and Audi in Poland, subsequently referred to as the Association.

### §2

The ethical standards of the Association's members stem from universally accepted ethical principles and moral norms.

### §3

The professional standards of the Association's members stem from the rules and norms accepted in Volkswagen and Audi dealer networks world-wide and from the business ethics standards defined in the present Code.

### §4

The Association's members shall act for the good of the customer, in accordance with the rules of honest competition, the present Code, and the resolutions and rulings of the Association.

### §5

The Association's members shall act with the aim of promoting the Volkswagen and Audi trademarks in the Polish market.

§6

The Association's members are bound together by care for the values shared by all dealers, and in particular for:

- improving efficiency;
- professional honour;
- positive cooperation (fair play);
- personal culture;
- loyalty;
- responsibility;
- professionalism;
- merchant honesty;
- reliability;
- the natural environment;
- promptness;
- integrity;
- a high quality of service;
- customer satisfaction.

§7

In order to implement the principles outlined in §2-§6, Association's members are obliged to create and consolidate a positive image of the Volkswagen and Audi trademarks in the Polish auto market. This aim is served by providing a high standard of customer service, taking care to preserve the good name of the company and the whole dealer network in the market as well as developing a positive climate for interpersonal relations within the company.

§8

In their activity, the Association's members shall follow the principle of loyalty towards the manufacturer, the exclusive importer and in mutual relations.

§9

Expressing negative opinions about the products, manufacturers, importer or other dealerships in outside contacts is considered a violation of ethical standards.

## §10

The Association's members are obligated to:

- comply with the law;
- comply with the principles of honest competition and protection of the good name of all Volkswagen and Audi dealerships in relations between companies within the network and outside the company;
- introduce the proper standards of conduct and behaviour towards customers among employees.

### Customer Service

## §11

A quality of service that distinguishes Association's members is the best way of developing a positive ethos and trademark image.

## §12

Customer satisfaction achieved by providing top-quality service in terms of sales, service maintenance, insurance and financial servicing of sales transactions shall be a subject of constant concern for Association members.

## §13

The Association's members shall serve customers in a professional, honest and polite manner, offering their knowledge, advice and assistance during the whole period of operation of a purchased vehicle. This holds both for person-to-person service and for correspondence, telephone conversations and electronic communications.

## §14

The Association's members are not allowed to refuse a customer service for reasons of physical handicap, family situation, nationality, political views, religious beliefs, gender, race or skin colour.

## §15

1.  The Association's members are obliged to protect the interests of their customers and ensure confidentiality of data and information about customers.

2. Confidentiality of data and information does not apply in data transfer between dealers if this could have an impact on the safety of services provided by the Association's members or if such is the ruling of the law.

### §16

The Association's members should eliminate practices jeopardizing customers' trust in the dealer profession.

## Cooperation of Dealers

### §17

With the best interest of the Association and their own in mind, dealers should share their knowledge and experience with other members of the Association, remain loyal towards the Association and participate actively in its work.

### §18

The Association's members shall comply with the principles of partnership cooperation in the auto market, offering one another support and assistance as colleagues.

### §19

1. The Association's members shall not make sales proposals and shall not carry out marketing within the scope of activity of other Association members.

In the special case of strategic customers, such activities are permissible, but only in coordination with the Dealer's Council and/or the dealer (dealers) of the region in question.

2. The content and form of advertising and promotional materials (exhibitions) as well as the method and place of their presentation must not depreciate the services offered by other dealers in the eyes of the public or harm the dealers' interests.

### §20

The Association's members accept as permissible only such actions that do not harm the interests and good name of other dealer-members of the Association and those that do not contradict the interests of customers.

## §21

In case of direct contact with the customer of another member of the Association, a dealer's further contacts with that customer should always take place with the knowledge of that member and on the terms agreed upon by the Association's members.

## §22

In case of any conduct contrary to the principles of the present Code on the part of a dealer, every member of the Association should bring it to the attention of the dealer in question. If such a remark is ineffective, the Association member should inform the Council of Dealers or file a complaint with the Association's Arbitration Court through the Council.

## §23

1.  Practices consisting in one dealership offering jobs to the employees of other dealerships operated by the Association's members, with better wages for comparable positions and similar duties (luring employees away), are prohibited and impermissible.
2.  When employees change their place of employment, the period from the termination of the employment contract with one workplace from the Volkswagen and Audi network to the commencement of an employment contract with another workplace from the network (grace period) must be at least:

- three months for managers;
- two months for other employees.

### Relations with Employees

## §24

The Association's members shall organize their employees' work in a way ensuring the employees satisfaction stemming from the fact that:

1.  the products and services sold are of the highest quality;
2.  this is done in an honest way, without misleading the customers;
3.  the work atmosphere is conducive to the employees working true to their conscience.

§25

The Association's members shall work towards consolidating the employees' sense of belonging to a dealership by promoting the principles of good cooperation and honest competition among the employees.

§26

The owners/managers of dealerships shall exercise constant supervision over employees' compliance with the rules defined in the present Code, and organize appropriate training courses with that aim, particularly in the case of new employees.

## Disciplinary Punishment and Resolving Disputes and Complaints

§27

1.   In case of failure to comply with the ethical principles defined in the present Code and the professional standards defined in the Appendix to the present Code, Association's members are subject to disciplinary punishment.
2.   Disciplinary punishments include:

- an admonition;
- a reprimand;
- a reprimand with warning;
- an order to compensate for damages to a specified value;
- an application to the importer to terminate the dealership agreement.

§28

1.   The proper organ of the Association for deciding about disciplinary punishment and resolving disputes involving the standards defined in the present Code is the Association's Arbitration Court.
2.   The procedure for reviewing cases by the Association's Arbitration Court is defined in the Court's Regulations.

§29

1.   In case of a dispute between dealers, an Association member can file a case against another member for reviewing by the Association's Arbitration Court.

2. The party filing a case or complaint should submit a written application to the Dealer's Council, together with the grounds for the dispute or complaint and the necessary documentation.

3. Upon completing a preliminary analysis of the dispute or complaint, the Dealer's Council shall pass the case on to the Association's Arbitration Court for reviewing, together with a statement of its position.

## Final Regulations

### §30

The present Code was approved by the Congress of Volkswagen and Audi Dealers on 4 December 1998.

### §31

Any changes to the Code require a resolution from the Congress of Dealers following a motion from the Dealer's Council.

## NOTES

1. The Centre is an agency of the Independent Commission Against Corruption, which recently celebrated its 25th anniversary.
2. I. Lazari-Pawlowska, 1992, 'Etyki zawodowe jako role spoleczne' (Professional Ethics as Social Roles), in I. Lazari-Pawlowska, *Etyka: Pisma wybrane* (Ethics: Selected Papers), Ossolineum, Wroclaw, p. 84.
3. K.E. Boulding, 1985, 'Etyka i biznes' (Ethics and Business), in *Ponad ekonomi* (Above Economics), PIW, Warsaw, p. 59.
4. Fédération Européene d'Associations Nationales d'Ingénieurs.
5. Prepared as part of the Association's ethics programme by Professor Wojciech W. Gasparski and Mr Adam Szewczyk, Chairman, the Dealer's Council. The code is published with the written agreement of the Polish Dealer Association Volkswagen – Audi.

# 12. Building moral competence in organizations: the difficult transition from hierarchical control to participative leadership

### Rafael Esteban and Jane Collier

## INTRODUCTION

All organizations nowadays must face the reality of change. Seismic shifts in organizational processes and practices are needed to generate the internal renewal necessary to cope with the pressures of external change. Hierarchical organizations in particular find this kind of adjustment difficult. Not only does the rigidity of their bureaucratic structures make it difficult to achieve the necessary adaptability, but uncertainty frustrates attempts to formulate and implement strategic planning. Judgement and entrepreneurial creativity must therefore be exercised at every level if the organization is to respond adequately to new challenges (Ghoshal and Bartlett, 1998; Wheatley, 1999; Senge, 1990), and this implies that new ways of managing and leading are required to facilitate the changes in processes and practices.

The transition from hierarchy to autonomy in change organizations is fraught with conceptual, practical and moral difficulties. Much has been written about the conceptual and practical aspects of the change process (Belasco, 1997; Hechscher and Donnelan, 1994; Thompson, 1997; Eccles, 1996; McWhinney, 1997), but little emphasis has been placed on the moral aspects. This chapter addresses that issue. We argue that the key to successful adaptability in the face of change is given by the degree of organizational 'moral competence'. Using metaphorical understandings drawn from complexity theory and chaos theory we characterize the 'transition' problems experienced by organizations moving into situations of organizational renewal in terms of necessary shifts in moral values. Our argument is supported by two case studies based on our experience of facilitating organizational change in one particular not-for-profit sector. Our experience of the first facilitation gave us an understanding of the pitfalls of transition from hierarchy to participative processes. The organization in this case failed to make the transition because it was not capable of letting go of the old ways of valuing and relating. The second facilitation (in another organization) happened eight months later, and here the experience was entirely different.

## COMPLEXITY AND CHAOS

Change organizations should not be theorized as discrete entities: they are best analysed as 'open systems' nested within, and responsive to, the wider environment (Collier and Esteban, 1999). Using analogies from natural sciences, they can be modelled as complex adaptive systems whose survival in change situations depends on their ability to achieve continual renewal (Stacey, 1996b). Complex adaptive systems in the natural world, such as ecosystems, are self-organizing: they adapt to their environment by developing capabilities which are appropriate to their survival and abandoning life forms which have become redundant – in other words, achieving 'requisite variety'. Furthermore, these systems are not passive victims of environmental pressures; they have the ability to learn, to recognise patterns and thus respond proactively to change. This enables them to use resources more effectively and to become more efficient at renewal (Wheatley, 1999, p. 83).

This natural-world analogy does not translate easily into the social world. For one thing, many organizations faced with the tidal waves of technological and economic change do not achieve renewal. Because they consider change as a threat to their integrity, because they are frightened that change will open the door to disorder and confusion, they may seek to perpetuate the old certainties and rigidities by strengthening hierarchical controls. Alternatively they may dissipate their energies in disordered external responses and confused internal reactions. These two 'panic' strategies reflect a mindset which sees no middle way between control on the one hand and disorder on the other; opting for either of these is ineffective and potentially suicidal.

However, it is possible to avoid the weaknesses of rigidity and the threat of disintegration if organizations opt for a 'middle way', if they 'let go' and allow initiative, creativity and autonomy to play their part maintaining the balance between responsiveness to changing external demands on the one hand and the need to align organizational purpose and integrity on the other. Holding that tension can be described metaphorically as 'surfing the edge of chaos' (Pascale, 1999). Each of the two 'pulls' – responsiveness to the external environment and adaptive purposefulness – provides a constraint that prevents the organization from going too far in the other direction. In the language of chaos theory, each acts as 'strange attractor' for the other; each provides the context that 'governs', or places limits on, the variation in behaviour of the other (Wheatley, 1998; Collier and Esteban, 1999). Organizational purposes, standards, expectations and vision 'govern' the responsiveness of the organization to external demands. The responsiveness to external change 'governs' the transformation of organizational purpose and integrity in the light of organizational exigencies and (human) capabilities.

These 'chaotic' organizations closely resemble complex adaptive systems. Firstly, since increasing complexity renders top-down control ineffective they tend to be to a greater or lesser extent self-organizing. They can maintain their position on the edge of chaos only in the measure that every agent, every organizational member, demonstrates adaptability, willingness to learn, and is prepared to exercise creativity, collaborative judgement, and responsibility (Youngblood, 1997). Self-organization requires participative structures which facilitate connectedness and communication. Connectedness allows the organization to generate new ways of being active in its environment and to find different kinds of activities consonant with its purpose. This 'emergence' creates the newness, difference, and self-renewal essential to sustainability and survival. Emergent organizations are 'learning organizations', not merely in the adaptive 'single loop' sense, but in the deeper 'double loop' sense of generating questions about existing understandings and presuppositions (Argyris, 1994; Argyris and Schon, 1996). So it is particularly important that people have the space to try new ideas, the freedom to experiment, and the permission to fail and learn from reflection on failures.

In participative organizations the conventional view of leadership as 'what leaders do' no longer applies: competence and vision, judgement and decision are 'fractal' qualities exercised by all at every level throughout the organization. Although institutionalized processes are needed to allow all members to share leadership and to exercise influence in the governing process, shared leadership is and remains a political process. Creative impulses have to be freed, their articulation has to be listened to and heard, ideas have to be formulated, gain acceptance, and 'sold' to the gatekeepers of the legitimate organization. This involves dialogue, and real dialogue is usually uncomfortable because people's mental maps and symbols are different (Bohm and Edwards, 1989). Certainties and expectations are frequently shattered by organizational renewal, and if trust is to flourish anxieties must be managed (Collier and Esteban, 2000). Once trust prevails creativity can begin to grow in a 'climate of generativity' (Kets de Vries, 1996).

New organizations are often prepared to live with 'chaotic' organizational processes. However, such processes are experienced as a threat by rigidly authoritarian organizations. Authoritarian organizations tend to fear conflict and tension: they try to avoid it by inspiring people to follow some common vision, share the same culture, and pull together. This is done at the cost of

removing the diversity that is the very raw material of creative activity. We
believe that the difficulties of moving from hierarchy to participation are
profound, and more resistant to good intentions than would appear at first
sight. The two cases we present here illustrate this point.

### The Processes and Politics of Organizational Transition: Two Case Studies

One of us was invited to facilitate the General Chapters of two Roman
Catholic religious societies (the second of these events took place eight
months after the first). Religious congregations in the Catholic Church have a
procedure whereby every six years a General Chapter is convened of
representatives, elected or *ex officio*, who meet together for several weeks,
usually in Rome. Chapters are essentially governance mechanisms; the aims
are to evaluate the state of the Congregation, to set guidelines for its work, and
to elect the team that will lead the group until the next Chapter. They are
preceded by Pre-capitular Assemblies which prepare the documents on which
the discussions are based. In a sense, therefore, General Chapters represent a
process of shared leadership whereby every member can influence the
direction of the Congregation. These 'organizations' provide real-life
examples of the evolution of participative processes: such examples are
usually very difficult to find (McLagan and Nel, 1997 p. 24).

For many centuries General Chapters constituted the primary means of
control in these hierarchical religious organizations. Their main aim was to
ensure fidelity to the past within organizations which at that time operated as
closed systems. However, the Second Vatican Council of the Roman Catholic
Church (1962–5) asked all religious congregations to accept the necessity of
'renewal' in a changing world. Since then many of these congregations have
tried to effect the transition from authoritarian hierarchical structures and
practices, and to adopt a participative style. Their General Chapters are
becoming the main means of the transformation to 'open systems' capable on
the one hand of responding to the needs of the world, while at the same time
maintaining their integrity of purpose. The two organizations discussed here
had already committed themselves to the perspective of renewal. In both
cases around 50 participants represented an organization of over 1000
members, and they worked together for four weeks. In both cases the
congregations accepted our proposal that the work of the Chapter should
be structured as a participative emerging process divided into four
phases:

1. responsiveness: discovery of new challenges and opportunities in the
   enviroment;

2. purposefulness: re-founding of the Society's identity and purpose in answer to members' aspirations and environmental challenges;
3. selection of the central management team entrusted with the nurturing of the new organizational shape;
4. reshaping of future strategies and structures.

The facilitator's job was to set and explain the boundaries and the dynamics of participation, and to help manage the emotions and the tensions that arise in such participative processes.

### 1. Globus and Easter: structural similarities

The first Chapter, which we shall call Globus, brought together three groups; the European (the founding and traditionally dominant group), the African, and the Asian, with another ten members coming from various countries of the South. The European members of Globus are now aging, and there are few active members, whereas the African and the Asian members are much younger. The work of the Chapter was done in language groups: the Europeans and Africans favoured French, Asians preferred English, and only about a third of the participants were comfortable in both languages. The second Chapter, which we shall call Easter, was a mix of an older 'founding' Western group and a strong, growing and younger Asian and African membership representing the future of the group.

Both congregations share similar traumatic tensions in their growth as multi-cultural and multi-ethnic groups with past stories of colonial and paternalistic attitudes of the Western group towards their younger non-Western members. Both groups had the same difficulties in communicating: in both cases French is the dominant language of the older Western group and English the dominant language of the younger, non-Western group. Only a minority of members in either group had full command of the two working languages (French and English).

On the face of it, therefore, the groups were similar, the events were similar, the context was identical, and the method of working was the same. But the outcome in each case was markedly different. We explain this difference in terms of the presence or absence of the moral competences necessary to effect successful transition from hierarchy to participation.

### 2. Globus and Easter: different outcomes

In the first phase of the Chapter participants attempted to create an institutional vision of Globus and its future in response to the felt need to move towards 'frontier situations' (religious frontiers in dialogue with other religions, ecclesial frontiers in primary evangelization and sociological frontiers of poverty, deprivation and injustice). This was done in a staged process which moved from intra-subjectivity (individual), through inter-subjectivity (the sharing in provincial and regional groupings), to the level of generic subjectivity (Weick, 1995), where group agreement was reached on the new challenges faced by the Congregation and on the need of renewing organizational purpose in line with those challenges.

There was a certain feeling of uneasiness during this exercise of operating as self-organizing groups. Many participants had no real experience of being given open-ended tasks, and there was anxiety about 'lack of control' of the process. However, the exercise produced inspiring texts which painted a picture of a rejuvenated congregation daring to engage courageously in frontier situations, even if underlying disagreements that threatened to surface at this level of sharing were pushed into the background by the felt need to reach 'consensus'.

In the second week the group task was to reflect on and redefine the Society's identity in the new situation. This reflection would pave the way for the election of the new directing team (a Superior General, a Vicar General and three Councillors), due to happen at the beginning of the third week. Although in the first week the need to entrust the management of the Congregation to the active and younger non-European membership had become obvious, it now appeared that certain members of the older Western group had the capacity to control the decision-making process and to block the process of renewal. The inevitable confrontation surfaced in the context of a discussion about the challenges of internationality in the Congregation. The non-European participants expressed their feelings of hurt at being kept in an inferior position by the traditionally dominant European group, while the Europeans, faced with the demand to 'decolonize' the Congregation, could barely disguise their paternalist attitudes towards their younger non-European colleagues and their indignation at being accused of holding colonialist attitudes. Denunciations of hidden agendas and power games were made: things became heated and the facilitator attempted to make the group aware of the lack of trust that had surfaced during their deliberations.

This intervention took place the evening before the elections were due to begin but it failed, as might be expected, to heal the mistrust. At the election of the Superior General the confrontation came to a head. The Asian group pushed for a Third World nominee, thereby signalling its expectation of a shift towards a younger leadership. They expected the backing of the African group. But the African group, threatened by what they interpreted as aggressivity in the Asian group, sided with the Europeans. This resulted in the election – again – of a European to head the Congregation. The transition hoped for by the majority of the participants had failed to materialize. This left the Asians disillusioned, the Africans ashamed, and the Europeans bruised. The Asians decided to withdraw *en bloc* as candidates for the remaining posts on the direction team, and the further process of the Chapter was blocked by the refusal of a sizeable group of members to continue with the election of the Councillors. To all intents and purposes the Chapter, as a creative participative effort of transition and renewal, had been short-circuited, leaving the group painfully split.

In the case of the Easter Chapter, the participative process of renewal happened without a hitch, with the new dynamism of the Third World demands for radical commitment and change blending creatively with the traditional thrust and capabilities of the group in a truly open and gently managed political process. Some of the success of the Easter Chapter may have been attributed to the increased experience of the facilitator and of the lessons learnt in the dramatic Globus Chapter. But, on reflection, we believe that the improved facilitation had only a marginal effect on the quality of the participative process, and that its success was due to the presence in the group as a whole of an organic set of moral capabilities for participation and shared leadership.

## The Pains and Dangers of Organizational Transition

This twofold experience demonstrates that the transition from hierarchy to participation is difficult and complex. General Chapters are a very good example of Winnicott's 'transitional space' (Winnicott, 1971), where normal activity is suspended and people try to make sense of the outer world through 'play' (Klein, 1975). People have the space and the freedom to express creative ideas and to indulge in collective 'sensemaking' (Weick, 1995). However, the institutionalization of creative intuitions and diverse and conflicting interests is not neat, controllable or predictable. It involves many processes and very complex interactions that deeply engage peoples' emotions and are therefore necessarily messy (Wheatley, 1998 p. 347; Stacey 1996a, p. 337). The more committed and passionate members are about the organization and its outcomes, the more this is likely to be the case. The underlying reason for this is that the process of strategic renewal involves destabilizing the system. This instability is destructive in that it threatens existing work patterns, structures and power positions. But it is also creative: it is a 'chrysalis' process where the pain of disintegration allows the organization to emerge 'renewed'.

Managing the conflicts and the emotions of renewal is one of the great challenges that change organizations face. Past governance systems are remarkably tenacious. This is even more so where those governance systems have been endowed with religious significance and divine approval. Even when a group has consciously undertaken the path of renewal in the search of participation, the old mechanical and control models maintain their grip on the system, and this manifests itself in rigidities and defensive routines. 'Every institution that has tried to entrench participative forms of government can attest to the sheer complexity and turbulence involved in making such a shift' (McLagan and Nel, 1995, p. 26). We identify four aspects of this process.

## 1.   The difficult move from control to trust

Hierarchical systems work on the basis of a system of control founded on a mistrust of freedom. 'Chaotic' organizations which need participative processes cannot prosper unless there is a climate of trust. Formal interactions (meetings, rituals) impose formalized behaviour in organizations, but in order to 'get a feel for' the climate of an organization we need to focus on the informal interactions of the members (Schneider, 1990). In the Globus case it was obvious to the facilitator how different were the spontaneous groupings (in corridors, dining room, recreation, outings) from the formal work groupings. The different 'families' (the three main groups) flocked together at every opportunity. Moreover, again and again, participants from all sides came to share with the facilitator their diffidence and suspicion towards members of the other groups. It was clear that the 'families' were very deeply ill at ease with one another: people were systematically misinterpreting the words and the actions of other groups and, worse still, even doubting their good will. The climate of the group was one of deep mistrust.

Trust and mistrust are like force fields that translate into the 'feel' and the 'smell' of a place. In the Globus Chapter the lack of trust of the older European members when faced with the call to change by the younger members was evident to the facilitator, but went unrecognized by the perpetrators who thought that they were the only ones who cared for the future of the congregation. Their need to control was manifest in the way they ensured that the direction of the group was kept in the hands of the dominant group, and that all decisions were couched in terms acceptable to the older 'founding' group. This generated a vicious circle of deepening mutual mistrust that was rife in the corridors, and visible in the way different groups flocked and plotted against one another and in the way disagreements surfaced violently in formal general assemblies in crucial moments of the process.

In the Easter Chapter, the 'smell' of the place was totally different. During the preparation of the Chapter and during the month that followed the facilitator never heard a disparaging comment and what is more important, the group showed a remarkable capacity to enter an emergent process of discernment and decision making where the boundaries were continually reset – in sensitivity to the unfolding of the process itself – by the Steering Committee in which the facilitator was continually present. Trusting 'emergence' is perhaps one of the most difficult attitudes to achieve for groups that have become used, in hierarchical organizations, to controlling the outcomes and thus short-circuiting the possibility of genuine participation. In spite of the apprehension and the insecurity expressed by many during the Chapter, the group showed a remarkable capacity to contain their emotions and an ability to 'go with the flow'. Moreover, the older Western group openly recognized the preparedness of the non-Westerners to take over the direction of the congregation, so that the election of the new executive was a very relaxed and joyful affair. Everything was done in a great atmosphere of mutual trust, and this allowed the gentle management of the emotions that arose normally from the renewal process.

## 2.  The difficult move from consensus to congruence

Hierarchical systems work on the basis of consensus: dissent is seen as dysfunctional and is not tolerated. Diversity is tolerated only in the measure that it does not endanger organizational consensus. But organizations which seek renewal need the creativity and newness that diversity brings, so that they need to encourage rather than suppress dissent. However, creativity and newness have to be 'governed' by organizational purpose and integrity. Achieving integration of purpose in the midst of diversity and creativity involves replacing the consensus imposed around a dominant ideology by congruence, the ability to 'fit' together even when there are differing viewpoints, and to align diverse interests by means of political processes (Kelly and Allison, 1998).

Both Globus and Easter were founded by Europeans who developed the dominant 'culture' of the organization. Membership of the groups has become more international and inter-racial, but new members have had to adapt to the dominant 'founding' culture. Both groups have reached the point where the younger non-European membership has reached a 'critical mass', and has started to demand a positive recognition of its identity in a genuine multi-cultural and multi-racial organization. The organization is therefore faced with the need of learning to live with dissent. The capability of thriving in a climate of dissent is particularly difficult to achieve in religious groups, where conflict arising from political group pressure and interaction is somehow seen as negative and is to be avoided.

The Globus case shows how challenging and upsetting it can be for a group built on consensus to realize that with the maturity of an organization, with increased internationality and with the diversification of situations and commitments, comes the chaos of complex political interaction. The Globus group was clearly not comfortable with the conflicts and the politics that diversity brings. Globus was faced not only with different personal points of view, but also with a divergence of interests and feelings: consensus was simply not possible any more. Coalitions promoting their particular interests developed and they engaged in a tense political process which threatened the cohesion of the group. The Globus Chapter floundered because of the insistence of the dominant 'founding' European group on achieving consensus, and their condemnation of the Asian group as 'disloyal' when the Asians demanded that the identity of the group within a fundamentally changed and changing situation be redefined.

In contrast, the Easter Congregation showed a great appreciation of the richness that dissent and diversity can bring to the group in a great variety of situations. Something remarkable had already happened in the preparation of the central theme of the Easter Chapter: the texts of the Chapter were prepared in two languages, and although they were the same texts they were given two very different stresses in the French and the English texts so as to reflect the divergent cultural and socio-economic contexts of the Congregation's experience. The Easter Chapter showed throughout the discernment and decision process a deep awareness of the need to take on board the creative tensions produced by the increasing cultural diversity in the Congregation. This confident and positive approach to cultural diversity manifested itself very vividly and beautifully in the rituals that punctuated the life of the Chapter. The Easter Chapter was clearly comfortable with diversity and with dissent. Actually, the notion of 'congruence' presented by the facilitator in the introductory reflection at the opening of the Chapter gave the group a conceptual tool to 'name' their desire to respect and exploit their diversity.

### 3.   The difficult move from asymmetry of power to mutuality

Hierarchical authoritarian systems are based on asymmetries of positional power. Genuine participative systems on the other hand are based on mutuality defined as equality of opportunity to exercise influence. The exercise of participation demands the ability to suspend hierarchies and to abandon power games. However, whereas suspending formal hierarchies for a while is relatively easy, recognizing inbuilt asymmetries and hidden power games is more difficult.

The Globus Chapter floundered because of an entrenched lack of mutuality among the members and their diverse coalitions. The 'espoused theory' of the group (Argyris and Schon, 1996) and of the practice of Chapters in general is the total equality and mutuality of all members and participants. But the 'theory in use' in this case sprang from an unrecognized and undiscussed asymmetry of power between the older European group and the younger Third World membership. The European group as a whole related to the younger non-European membership from the perspective of a superiority complex grounded in the perceived right to protect the foundational 'charism' of the Congregation. This generated an anxiety concerning the potential future of the Congregation under non-Western direction; the classic belief that the colonized are never 'ready' to take over translates here into the view that they cannot be trusted to respect the 'charism' of the founders. The anxiety of the Europeans deepened when Third World members expressed the frustration and the feelings of inferiority inculcated by generations of dependence. Their frustration was translated into an overstatement of their case and into an impatience for radical change that seemed to lend support to their elders' worst fears.

The real problem is that the inbuilt asymmetry of power has not been recognized by the dominant group. The Europeans have made superhuman efforts to adapt to Third World cultures. Their attitudes are a world away from the racism and the superiority complex dominant still in their Western countries of origin. But they cannot see themselves as their non-European colleagues see them. Many non-European members, who have memories of having been treated as inferior, continue to feel and to resent very deeply the paternalism, the superiority and the lack of trust of the older European group. They tend to express their feelings in the strong language of 'colonialism and neo-colonialism'. The older Europeans felt hurt when their paternalist attitudes and their superiority complex were openly challenged. But their reaction proved exactly the point that the non-Europeans were trying to make. The Europeans, accused the non-Europeans of ingratitude. 'After all we have done for them, they do this to us' is a classic reaction of parents to their children's criticism. Faced with criticism, the dominant group went into denial and into defensive routines, blaming the Third World members for 'breaking the peace'.

The Easter Chapter was remarkable for the way in which the 'founding' Western group was prepared to let go of their influence on the direction and priorities of the organization and to recognize the shift in the centre of gravity of the organization to the non-Western membership. In fact, it was the non-Western context of the organization's operations that provided the motives and the priorities for a renewed strategy which challenged the traditional organizational strategy. There was clearly an acknowledgement by the Westerners that they had to diminish in order to let the non-Westerners grow. All this was made possible because the vast majority of the members of the Chapter were prepared to put the common interest before personal and constituent group interests.

A recurring theme in the Easter Chapter was the need to nurture the 'fraternal' character of the congregation. In fact this was a Chapter of a group of Brothers, which originated as a breakaway group from a mixed Congregation of Brothers and Priests. This breakaway had happened because the Brothers had been kept in a subordinate, inferior position by the Priests. We wonder if this 'foundational' traumatic experience has not in fact given to the Brothers a keen awareness of the dangers of the abuse of positional power and a commitment to a genuine fraternity and mutuality in their work relationships. On the other hand, it may be the case that the Globus Chapter demonstrates how deep is the addiction to power among priests in the Catholic Church (Crosby, 1991) and how difficult it may be for a group with a clerical culture to embark on genuine participation.

## 4.    The difficult move from rigidity to tolerance

All organizations need stability. But while hierarchical authoritarian organizations achieve stability by imposing a rigidity grounded in fear of disorder, participative organizations achieve stability by developing the ability to navigate the 'edge of chaos' between rigidity and disorder. In other words, they manage the continuous tension between the search for coherence or 'fit', and the drive for diversity or 'split'. Every organization aims to achieve 'fit' in terms of the integration between what is desirable in terms of purpose and objective on the one hand and what is possible in terms of resources on the other. But a perfect 'fit' guarantees stagnation and atrophy, since nothing new is tried. Change organizations must engage with the new and the diverse; they must respond to the differentiating pressures and demands of the environment, but not to the extent that they lose sight of organizational intent and sense of direction. The managing of this tension between 'fit' and 'split' creates 'stretch', the quality which allows the organization to navigate the turbulence of change, and extends the capabilities and horizons of the organization (Hamel and Pralahad, 1994).

Rigidity is the fundamental characteristic of organizations' intent solely in continuity and in the conservation of the past. It manifests itself in intolerance towards change, in the setting of rigid identity boundaries and in preoccupations with legalism and with the elimination of ambiguities. In the Globus Chapter the lack of dynamism of the older group, together with their perceptions of the identity of the organization as 'European', produced a resistance to the changes in direction and priorities demanded by the more dynamic, younger non-Western groups. A strict subservience to a rigid procedure was in fact used as a method of control by the dominant Western group intent on avoiding change. Their insistence on a procedure which discussed and voted every comma and every word was in fact a way of emasculating the thrust of the more dynamic and challenging proposals coming from the non-Westerners. This happened in spite of the efforts of the facilitator to suggest the need to accept texts in their global meaning without too much preoccupation with grammar and syntax.

The Globus Chapter thus produced a split but failed to find a renewed fit, and the Congregation is now stuck in the most painful and dangerous stage of renewal. The group is polarized by the intolerance between the 'dissenters' who are creating a 'split' in their longing to 'stretch' the organization towards a new 'fit' and those who are clinging to the old 'fit' while giving lip service to a belief in renewal. Globus will need to unlock the process by dealing with the hurts, past and present, which lie at the root of the blockage. If this tolerance is not achieved, the split may well harden, draining organizational dynamism and eventually resulting in organizational disintegration.

By contrast, the Easter Chapter showed the suppleness and tolerance needed for participative purposing and decision making. This suppleness, in the context of a robust confidence in the historical dynamism of the organization, proved invaluable in establishing the capacity of the group to undertake a participative emergent process of change and renewal. A rigid procedure for the taking of decisions and the drawing of texts was in fact approved at the beginning of the Chapter, but very quickly the group agreed to sideline the originally approved procedure in order to draw up inspirational texts and to accept decisions in their general sense, thereby accepting the fuzziness and ambiguity that comes with congruence. The group also showed a great capacity to manage with great gentleness the tensions produced by the emotions and anxieties inherent in a genuine process of renewal. The Easter Chapter also proved its ability to live with fuzzy boundaries by inviting lay representatives of the various organizations with which they collaborate and giving them an active role in an extended session of the Chapter which considered the dynamics of sharing the primary task and strategic collaboration. This invitation constituted a true novelty in the practice of General Chapters.

## Participation, Moral Competence and Awareness

We are increasingly aware of the fact that the 'forms of authoritarian governance that have characterized most of the world's institutions for three thousand years are immoral and fundamentally flawed' (McLagan and Nel, 1995, p. 27), and that 'moral competence' in organizations must be based on the human freedom and creativity of participative organizations. But the transition from authoritarianism to participation is difficult and often painful. It becomes clear that the values and attitudes that characterize the authoritarian hierarchical organization – consensus, control, asymmetry, rigidity – constitute an organic whole and make these organizations morally incompetent to undertake a process of participative renewal. In order to become participative, organizations must undergo a radical conversion and embrace the values and attitudes that we have identified – congruence, trust, mutuality and tolerance – that produce the moral competence to thrive in a situation of continuous change and emergent renewal.

The transition from hierarchy to participation has therefore to be based on a profound change of organizational 'mind' and 'heart', a personal and organizational 'conversion' of presuppositions, values and attitudes

(Lonergan, 1971; Collier, 1990). On the cognitive level there must be a reinterpretation of previous understandings of what it means to 'organize'. On the normative level new values must generate a reevaluation of priorities. On the social level new ways of relating to others must support the processes of shared leadership. 'Conversion' is the prerequisite for this difficult transition, but it has to come from within the organization – it cannot be imposed from the top.

It is also essential for organizations embarking on the transition to develop new capabilities and skills. Members need to develop capabilities of dialogue and a positive tolerance of diversity that will allow people to feel comfortable with dissent and with the attendant conflicts. This will allow for friendly, gentle politics in the process of institutionalizing personal insights and group interests. It may also be necessary for a facilitator to 'hold the context' of dialogue (Senge, 1990 p. 243). Underlying all this is the need to develop and deepen self-awareness. Through self-awareness people can become sensitive to their own prejudices and take stock of feelings so as to neutralize their destructive potential. The unlocking of self-awareness is a painful process, but it is necessary in order to bring to the surface the roots of the mistrust that can threaten the integrity of any community and its future survival.

We identified the lack of such awareness in the Globus Chapter as the main cause for the failure of developing the moral attitudes and competence needed for genuine participation. The people of the Globus Chapter proclaimed their commitment to participation, but they showed their moral incompetence by their blind adherence to deeply ingrained authoritarian attitudes and practices. The success of the Easter Chapter seems to validate our identification of the moral competence needed for a participative culture in organizations and for the exercise of shared leadership.

# REFERENCES

Argyris, C. (1994), *On Organizational Learning*, Cambridge, MA: Blackwell Publishers, Inc.

Argyris, C. and Schon, D. (1996), *Organizational Learning II: Theory, Method and Practice*, Reading, Mass: Wokingham, Adison Wesley.

Belasco, J. (1997), *Teaching the Elephant to Dance: Empowering Change in Your Organization*, London: Century Business.

Bohannan, P. (1995), *How Culture Works*, New York: The Free Press.

Bohm, D. and Edwards, F.D. (1989), *Science, Order and Creativity*, London: Routledge.

Collier, J. (1990), *The Culture of Economism: an Exploration of Barriers to Faith-as-Praxis*, Frankfurt: Peter Lang.

Collier, J. and Esteban, R. (1998), *From Complicity to Encounter: the Church and the Culture of Economism*, Harrisburg, PA: Trinity Press International.

Collier, J. and Esteban, R. (1999), 'Governance in the Participative Organization: Freedom, Creativity and Ethics', *Journal of Business Ethics*, **21**, 173-188. Also as Judge Institute of Management Studies Working Paper 3/99.

Collier, J. and Esteban, R. (2000), 'Systemic Leadership: Ethical and Effective', *The Leadership and Organization Development Journal*, **21**(4), 207–215.

Crosby, M.H. (1991), *The Dysfunctional Church: Addiction and Codependency in the Family of Catholicism*, Notre Dame, Indiana: Ave Maria Press.

Eccles, T. (1994), *Succeeding with Change*, London: McGraw-Hill.

Eccles, T. (1996), *Succeeding with Change: Implementing Action-driven Strategies*, London: McGraw-Hill.

Ghoshal S. and Bartlett, C.A. (1998), *The Individualised Corporation*, London: Heinemann.

Hamel, G. and Pralahad, C.K. (1994), *Competing for the Future*, Boston: Harvard Business School Press.

Hechscher, C. and A. Donnelan (1994), *The Post-bureaucratic Organization: New Perspectives on Organizational Change*, London: Sage.

Kets de Vries, M.F.R. (1996), 'Leadership for Creativity: Generating Peak Experiences', INSEAD Working Paper 1996/62.

Kelly, S. and Allison, M.A. (1998), *The Complexity Advantage*, New York: McGraw-Hill.

Klein, M. (1975), *The Psychoanalysis of Children*, London: Hogarth Press.

Lonergan, B. (1971), *Method in Theology*, London: Darton, Longman and Todd.

McLagan, P. and Nell, C. (1997), *The Age of Participation*, San Fransisco: Berrett-Koehler Publishers.

McWhinney, W. (1997), *Creating Paths of Change*, 2nd ed., London: Sage.

Pascale, R. (1999), 'Surfing the edge of chaos', *Sloan Management Review*, **40**(3), 83–94.

Schneider, B. (ed.) (1990), *Organizational Climate and Culture*, San Francisco: Jossey Bass.

Senge, P.M. (1990), *The Fifth Discipline: the Art and Practice of the Learning Organization*, New York: Doubleday.

Stacey, R.D. (1996a), *Strategic Management and Organisational Dynamics*, 2nd ed., London: Pitman Publishing.

Stacey, R.D. (1996b), *Complexity and Creativity in Organizations*, San Francisco: Berrett-Koehler Publications.

Thompson, J.L. (1997), *Strategic Management: Awareness and Change*, London: International Thomson.

Weick, K.E. (1995), *Sensemaking in Organizations*, London: Sage.

Wheatley, M. (1999), *Leadership and the New Science*, 2nd ed., San Francisco: Berrett-Koehler.

Winnicott, D.W. (1971), *The Maturational Process and the Facilitating Environment*, London: Hogarth Press.

Youngblood, M. (1997), 'Leadership at the Edge of Chaos: from Control to Creativity', *Strategy and Leadership*, Sept/Oct, 8-14.

# 13.  National champions in a unified market: the BSCH–Champalimaud case

## Alejo José G. Sison

The European Union charter guarantees the free movement of goods, services, capital and people among member states. Yet there is a very strong resistance not only to transnational mergers and acquisitions, but even to alliances among corporations. This is especially true in sectors deemed politically sensitive, as finance. This chapter relates how and why the BSCH–Champalimaud strategic alliance failed, due to the intervention of the Portuguese government, basically. Although the European Commission claimed victory for the outcome, its jurisdiction over such economic transactions was, in theory and in practice, far from being definitively upheld.

Rather than argue in favour or against 'national champions' and 'unified markets', we intend to provide a basis for the discussion of the ethical issues involved. We are concerned particularly with the duplicity of actors who pay lip-service to free markets, liberalization, deregulation, privatization and fair competition, while implementing measures that are protectionist, interventionist, discriminatory, populist and perhaps, even corrupt. How could privatization be compatible with government ownership of golden shares, or free markets with state subsidies and tax-breaks? How could deregulation coexist with increased bureaucracy, or the pursuit of economic efficiency with the protection of social, cultural and political interests? Could sovereignty be shared by a nation state, the repository of our loyalties and sentiments, and an economic union, that appeals to a cosmopolitan sense of justice and reason?

## MISE EN SCÈNE

Banco Santander Central Hispano (BSCH) resulted from the merger in January 1999, between Banco Santander and Banco Central Hispano. The merger sought the advantages of scale in a new environment characterized by globalization, the unification of the European market, the introduction of the euro and the use of net technologies. It was the top Spanish bank in assets and market capitalization, with important stakes in construction, real estate, energy and telecommunications. It was also the prime financial group in Latin America, managing 15 banks in 11 different countries. Within the euro zone, it ranked third in market capitalization and tenth in assets.[1] Apart from the Botín family, its major shareholders included the Royal Bank of Scotland, Assicurazioni Generali, San Paolo-IMI, Commerzbank, Merrill Lynch International and Metropolitan Life. Emilio Botín and José María Amusátegui became the new bank's Co-Presidents.

Antonio Champalimaud is the patriarch of one of the three families that dominated the Portuguese economy during the Salazar dictatorship. In 1960 the Champalimaud Industrial Group, which originally dealt in cement and steel, obtained control of the Banco Pinto and Sotto Mayor (BPSM). In 1968 the Group assumed majority stakes in two insurance companies, Mundial and Confiança. With the 'revolution of the carnations' that ended the 42-year dictatorship in 1974, Champalimaud was forced to flee to Brazil. In 1975 banks and insurance companies were nationalized. In 1978 Mundial and Confiança, still under government control, merged to form Mundial Confiança (MC). In 1992 MC was re-privatized and Champalimaud regained his dominant position. In 1994 MC bought 80 per cent of BPSM and together they acquired 50 per cent of Banco Totta and Açores (BTA) in the following year. Since 1992, BTA has been the largest shareholder of Crédito Predial Portugués (CPP) with 43.4 per cent. In 1996 MC, through BPSM, secured 97.23 per cent of Banco Chemical Finance (BCF) and increased its stakes in BTA to 56.4 per cent. In 1998 MC participated in the buy-out of CPP, raising its holdings to 70.57 per cent. At the same time, BPSM acquired 94.4 per cent of BTA through a share swap. As a result, MC was able to restructure its participation in BPSM to 58.3 per cent. In 1999, therefore, the Champalimaud Group consisted of the MC insurance firm as its flagship, two universal banks, BPSM and BTA, an investment bank, BCP, and a mortgage and lending bank, CPP. It was the third largest financial institution in Portugal, in terms of both assets and market capitalization.

The European Economic Community (EEC) began with the signing of the Treaty of Rome in March 1957. It sought to raise the standard of living and strengthen relations among member states by establishing a common market and common economic policies. In article 3 of the Treaty of Rome the EEC committed itself, among other things, to (a) the abolition of obstacles to freedom of movement for persons, services and capital; (b) the institution of a system insuring competition; and (c) the approximation of the laws of member states for the proper functioning of the common market. The four main institutions of the EEC were also founded: the Commission as the executive organ, which initiates and implements policies; the Council of Ministers, which decides on the proposals of the Commission; the Parliament, which plays an advisory role, and the Court of Justice, which interprets decisions and provisions under dispute. The Commission is composed of a President, Vice-Presidents and various other Commissioners for areas as Competition, Internal Market, Financial Services, Taxation and so on.

Spain and Portugal joined the EEC together in January 1986. The EEC became the European Union (EU) through the 'Treaty on European Union' approved in Maastricht in December 1991. However, the Maastricht Treaty did not come into force until after its ratification by national parliaments in November 1993. The Maastricht Treaty contained two major sets of provisions: those aimed at an economic and monetary union; and those geared towards a political union. The latter included directives for common foreign and defence policies and union citizenship. Likewise, the Maastricht Treaty granted the European Court of Justice the right to impose fines on member states for failing to implement its rulings. The last major EU Treaty was signed in Amsterdam in October 1997. The Amsterdam Treaty introduced amendments so that matters as judicial cooperation, the Schengen Agreement, the Social Policy, the Common Foreign and Security Policy and so on be fully integrated into the Union framework.

## CHRONICLE OF EVENTS

*7 June 1999*   Scarcely three weeks after its divorce from Banco Comercial Portugues (BCP), BSCH finds a new partner in the Champalimaud Group. The BSCH Co-Presidents, Amusátegui and Botín, sign a deal with Antonio Champalimaud in which BSCH receives 40 per cent of the Champalimaud Holding in exchange for 1.6 per cent of BSCH shares. Through MC, Antonio Champalimaud controls BPSM, BTA, CPP and BCF. In addition, BSCH outrightly receives 13.3 per cent of BPSM in exchange for 48 per cent of Banco Santander Portugal (BSP) and 20 per cent of Banco Brasil Noroeste (BBN).

*18 June 1999*   The Portuguese government headed by Antonio Guterres vetoes the BSCH–Champalimaud deal in defence of 'national interests'. The decision was reached after initial inquiries carried out by the Finance Ministry, the Attorney General's Office, the Bank of Portugal, the Securities and Exchange Commission (SEC) and the Portuguese Insurance Institute. Supposedly, the deal violates a regulation prohibiting foreign companies from acquiring more than 20 per cent of local insurance firms.

Once the veto was made public, Jorge Jardim Gonçalves, BCP president, announce a hostile takeover bid of MC 'to support the competitiveness of the national financial system' and 'to protect the interests of the market'. BCP offers 2.02 shares for each MC share, representing an 80 per cent premium over MC's last quoted price.

*21 June 1999*  Mario Monti, the European Internal Market and Financial Services Commissioner, begins inquiries on the Portuguese veto. On 25 June 1999, he informs the Portuguese government that the veto violates EU laws, in particular, those referring to the freedom of establishment and the free movement of capital.

*22 June 1999*  The Portuguese Insurance Institute limits the voting rights of BSCH, theoretically the owner of around 20 per cent of MC, to 10 per cent. Champalimaud informs the SEC that a lien exists on 51.1 per cent of MC shares. In principle, this restriction hinders their sale.

*28 June 1999*  Taking advantage of the EU Latin American and Carribean Summit in Rio de Janeiro, Abel Matutes, the Spanish Foreign Minister, meets with Jaime Gama, his Portuguese Colleague, in an attempt to find a diplomatic solution to the BSCH-Champalimaud case.

*30 June 1999*  The European Competition Commissioner, Karel Van Miert, informs the Portuguese government that the BSCH-Champalimaud deal, given its Union-wide dimension, falls exclusively under his competence.

*20 July 1999*  After considering the allegations of the Portuguese Finance Ministry and finding these unsatisfactory, the European Commission formally suspends the veto over the BSCH-Champalimaud alliance, with effects retroactive to 17 June 1999. By the same stroke, the Commission invalidates the Portuguese Insurance Institute ruling that limits BSCH-Champalimaud voting rights in MC.

BCP extends its takeover bid to two of the Champalimaud banks. BCP offers 25 shares for 27 of BPSM or its cash equivalent (23.156 euros). For CPP, BCP offers a cash equivalent of 14.35 euros per share. These offers represent a 40 per cent premium over the current prices of BPSM and CPP. Lastly, BCP promises to pay BTA minority shareholders 26.136 euros per share or 80 per cent more than the previous going rate.

*25 July 1999*  The Portuguese Attorney General's Office submits a report to the Ministry of Finance informing of irregularities in the Champalimaud Group. Apparently the Champalimaud banks are controlled by two foreign groups, Baliana Trading Limited, registered in Dublin, and Corporación

Ultramar de Inversiones, registered in Montevideo. However, these foreign groups own only an insignificant number of shares in the banks. The Champalimaud Group is alleged to owe these firms more than 32 billion escudos. Furthermore, the share registries of the Champalimaud Group have been blank since 1994 and no written records of its Board Resolutions could be found.

*3 August 1999*  The European Commission authorizes the BSCH–Champalimaud alliance, but falls short of annulling the Portuguese government veto. Portuguese law allows state authorities to maintain the veto until the end of September, 1999, and the Commission wishes to respect this provision.

*8 September 1999*  Van Miert initiates legal proceedings that would allow him to file a fast-track suit against Portugal in the European Court of Justice. These proceedings will be added to those began earlier by the Internal Market Commissioner, Monti.

*15 September 1999*  Antonio Champalimaud files several suits in the Supreme Administrative Court of Portugal seeking the annulment of the Finance Ministry and Portuguese Insurance Institute resolutions. He argues his case on the basis of the authorization received from the European Commission.

*24 September 1999*  The Bank of Portugal issues its own veto. The fact that the BSCH–Champalimaud alliance does not have a clear majority in the MC voting rights produces a 'power void' in the banks that this insurance firm controls. As a result, the 'healthy and sane management' of these banks would be put in jeopardy, if the alliance were allowed to push through.

Upon learning of the Bank of Portugal's decision, Antonio Champalimaud for the first time wavers and admits the possibility of breaking the deal with BSCH.

*10 October 1999*  Antonio Guterres is re-elected Prime Minister of the Portuguese government.

*20 October 1999*  The European Commission annuls the Portuguese veto declaring it illegal.

*28 October 1999*  The Supreme Administrative Court of Portugal rejects Antonio Champalimaud's petitions for the lifting of the government vetoes.

*29 October 1999* BCP formalizes its bid for the entire Champalimaud Group at the Portuguese SEC.

*3 November 1999* The European Commission files a suit against the Portuguese government at the European Court of Justice in Luxembourg.

## ISSUES, ARGUMENTS AND REBUTTALS

There are two main parties in the conflict. The Portuguese government and BCP defend the cause of a 'national champion' in the financial sector, whereas the European Commission together with BSCH, the Champalimaud Group and the Spanish government struggle to protect what they consider to be the bedrock of a unified market. Unless this distinction is clear, one could easily get lost in the welter of claims and counter-claims made by both sides.

The first objection presented by the Portuguese government refers to the resale restrictions of newly privatized corporations such as BPSM. A clause prohibits the Champalimaud Group from selling 51 per cent of BPSM within five years of its purchase. Any transaction requiring an exemption could only be carried out with an authorization from the Finance Ministry. This prohibition is effective until November 1999. However, the Champalimaud Group signed the deal with BSCH on 7 June 1999, and failed to ask permission from the Finance Ministry until 11 June 1999.

Related to this first objection, but rarely cited by either party, are the events surrounding Champalimaud's purchase of BTA in 1995. In February 1995, the five most senior members of the Portuguese SEC resigned after the government waived takeover rules, thus allowing Champalimaud to buy 50 per cent of BTA without bidding for the rest of the shares. Champalimaud bought the BTA shares from Spain's Banesto, then already under the control of Botín's Banco Santander.

In May 1999, an inquiry by the Conservatives into alleged 'illicit and criminal dealings' in the BTA and MC privatizations was blocked in parliament by Social Democrats and Socialists. Declarations by Mario Soares (the Socialist Prime Minister during those privatizations) that Champalimaud had been 'pampered' by the Portuguese democracy fanned the flames of suspicion over the deals and the former government's probable complicity. The Conservatives remain firm in their belief of 'unfair practices' and a 'cover-up' although, at present, this may be impossible to prove.

Furthermore, as revealed in a meeting on 11 June 1999, among the Prime Minister, Antonio Guterres, the Finance Minister, Antonio Sousa Franco and the presidents of the major Portuguese banks, a 'gentleman's agreement' existed that Champalimaud would first inform his colleagues – particularly

Arturo Santos Silva of Banco Portugues do Investimento – of any intention to sell, in order to keep his holdings in the hands of his co-nationals. This understanding was reached sometime in the autumn of 1998. Besides, Antonio Champalimaud's son and BPSM President, Luis, apparently assured the Portuguese Chief Executive on 7 June 1999 that they would never sell important packets of shares to foreigners.

A second objection was raised, not directly by the Portuguese government, but by the minority shareholders in MC. They claimed that they had been unjustly deprived of the opportunity to exchange their shares for those of BSCH. They argued that the equity swap should have been made through a public offer, available to all MC shareholders. They also complained about the lack of information, vital to their own interests, regarding the scope and conditions of the deal. In September 1999, a group of American and British institutional investors accounting for 15 to 20 per cent of MC initiated an investigation of its Board. This was done with a view to possibly calling a General Shareholders' Meeting and soliciting changes among the Board members. Portuguese law allows for such meetings to be held, whenever requested by more than 5 per cent of the shareholders.

A third difficulty came by way of the Portuguese SEC, which on 14 June 1999 suspended the trading of Champalimaud shares as a precautionary measure. (Several other suspensions of trading were to follow.) This was occasioned by the great disparity observed in the equity swap: Champalimaud receives shares for the value of $660 million, whereas BSCH only receives $311 million worth of stocks. This led one to suspect that BSCH had assured itself the control of the Champalimaud Group through a call option. Another strange detail was that Antonio Horta Osorio, President of BSP and a man of Botín's confidence, was reported to assume the top posts in Champalimaud's BPSM, BTA and CPP. However, without further explanations, trading was resumed in the Lisbon bourse on the following day.

Fourthly, when the Portuguese government announced its veto, the reason cited was an Insurance Institute regulation that prohibited foreign companies from owning more than 20 per cent of local firms. This figure was more or less what BSCH came to hold by acquiring 40 per cent of the Champalimaud Group, which in turn owned MC. The Portuguese Insurance Institute reacted by limiting the voting rights of BSCH in MC to approximately half of its holdings or 10 per cent. Such a measure was supposed to facilitate the 'government-sponsored' takeover by Jorge Jardim Gonçalves's BCP. But as it turned out, a lien existed on 51.1 per cent of MC shares which serve as collateral for a syndicated loan with Caixa Geral de Depositos (CGD) and Espirito Santo. That loan was formalized in November 1994, and its final amortization of $121 million is due in November 2004. For this reason MC requested that the SEC disallow BCP's takeover attempt, but to no avail.

Similarly, the Insurance Institute maintained its course and in early July 1999, it also reduced the Champalimaud Group's voting rights in MC. In the end, the combined voting rights of BSCH–Champalimaud in MC were down to about half of their share holdings or 23.7 per cent.

In the fifth place, the Bank of Portugal opposed the deal on the grounds that it created a 'power vacuum' within the top management of BPSM, BTA, CPP and BCF. This claim was founded on the reduced combined voting rights of BSCH–Champalimaud in MC, on which the control of the aforementioned banks depended. If the deal were to proceed, it was not clear who should assume ultimate responsibility over the banks. Yet this obstacle depended entirely on the Insurance Institute's controversial rulings.

The Portuguese government had always interpreted the equity swap between BSCH and the Champalimaud Group not as a mere 'strategic alliance', but as a full-blown acquisition of the latter by the former. Hence its insistence that a formal takeover bid be filed with the SEC, and its unofficial support of the local candidate BCP as the 'white knight'. (In theory, the Lisbon SEC could reject a takeover bid if it could demonstrate any positive intervention by government.) Hovering was the fear that BSCH and Champalimaud connive in creating a holding, proceed with some asset-stripping to increase its value, then sell off at the first opportunity to reap fat profits. Thus the accusation of 'short-termism'.

In the sixth place, the Attorney General's Office also added motives for the government's objections. Firstly, with the dubious links it had discovered between the Champalimaud banks and companies registered in Dublin and Montevideo, and secondly, with the irregularities found in the Champalimaud Board records.

On a personal plane, the Portuguese Finance Minister Antonio Sousa Franco, at the beginning of the controversy, accused Commissioner Van Miert of acting at the service of 'private interests'. This was because Van Miert's spokesperson, Stefan Rating, was married to a lawyer working for the Uria & Menéndez Law Firm, then representing BSCII interests in Brussels. However, the Commission strongly denied the involvement of any female lawyer in the BSCH–Champalimaud proceedings.

There were likewise apprehensions that Prime Minister Antonio Guterres was making use of the BSCH–Champalimaud case as a rallying point, since he was due for re-election in October, and nationalist causes haul in votes. Although such conjectures are extremely difficult to confirm, the fact is that Antonio Sousa Franco was among the first to leave the new Guterres cabinet. Nonetheless, Joaquim Pina Moura, Antonio Sousa Franco's successor, repeatedly declared that he would continue with the veto because it was the government's decision and not his predecessor's personal whim.

The respective foreign ministries of the Spanish and Portuguese governments tried to contain the conflict by acknowledging the autonomy and prudence of the Courts and other deciding bodies. They wanted to prevent the BSCH–Champalimaud affair from straining other aspects of their countries' bilateral relations.

Yet protests also arose from other countries, even from outside the EU. Chile, France and Italy joined Portugal in raising objections. On 17 May 1999, Banco Central of Chile agreed to sell its 35.4 per cent stake in Banco Santiago to BSCH, raising the latter's share to 78.9 per cent. This would enhance BSCH's dominance in the Chilean market to 28.2 per cent. Previously, BSCH already was a major player through Banco Santander Chile, that country's second largest. At the same time, fears spread in Paris that BSCH could become Société Générale's (SG) 'white knight', thwarting the double hostile takeover bid launched by the Banque Nationale de Paris (BNP) over SG and Paribas. Immediately the French government announced that it would not tolerate any foreign meddling in its domestic financial affairs. Nevertheless, exploratory talks for an equity swap wherein BSCH could raise its stakes in SG from 5.1 to 10 per cent continued. And finally, the deal likewise provoked uneasiness among three of BSCH's major shareholders, Assicurazioni Generali (which controls Mediobanca), San Paolo-IMI and Metropolitan Life, for they competed against each other in Italy's banking and insurance markets. The alliance could spell even more problems for BSCH's already complicated share structure.[2]

Foreseeably, the BSCH–Champalimaud alliance would also encounter serious obstacles from labour groups. BSCH had already planned to lay off 4150 employees above 52 years old in 1999. By the end of 2000, it should have closed down 1000 branches among its three brands, Banesto, Banco Central Hispano and Banco Santander, in order to meet its cost-cutting targets. The alliance with the Champalimaud banks could only mean more redundancies and lay-offs, in already difficult labour markets such as those of Spain and Portugal.

BSCH and Champalimaud have always found in the European Commission their strongest ally. For then Internal Market Commissioner Monti, the Portuguese government veto goes against the freedom of establishment of services (banking, insurance and so on) and the free movement of capital. Besides, in accordance with the principle of institutional loyalty contained in article 10 of the Union Treaty, Portugal should have first consulted with the Commission before issuing its veto.

For then Competition Commissioner Van Miert, any decision over the equity swap belongs exclusively to his Office and not to the Portuguese government, which should abstain from applying national laws to the Union-wide integration of corporations. He bases his argument on article 21 of the normative 4064/89 concerning the control of the corporate consolidation. This article lists only three exceptions in which a national government could intervene: to assure public security, in the case of mass media, and when the stability of the financial system is threatened or the legality of the transaction is suspect. He expressed serious doubts that Portugal could justify its veto on the merits of any of these grounds. Besides, the Competition Commissioner agrees with the two partners in the alliance that their combined market share in Portugal's financial sector only adds up to 19 per cent, a shade below the 20 per cent permitted by the Antitrust Laws.

There was a consensus between the Internal Market and the Competition Commissioners in the steps taken against the Portuguese government, from the suspension of the veto to its annulment, and finally, to the filing of charges in the European Court of Justice. Such resolve was not affected even by the changes in the Commission in September 1999, when Van Miert stepped down and Monti took his place. The new Internal Market Commissioner, Fritz Boelkestein, supported the efforts of his predecessor, affirming that he would not permit the defence of national interests to interfere with the restructuring of financial services within the EU.

Antonio Champalimaud has always claimed that he has never sold shares of his companies to BSCH. The transaction consisted in an equity swap, not a merger, let alone a sell-out. His group would still keep 60 per cent of MC and the control of its Board. Therefore, there is no reason to fear a 'power void' in the governance of the financial institutions dependent on MC. These banks and insurance companies are still very much in Portuguese hands. He believed that Portugal would come out as the winner in the deal, because of his group's increased stakes in BSP and BBN, in line with its internationalization strategy. Understandably, he protested over the doubts cast on his credibility and patriotism. In turn, he has been highly critical of the Portuguese government's unofficial support of BCP in its hostile takeover bid. He has even remarked that such bids could not be realized with local resources alone and without foreign support.

**Preparing for a Showdown**

The filing of charges by the European Commission against Portugal in early November dashed hopes that the changes within both the Commission and the Portuguese Cabinet would somehow ease the conflict. There was hardly anything left to do than to prepare for an unprecedented showdown between Brussels and Lisbon.

However, in late September, Champalimaud 'blinked' and for the first time admitted the possibility of reneging on the alliance. Though it turned out to be a bluff, the public was afforded a peak into the deal's limitations and exit strategies. Firstly, either party could unilaterally back out without paying damages if, by 7 March 2000, the alliance fails to receive approval from the Portuguese government. Secondly, the target date for the finalization of the equity swap would be 30 June 2000 and shares in the consortium controlling 51 per cent of MC could not be sold until after two years thence. Thirdly, BSCH could also back out from the agreement if Champalimaud were to object to the acquisition, through their joint holding, of other financial institutions in the Portuguese market. Fourthly, a minimum of seven members would constitute the MC Board, four from Champalimaud and three from BSCH. Finally, the Champalimaud family would hold the 'rights of first refusal' were BSCH to sell its shares, so that the consortium could continue in Portuguese ownership.

The prospects of the European Commission's suit against Portugal were not very heartening. The Luxembourg Court usually takes one to two years to decide on such cases, which is beyond the agreed time frame for the consolidation of the alliance. In order not to render its efforts futile, the Commission found itself forced to request a quick solution and for 'provisional measures', petitions which the European Court of Justice is under no obligation to grant.

## A Solomonic Solution?

*10-11 November 1999*   The new Portuguese Finance Minister, Joaquim Pina Moura, introduces modifications to the BSCH–Champalimaud deal acceptable to the major parties. With the approval of the Portuguese government, BSCH makes a friendly takeover bid for the whole of MC, paying Champalimaud about $1.6 billion in cash and shares. This is above MC's current market value of $1.2 billion. In exchange for the divestiture, Antonio Champalimaud becomes one of BSCH's majority owners with shareholdings between 3 to 3.5 per cent of the total. BSCH then sells MC and BPSM to CGD, a government institution, while it keeps 100 per cent of BTA and CPP. BSCH and CGD become the protagonists of a new 'Treaty of Tordesillas', this time engineered by the Portuguese Finance Minister.

Surprisingly, these terms are very similar to the proposals made by the previous Finance Minister, Antonio Sousa Franco, in mid-September and rejected by Champalimaud. Sousa Franco then suggested that MC and BTA remain under Portuguese control.

Meanwhile, BCP maintains its takeover bid for the entire Champalimaud Group. Most likely, BCP would buy MC from the CGD in the end. Although the Portuguese government ipso facto has lifted its veto, the EU Commission still keeps its suit in Luxembourg. Nevertheless, the Competition Commissioner Monti expresses satisfaction over the turn of events.

Hardly had the news of the agreement reached public domain, when commentators hastened to call it 'Solomonic'. The BSCH Co-Presidents, Botín and Amusátegui, jointly congratulated the Portuguese government for 'fulfilling its mission responsibly and wisely', paving the way for a solution that was 'good for Europe, good for Portugal, good for Spain, and good for BSCH'.[3] They had sound reasons for saying so. They may have lost 40 per cent of the Champalimaud Group, but they have gained in exchange 100 per cent of two of its banks, BTA and CPP. They have risen to the fourth place among Portugal's biggest financial groups, thanks to their previous holdings in BSP and in Banco Santander de Negocios. Undoubtedly, this was a step forward in their strategy of becoming a 'pan-European' bank, through alliances and acquisitions.

Champalimaud was of a different opinion altogether. Despite divesting of his shares at a considerable premium and gaining a stronghold in the BSCH board, he lamented that the Portuguese government was unable to understand his vision for the erstwhile Champalimaud Group. He keenly felt the loss of BTA and CPP to foreign control. He insisted that this could have been avoided had the government allowed his original plan to materialize.

Certainly, it was the Portuguese government that held and turned the key that undid the lock. From the very beginning, the Portuguese government was highly criticized for its glaring protectionism and parochial approach. But the veto did not speak very well of the Portuguese banks and bankers either. They were perceived as whiners who, because of their inability to get their act together and consolidate into a decent European institution, in the end had to take recourse to government. Government interventionism was shown firstly, in the priming of BCP as an acceptable 'white knight', and later, in the summoning of CGD, Portugal's largest bank, to divide the spoils of the Champalimaud Group together with BSCH. Even the minority shareholders of MC expressed disgust at the government's resorting to a public financial institution as CGD to bail out Champalimaud's interests. These investors knew a better offer could be expected from a private entity such as BCP. BCP may be the only real loser, having been hung to dry by government. It could only hope for better treatment from CGD in the future, if and when CGD finally decides to sell the remnants of MC.

In resolving the deadlock, Pina Moura's diplomatic approach was more effective than Sousa Franco's unrelenting adversarial stance. Portugal was pressed for a quick solution because it was slated to assume EU Presidency in January 2000, and it would indeed be strange if by then it still had cases pending at the Luxembourg Court. The words of the Portuguese President Jorge Sampaio praising the 'strategic vision' of his government reflected its degree of self-satisfaction for the decision.[4] The sovereignty of the Portuguese nation over its economic and financial affairs has been safeguarded and the original BSCH–Champalimaud transaction has been re-engineered to the government's bidding.

Surprisingly, European Competition Commissioner Monti likewise claimed success. After all, the Portuguese government lifted its veto as the European Commission had insisted. That in itself could be taken as an acknowledgement of the Commission's exclusive competence over the consolidation of corporations. The two principles of the free movement of capital and the freedom of establishment within the Union were also preserved. And just in case something in the new deal goes against the EU normatives, the suit in Luxembourg could still follow its course. For practicality's sake, though, the suit could be shelved because the bone of contention, Portugal's veto, has already disappeared.

But has it, really? Is it not bound to resurface, in one form or another, in finance or some other sector, within Portugal or elsewhere in the EU? That rival parties – each protecting its own interests, incompatible with that of others – contend that they have won leaves a lot of ground for scepticism. It is impossible that opposing factions win the same war ... Unless the real problem concerning political sovereignty – the nation state's (Portugal's) or the (European) Union's? – has been wilfully ignored, obviated, side-tracked and bypassed. Which means that there has been no genuine desire for a solution, or that it is a question best left unanswered. So much then for 'Solomonic judgements'...

## NOTES

1. On 17 December 1999, BSCH, with a market capitalization of 43 674 million euros, surpassed Deutsche Bank's 42 900 million euros, and thus became the top bank in the euro zone.
2. What follows are the most recent developments in BSCH's buying spree: on 27 November 1999, the Royal Bank of Scotland, of which BSCH is the largest investor, launched an unsolicited $42.5 billion bid for National Westminster Bank, Britain's third largest. BSCH committed itself to buy £1.2 billion of Royal Bank of Scotland shares to finance the deal. In exchange, BSCH would receive a 6.5 per cent stake in the combined company. Two weeks later, this time in France, Société Générale, in which BSCH holds a 5.1 per cent stake, announced its acquisition of 3.8 per cent of Crédit Lyonnais, thus becoming its biggest stockholder.
3. Compare this optimism with the results of a KPMG study on cross-border mergers. The report examined 107 major deals between 1996 and 1998, interviewing senior managers and comparing share price movements with those of competitors for the first year after the merger. Fifty-three per cent of the deals destroyed value, 30 per cent produced no discernible difference and only 17 per cent added value for the investors. Cultural affinity seems to be the key: mergers between American and British companies were 45 per cent better than the average success rate, while mergers between American and continental European companies were 11 per cent below average.
4. An OECD special report published in October 1999 corroborates Portugal's remarkable economic performance, particularly in the financial sector: 'The transformation of the financial system is likely to have had important spill-over effects on the rest of the economy

and no doubt played a major role in Portugal's good macroeconomic performance of the past few years, leading to participation in EMU'. Certainly, this improvement could have been the result of EU directives concerning interest rate deregulation, liberalization of the regulatory framework, privatization, modernization of monetary policy instruments and the freeing of international capital movements. The report adds that financial reform in Portugal 'has not been accompanied by a boom-bust cycle associated with the deterioration of credit quality and the failure of institutions ... Avoiding such an outcome has been the result of adequate supervision, cautious sequencing, and the pursuit of prudent macroeconomic policies'.

# REFERENCES

Reports from ABC (Madrid), El Mundo (Madrid), El País (Madrid), La Actualidad Económica (Madrid) and The Economist (London).
Leonard, Dick (1998), *Guide to the European Union*, London: The Economist and Profile Books.
Banco Santander Central Hispano (BSCH), http://www.bsch.es
Banco Totta and Açores, http://www.bta.pt
European Union, http://www.europa.eu.int

# 14. 'Green' business practices: why should companies get involved?

## Eleanor O'Higgins and Eamonn J. Harrigan

Corporations are increasingly being called to account for their actions with respect to the physical environment, to champion the realization of 'sustainable development' – the creative reconciliation of present economic growth with the preservation of our planet for future economic growth.

How is a reconciliation between the present exploitation and future conservation of the environment enacted within individual firms? This chapter reports on exploratory research to ascertain the reasons that businesses actively undertake 'green' measures, and the benefits derived from doing so. The stakeholder context is used as a framework.

Business is under pressure from stakeholders to take environmental concerns seriously. In this regard, the main stakeholders and issues centre around legislation, competitive advantage, customers, owners, financiers, employees, environmental pressure groups and the media. The environment itself may also be regarded as a stakeholder (Figure 14.1).

## LEGISLATION

In the free market economy, 'the theory of the commons' provides the justification for environmental legislation – individuals maximize their gains by destroying collectively owned resources such as the environment. This is the 'free-rider' problem – the incentive to pollute if you do not pay for it. Legislation attempts to eliminate the free-rider problem by forcing companies to internalize environmental degradation costs (Velasquez, 1998). On a long-term basis, Gladwin (1999) argues that human life on our planet will deteriorate if business and strategy become detached from the biosphere.

Worldwide, three phases of legislative development are identified in the last 30 years: 1970s – pollution control, 1980s – compliance with legislation, 1990s – prevention.

In Europe, the European Union (EU), is increasingly driving the environmental policies of member states. To date there have been five

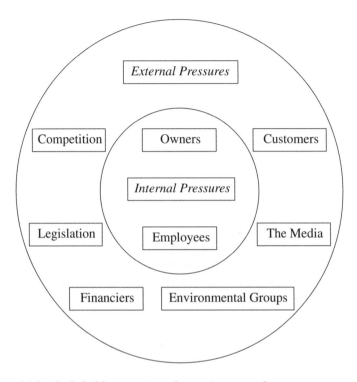

*Figure 14.1   Stakeholder pressures for environmental management*

European Environmental Action Programmes, between 1973 and the present.

The Fifth Programme (1993–2000) is the most proactive. It introduces the idea of 'sustainable development' – meeting the needs of the present generation without compromising the ability of future generations to meet their needs. While recognizing economic growth as necessary to meet people's aspirations for a better lifestyle, competitiveness must be grounded in a proactive stance based on the adoption of cleaner technologies and the development of markets for green products.

This Programme provides two key market-based tools to complement and reinforce legislation:

*Eco-labelling scheme*   This is a market-based instrument to promote purchase of environmentally friendly products. The Eco label is awarded to individual products on the basis of definitions of product groups and related ecological criteria. Ecological criteria for each product group are defined on the basis of a 'cradle to grave' assessment of the environmental impact of the product group and developed on a scientific objective basis, after a comprehensive technical study and full consultation with environment, consumer, and industry experts.

*Eco Management and Audit Scheme (EMAS)*   This is a framework for companies to assess environmental impact and commit to a policy of reduction. It encourages regular published progress reports, and is voluntary at present. However, so far companies find the procedures and reporting requirements of EMAS cumbersome and overly elaborate. Moreover, the responses of important stakeholders to companies taking up EMAS – customers and investors – were lukewarm or indifferent (Steger, 2000). The environmental benefits of EMAS are not superior to those enjoyed by companies following simpler environmental systems, such as ISO 14001. Indeed, ISO 14001 is becoming the de facto international corporate environmental management standard.

In Ireland, as an EU member, the main drivers of environmental legislation are the EU Environmental Action Programmes. In 1994 the government committed itself to a national sustainable development strategy. Noteworthy milestones in Ireland's legislative journey to sustainability include the establishment of the Government Environment Information Service (ENFO) in 1990, the EPA Act of 1992 instituting the Environmental Protection Agency (EPA), publication of Irish Environmental Management System IS 310 by the National Standards Authority of Ireland (NSAI) in 1994 and the adoption of the EU EMAS in 1995.

A menu of initiatives in Ireland, current and proposed, clearly demonstrates the growth in importance of environmental issues in the last ten years. Included are such diverse measures as:

- annual 'Better Environment Awards' for industry;
- ISO 14001 – the international standard for environmental management systems. Approximately 60 organizations have been certified in Ireland;
- eco-labelling – over 200 products have been awarded an Eco label;
- grants for environmental auditing and studies on environmentally superior products;
- the Irish Business and Employers Confederation (IBEC) encourages member companies to achieve environmental excellence alongside an information service to members and a range of consultancy services;
- a national hazardous waste management plan;
- publication of a government policy report on sustainability (Department of the Environment, 1997).

# COMPETITIVE ADVANTAGE

In a link between the notion of competitive advantage and legislation, Rugman and Verbeke (2000) argue that firms may attempt to develop a dynamic capability in dealing with government and regulation, ranging from forestalling or influencing upcoming legislation in their favour, all the way to becoming a 'model' corporation in the eyes of government. For multi-nationals, the challenge is even greater, as they have to develop an internationally transferable green capability.

At the firm level, in an analysis of the relationship between competitiveness and regulation, Porter and van der Linde (1995) have argued that companies should move beyond prevention to innovation that addresses the root causes of pollution, by improving resource productivity to avert wastage in the first place. This approach offers competitive advantage in its own right. However, legislation is still necessary to provoke companies to seek and initiate the innovation that will reduce waste and promote customer value.

When a small company perspective is taken, the necessity for legislation becomes even more pressing. Tilley (2000) showed that the level of eco literacy was very low in a sample of 60 engineering firms in the Leeds, UK area. Their small size often puts them below compliance requirements necessary for larger firms, and they are unlikely to invest in green measures that do not offer an obvious and immediate pay-off.

Similar to Porter and van der Linde, Vasanthakumar (1996) has argued that proper environmental management leads to competitive advantage in areas like design, production, packaging, marketing, labelling and communication.

Reinhardt (1999) outlined five 'green' approaches to competitive advantage: (1) differentiating products, thus commanding higher prices; (2) shaping industry rules that penalize non-green competitors; (3) cutting costs through environmental measures; (4) managing environmental risk; and (5) making systemic changes that redefine competition.

The argument for competitive advantage through environmental management is advocated in the report of The Performance Group (1998), a consortium including Deutsche Bank, Electrolux, Gerling Group of Insurance Companies, ICI, Monsanto, Unilever and Volvo. This group gathered in 1997 to answer the question 'Is there a link between sustainable strategies and shareholder value?' Their conclusion is that, while unable to provide definitive proof of such a link, it appears that there is an indirect link which acts through a multitude of other factors. It is especially through improvements in reputation, increases in innovative capacity, savings through efficiency gains, and improved market advantage through better awareness of stakeholders' and customers' perceptions and needs that increased shareholder value can be realized.

This view is echoed by Escoubes (1999) who declares that environmental strategy can be converted from being a source of costs into a source of market value creation, through systematic stakeholder management. Hard evidence for the benefits of environmental management is put forward in a study by Russo and Fouts (1997) whereby firms with the highest levels of environmental performance are more profitable than those with lesser attention to 'green' matters.

In Ireland, sustainable development offers opportunities to enhance the marketing of key natural resource-based industries and to exploit the fast-growing world market for environmental goods and services. Ireland is ideally placed to reap the rewards of a 'green' approach in areas such as eco tourism and sustainable farming (Sheerin, 1997).

## CUSTOMERS

Customers have become more interested in the environmental pedigree of their purchases. As the level of knowledge of environmental issues expands, it is incumbent on businesses to recognize the risks inherent in selling products which do not meet consumers' green expectations. Even in developing countries, where air and water pollution are rampant, consumers have become more vociferous in insisting that business take responsibility for providing a clean and safe environment (*The Economist*, 2000).

An EPA study on Irish Citizens and the Environment (Faughnan and McCabe, 1998) outlines five thematic areas:

- *Environmental protection and economic growth* Support for environmental protection, when juxtaposed with economic growth, was greater among respondents who were younger, had relatively large personal incomes and higher levels of educational attainment.
- *Environmental knowledge and concerns* Irish results ranked among the lowest of the countries examined.
- *Environmental behaviour* In a number of different areas including sorting of recyclable rubbish; purchasing and eating patterns; attention to packaging and labelling; patterns of car use; and the use of heat and light in the home, no country depicted a high level of environmentally friendly behaviour in all aspects, but Irish respondents were decidedly less active.
- *Environmental policy preferences* Provides data on the willingness of people to 'pay' for environmental protection whether in behavioural or fiscal terms. Overall, Irish respondents were less receptive than their European counterparts to paying for such measures.

- *Role of national government and EU in environmental protection*
  Irish respondents were strongly in favour of a regulatory approach to
  business, with 90 per cent stating the government should pass laws,
  even if these interfere with the rights of business enterprises.

The survey clearly indicates that, while Irish consumers lag behind their
European counterparts on environmental behaviour, the pattern is changing as
consumers become more educated and affluent. Irish businesses will
increasingly have to behave in an environmentally responsible fashion to
satisfy their customers.

## OWNERS AND FINANCIERS

Socially responsible investing appears to be a growing phenomenon.
Companies that are especially environmentally conscious are often granted
special approval by ethical investors (Kreuze, Newell and Newell, 1996).
Studies, mostly from the USA, have found a significant correlation between
the environmental credentials of companies and share performance (Houlder,
1999a). While it can be argued that these companies are better managed and
therefore more profitable, the basic point, however, is that companies
normally only undertake 'green' actions if they make business sense, in a spirit
of enlightened self-interest.

## EMPLOYEES

In many companies, the pressure to adopt sound environmental policies
may come initially from the workforce. Managers, too, often want to have an
environmental record to be proud of. Another consideration is that a business
relies on its employees to carry out its strategies, so employee involvement in
environmental strategy is essential (The Performance Group, 1998).

## ENVIRONMENTAL PRESSURE GROUPS

Pressure groups such as Greenpeace and Friends of the Earth have proved to
be powerful adversaries to business. Recently, such groups have widened their
nets to focus on financial institutions which are judged to have taken
insufficient account of environmental issues in their lending decisions. A
serious worry for banks is the risk of being held responsible for site clean-up
costs if a bank forecloses on a defaulting company (Houlder, 1999b). Latterly,

environmental pressure groups have tried to develop a more constructive relationship with companies to discuss solutions to environmental problems (Houlder, 1999c).

## THE MEDIA

Environmental pressure groups have become expert in their dealings with the media. Businesses are under pressure from the media to behave in an environmentally responsible way, or risk a flood of bad publicity and a damaged reputation. The recognition of the value of a good environmental reputation is inherently a recognition of the requirement to deal properly with the media.

The opposite also applies, environmental good news stories make the papers and businesses can harvest invaluable publicity. Electric cars, high-yielding willow plantations, and 'clean' coal are examples of products which have been given favourable publicity in the financial press (Griffiths, 1999; Henderson and Guild, 1999; Houlder, 1999d; Houlder, 1999e).

## THE ENVIRONMENT AS STAKEHOLDER

It is argued that pressures on business should be taken further. In theory, as a major contributor to economic performance, the environment itself should be deemed a stakeholder by business and society, as well as through the interests of future generations – the concept of 'sustainability' (Velasquez, 1998). In practice, companies could consider establishing an environmental consultative committee or appointing a director with specific environmental responsibility (Jacobs, 1997). While the environment cannot be given a direct financial stake in a company, it is still possible for companies to set aside funds for future generations. The environment as stakeholder perspective has an impact on the traditional economy-environment concept. The idea of 'green' taxes, for resource use and pollution, has gained credence.

## RESEARCH STUDY

### Interview Sample

The sample consisted of 19 companies, eight of which are subsidiaries of foreign MNCs. They were selected on grounds of a proven record in environmental management. This consisted of participation and recognition in one of a number of environmental initiatives sponsored either by the Irish

Department of the Environment or the EU. Generally, these schemes seek to promote environmentally friendly processes in both manufacturing and service companies. Projects are designed to reduce waste, save energy and control pollution. The sectors represented by these companies include pharmaceuticals, chemicals, food processing, printing and a tannery.

The interviewees were the companies' environmental managers, meaning any individual who has environmental management as a substantial part of his or her job responsibilities. The interview route was selected rather than survey methods as the research was exploratory in nature. The interviews can be described as semi-structured. The respondents were presented with a menu of choices for some questions, but also 'options' to give additional other information or comments.

**Interview Design**

The interview was comprised of three broad questions concerning the motivations for environmental management and the benefits accruing.

**Question 1**   Designed to ascertain the reasons for undertaking environmental management. A list of nine possible reasons was presented plus an 'other' option. Respondents were asked to state which, if any, of these reasons apply. The list comprises:

- government incentives;
- compliance with legislation;
- revenue increases;
- cost savings;
- need to ameliorate environmental problems;
- protection of reputation;
- avoidance of liabilities;
- competitive reasons – expectations of customers;
- investor/lender pressure.

**Question 2**   Designed to assess the extent of the benefits realized due to implementing environmental management. A list of four possible benefits is presented plus an 'other' option. Respondents were asked to state which, if any, of the benefits have accrued.

- increased revenue;
- decreased cost;
- improved reputation;
- improved access to finance.

**Question 3**  Designed to ascertain the timing of realization of possible benefits, whether short, medium or long term.

**Question 4**  A closing question, asking for additional comments or observations the respondents might have in the broad area of environmental management, based on their experiences.

## RESULTS

### Question 1   For what reason is the company undertaking active environmental management (Table 14.1a)?

*Table 14.1a   Reasons for undertaking environmental management*

| Alternative | Respondents (percentage) |
|---|---|
| Government incentives | 0 |
| Compliance with legislation | 15 (79%) |
| Revenue increases | 3 (16%) |
| Cost savings | 6 (32%) |
| Eliminate environmental problems | 5 (26%) |
| Protection of reputation | 4 (21%) |
| Avoidance of liabilities | 3 (16%) |
| Competitive reasons – customer expectations | 7 (37%) |
| Investor/lender pressure | 1 (5%) |
| Other | 15 (79%) |

The 'other' option elicited the answers as shown in Tables 14.1b.

*Table 14.1b   Breakdown of 'other' reasons*

| Reason | Respondents (percentage) |
|---|---|
| Corporate policy/pressure from headquarters | 6 (32%) |
| Sales and marketing drivers/multinational customers | 4 (21%) |
| 'Good neighbour' | 4 (21%) |
| Increase efficiency | 1 (5%) |
| Pressure from employees | 1 (5%) |

The main conclusions from the above results can be summarized as:

- Legislation is the primary reason.
- Competitive/customer pressures are also highly important.
- Corporate pressures and MNC customers impact heavily on subsidiaries.
- Cost reductions and revenue increases are of moderate importance.
- Government incentive schemes make little impact.

**Question 2   What, if any, benefits have accrued from the implementation of environmental management (Table 14.2a)?**

*Table 14.2a   Benefits from implementation of environmental management*

| Benefit | Respondents (percentage) |
| --- | --- |
| Increased revenues | 3 (16%) |
| Decreased costs | 10 (53%) |
| Improved reputation | 8 (42%) |
| Increased access to finance | 5 (26%) |
| Other | 15 (79%) |

The 'other' option in Table 1 elicited the following answers:

*Table 14.2b   Breakdown of 'other' benefits*

| Benefits stated | Respondents (percentage) |
| --- | --- |
| Compliance with legislation | 6 (32%) |
| Waste reduction/decreased energy consumption | 5 (26%) |
| Improved management commitment to environmental management and better awareness among staff | 2 (11%) |
| Increased revenues through sales of waste products | 2 (11%) |
| Improved processes, efficiency and better housekeeping | 2 (11%) |
| Reduced environmental impact/ benefits to whole community | 2 (11%) |
| Increased customer satisfaction | 1 (5%) |
| Grant income | 1 (5%) |

The main conclusions from the results of question 2 are:

- Cost reductions through waste reduction and energy efficiency are the main tangible benefits.
- Improved reputation is an important intangible benefit.
- Compliance with legislation is reaffirmed as an important driver.
- Costs may increase in order to comply with legislation.

**Question 3  Are the benefits realizable in the short, medium or long term (Table 14.3)?**

*Table 14.3  Time frame for results of environmental management*

| Time frame | Respondents (percentage) |
| --- | --- |
| Short term | 12 (63%) |
| Medium term | 5 (26%) |
| Long term | 17 (89%) |

Most respondents (89 per cent) view environmental investment as a long-term prospect with returns mainly in the distant future, although more than half also perceive benefits in the short term.

**Question 4  Have you any general comments or observations, based on your experience of environmental management?**

The most appropriate way to present the results in this instance is in bullet point form:

- 'Interest from colleges, schools and County Councils in our waste water treatment system, with several groups coming to visit'.
- 'Used as a basis for environmental benchmarking tools'.
- 'Reduction in waste to landfill, recycling of metal drums, recycling of solvents. Prior to this we disposed of hazardous waste through the UK. Returnable packaging gives benefit to customers'.
- 'Our neighbours are happy. There is a lot of interaction with the local community through sponsorship of school competitions. Therefore, we foster environmental awareness'.
- 'An unusual benefit is that the company has been used as a case study for environmental management; therefore we have good publicity'.
- 'Better reputation combined with more input from employees'.

- 'We have achieved cost savings through rationalizing energy costs. We now reuse coke we used to dispose of'.
- 'It has been positive in relation to our own employees and has given the public a positive perception of the company'.
- 'Disciplines have been imposed and standards set for management'.
- 'Better system of waste collection has meant the surrounding area is tidier'.
- 'To some extent it has heightened awareness (of environmental issues)'.
- 'Waste minimization – both hazardous and non-hazardous waste through reuse. Return to suppliers of empty drums. Composting of organic waste. Energy auditing and resource monitoring have identified savings'.
- 'Our neighbours are happier to have us around. We are now highly regarded in the locality'.
- 'Very important for our customers, most of whom are multinationals'.

Generally, these comments capture some of the key benefits of implementing environmental management.

- waste minimization and energy savings;
- improved reputation;
- better management;
- more satisfied customers;
- happier neighbours.

While most respondents focused on benefits, three companies clearly made the point that environmental management may incur more costs than tangible benefits. Their comments illustrate the difficulty of accurately quantifying the costs and benefits of environmental management:

- 'IPC has led to cost increases, but not decreases. It involves a lot of monitoring. The costs associated may be larger than the benefits'.
- 'Not much quantifiable benefit, but the experience has been valuable'.
- 'There has been a significant capital investment. However this may have been done irrespective of the needs of environmental management'.

## DISCUSSION

Compliance with legislation is the primary reason for undertaking environmental management. The importance of legislation confirms the assertion by Brennan (1997) that this is the single most important driver of environmentally friendly industry behaviour.

Competitive reasons are ranked highly by 58 per cent (11) of respondents when the detailed 'other' responses are analysed and included. These companies cite sales and marketing drivers and particular mention is made of the importance of multinational customers. This finding is consistent with a constant contention in the literature that greenness is becoming a potent strategic marketing weapon.

Among the perceived benefits, improved reputation is noted as important by 42 per cent (8) of respondents. This contrasts markedly with question 1 in which only 21 per cent (4) of the respondents specified 'protection of reputation' as a reason for undertaking environmental management. This suggests that the companies surveyed may be more concerned with building a reputation for positive competitive reasons, as the emphasis is on improvement rather than protection.

The protection of reputation and avoidance of liabilities were given as reasons by 21 per cent and 16 per cent respectively. Given that this survey is conducted among companies noted for a good environmental record, the relative unconcern for reputational liabilities may indicate a low expectation of claims and fines. Also, it may indicate a less-developed judicial system in Ireland the area of environmental law. This finding complies with the assertion in the Faughnan and McCabe (1998) study that overall, Irish respondents perform relatively poorly in most domains when it comes to 'greenness', particularly in relation to knowledge of environmental issues, environmentally sensitive consumer behaviours and resistance to fiscal measures to tackle environmental problems.

Cost savings and efficiency increases also feature in the literature as prominent reasons for environmental management (Vasanthakumar, 1996). This survey indicates that 37 per cent (7) (including the analysis of 'other') Irish companies that agree, appears low when compared to the importance attached to this reason in the literature. However, it turns out decreased costs are noted by 53 per cent (10) respondents as a major benefit. The cost reductions are gained through improved management of waste and energy consumption. These savings are likely to be the result of simple changes, such as improved housekeeping. Nonetheless they are essential to give the necessary financial reinforcement to the environmental management effort.

An overall need to ameliorate environmental problems was considered important by only 26 per cent (5) of companies surveyed. This confirms that economic considerations take precedence, and that goodwill towards the environment is in itself not sufficient to ensure proper environmental management. Possible revenue increases for 'green' management are cited by only 16 per cent (3) companies as relevant. This indicates that market-based instruments, such as the Eco label scheme, which are intended to act in concert with legislation, are not viewed by these companies as important. It certainly appears that grants are not sufficient to encourage companies to pursue active environmental management.

The lack of importance attached to government incentives, with no companies choosing this alternative, has important implications for government policy in this area. If legislation can be viewed as the stick and incentives the carrot, it seems that the stick is a much more effective tool of government strategy for the environment. The carrot, as currently constituted in the form of grant aid is useful for the publicity generated, but does not alone appear to be a sufficient reason for companies to actively manage the environment. The evidence of this study supports the Porter and van der Linde (1995) contention that externally imposed regulation is necessary to push companies to take up environmentally friendly practices. However, in most cases, once the companies have complied, they discover the strategic and economic benefits that accrue, and thereby the process should become self-reinforcing.

There appears to be little credence given to the notion that investor/lender pressure is an important factor in influencing environmental management as only one of the respondents cited this reason, in contrast to the assertion by Kreuze, Newell and Newell (1996).

The environmental policy of the subsidiaries of multinationals is driven by their parent companies, and their standards are set by legislation and norms in the parent country. This is consistent with the findings of Rugman and Verbeke (2000), where four of their six companies studied transferred their environmental practices to their international subsidiaries. Thus, pressure from business network partners outside Ireland may act as an increasing catalyst for 'green' management in a small open economy, highly dependent on foreign direct investment, as is Ireland.

Four respondents cite the necessity to be a 'good neighbour' or a 'good citizen'. This is particularly relevant when the plants are situated in rural communities. A spin-off benefit is integration of business and community institutions.

Employees do not appear to have a major effect on environmental management although one service company noted that the initial move towards being 'greener' came from staff pressure, motivated by knowledge that customers expected the establishment to be more environmentally friendly than it actually was at the time.

Most respondents (89 per cent) view environmental investment as a long-term prospect with returns mainly in the distant future. This has important implications for the financial planning of capital expenditure decisions. If only short- and medium-term cash flows are taken into account in projections and if high discount rates are used, then environmental investments which pay off only in later years will be disadvantaged. Thus, there is a discrepancy when most respondents viewed environmental management as a long-term investment and a short-term stance is taken by decision makers. This is compounded by problems of quantification of environmental benefits, whether short, medium or long term.

The differential impact of various stakeholders is summarized in Figure 14.2.

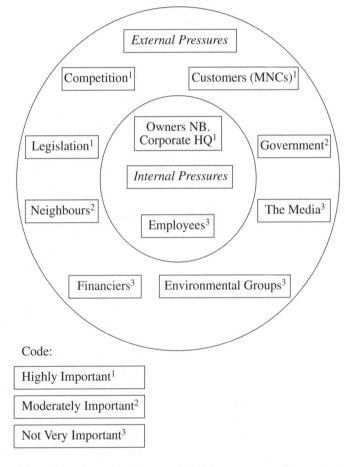

*Figure 14.2   Intensity of various stakeholder pressures for environmental management*

In conclusion, while legislation and competition constitute strong initial pressures for environmental management, companies engaging in green practices realize other benefits, once they get involved, especially in the area of cost savings and improved reputation. The latter is seen as building long-term competitiveness. In Ireland, foreign trading partners and MNC headquarters also provoke environmental management. The study results suggest which levers are effective in encouraging the initial introduction of sustainable business practices, and subsequently, which ones reinforce their continuation for the sake of enlightened self-interest.

## REFERENCES

Brennan, F. (1997), *Green and Competitive: Environmental Management - The Proactive Approach*, Dublin, Ireland: MBA Thesis, University College Dublin.

Department of the Environment (1997), *Sustainable Development: A Strategy for Ireland*, Dublin, Ireland: Government Publications Office.

*Economist* (2000), 'How green is your market?', January 8, 76.

Escoubes, F. (1999), 'A framework for managing environmental strategy', *Business Strategy Review*, **10**(2), 61-66.

Faughnan, P. and B. McCabe (1998), 'Irish citizens and the environment: A cross national study of environmental attitudes, perceptions and behaviors', *Environmental Protection Agency Desk Study Report No. 2*.

Gladwin, T.N. (1999), 'A call for sustainable development', *FT Mastering Strategy*, Part 12 (13 December), 2-4.

Griffiths, J. (1999), 'The clean, mean electric machine', *Financial Times*, March 29.

Henderson, C. and A. Guild (1999), 'New generation that comes out of the Woodwork', *Financial Times*, March 9.

Houlder, V. (1999a), 'Ecological wake-up call for fund managers', *Financial Times*, January 25.

Houlder, V. (1999b), 'Ecowarriors make peace', *Financial Times*, April 13.

Houlder, V. (1999c), 'Green guns turn on the financiers', *Financial Times*, February 9.

Houlder, V. (1999d), 'Clean coal producers to target £30bn exports', *Financial Times*, April 19.

Houlder, V. (1999e), 'Green idea ready to take root at school', *Financial Times*, February 1.

Jacobs, M. (1997), 'The environment as stakeholder', *Business Strategy Review*, **8**(2), pp. 25-28.

Kreuze, J., G. Newell and S. Newell (1996), 'What companies are reporting', *Management Accounting (USA)*, **78**, 1, pp. 37-42.

Performance Group (1998), *Sustainable Strategies for Value Creation*.

Porter, M.E. and C. van der Linde (1995), Green and competitive: Ending the stalemate', *Harvard Business Review*, September-October, 120-134.

Reinhardt, F.L. (1999), 'Bringing the environment down to earth', *Harvard Business Review*, July-August, 149-157.

Rugman, A.M. and A. Verbeke (2000), Six cases of corporate strategic responses to environmental regulation', *European Management Journal*, **18**(4), 377-385.

Russo, M. and P. Fouts (1997), 'A resource based perspective on corporate environmental performance and profitability', *Academy of Management Journal*, **40**(3), 534–559.

Sheerin, J. (1997), *Successful Environmental Management*, Sligo, Ireland: Enviro Eire.

Steger, U. (2000), 'Environmental management systems: Empirical evidence and further perspectives', *European Management Journal*, **18**(1), 23–37.

Tilley, F. (2000), 'Small firm environmental ethics: How deep do they go?', *Business Ethics: A European Review*, **9**(1), 31–41.

Vasanthakumar, B.V. (1996), *The Green Corporation: The Next Competitive Advantage*, Westport Connecticut, USA: Quorum Books, Greenwood Publishing Group, Inc.

Velasquez, M.G. (1998), *Business Ethics - Concepts and Cases* (4th edn), Upper Saddle River, New Jersey, USA: Prentice Hall.

# 15. Corporate ethics and social responsibility: principles and practice at Siemens AG

## Gerhard Hütter

## 1 INTRODUCTION: BRIEF PROFILE OF SIEMENS

A brief profile of Siemens is shown in Box 15.1.

---

### BOX 15.1  BRIEF PROFILE OF SIEMENS

- Founded in 1847.
- Comprehensive product range – from mobile phones to power plants. Business segments: Information and Communications, Energy, Automation and Control, Transportation, Health Care, Components, Lighting, Financial Services.
- Net sales approaching DM135 billion.
- Operates in approximately 190 countries.
- 570 000 shareholders.
- More than 440 000 employees, some 190 000 in Germany.

---

## 2 CORPORATE CULTURE AND SELF-UNDERSTANDING OF SIEMENS

Siemens' corporate culture is formed by the

### 2.1  Values of Company Founder, Werner von Siemens

as recorded in numerous personal letters and written statements: *pioneering spirit, technological progress, financial success and social responsibility.* These values, which have dominated the company throughout its history, were clearly reaffirmed in 1997 when the new Corporate Principles were drawn up; and by the

### 2.2   Core Products and Services of Siemens

As early as the middle of the nineteenth century, Europe's national markets were already too limited for the company's early activities in the communications (telegraphy) and power generation spheres. This explains why Siemens was an international company from its inception, maintaining branch offices in England and Russia and implementing international projects just a few years after the company was founded.

Both areas of business activity required long-term commitment and a continuous presence in various national economies. Today, Siemens is active in some 190 countries and can look back on a history of more than 100 years in many of these countries.

Electrical engineering and its applications have always had a marked effect on society as agents of change and innovation, and Werner von Siemens was aware of this dynamic effect and its social consequences. Today, too, Siemens' business segments – Information and Communications, Automation and Control, Power, Transportation, Medical, Lighting, Components and Financial Services – are key fields shaping modern societies and exhibit tremendous continued dynamism.

As a provider of infrastructure, for a long time Siemens was close to political institutions, with the state being the main contractor in the communications, transportation and energy sectors in many countries until just a few years ago. This is one reason Siemens' corporate culture has a marked sociopolitical orientation.

## 3   ETHICAL STANDARDS IN BUSINESS AND AT THE COMPANY

In developed societies, the economy is subject to many binding standards and regulations. Under the system of business and corporate ethics at Siemens, Box 15.2 illustrates the categories of standards that apply –

---

### BOX 15.2   CATEGORIES OF STANDARDS AT SIEMENS

- State-imposed standards.
- Non-state regulations.
- Corporate ethics: values, principles, guidelines, rules of conduct.
- Personal values and individual morals.

---

### 3.1 State-imposed Standards

In concrete terms, government-imposed standards are laws and ordinances that touch on virtually all areas of corporate activity, setting norms, regulating processes and establishing relationships. These include industrial law, contract law, antitrust law, environmental legislation, technical standards, safety standards, liability laws and extensive approval procedures for investments.

All of these standards and regulations embody ethical concepts, for instance, the nature of the work process, production of goods or relationship between manufacturer and customer. The organization of the economy is a social task, a central task of the state.

In practice, international and global companies encounter a multitude of difficulties in observing state standards and regulations. Companies are confronted with supranational claims and standards (from such bodies as the EU, UN, OECD and WTO), as well as national, regional and municipal laws and ordinances which are by no means always consistent and free of contradictions. Moreover, companies operate within economic systems that exhibit varying degrees of regulation and – depending on the culture in question – different value sets and, accordingly, different ideas about what constitutes ethical conduct in the context of economic activity.

### 3.2 Non-state Regulations

After state legislation, the second level of standards that affects the business world is non-state regulations, such as collective agreements, industry standards, quality and safety standards and agreements with non-governmental organizations (NGOs).

Within an industry, companies set standards through contractual agreements, for instance, by voluntarily entering into a joint agreement to exceed state standards for environmental protection. While collective agreements are probably the most widespread provisions of this nature, industry-wide environmental regulations and safety standards are also very important.

### 3.3 Corporate Ethics: Values, Principles, Guidelines and Rules for Conduct

The third level is the rules for conduct, both internally for employees, and externally for dealing with customers, business partners and the general public, which we feel all companies must define.

A company has to communicate its guiding principles and perception of itself clearly and unambiguously. General social standards and expectations for behaviour are set forth in detail in corporate principles and mandatory management and behaviour principles for the company's area of responsibility.

Employees have a right to know what company, what values and what aims they are working for. This is the cornerstone of all motivation and commitment. A broad consensus regarding the values and aims of the company is the basis for decentralized, business- and customer-oriented corporate leadership that empowers employees and managers alike to make decisions.

Corporate principles or corporate ethics continue the development of standards and organizational structures at the company, shaping a company's perception of itself and its corporate culture and making them tools for meeting challenges or rising to the occasion when outstanding efforts are required.

For their part, society, politicians and the general public want to be able to judge a company's behaviour, particularly in situations where it is not or cannot be controlled, for example, in new fields of business or technologies where legal regulations are not yet in place (such as genetic engineering or legal protection on the Internet). Society expects companies to be reliable in the sense of general ethical standards – a prerequisite for that valuable entity *trust* and a sustained positive *image*. Within the framework of a communication society, *moral* behaviour has become a competitive factor.

Fundamental statements on corporate ethics – corporate principles, corporate values, or principles for behaviour – give companies considerable leeway to define themselves for the general public and in their markets in the competitive arena, and companies must exploit this scope. It is not enough to observe simply the minimum legal requirements. A company can portray itself as a moral 'pioneer' by voluntarily committing itself to fulfil new standards.

### 3.4   Personal Values and Morals of Employees and Managers

The personal values and individual morals of employees are the fourth level of standard and the basis for implementing all the other standards and regulations. Every organization and every company proceeds on the assumption that people have an internalized set of values and morals which are passed on in a social context and have an effect on society. Without this assumption, life in society or the management of a company would be inconceivable. Since it is so natural and self-evident, the key importance of *individual* values and *personal* morals for the economy is generally underestimated, except when problems, unacceptable conduct or serious conflicts arise.

Individual employees orient their behaviour according to very personal values, their experience, interests and degree of identification with the company. Levels of commitment to one's profession, business and company vary, with employees exhibiting varying degrees of willingness to assume responsibility. However, frequently the entire company must bear the consequences of inappropriate conduct on the part of an individual. Only individuals can ultimately bear moral responsibility, and since they make decisions by weighing up what is important, companies have to consciously count on the personal ethics and conscience of each and every employee.

On the other hand, the plethora of laws, standards, ordinances and agreements relating to economic activity clearly demonstrates the importance of the ethical aspect of the basic order. In a free society with a market economy, all economic activity is dependent on the individual's moral conduct and a functioning basic order, that is to say, accepted 'institutional' ethics. This means that companies must:

- continually address the matter of their employees' and managers' personal values, motivation and individual morals; and
- actively participate as corporate citizens in the political process of shaping the political and social order.

## 4   ETHICAL STANDARDS AND IMPLEMENTATION AT SIEMENS

Corporate ethics at Siemens - that is, the mandatory statements and standards - cannot be reduced simply to the Corporate Principles or a condensed mission statement. In practice, our values, obligations and target behaviour are shaped, reflected and implemented at the levels shown in Box 15.3.

---

### BOX 15.3   SIEMENS' LEVELS OF ETHICAL STANDARDS AND IMPLEMENTATION

- The Corporate Principles.
- Rules of business conduct for Siemens' employees.
- Guidelines and circulars (such as the company's environmental guidelines).
- Management tools and training.
- Communication, sociopolitical seminars.

---

### 4.1   The Corporate Principles

Siemens' new Corporate Principles, the umbrella for all value statements at the company worldwide, were drawn up as part of the Siemens Identity project conducted in preparation for the company's 150th anniversary in 1997. Against the backdrop of the deep and lasting changes being wrought at the company by the globalization of the economy, project members had the task of working out the implicit core values of Siemens' corporate culture and portraying Siemens' identity in such a way as to make it fertile ground for the company's continued development.

The theory: the larger a company is, the more globally it acts and the more decentralized its leadership must be, the more important common set of values is for an outstanding culture of achievement and the requisite commitment on the part of its employees. An extensive survey among employees and managers was conducted to obtain answers to the following questions:

- What values do Siemens' employees hold? What motivates them?
- Are there values shared by all employees, regardless of function, responsibility, group, region, nationality and culture?
- Which characteristic values or features do employees attribute to Siemens?
- What is their actual experience at their workplace?

Survey participants included 2500 managers and 5600 employees from 11 countries and all levels of responsibility. Seven value profiles emerged with surprising clarity from the results, sets of values which represent a particular form of behaviour and were specified by employees more than other values. It was on the basis of these profiles that the seven Corporate Principles were formulated.

What is important about the new principles?

- They are much more legitimate than an arbitrarily formulated statement, since they represent employees' values.
- They bring together the positive values of employees and of the company as the core of the company's identity and culture, and support corporate strategy.
- They make implicit values explicit, and therefore communicable and practicable.

These seven Corporate Principles are illustrated in Figure 15.1 and Box 15.4, respectively.

We see the Corporate Principles not as a complete work but as a work in progress, a crystallization point and common point of reference that promotes the active, conscious interplay between personal values and the company's principles.

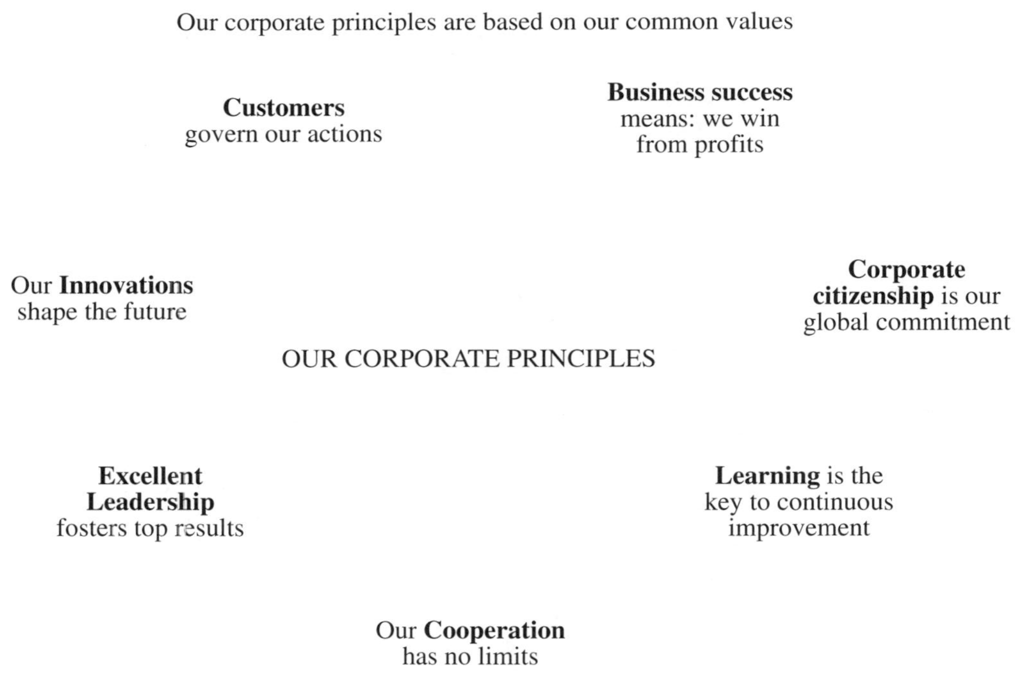

Our corporate principles are based on our common values

**Business success**
means: we win
from profits

**Corporate
citizenship** is our
global commitment

**Customers**
govern our actions

OUR CORPORATE PRINCIPLES

**Learning** is the
key to continuous
improvement

Our **Innovations**
shape the future

**Excellent
Leadership**
fosters top results

Our **Cooperation**
has no limits

*Figure 15.1   Siemens' Corporate Principles*

## BOX 15.4   THE SEVEN CORPORATE PRINCIPLES OF SIEMENS

**Customers** govern our actions

Our top priority is to provide outstanding value to our customers, since ultimately our success depends on their satisfaction. We provide solutions that enable our customers to achieve their objectives faster, more easily and more efficiently.

Our **Innovations** shape the future

We put new ideas to work, creating innovative products and services to benefit our customers. We encourage experimentation and imagination. Our creativity and willingness to take risks enable us to build an environment in which promising ideas can be quickly turned into successful solutions. We also promote and draw on others' ideas.

**Business success** means: we win from profits

International competition is our benchmark. We work to achieve profits while striving for industry leadership and a steady increase in economic value added. This gives us the entrepreneurial freedom we need and makes us a trusted partner. To ensure financial success, we optimize time, quality and cost in all our work.

**Excellent leadership** fosters top results

Our managers set clear, ambitious and inspiring goals. We always strive to surpass ourselves. If we don't, others will. By leading on the basis of trust, we empower our people to make their own decisions. We demonstrate courage and conviction when introducing necessary changes. Our managers serve as role models in everything they do.

**Learning** is the key to continuous improvement

We always measure ourselves against the world's best. Each of us strives to learn continuously. We welcome and offer open feedback and also learn from our mistakes. We are quicker than others at identifying new opportunities and adapting our solutions, organization and our behaviour accordingly. We are building an international network of knowledge in which everyone gives and takes.

Our **Cooperation** has no limits

We are a global company and draw on our worldwide capabilities. This makes us the best team on the playing field. All our thoughts and actions stem from a sense of responsibility when it comes to achieving our common goal. Our cooperation is characterized by trust, personal integrity, mutual respect and open communication.

**Corporate citizenship** is our global commitment

Our knowledge and our solutions help create a better world. We are committed to protecting our environment. We are a respected corporate citizen in all countries in which we do business. We safeguard our people's future through training and continuing education. Integrity guides our conduct towards business partners, colleagues, shareholders and the general public. Cultural differences enrich our organization.

## 4.2   Rules of Conduct for Siemens' Employees

The second level of ethical statements, also valid throughout the company, relates directly to the most important legal foundations in most countries and in international business transactions. *The Rules of Conduct for Siemens' Employees* (Box 15.5) are more than merely minimal behavioural standards

## BOX 15.5   LETTER OF RULES OF CONDUCT FOR SIEMENS' EMPLOYEES

ZV                                    Munich W, 31st August 1998

Distribution:
Chairmen of the Supervisory and Managing Boards; Executive Vice Presidents, Senior Vice Presidents; Group Executive Management, Vice Presidents; Management of Corporate Offices, Services; Management of Regional Companies, Representative Offices; Siemens Companies; Siemens Corporation; Position levels 1-4; Central Works Council; Human Resources

**Rules of conduct for Siemens' employees**

Siemens' employees around the world work for the benefit of the company as an integrated part of the local economy, and with attention to and respect for the cultural and social values in each country.

As a globally active company we have prepared a set of international guidelines governing the conduct of employees that are valid across all borders.

These guidelines are consistent with our new corporate principles and also help to impress upon our customers and the general public our resolve always to be honest and fair, and to abide by the law.

We ask you personally to ensure in your own behavior and that of the employees within your area of responsibility that these principles of conduct are strictly adhered to in business relations.

Should any questions arise, please address these either to your human resources department or to the legal department of your group or region.

Encl.

sgd. v. Pierer          sgd. Pribilla

that we take for granted. The important point is that the company – in a clear and binding form – demands the consistent observance of certain standards in all countries where it does business, even though the legal status and practice of these ethical standards varies from country to country. The *Rules of Conduct for Siemens' Employees* (Box 15.6) must be signed by managers and are part of the employment contract.

## BOX 15.6    RULES OF CONDUCT FOR SIEMENS' EMPLOYEES

Siemens' employees around the world work for the benefit of the company as an integrated part of the local economy and with attention to and respect for the cultural and social values in each country. The following rules of conduct apply to all employees throughout the world.

1.  Employees shall obey the laws and regulations of the legal systems within which they are acting.

2.  Employees should be concerned with the good reputation of Siemens in each country. In all aspects of performing their jobs, they are to focus on maintaining the good reputation of, and respect for, the company.

3.  Employees are to act honestly, fairly and with integrity towards other employees, the company and business partners.

4.  Employees may not discriminate, especially with regard to race, religion, age, or sex. Sexual harassment is forbidden.

5.  Employees are to observe the rules of fair and open competition.

6.  Employees may not misuse their company positions. In particular, employees are not to take, allow others to take, or give to third parties any unauthorized benefits.

7.  Employees are to protect the tangible and intangible assets of the company. The facilities and equipment of the company may be used only for business purposes. All data, documents and records are to be properly and accurately stated and recorded truthfully.

8.  Employees may not use or transfer proprietary information available at the company without proper authorization. Improper use of insider knowledge is prohibited. Confidential data is to be protected.

9.  Employees are to observe the applicable security and safety regulations.

10. Employees are not to conduct outside business activities or have outside business interests which could be detrimental to their job performance for the company or to their loyalty to the company.

Please address any questions or problems which may arise in connection with the rules of conduct to the respective Siemens Group Compliance Officer or to the Legal Department.

### 4.3   Guidelines and Circulars

Internal guidelines and circulars from the Corporate Management and Super-visory Board or Central Offices also have a normative function. Here the content and extent of the regulations can differ greatly: circulars define a particular form of behaviour for the whole company, the business segments, regions or countries, for particular subjects or areas of work in order to comply with or implement legal standards and/or guarantee the functions of the company.

*Examples*   Environmental protection, data protection, technical and work security, social security, internal reporting and so on.

Circulars are thus above all the company's means of setting standards in response to the requirements of the moment. They can be occasioned by changes in the law, by new technical or scientific findings or by changes in social values.

Environmental protection is particularly important here because of its high priority as a social issue and its significance for the company. Siemens has therefore also a special *Environmental Protection Principles and Technical Safety* office responsible for issuing environmental principles (Box 15.7) and detailed guidelines (Box 15.8) and implementation regulations, which are also internationally binding.

---

### BOX 15.7   SIEMENS' ENVIRONMENTAL PRINCIPLES

**Environmental Mission Statement**

Our knowledge and our solutions are helping to create a better world. We have a responsibility to the wider community and we are committed to environmental protection.

In our global operations, featuring a great diversity of processes, products and services, our company is concerned with sustaining the natural resources essential to life. We view the economy, environmental protection and social responsibility as three key factors carrying equal weight in a liberal world market.

We support the dissemination of knowledge needed for sustainable development through the transfer of knowledge in the fields of management and technology, wherever we operate as a company. For us, sustainable development in environmental protection means careful use of natural resources, which is why we assess possible environmental impacts in the early stages of product and process development. It is our aim to avoid pollution altogether or to reduce it to a minimum, above and beyond statutory requirements.

sgd.

Dr. Heinrich v. Pierer
President and Chief Executive Officer Siemens AG

Dr. Edward G. Krubasik
Member of the Managing Board Siemens AG,
responsible for Environmental Protection and Technical Safety

## BOX 15.8   SIEMENS' DETAILED GUIDELINES

**Guidelines**

**Corporate Responsibility**

The environmental policy of the company is based on its responsibility to humans and to the environment. The purpose of environmental protection and technical safety is to avoid hazards and to minimize risks.

**Guidelines**

The following guidelines form the basis for implementing environmental policy in the company:

- We work continuously toward reducing the burden on the environment, toward minimizing associated risks and toward lowering the use of energy and resources, above and beyond the legal requirements.
- We take appropriate precautions to avoid environmental hazards and to prevent damage to the environment.
- Potential impact on the environment is assessed and incorporated in product and process planning at the earliest possible stage.
- By applying appropriate management, we ensure that our environmental policy is implemented effectively. The technical

and organizational procedures required to do this are monitored regularly and constantly further developed.

- Each employee is required to act in an environmentally conscious manner. It is the constant duty of management to increase and encourage awareness of responsibility at all levels.
- We work with our business partners to promote conformity with similar objectives and we work in a spirit of cooperation with the relevant authorities.
- We inform the public of the impact on the environment caused by the company and our activities related to the environment. We supply our customers with information on ways to minimize any potentially adverse environmental impacts of our products.

The duties arising from these guidelines must be performed throughout the company as an integral part of corporate policy. This applies to each aspect, from purchasing and development, design and production to sales and service.

Environmental protection and technical safety are the concerns of every employee in the company. Compliance with legal requirements is an absolute priority. Our efforts to avoid pollution or to reduce it to a minimum extend beyond statutory requirements, however. One of the functions of management is to create the conditions where due consideration is given to personal safety and environmental protection in every area of activity.

### 4.4   Leadership and Communications

The above values, standards and behavioural goals do not exist in a vacuum but are systematically anchored in personnel management instruments which Siemens has revised completely in recent years. The value statements of the Corporate Principles, for example, are also brought in at management level in the EFA dialogue (employee assessment) and the management dialogue (between employee and manager on management performance). The standardized employee survey that is conducted at regular intervals is also based on the Corporate Principles. Here the employees state the extent to which they think the goals and requirements of the Corporate Principles are being met. By linking the behavioural goals with the instruments of personnel management, concrete results can be achieved which can be checked and measured.

*Implementation of the Corporate Principles* Continuous communication of the core values of the Siemens culture is essential if they are to have a real and lasting effect on the day-to-day workings of the company. This is initially achieved with brochures, fliers and posters, workshops and projects, but in the longer term with the instruments of internal communications, in particular the employee magazine *Siemens World* and the management publication *News and Views*, but increasingly also via the Siemens intranet.

The Corporate Principles and behavioural regulations are integrated into the various stages of management training and also feature in the *Sociopolitical Seminars*.

## 5  SOCIAL RESPONSIBILITY: EXAMPLES OF PRACTICE

### 5.1  Siemens' Social Commitment

Companies automatically become more 'political' in the sense of 'active involvement as citizens'. Active commitment and constructive contributions are expected to an increasing extent where state institutions have been forced for financial reasons to cut back, or have lost certain regulatory functions because of the pace of change.

Through its decentral structure and global presence alone, Siemens' social commitment has taken on a multitude of forms, as this function is being implemented both centrally and by the regions and locations. There are nevertheless clear priorities, subjects and projects to which Siemens traditionally feels committed. These include the following:

- *Support for education and training* continuous cooperation with schools, universities and other educational institutions; projects, internships, case studies of companies and competitions with students and teachers, workshops with young multipliers. In Germany alone Siemens works with 130 partner schools, among them over 30 which bear the name of Siemens. Current main topics are innovation and technology, multimedia and environmental protection.
- *The 'Youth and Knowledge' advancement programme* This programme, initiated on the occasion of the company's 150th anniversary in 1997, consists of educational projects in European schools on the subjects of technology and economics, scholarships for students from Eastern Europe and Asia to take master's degrees at German universities and colleges, doctoral and research scholarships including prizes for work of outstanding excellence and support for places of higher education all over the world.

A better understanding of the next generation in many countries, the international 'scientific community' of tomorrow, is the goal of this programme, in which a total of approximately DM50 million is being invested.

- *Cultural promotion* is an established tradition at Siemens. Three foundations promote study of the sciences, art and modern music. The Ernst-von-Siemens Foundation awards a substantial prize for music.

   Siemens AG has in addition introduced its own programme for arts projects, which does not simply passively support such projects but encourages and promotes new productions. The Siemens Cultural Programme develops ideas of its own, focusing on modern art and its introduction to the public.

- Support of employees who are standing for *public office* or already occupy such a position. Flexible regulations make it possible for them to combine work and public office. Siemens itself of course observes strict political neutrality.

- *Donations*  In the last fiscal year Siemens AG donated DM16.4 million, of which DM4.7 million went to support research, technology and natural sciences (places of higher education) and DM11.7 million was donated for a wide spectrum of cultural, educational or caritative purposes.

These are only a few examples of Siemens' social commitments worldwide.

### 5.2   Public–Private Partnership

At the end of section 3, it was mentioned that companies should participate politically as corporate citizens in the process of shaping the political and social order. We have been doing this in many ways at the point where politics and business coincide, so far mainly in an advisory capacity.

   In the future, cooperation between companies and public bodies – public–private partnerships – will become increasingly important. Work will be distributed in binding partner networks where each side contributes its specific skills and strengths. Examples of this type of cooperation are the design, organization and implementation of occupational training, in particular with respect to new training courses. Or cooperation in university research, concentrating on the generation of knowledge and its successful marketing and evaluation.

### 5.3   Sociopolitical Seminars for Management Personnel

The *Sociopolitical Seminars* give employees and management personnel the opportunity to reflect on social questions in the context of global business and Siemens' company goals. Information provided by speakers from inside and outside the company, role play and subsequent discussions make the participants aware of the far-reaching nature of particular social issues and the communication requirements and ethical aspects of their own business activities.

## 6   CONCLUSION

The central concept of Siemens' Corporate Principles, management ethics and corporate culture is *responsibility*. It is an overall responsibility: towards the company, the environment and society. Siemens trusts each employee to be responsible, and deliberately avoids hampering individual decision-making by too many regulations.

Management personnel in particular must be allowed scope for the decisions they have to make under a very wide variety of circumstances. We cannot relieve them of their personal responsibility, however detailed our standards and rules for behaviour may be.

For this reason Siemens attaches great importance to the personal development of our colleagues and management personnel, to their knowledge and insight and to an ethically rational understanding of business and society. Supported by the quality of our Internal Communications, Continuing Education and Management Training, and an extensive dialogue with our social environment, these goals have clear priority over fixed rules, formal routines and controls.

The concept of responsibility would however be worthless, because it would be too vague, if it was not seen within the framework of the values to which Siemens is committed, the Corporate Principles, which provide the context for the achievement of the company's goals.

# 16. Cultural differences of values-driven management: the value-management programmes of the General Electric Company and Siemens AG*

## Eberhard Schnebel

## 1  INTRODUCTION

The managerial focus on ethics is both founded on cultural roots and related to the organizational structure of the company. This is the initial position for companies like General Electric Company, USA (GE) or Siemens AG, Germany (SIEMENS) working with top-down value management systems. Both companies implement management tools which guarantee the communication of the corporate principles as well as the consideration and integration of individual preferences. There is, however, a fundamental distinction in the understanding of ethics that is related to a different interpretation of guidelines and principles in the working processes. There are thus specific differences in the way they deal with values. Different interactions due to either informal or instrumental approaches determine the prevailing character of their corporate activities to achieve a management driven by ethical values.

The following case study refers to the processes of value management in GE and SIEMENS. Specific differences and characteristics between GE and SIEMENS are clearly related to their different organizational, traditional and cultural background. GE implemented corporate values to determine employees' behaviour and managerial cooperation in the company and to ensure the compliance with rules and instructions. Value-communication in SIEMENS however is an expression of corporate culture to create and retain a 'common spirit'. Both styles show a significant personal notion of responsibility next to values-based target criteria for business activities in the particular management systems.

*The helpful assistance of General Electric Company and Siemens AG is gratefully acknowledged.

# 2   MANAGEMENT OF VALUES IN GE

## 2.1   Main Interest: Management of Core Business Ideas and Preferred Behaviour

GEC, one of the world's biggest players in electronic and technology products, is an outstanding example for the interlock of economic considerations, ethical systems and sound organizational rules in management. GE likes to define a management system beyond cultural and individual differences that integrates values-driven aspects to increase corporate success. Since Jack Welsh took the job as Chief Executive Officer (CEO) in 1981 GE developed a unique value management programme to optimize and to empower the cooperation and collaboration of the GE managers. They spread the basic values they wanted to take seriously in all conferences and to all employees. The basic task of this corporate value management system is to improve the success of the company's businesses inside GE and to avoid complications with ethical behaviour in the international context.

## 2.2   The Implementation Process

The first step was to define the fundamental operating behaviour and responsibilities the executive board determined as the most important factors for the success of the company in a fast-changing business world. Then GE developed a corporate value system, and adjusted the goals to the demands of these values (Figure 16.1). More and more the values 'evolved from philosophical, "soft" concepts into behaviors that deliver hard results, and they are the reason for both today's success and the enomous potential we see for tomorrow' (GE, 1995).

GE first produced a Business Strategy, which is based on the guideline 'Be No. 1 or No. 2 in your global business, or fix, sell or close' and on four basic principles: speed, simplicity, self-confidence, and integrity (GE, 1995; GE, 1996). These principles had been worked out to be the company values, published in the 1999 GE Annual Report (1999a) and in the Internet Homepage of GE (Box 16.1)

## 2.3   Commitment of Integrity

The very core of the value management system is the Commitment to Integrity, a document designed to mediate the ethical behaviour expected from all employees and to support the credibility of the value management system. It is innovative by putting rules and regulations into action for the goal of creating economic value and acting by ethical principles (Box 16.2 and Wolff,

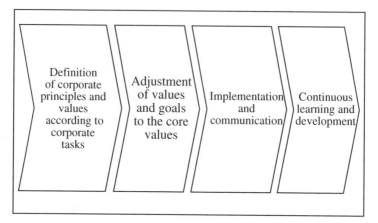

*Figure 16.1    Sequence of the GE value implementation process*

## BOX 16.1    THE VALUES OF GE

**GE Leaders ... Always with unyielding integrity ...**

- Are **passionately focused** on driving customer success.
- Live Six Sigma Quality ... ensure that the **customer is always its first beneficiary** ... and use it to accelerate growth.
- Insist on **excellence** and are intolerant of bureaucracy.
- Act in a boundaryless fashion ... always search for and apply the **best ideas** regardless of their source.
- Prize global intellectual capital and the **people** that provide it ... build diverse teams to maximize it.
- See change for the growth opportunities it brings ... i.e., **'e-Business'**.
- Create a clear, simple, **customer-centred vision** ... and continually renew and refresh its execution.
- Create an environment of 'stretch', excitement, informality and **trust** ... reward improvements ... and celebrate results.
- Demonstrate ... always with infectious enthusiasm for the customer ... **the '4-E's' of GE leadership**: the personal **Energy** to welcome and deal with the speed of change ... the ability to create an atmosphere that **Energizes** others ... the **Edge** to make difficult decisions ... and the ability to consistently **Execute**.

## BOX 16.2   GE's COMMITMENT OF INTEGRITY

### A Commitment To Integrigy

GE is dedicated to the highest standards of integrity. Through our policies and actions, we seek performance and a reputation reflecting the very best we can achieve – a company that both creates economic value and acts by ethical principle. But when the issue is ethics, it is better that profits be lost than corners cut or rules bent.

The company must respect and respond to diverse responsibilities and interests. GE – and the individuals who comprise it – are accountable to laws and regulations, to standards of ethics and excellence; to customers and fellow employees; and to the communities and nations in which we work and to whom we sell.

A number of company policies have been issued which not only address specific standards of ethical conduct but outline the process by which these commitments are to be met. Living by these rules – and the values they express – is the most serious responsibility a GE employee undertakes. Employees must understand that they alone are responsible for their acts and omissions.

Ensuring that a commitment to ethical values remains the vital force within our company requires more than adherence to internal policies and to external laws and regulations. In all situations, we expect our employees to be guided by a sense of honor and motivated by a spirit of integrity.

All employees are expected to live by the highest standards of ethical conduct in their relationships with each other, the company, customers, and the public. If they perceive lapses in those standards, they are expected to report them to their superiors. Employees who prefer to report possible violations of laws or company policies to someone outside their business may contact, on a confidential basis, the Corporate Ombudsman. In every case, if confronted with apparent conflicts between the demands of their jobs and the highest standards of conduct, employees should be guided by their sense of honor until the inconsistency has been reconciled. GE employees are expected to be as vigilantly ethical as they are aggressively entrepreneurial.

It is a managerial responsibility to make ethical behavior and efficient performance complementary. Good managers measure excellence by qualitative values as well as by quantitative results, motivating employees to 'do the right thing' while 'doing things right.' They must encourage all employees to be alert to ethical ambiguity and to ask tough questions, and must respond promptly to employee concerns about possible violations of laws and regulations. We look to management to uphold company policies and standards, and to set the example by instilling a spirit of honor in the workplace.

It is a leadership responsibility to sustain an open, accountable environment where such a spirit of honor can thrive. For only in such an environment can a spirit prevail by which every individual member of the GE community shares responsibility for the integrity of the institution as a whole.

These common values and mutual responsibilities provide the framework for specific standards consistent with our commitments to openness, fairness, and respect for customers and communities. Yet prescribing policies is never more than a beginning; fulfilling them must always be a way of life in GE. Integrity is not an occasional requirement but a continuing commitment. It erodes when it is not reinforced; it weakens if it is not applied, as a living standard, to new issues and situations.

GE and each individual employee together pledge to comply with these policies to the best of their ability.

**John F. Welch, Jr.**
Chairman of the Board and Chief Executive Officer
**Lawrence A. Bossidy**
Vice Chairman of the Board and Executive Officer
**Edward E. Hood, Jr.**
Vice Chairman of the Board and Executive Officer

---

1995). For that reason the management defines precisely the means of ethical topics by connecting them to the guidelines and rules: 'When the issue is ethics, it is better that profits be lost than corners cut or rules bent'. Due to this relationship of ethical standards and guidelines, GE has the possibility to install a reporting system for ethical conduct: 'All employees are expected to live by the highest standards of ethical conduct in their relationship with each other, the company, the customer and the public. If they perceive lapses in those standards, they are expected to report them to their superiors'. The combination of ethical behaviour with its expression in guidelines makes possible the announcement and confidential whistle-blowing on actual and possible violations. And it structures investigations and analysis of ethical misconduct: 'Employees who prefer to report possible violations of laws or company policies to someone outside their business may contact, on a confidential basis, the Corporate Ombudsman'.

The Commitment to Integrity also emphasizes different areas of individual responsibility in the company, related to the function a person might have. First there is the area of individual responsibility of each single employee: 'Employees must understand that they alone are responsible for their acts and omissions.' On the areas of management and leadership this individual responsibility means the creation of possibilities to act ethically: 'It is a managerial responsibility to make ethical behavior and efficient performance complementary ... It is a leadership responsibility to sustain an open, accountable environment where such a spirit of honor can thrive'. In 1999 GE established a comprehensive Integrity Guideline of 'the spirit and the letter of our commitment'. In 95 pages it explains in a very detailed description the understanding of 'Integrity' in GE in the following chapters (GE, 1999b):

1. Statement of Integrity; How to use this booklet
2. How to handle a concern
3. Working with Customers and Suppliers
4. Government Business
5. Fair Competition
6. In the GE Community
7. Your Personal Integrity
8. What to watch out for
9. Where to find help.

### 2.4 Emphasis on Quality Management and Organizational Instructions

The GE business ethics programme is a set of organizational guidelines, policies and rules. The programme develops a few instructions in behaviour that is required for a successful career in GE. In addition, GE introduced the Six Sigma programme that emphasizes moving every process that touches the customers – every product and service – towards near perfect quality. This total quality management programme links the value management of GE with change processes and re-engineering efforts. Work in Six Sigma projects consists of five basic activities: defining, measuring, analysing, improving and controlling processes. Several management tools are supported:

1.  GE – policy – guidelines;
2.  guidelines for the division;
3.  Codes of Conduct for the division;
4.  policies and procedures regarding special areas of quality, style and sorts of business;
5.  business instructions;
6.  training and education.

Human resource management supports these efforts in order to achieve a management programme that integrates all tools into one big, successful, overall management system. This includes cultural change processes, change acceleration processes and a core leadership development programme.

### 2.5   Consequent Conversion of Values into Leadership

Managerial quality is evaluated with regard to values and to results. Only managers making good business results under application of corporate values are desirable (Figure 16.2). Four dimensions of value measurement evaluate the values and the behaviour of each manager and leader of GE: senior management, colleagues, the human resource department and assistant employees or co-workers. This management adjustment programme led to important changes. Due to the close relation of the value management programme to its internal formal guidelines, GE is able

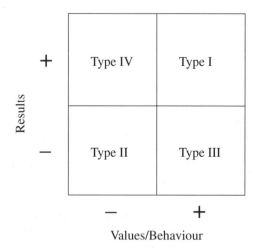

*Figure 16.2    Results*

to check the behaviour of single managers. GE defined a master profile of a manager, how he or she furthered or blocked the GE values, against which everybody is measured and adjusted. This profile contains four styles of managers:

> *Type I* not only delivers on performance commitments, but believes in and furthers GE's small-company values. The trajectory of this group is 'onward and upward,' and the men and women who comprise it will represent the core of our senior leadership into the next century. *Type II* does not meet commitments, nor share our values – nor last long at GE. *Type III* believes in the values but sometimes misses commitments. We encourage taking swings, and Type III is typically given another chance. *Type IV* delivers short-term results. But Type IV's do so without regard to values and, in fact, often diminish them by grinding people down, squeezing them, stifling them. Some of these learned to change; most couldn't. The decision to begin removing Type IV's was a watershed – the ultimate test of our ability to 'walk the talk', but it had to be done if we wanted GE people to be open, to speak up, to share, and to act boldly outside traditional 'lines of authority' and 'functional boxes' in this new learning, sharing environment (GE, 1996)

## 2.6 Controlling and Reporting

GE calls itself a 'values-driven organization' - inasmuch as values manifest as the rules and principles of the company's guidelines. Under these conditions, GE is led by values, planned by values and controlled by values. The means of these values finds its expression in the formal guidelines. And in this sense values are the second pillar of strategic management at GE, along with financial control. Well-established codes and organizational institutions like hotlines, Ethics Officers and other instruments ensure the reporting about disregard of values in leadership and day-to-day business. The proceeds and the spirit of this reporting are summarized in the chapter 'How to handle a concern': 'First, define your concern ... Second, raise the concern ... The whole idea is to speak up'. In addition GE provides established channels inside both the local companies and the GE Corporation – 'for reporting or supplying information about a policy concern' (GE, 1999b, p. 11). In addition, with the regular evaluation of the managers' values as a task of leadership, GE integrated many impulses of traditional compliance strategies and innovative integrity approaches.[1] This is why the CEO of GE emphasizes the term leadership by values: 'We are not leading by numbers but by values, which we convert into behaviour. If the values are all right, the results are all right. GE lives on fast exchange of good ideas across boundaries of departments and corporations. We call this boundaryless management' (GE Annual Report 1995) (Jack Welch).

# 3   MANAGEMENT OF VALUES IN SIEMENS

### 3.1   Main Interest: Communication of Intrinsic Values

The motivation of SIEMENS was the integration of cultural and individual peculiarities into the corporate communication processes. More than optimizing the fundamental corporate structure, the value management process at SIEMENS is driven to optimize soft facts of communication like the corporate culture. SIEMENS took calculated measures to avoid complications with ethical behaviour in the international context and to integrate people with different ideas into the 'SIEMENS family'. As a side-effect, value management should improve the success of the company's businesses. Such a management of intrinsic values of the managerial and organizational approach requires highly developed informal structures. These informal structures are part of the tradition of SEMENS:

1.  Focus on financial results with strict financial control
2.  Strategic and technical management without consideration of values
3.  Realization of strategic orders vithout support of ethical values
4.  Clear managerial focus on technical and economical contexts
5.  Focus on individual personal development
6.  Top management is recruited from complete SIEMENS careers

### 3.2   SIEMENS' Corporate Values and the Implementation Process

Emphasis on intrinsic business ethics relates to three aspects, which belong to the history of SIEMENS since 1848: SIEMENS sees the whole corporation as family; they have a strong obligation to traditions and continuity inside the structures of the company is very important. Accordingly, corporate principles at SIEMENS expresses their cultural philosophy in general terms without concrete rules and only has an informal connection to other leadership tools. This means that, up to now, there is no concrete Commitment of Integrity for connecting corporate values to other leadership tools.

As a result, SIEMENS' corporate principles express only general economic rules (Box 16.3). They are defined less to drive the companies' businesses than to cover the orientation for employees working in SIEMENS in general. This is founded in the development process, where the applied SIEMENS values and the preferred values of the employees had been summarized and approved by the executive board.

With regard to the importance of intrinsic and cultural values inside the informal structures at SIEMENS, the management decided first to evaluate the prevailing values of the SIEMENS employees. To increase the identification

## BOX 16.3 CORPORATE PRINCIPLES OF SIEMENS

**Customers** govern our actions

Our top priority is to provide outstanding value to our customers, since ultimately our success depends on their satisfaction. We provide solutions that enable our customers to achieve their objectives faster, easier and more efficiently.

Our **Innovations** shape the future

We put new ideas to work, creating innovative products and services to benefit our customers. We encourage experimentation and imagination. Our creativity and willingness to take risks enable us to build an environment in which promising ideas can be quickly turned into successful solutions. We also promote and draw on others' ideas.

**Business success** means: we win from profits

International competition is our benchmark. We work to achieve profits while striving for industry leadership and a steady increase in economic value added. This gives us the entrepreneurial freedom we need and makes us a trusted partner. To ensure financial success, we optimize time, quality and cost in all our work.

**Excellent Leadership** fosters top results

Our managers set clear, ambitious and inspiring goals. We always strive to surpass ourselves. If we don't, others will. By leading on the basis of trust, we empower our people to make their own decisions. We demonstrate courage and conviction when introducing necessary changes. Our managers serve as role models in everything they do.

**Learning** is the key to continuous improvement

We always measure ourselves against the world's best. Each of us strives to learn continuously. We welcome and offer open feedback and also learn from our mistakes. We are quicker than others at identifying new opportunities and adapting our solutions, organization and our behavior accordingly. We are building an international network of knowledge in which everyone gives and takes.

Our **Cooperation** has no limits

We are a global company and draw on our worldwide capabilities. This makes us the best team on the playing field. All our thoughts and actions stem from a sense of responsibility when it comes to achieving our common goal. Our cooperation is characterized by trust, personal integrity, mutual respect and open communication.

**Corporate citizenship** is our global commitment

Our knowledge and our solutions help create a better world. We are committed to protecting our environment. We are a respected corporate citizen in all countries in which we do business. We safeguard our people's future through training and continuing education. Integrity guides our conduct toward our business partners, colleagues, shareholders and the general public. Cultural differences enrich our organization.

of the employees with the SIEMENS values, the corporate principles should be an expression of the values the employees want to have in SIEMENS. So SIEMENS started a worldwide, company-wide 'value poll', where they interviewed all SIEMENS' managers. After this they adjusted these values to the business goals of the company and developed a large set of corporate principles with detailed and comprehensive explanations (Figure 16.3).

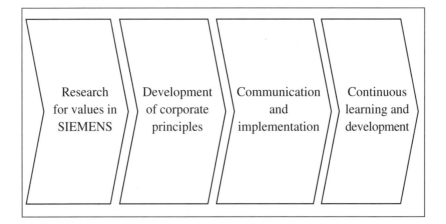

*Figure 16.3   Sequence of the SIEMENS value implementation process*

### 3.3 Management Lines as Channels of Communication

At the same time SIEMENS defined its value-table and extended its communication instruments to guarantee the communication of this value-framework. In the form of a second management system, these lines are established next to classical decision-making processes to establish a value-oriented conversation. Because it is a communication system, its goal is the creation of value-consciousness related to principles and values. Its emphasis is more on informal correspondence of personal values, preferred organizational values and corporate reality than on the commitment to a guideline. And it includes the idea that employees should live their own values.

SIEMENS' corporate principles are embedded in a set of organizational steps to support this process. Training, values-oriented projects and the study of best practice cases are established, among other tools, to communicate the possible tension between individual values and the corporate reality. Because corporate principles should articulate core convictions at SIEMENS, discussions on corporate values on all managerial levels, and within every branch, take part regularly. These are supported by the communication of best practice cases to illustrate integrity in behaviour. In addition there are projects to train the individual adjustment of the personal style of management to corporate principles and values-based training for individual development and individual objectives. Periodic surveys on corporate values and team values check the informal agreement of basic corporate principles by employees. These steps help to integrate the company principles into the leadership framework and managerial tools.

### 3.4 Management Tools Leveraged by Intrinsic Values

At SIEMENS the various management tools implicitly involve value management to a differing degree. In general, strategic planning and controlling works independent of value management and value communication. As a consequence, divisional success is measured as a factor of the ranking in the marketplace and of the contribution to profit but not as an expression of core values. Management by objectives works without values due to the fact that divisional objectives are not combined with corporate values and principles. There is also no structured relation between values and the success of the organizational elements of the company. More than this, there is an important emphasis on personality in management techniques. The systems and regulations that are adjusted to support and to promote the values and the behaviour of the corporate principles include the whole range of:

1.  Accounting, controlling and corporate planning
2.  Communication systems
3.  Assessment and feedback systems
4.  Careers and incentive systems
5.  Salary systems, time accounting systems
6.  ISO 9000; Guidelines of the European Foundation of Quality Management
7.  TOP (Time Optimized Processes) – Process
8.  Status symbols
9.  Entertainment expenses and travelling expenses
10. Managerial conversations.

One main focus is the screening of current management tools in the organization. Each management tool should be related to the demands of the corporate Principles of Leadership as shown below (Table 16.1). But there is no strict analysis undertaken in order to impose sanctions against managers who do not care for the corporate principles.

### 3.5  Communicational Requirements and Measurement of Managerial Results

In SIEMENS there is no strict managerial relation between leadership values and operational results. The evaluation of managerial quality works in principle with regard to results. Managers who achieve good business results are always desirable and results are the main focus of leadership. Values and corporate principles have to grow only inside the managers' behaviour without any strategic control – they are only part of corporate communication. There is no advised and authorized ombudsman and there is no hotline or other mechanism for the employees to communicate misbehaviour. Up to the year 2000 there had not been a written Code of Conduct, including objective criteria to evaluate behaviour of employees, though SIEMENS plans to establish code and reporting channels in 2001.

## 4   ANALYSIS OF ECONOMICAL, ORGANIZATIONAL AND ETHICAL INTERESTS

### 4.1  Main Differences

The differences in the ethic management systems of GE and SIEMENS belong to different ideas about the role of ethics in organizations.[2] For GE, as part of the US tradition, the management of ethics relates to the keeping of explicit

Table 16.1 *Checklist for the conversion of corporate principles into leadership tools*

SIEMENS principles of leadership — Management tools and systems

| SIEMENS principles of leadership | Interview of employee | Framework of leadership | Conversation for supervision | Management by objectives | Framework for Salary (EFA) | Salary Incentive | Processes and Standards of Quality Management | Balanced Scorecard | Quarterly managerial conversations |
|---|---|---|---|---|---|---|---|---|---|
| **Customers** govern our actions | | | | | | | | | |
| Our **innovations** shape the future | | | | | | | | | |
| **Business success** means: we win from profits | | | | | | | | | |
| **Excellent leadership** fosters top results | | | | | | | | | |
| **Learning** is the key to continuous improvement | | | | | | | | | |
| Our **Co-operation** has no limits | | | | | | | | | |
| **Corporate citizenship** is our global commitment | | | | | | | | | |

meanings of concrete and sound rules. The corporate principles are the peak of all rules and guidelines, which determine managerial structures and work flows. The safeguarding of the commitment of employees to these rules, the development of their behaviour according to these rules and the evolution of areas including potential conflicts are therefore the main topics. GE develops leadership tools to handle the soft facts of concrete organizational problems. They integrated a value management system as the core system to communicate their strategic orientation and impulses with concrete and measurable effects on the behaviour of their employees. Value management in GE is therefore a main component of quality management, as shown by its close relation to the Six Sigma programme. This creates the opportunity to control even the soft elements of their strategic success. More than a tool to communicate the corporate spirit, the GE value management system is the core leadership tool to develop and to plan changes of the company in all branches. Value management in GE belongs to the core business drivers of the GE strategy and therefore its details increase competitive advantage.

For SIEMENS, as part of European tradition, ethical behaviour means the structuring of individual commitment to soft rules and a common basic feeling. The area of values is only partly determined by concrete rules and belongs mainly to individual freedom. Therefore its organizational guidelines for the work flow are not primarily part of ethic management. Management of values in this sense is the management of soft facts inside the company, related to personal space. Its task is to create a realm of homogenous ideas and a sphere of shared values. It requires a sensible consideration of traditional and cultural value systems and the cautious integration of similar impacts of values (Figure 16.4). The management of SIEMENS AG maintains a high sensitivity to the traditional roots of the company and its integrity within their own society. The top management takes care to keep local cultural and individual differences as a factor of success of their business – in Germany as well as in other local branches. Flexibility, the ability to change, is not a particular factor of management of the corporate design of SIEMENS. Nevertheless they have innovative inventions and products and a clear corporate strategy. SIEMENS relies more on the individual flexibility and responsibility of managers than on the organizational integration of these managers.

### 4.2  Aspects of Corporate Culture

*Homogeneous ethical behaviour* plays an important role for the success of both companies in all levels of management. Therefore they take great care in communicating and educating all employees in their corporate values and principles. High emphasis of value agreement on all levels of the executive

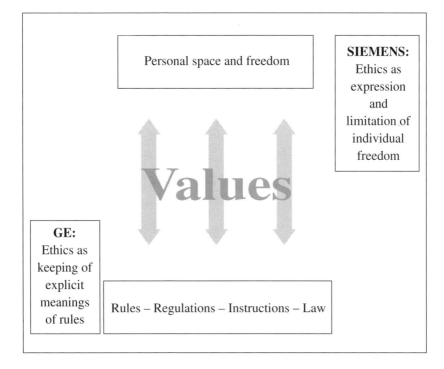

*Figure 16.4    Meaning of ethics in organizations*

management and in all branches is expected – although they require a high level of agreement of management with corporate principles and values. Due to this task, the core values of both companies are defined in a very wide and general sense. They may be founded on the more formal and catchy principles of GE, according to a pronounced high identification of the employees and the management with the company and its goals in GE.

*Individual integrity in society and company* is striven for as a guarantee to the success of the company. In both companies individuals receive their responsibilities from the grade to which they are linked. This question of integrity – that is whether employees work and behave as good citizens – has its strength and weakness in both companies; it seems to be independent from their value management systems. Only the orientation of freedom and individual responsibility has a different relation to either corporate or cultural values (Figure. 16.5) The task of SIEMENS is to respect and to integrate multinational and multicultural specifications of values into the organizational structure. The homogenous global languages of business communication to this purpose are financial and technical reports, whereas business principles

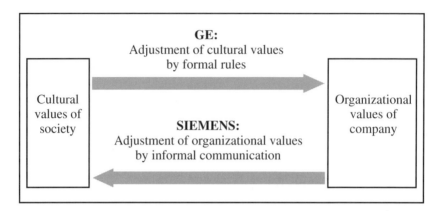

*Figure 16.5   Difference of value adjustment*

are very general and open, creating more implicit meanings of value management.

*Personality and individual responsibility* is used in the GE case to develop the organizational principles and business and in the SIEMENS case to undertake independent cultural-specific ethical responsibility. Individual personality is of high importance in both cases, though in different directions: while in SIEMENS it is required to derive ethical behaviour in day-to-day management out of corporate principles, in GE it is used to stimulate and to improve the principles of day-to-day management. Individual personality and individual responsibility in borderline cases gets more attention in the management of SIEMENS.

A highly *homogeneous corporate culture* and working atmosphere all over the world is one of the most noticeable characteristics of the SIEMENS company. The employees are all 'SIEMENS members' and take responsibility for their work out of this situation. This intrinsic attribute of SIEMENS was in the past not really visible, it was latent. The approach of working with ethical values as an aspect of corporate communication more than as an aspect of personnel management has is roots in care for this intrinsic self-confidence. In GE there is a graduated identification of employees with their company. Its employees do their jobs regardless of whether they feel themselves to be members of a worldwide community or not, though in GE there is a pronounced high capability to think and work beyond rules and regulations, more than in SIEMENS, where it is related to individual space. This relates to the established codes and reporting structures of the GE organization. Due to their pronounced values GE is able to shift its values according to the fast changing requirements of businesses and society.

## 4.3 Aspects of Leadership Principles

Leadership tools of value management in SIEMENS primarily focus on the development of individual personality and personal ethical responsibility. They are primarily tools of *internal communication*. Therefore SIEMENS emphasizes that the intrinsic morality of every action in science and business has to be a matter of education and awareness and the informal corporate structures enshrine the awareness of this morality. This requires a closely defined corporate ethical culture for doing business based on informal channels without established and precise leadership tools. But if the company gets very diversified, like SIEMENS, the lack of established instruments of value orientation becomes a problem of leadership, because the top management has to lead more and more goal-oriented and prescriptively in all branches.

Leadership tools of value management in GE concentrate on the definition of internal cooperation and behaviour. GE fixes the style of management they expect and simultaneously the borderline of behaviour it will not tolerate. GE expects everybody to share its principles in this sense. Leadership in GE is the definition and adjustment of these values and principles and therefore it is more important to lead than to manage. The means of GE value management is the core leadership tool to communicate the vision, the mission and the strategy of a company. It has its duty to *ensure the commitment and knowledge* of all rules that are necessary for the corporate function. And therefore value management is the core competence of GE's internal knowledge management.

These differences are expressed in respective *organizational and managerial structures*, which can be represented as in Figure 16.6. It illustrates how GE manages its values in combination with its business planning and leadership planning and in addition to controlling and reporting instruments. The management of principles in SIEMENS is a kind of public style without a direct link to other managerial tools. Therefore value management is mainly a task of internal communication. Values in SIEMENS are expressed as a kind of attitude and character, and business planning processes, in an instrumental sense, lack any values-based controlling and reporting instruments. However, both organizational approaches have its advantages and its strength.[3]

## 4.4 Aspects of Organizational Structure, Formal Rules and Leadership Tools

Corporate values and principles of GE are related directly to the requirements of the present company's business success, whereas SIEMENS pronounces general cultural implications of 'good and fair business'. According to this, *organizational flexibility* for the integration of new styles of working, new

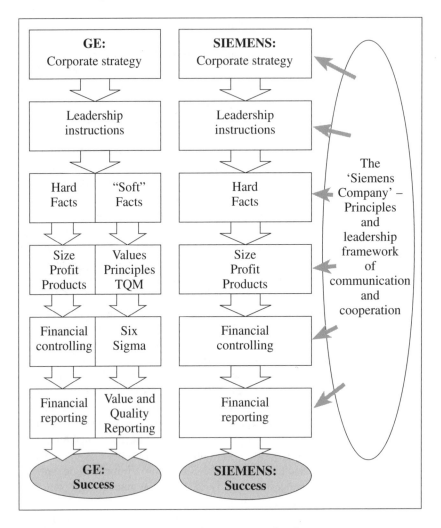

*Figure 16.6    Strategic managerial structure and value management*

teams and new cultural aspects is well developed in the GE value management system. This leads to a high flexibility to change or shift values and their alignment within the workforce. GE insists on this values shift in accordance with changes in business requirements. SIEMENS shows instead more willingness, ways and abilities to manage and implement changes in line with the importance of cultural characteristics for the success of the organization. SIEMENS depends on the adjustment of organizational stuctures to existing cultural values.

An important point for GE is *value adjustment,* the function of values shift due to changing markets and needs, which works very rapidly in GE and require highly developed organizational structures to deal with values and ethics. SIEMENS however, sees no need for rapid values shifts on account of changing business requirements. Due to its more cultural understanding of individual values SIEMENS relies on the distinction between hard business facts and value communication. Thus value adjustment in SIEMENS works very slowly.

Values in GE are very *explicit.* They do not refer merely to general ideas about good business performance, but name concrete specifications for 'GE thinking' and 'GE behaviour'. They shape a basis of explicit values to relate contracts and controlling instruments precisely to the goals and tasks of the company. The preferred values are safeguarded with different leadership techniques to keep the GE management close together. SIEMENS, in contrast, defines a wide range of values with borderlines of unacceptable behaviour. Its values are more *implicit.*

These circumstances are related to *value controlling systems*: how seriously the management safeguards the corporation against misconduct and misbehaviour. In this respect GE works very instrumentally in that it defines when and how and to which grade compliance with values is achieved. SIEMENS works more with informal tools to communicate and train the most important and sensitive values.

In the end, both companies demonstrate the *importance of informal structures* in general to communicate and supervise values: GE stresses the importance of informal structures to communicate and discuss corporate values in close conjunction with its business strategies, SIEMENS uses them to communicate the sense and compliance with the corporate values.

## 5   CONCLUSION

Similarities between the value management systems of GE and SIEMENS agree with the common opinion that two similar companies in similar businesses, similar markets and similar grades of globalization relate to comparable management ideas, if they stress the term value management. But due to their history and due to the different cultures, from which the two companies originate, there are significant differences. It is not possible to judge whose way of management is more adequate to ensure these companies business success in the near and far future – whether the more informal way of SIEMENS or the more instrumental way of GE. Insights into the way these companies deal with ethical values may increase the ability in leadership to decide on a suitable style of dealing with ethical or values-based topics.

## NOTES

1. For a specific determination of the difference between compliance-based and integrity-based strategies of values-driven management see Paine (1994).
2. The role and influence of unions for the employment policy of companies has been very important in the past in Germany. But observing and judging values-based management systems from the perspective of 'careers' rather than by ways of 'duty', 'function' and 'employment' changes the subject. The historic and present work of unions has only a small influence. The way managers are protected and influenced and the way managers occupy positions of leadership is not determined by the work of unions. Instead, unions confine themselves to employment rights, cancellations, and so on.
3. From a sociological point of view there is no reason to claim an advantage for formal or informal, instrumental or communicational aspects of leadership to guarantee the success of organizations and their survival (Luhmann, 2000, pp. 183 ff. and pp. 256 ff.). Economical theories however prefer formal and instrumental approaches to manage and structure organizations successfully due to deterministic approaches (Wolff, 1999; Wuttke, 2000). In the end preferences for one or the other way of values-driven management are a point of leadership style more than of leadership quality or of right and wrong, though there is still the question of the managing initiative (Paine, 1994).

## REFERENCES

Byrne, John A. (1998), How Jack Welch Runs GE, *Business Week*, 8 June.

Dahm, Karl-Wilhelm (1988), *Ethische Erziehung von Führungskräften?* Die US-amerikanische Corporate-Ethics-Bewegung, Bochum.

Deutsch, Claudia H. (1998), 'Six Sigma Enlightenment. Managers Seek Corporate Nirvana Through Quality Control', *The New York Times*, 7 December.

Driscoll, Dawn-Marie and W. Michael Hoffman (2000), *Ethics Matters: How to Implement Values-Driven Management*. Waltham, Massachusetts, Bentley College.

Egon Zehnder International (1997), 'Face to Face: Jack Welch', *Focus*, Vol. 1, Issue 1/97, New York, Egon Zehnder International Inc.

General Electric (1995), Annual Report 1994, Fairfield, Connecticut, General Electric Company.

General Electric (1996), Annual Report 1995, Fairfield, Connecticut, General Electric Company.

General Electric (1997), Annual Report 1996, Fairfield, Connecticut, General Electric Company.

General Electric (1998), Annual Report 1997, Fairfield, Connecticut, General Electric Company.

General Electric (1999a), Annual Report 1998, Fairfield, Connecticut, General Electric Company.

General Electric (1999b), Integrity: The Spirit and Letter of Our Commitment, Fairfield, Connecticut, General Electric Company.

General Electric (2000), Annual Report 1999, Fairfield, Connecticut, General Electric Company.

Hall, Brian P. (1995), *Values Shift, A Guide to Personal and Organizational Transformation*, Rockport, Massachusetts, Twinlights Publishing.

Luhmann, Niklas (2000), *Organisation und Entscheidung*, Wiesbaden, Westdeutscher Verlag.

Paine, Lynn Sharp (1994), 'Managing for Organizational Integrity', *Harvard Business Review*, Vol. 72, Issue 2, March/April, pp. 106–117.

Palazzo, Bettina (2000), *Interkulturelle Unternehmensethik. Deutsche und amerikanische Modelle im Vergleich*, Wiesbaden, Gabler.

Schnebel, Eberhard (1997), *Management – Werte – Organisation. Ethische Aufgaben im Management der Industrie*, Wiesbaden, Westdeutscher Verlag.

Siemens AG (1995), TOP-Projekte, München, Siemens Aktiengesellschaft.

Siemens AG (1996), EFA-Programm, München, Siemens Aktiengesellschaft.

Siemens AG (1997), 150 Years of Siemens. The Company from 1847 to 1997, München, Siemens Aktiengesellschaft.

Siemens AG (1998), Annual Report 1997, München, Siemens Aktiengesellschaft.

Siemens AG (1999a), Annual Report 1998, München, Siemens Aktiengesellschaft.

Siemens AG (1999b), Unternehmenswerte, München, Siemens Aktiengesellschaft.

Siemens AG (2000), Annual Report 1999, München, Siemens Aktiengesellschaft.

Slater, Robert (1999), *Jack Welch and the GE-Way*, New York, McGraw-Hill.

Welch, Jack (1997), 'A Learning Company and Its Quest for Six Sigma', Executive Speech Reprints, Fairfield, Connecticut, General Electric Company.

Welch, Jack (1998), 'Three Roads to Growth', Executive Speech Reprints, Fairfield, Connecticut, General Electric Company.

Welch, Jack (1999), 'GE and the Internet', Executive Speech Reprints, Fairfield, Connecticut, General Electric Company.

Wolff, Birgitta (1995), *Organisation durch Verträge,* Wiesbaden, Gabler.

Wolff, Birgitta (1999), *Anreizkompatible Reorganisation von Unternehmen*, Frankfurt a. M., Schäffer-Poeschel

Wuttke, Stephan (2000), *Verantwortung und Controlling. Controlling zur Förderung verantwortlichen Handelns*, Frankfurt a. M., Lang.

# 17.  From attitude to action: strategy for development of values and attitudes

## Christen Andreas Larsen

## INTRODUCTION

The Eidsvåg/Salhus municipality is one of 12 municipalities in Bergen. Eidsvåg/Salhus had approximately 14 200 residents as of 1997. A large portion of the municipality is an urban area consisting of detached and semi-detached homes. The living pattern is stable. The municipality is organized in four departments: Municipal Administration, Health Services, Social Welfare and Nursing and Care. The municipality is the smallest in Bergen when measured in number of employees, with 250 employees in 168 positions.

The idea for a project on 'ethics' originated from the municipality's application to the Council Training Fund (Kommunens Opplæringsfond) for funds to train unskilled health services workers in handling confidentiality issues. The Fund expressed an interest in our application and further discussions led to the development of the project.

The problem in managing confidentiality issues in a professional manner is that in many cases they are linked to an ethical dilemma. This recognition by the municipal management led them to act on their desire to place ethics in focus. Eidsvåg/Salhus municipality had prioritized quality assurance in their 1993–1995 strategic plan. In 1994, each professional department was to develop quality requirements for their services. Ethics and confidentiality are central areas within quality assurance. The municipality wanted to place ethics and confidentiality on the agenda, also as specific items.

It was important that the project plan have realistic expectations with respect to the participants' contribution as they were also responsible for maintaining day-to-day services. One of the project's goals was to generate organizational knowledge that could be used in other contexts. It was also desired that the project plans be incorporated into already existing plans.

# ETHICS IS A 'LEADERSHIP RESPONSIBILITY'

The challenge was to develop an organization where ethical norms and values were included as part of the municipality's 'strategy and ongoing actions'. The values had to be taken seriously and provide a common base for all municipal employees. It was important that the senior management team was active in the development of the values and took responsibility for the values that the municipality stood for. An ownership for and commitment to the values by municipal employees had to be established. The senior management team had to live up to the values and monitor that everybody else followed them. There had to be a close connection between words and actions.

Emphasis was put on the following:

- **Honesty and openness**
  Information, communication and behaviour shall be open and honest. One shall have the courage and desire to engage in a constructive exchange of opinions. Everyone has the right to expect honest and direct feedback.
- **Trust**
  All coworkers shall work such that the organization is perceived as being credible and deserving of trust.
- **Loyalty**
  Employees shall be loyal to all resolutions, goals, plans and decisions and work actively to their fulfilment.
- **Responsibility**
  Everyone must take initiative and show responsibility for their actions and their areas of responsibility.
- **Cooperation**
  Each employee is solely responsible for their relationships with other organizations and shall contribute to the success of others.
- **Creativity**
  Everyone is to actively contribute to a safe working environment while maintaining room for ideas and innovative action.

# OBJECTIVES FOR THE PROJECT

*'Create an awareness of attitudes and ethics through education and process-oriented action'.*

There is a danger that, given continually tighter economic constraints and increased work pressure, it is perceived that financial considerations are given higher priority than the evaluations of professionals or the quality of the service performed. Within the health and social welfare sector it has been observed that individual rights play a larger role, while the general care for others may be neglected. The municipality wanted to follow this up with the employees by defining values and making attitudes more visible.

In the Eidsvåg/Salhus municipality, as in other areas of health and social services, it is difficult to give priority to internal projects, especially for those individuals providing front-line services. For example, closing the local heath station or reducing home care may be necessary in order to free the time needed to undertake such projects. When such projects are undertaken, the reasons for starting the project need to be well founded and the expected value to be gained should be as large as possible.

Eidsvåg/Salhus municipality formulated the following *objectves* for the project:

- Set ethical standards for the municipality.
- Increase competence to master ethical dilemmas.
- Provide management insights into process-oriented work.

The municipality did not want ethics to be seen as a fad that was 'in' for a short period and then forgotten. The ethical standards are intended to be the attitudes the municipal leadership stand for and all the employees should adhere to. Through the project, the municipality's goal was that the management team and staff would be more capable of identifying an ethical dilemma, taking a standpoint and then making an educated choice. *The municipality felt that insight into process-oriented work would have added value to other development work as well as strengthening the municipality's leadership.*

## ORGANIZATION

The project had to, as far as possible, follow the existing reporting structure. It was necessary to retain outside help to assist with the coordination of the work, lectures, process work, development of questionnaire and internal marketing activities. Joint actions ensure that the project encompasses the whole municipality, as well as taking on subjects/themes with common interests. Internal marketing focused on all departments as well as special interests.

When starting the ethics project, the senior management team wanted to place ethics on the agenda. It commenced the process within its own groups. A priest and a political scientist were invited to provide both their personal and academic points of view on 'attitudes and values'.[1]

The result of the first meeting was that the project should be anchored in the ethical standards for the municipality. In addition, it was deemed desirable to include an external advisor in the project. In a subsequent meeting the senior management team defined the project plan. The following subjects were discussed: approach for the project, goal for the project, organization, design, progress, value foundation, employers political profile, approach for the sub-projects and task for stage two.

The project plan was rooted in the subjects mentioned above. The process within the senior management team was difficult at times. It became apparent that individual members of the senior management team did not have the project 'under their skin' as much as one had hoped. The process was intended to deal with the fact that we, as top leaders in the municipality, had to support the project.

## Approach to the Project: Value Foundation – Approach

It was important to lay the groundwork for a value foundation. It was also important to have a common understanding and attitude towards ethics in the municipality. A common set of values for employees and clients would create similar attitudes and understanding was desired.

The complete approach comprises: overall standards of values, employer's political value foundation and basic view of management. This project was aimed towards three main areas:

1. to set an ethical standard for the municipality;
2. confidentiality and disclosure;
3. manage the conflict between professional ethics and values and financial constraints.

## Value Foundation

To bring up some important assumptions and fundamentals on which the 'ethics project' rests and at the same time establish a basis for a discussion on values in each department, the following outlines the starting point for the 'ethics project'.

The value foundation for the project was developed during a seminar where only members of the senior management team participated. During this seminar there were nine value foundations that everyone supported.

1. **Personal worth**
   Each person is unique and has the same worth regardless of position, cultural background, or view on life.

2. **Contribution**
   Everyone has the right to be heard and to be part of decisions that affect one's situation.
3. **Protection of privacy**
   We shall respect and protect the privacy of each individual.
4. **Clients shall be ethically in focus**
   Our services shall be adapted to each client, based on a professional evaluation and in conformity with the applicable legal guidelines.
5. **Information**
   We shall give our clients confidence that our employees have a duty to give the proper information and/or referrals.
6. **Accessibility**
   We shall be accessible to and act credibly with our clients.
7. **Advice and guidance**
   Clients have a right to adequate advice and guidance about their rights.
8. **Administrational practice**
   We shall ensure that good administrative practice provides:

   - legal protection;
   - equality and justice;
   - open assessments.

9. **Loyalty**

   - We shall be loyal to the organization's goals and interests.
   - Loyalty assumes mutual respect for each other.
   - Loyalty is to argue clearly for one's position before decisions are made and to be heard.
   - After a decision is made, the decision is actively supported even if one would have preferred a different outcome.
   - Loyalty is to address criticism where it belongs.
   - Loyalty is to clearly state when the conditions for doing a good job are not present.

**Goal limits**

Goal limits are defined as areas within each professional's ethical dimensions. One desires also to have common ethical attitudes within:

a. occupational ethics;
b. work ethics;
c. administrative ethics.

The case described below in Box 17.1 illustrates one of the many dilemmas that health care workers are confronted with each working day. The example also attempts to bring forward the different ethical dimensions one encounters between the different departments in public health care.

---

## BOX 17.1  CASE STUDY OF A HEALTH CARE WORKER

SHOULD THIS CASE BE REPORTED TO CHILD WELFARE SERVICES?

Stian: 2 years 6 months old
Mother: Beate, 21 years old

Mother's background:

Beate's home had been characterized by her father's alcohol problems. Her mother struggled to make the practical and economic aspects of the family function properly. Beate had a learning disability in school and was truant for part of her secondary schooling. She completed secondary schooling (nine years) with poor grades. In the first few years following secondary school, Beate spent a considerable amount of time in a drug environment, without being able to tell how often she used drugs.

Beate's family had periodic contact with the social welfare office, and between the age of 13 to 16 Beate had a contact person with whom she developed a good relationship.

Beate and Stian's father lived together during the first six months following Stian's birth. The child's father then informed Beate that he no longer wanted any contact with either Beate or Stian.

Beate currently has a boyfriend who occasionally lives with her.

Present status:

Beate has had good contact with the public health nurse subsequent to Stian's birth. She has turned up for all the appointments and has contacted the nurse on those few occasions when Stian was ill.

The public health nurse has, in due course, got the impression that the mother feels tired and unwell. Beate feels unsure with respect to her daily responsibility for Stian and in addition feels that he is demanding and difficult to control. Beate has also stated that her boyfriend occasionally drinks too much alcohol and that he has been violent towards her.

> The public health nurse has not observed any abnormal or worrying signs regarding Stian's development.
>
> Possible actions:
>
> Report as concern case to child welfare services without mother's consent. Encourage Beate to voluntarily make contact with child welfare services. Obtain consent from mother to report case to child welfare services. Wait until one can document physical or psychological damage.

The client shall be ethically in focus. In other words, all the client's needs should be focused on in such a manner that they are not overshadowed by professional or personal issues. It can often appear that the clients are there for the employees. The relationship between employee rights and professional ethics can often be an ethical dilemma. Take for example shift work, where the personnel's rights often go against professional ethics.

### Comfort in Managing Ethical Dilemmas

a.   Individual
b.   Organizational

One often encounters ethical dilemmas between the clients' rights and the limited amount of resources within the public heath care system. In order to manage the ethical dilemmas that arise in such work-related cases, it is important that the employee has the necessary knowledge and possibility of working through the dilemma in a formalized forum. It has been shown that employees who constantly feel inadequate in their jobs are those most vulnerable to burnout.

It was felt that something had to be done so that the personnel had a forum to discuss the daily ethical challenges they faced.

### Cooperation across Professions/Occupations

Many clients receive services from several administrative levels and departments. In a number of cases the lack of cooperation between the different departments is a direct impediment to proper treatment. There are many examples of this. Within the municipality this was especially the case between the Health Care department, Social Welfare department and Nursing department. It was therefore decided that cooperation across these departments should be strengthened. The challenge was to obtain cooperation across the professions in order to give the clients 'total service'. If this could be accomplished the reward would be better use of the professional capacity as well as savings with respect to use of time and financial resources. This would also provide short- and long-term benefits to the clients. To gain cooperation across professions and disciplines is a challenge within the Health Care sector as the disciplines are not trained to work as a team and are the largest in number. This is often seen when working with doctors as they are trained to give a diagnosis and must therefore trust their own decisions.

Being able to come to a *single* place that could take care of all the clients' needs without having to go from department to department would enable clients to receive quicker treatment for their problems.

## Ethics Integrated into Daily Work

To integrate ethics into daily work is a big challenge. It is important that ethics do not become a fad, but rather become an integrated part of the municipality's culture.

### Quality assurance routines[2]

Routines for quality control of the work performed were established. This was an overall requirement for all activities. Those items taken up in the project would be anchored in 'ethics' or a culture/attitude that should be the pervading method of thought to guide our actions and relationships with our clients.

### Forum for the handling of ethical questions

In order to meet the individuals' needs to discuss subjects related to ethical questions, work was started to organize discussion forums.

### Routines for follow-up

Project controls were included in the ordinary follow-up and were established prior to beginning the project. There was a quarterly follow-up in the beginning, while later, when it was felt that the project was set in the organization, the follow-up would be every four months.

Subsequently, the actions were incorporated into each department's action plan. These action plans were further anchored in the municipality's strategic plans.

### Process handbook

A process memo was developed. This would be the basis for a handbook on how the process should occur within the municipality's different departments. Thus each employee had a guide for the process under the entire duration of the project.

## Objectives for the project

The senior management team summarized the project's objectives in five points:

1. Clients of municipal services shall be met with dignity and respect.
2. All municipal employees shall have the confidence to handle their own work situation.
3. We shall show the will to cooperate and have respect for each other's competence.
4. The municipality's values shall provide the foundation of daily work.
5. The ethics project shall provide knowledge on work methods and processes.

## Project Design

By project design one means how the project shall be undertaken in the municipality, including planning, implementation and profiling of the project. It is important that this is made clear to all municipal employees before starting the project.

The different phases of the project design are outlined in Table 17.1.

*Table 17.1   Different phases of project design*

| Planning | | Implementation | | Profiling | |
|---|---|---|---|---|---|
| 1. | Value foundation | 1. | Challenges | 1. | Common attitudes |
| a. | Overall standard | a. | Charting – status | a. | Joint profiling |
| | Attitude to professional ethics Client focus | b. | Prioritizing | b. | Follow-up |
| b. | Trade culture | 2. | Leadership/steering | 2. | Mastering ethical dilemmas |
| | Basic view of clients | a. | Leader roles | a. | Individually |
| | Basic view of cooperation Basic view of management | b. | Profile | b. | Organizational level |
| c. | Employers political value platform | | | | |
| 2. | Approach/sub-projects | | | | |
| a. | Prioritizing common projects | 3. | Identifying potential for improvement | 4. Action plans | |

| Planning | Implementation | Profiling |
|---|---|---|
| b. Projects in the discipline departments Ethics and confidentiality Ethics and quality in communications Information | a. Solutions for own department<br>b. At the municipal level | a. Common for all<br>b. At the departmental level |
| 3. Process Handbook Contribution in the form of:<br>a. Documentation<br>b. Work methods/ process-oriented work<br>c. Situation-oriented apprentice process | 4. Development of attitudes<br>a. Across professions<br>b. In own department | 4. Cooperation quality across professions/ occupations<br>5. Quality assurance<br>a. Forum for follow-up<br>b. Evaluation<br>c. Organizational |

**Work Form and Methods**

A work guide was developed which included the project methods that were to be utilized. The guide described the different approaches. The primary purpose was to prepare for the different processes. The leaders were trained to run the processes in their departments.

**Training of managers/middle managers as 'motors' in process work**
The municipality has 23 managers with personnel responsibility. One of the goals for the project was to teach these managers 'process work' through practical experience. It was therefore decided that each manager would lead the work in their own groups, be the driving force and be responsible for developing a commitment and understanding for the project given that they themselves had participated in laying its foundations. Because of this it was decided to put the most effort into this group.

**An integrated approach**
By an integrated approach the following is intended:

- Common set of values:      Clients
- Cooperation:      Employees

- Administration:                    Management
- Employer's policies:               Personnel administration

With the term 'employer's policies', the goal was to continue to keep the best of the current personnel administrations, but at the same time reinforce the employer's main guiding and proactive responsibilities in a much stronger manner. The term 'employer's policies' places the responsibility and focus where they belong, on attitudes, will and action. In this sense there is a shift in perspective from a judicial approach based on the employer's rights and duties, to a proactive style that strives to release the organization's human potential. Concurrently, this ambition is made an overall management responsibility. Such an 'employer's policy' is important for the realization of the organization's goals. 'Employer's policies' are the basic values the organization has approved and which indicate how to create the framework for the employees to develop responsibility, enthusiasm and pride in work performed and the municipality as a workplace. Those that have experienced the release of energy in an organization know that this is the foremost challenge faced by leaders. They have seen the enormous rewards and have discovered which part of the organization has the largest potential.

## Ethics

- Values                    Understanding
- Ethical approaches         Transparency of action
- Ethical dilemma            Mastering and growth

The value set presents a vision where the possibility for and the willpower, engagement and motivation are the driving forces behind an individual's organizational knowledge. In addition, it says something about the social changes, movements and principal attitudes towards the relationship between policy and administration. Shared values among employees will lead to similar approaches for all users of services. This will lead to equal treatment of all. Common values will, in the long run, give the clients security. Taking the clients seriously will create good relationships between the clients, their families and the employees. In order to create a safe framework for the clients and the employees it is a condition that there is a common understanding of the problems and challenges. It is important in daily work to have the ability to admit that one may have an ethical problem, make this known and discuss it without feeling shameful or incompetent. For employees to be able to master ethical dilemmas, it is important that they experience a supportive environment which allows personal growth.

## Methodology

### 'From attitude to action'

Guidelines were developed as to how each department was to undertake project work. The staff contributed in prioritizing areas and problems with regard to the value foundation. From this, a simple situation was chosen to illustrate how the values could, in practice, be put to a test.

Further, current standards and consequences were described as well as handling the reporting of goals and standards. This was done so that everyone understood the goals and standards which were used and therefore would be able to measure the consequences against each other. A lot of emphasis was put on evaluations. Each project group was to establish milestones and specify what should be measured to see if a pre-defined standard was met. For the project group to have ownership of the methodology it was extremely important that there was agreement in the group on the methods in order to have a common approach and follow-up procedure.

### Attitude and awareness discussion

All groups had discussions on attitudes. These discussions helped create an awareness of where the attitudes of each group needed work. Consequently, a common action plan was to be developed for the prioritized areas.

### Focus on open forums

Putting a focus on open forums provides each employee with the possibility to discuss any daily dilemmas they may encounter. One can employ forums like staff meetings, personnel evaluation meetings to make ethical dilemmas known. It was the intention to utilize the established forums for discussions with personnel and not to subject employees to additional meetings. It was important to utilize existing forums in order to promote the discussion of the different problems as they arose.

Being able to set time aside for colleagues when they needed to discuss daily dilemmas was a challenge. Being aware of the critical conditions the employees were working under and getting this information to the right person at the right level was seen as extremely important.

### Leadership style that releases energy

If one wants to establish openness in the groups, it is important that the leader is aware of his role and how one should lead an organization. A lot of effort was put into teaching a leadership style that released energy.

To achieve this it is important to be open, clear, authoritative, approachable and not to overlook a participate style. When these conditions are met the employees can feel secure with their leader and make use of the energy that lies in the group. A leader who understands and masters the dynamics of leading in this manner will be able to bring forward the different sides of an organization's potential to develop process work. A leader who does this will have the employee's trust and only then will have the possibility to succeed.

## PROCESS WORK

To ensure that a good process was followed throughout the project a 'process memo' was developed to guide the project work. It was seen as expedient that one should incorporate a method for process work that could be used in other projects. One of the project's goals was to train employees to use process-oriented methodology in development work within the organization.

*Work processes are based on:*
The project work should take place with the smallest department forming the project team as it is easier to perform awareness enhancement in small groups. Emphasis was put on self-study by taking up concrete situations that arose daily, for example an ethical dilemma. Deliberately utilizing each other's competency, both on the professional and personal level, was seen as very important. To get employees deeply involved in process work is important as it makes them responsible and committed to each member of the group.

## IMPLEMENTATION

### Joint Acknowledgement

Joint acknowledgement by the group was emphasized as one of the most important conditions. The departments were encouraged to use time to describe their experiences so that they may utilize them more effectively in process work and to establish a common reference point or a common point of view.

### Deliberate Freeing and Use of the Groups' Competency and Experience

Groups identified their competency and experience by describing and taking part in the internal discussions of problems. The goal was that the group members would utilize their competency and experience in the project. Further, this activity improves the group's constructive ability to build learning into the process.

**Openness and Security**

By focusing on group dynamics when problems arise, as well as establishing rules for cooperation, one develops constructive and solution-oriented approaches. These were developed within the individual work groups. This was done so that each group would have ownership of the results while establishing a method of working. In addition, it was important to maintain the respect for each individual and enhance the group work process. It is also important that the group learn to differentiate between problems. Not all problems can be handled in group forums, rather other forums may be more appropriate.

**Managing Tension**

There had to be constructive alternatives to turn negative initiatives into positive ones or, failing this, to find alternative forums. The groups were informed that it is normal to have conflicts and to focus on providing a proper process for their resolution. In this process one consciously applied tools such as discussions and sharing in the resolution process. It is also important to take advantage of the group's positive energy.

**Learning by Discovering Oneself through the Process**

The group must work in a climate of constructive reflection of their actions. In order to achieve this the group's method of working had to be revised, by introducing rules and agreeing on a foundation. This was important to ensure that each member of the group felt comfortable. This helps in developing a reflective climate in the group.

**Use 'Socratic' method**

The project group had to actively use the 'why?' formulation to bring to the forefront the various group member's knowledge and experience. Knowledge and experience can be used as an instrument for focusing and steering as well as motivating action and creativity in the group.

In order to illustrate what is meant with this method, I quote from Socrates' defence (as translated from Norwegian):

Each individual must find the truth from within oneself. That which he can do is only to be a 'midwife' for others' thoughts. And it is through discussion that he can get others to think, think not Socrates' thoughts, but their own. By Socratic questioning, ever more aggressive and ever more precise questions the opposition will be forced to clarify their own standpoint.

### Concretizing as a Means

One must not be afraid to challenge thoughts that appear to be castles in the air or pure intellectualization. Action demands a practical, concrete and down-to-earth work style. Thought can be complicated – actions must be simple.

### Attitude and Behaviour must be Linked

One must ask oneself the following questions:

- What does this mean to me?
- How does this impact the work I perform?
- How does this affect the relationship I have with my colleagues?

One must also ask oneself the following questions:

- How do I demonstrate attitude through behaviour?
- How can one demonstrate a specific attitude in a specific situation? To become proficient, one has to train under different situations, discuss situations that arise and present them for discussion in groups.

## DELIBERATE ATTITUDE TOWARDS PROBLEMS

Training oneself to take a deliberate approach to solving problems is critical. We saw it as beneficial to use the small working groups to undertake this type of process work. In cooperation with the leaders, the following list was developed for the groups to use in their project work.

| FROM: | TO: |
|---|---|
| Defensive | Offensive |
| Problem | Solution |
| Adversary | Partner |
| Past | Future |

| | |
|---|---|
| Deviation | Normality |
| Discussion | Sharing |
| Monologue | Dialogue |
| Individual solutions | Group solutions |
| Denying responsibility | Commitment |
| Blame it on others | We will sort this out |

**Control Techniques in Process Work**

The process design was adapted to suit the problem area and participants. Emphasis was put on using questions as a steering mechanism. To develop a basic attitude based on listening to each other was important. In many processes this can be a pitfall which prevents one from progressing. When challenges presented themselves, each individual was allowed time to stop and reflect. Keeping the right level of excitement in the group was important. We defined the right level of excitement as the level needed to secure progress in the group. It was important that the groups managed the different stages of group development: forming, storming, norming, performing and adjourning. When the group reached a difficult discussion, sharing was employed as a technique to get an overview of the problem and to use this as raw material for 'new' problems.

# MY CHALLENGES AS LEADER OF A TOTAL ORGANIZATIONAL PROJECT

Being a leader meant being the 'locomotive' for a project that was undertaken concurrently with the organization's daily operations. This made for some tough days. In the different phases I had to take responsibility. The motivation of individuals varied during the process, something that was occasionally difficult to accept. The middle managers became exhausted and needed my help. The biggest challenge in the process was to be the person that everyone meant should have all the answers. It must be noted that these periods were brief.

I challenged my management team to participate in developing the value foundation for the 'ethics project' before we involved the entire municipality. In my opinion it is clearly a management challenge to start a project of this type and then to give clear guidelines. At a later stage in the project I received feedback that the middle managers wanted to participate in the development of the value foundation. The group would have been too large and such a process would have been too difficult to carry out.

In my assessment the responsibility for a project with such a fundamental subject must rest with higher management. After having completed the project, I am certain that I chose correctly when assigning the responsibility for developing the 'value foundation' to the senior management team.

After the seminar's first day, a new seminar was scheduled for the senior management team in which an external facilitator was present so that everyone would be free to participate in the discussions. This was a deliberate choice on my part. We also felt it was necessary to have an external advisor throughout the project planning phase. We wanted to run the project within the day-to-day operations.

One of the other challenges was not to take control, but to let the process work. This demands time and maturity, especially for those whose style it is to get the desired results. I was often placed in a dilemma as to how to handle those who wanted to go in a different direction than had been agreed upon. How does one get them back on track?

In these situations is was helpful to review the cases that had been developed as a way of securing the methodology. It was my task to be a guide and a partner without taking over.

In certain instances within my management group, I was more of a 'coach' for certain individual group members than for others. I believe that much of what I experienced as a leader could have been avoided by running the project outside the daily operations.

It was important for me as a leader to truly believe in the value foundation that was the platform for the project. There were occasional discussions about certain areas of the value foundation and some wanted to change parts of it. I believe, in retrospect, that it was absolutely necessary to stick with the project's value foundation that we had agreed upon at the start.

The different challenges that I, as a leader, faced throughout the project period, were occasionally difficult as I did not have anyone by my side to discuss what was strategically correct to do in the different situations. To be a top manager in an organization is a lonely job during daily work, but in a situation where one is running a project on ethics and ethical values, the demands on a leader are even larger. Everyone measured me up against the project objectives.

If I had not had the authority that I have as Director of Health Administration in Bergen, it would have been difficult to get the acceptance necessary to carry out a project of this magnitude. That is to say that one has freedom within the given boundaries, but also has the responsibility that goes along with this. The trade unions supported the project. If it had not been for this support and the broad authority, this project would have most likely not been started. I am grateful for all the support and help from all of those who have contributed to the accomplishment of the ethics project.

## PROJECT CONCLUSION

### The Way Forward

The ethics project in the Eidsvåg/Salhus municipality was concluded in 1996. It was an extensive project both in time and ground covered. The project lasted for a year and a half and all employees were involved to varying degrees. It was demanding both time-wise, work-wise and personally. One could not ignore the fact that many let out a sigh of relief when the project's active phase was completed.

A final review showed that almost all of the sub-projects were completed and the results were incorporated into municipal plans. This will secure the municipality's intentions that the ethics project should not be a short-term fad (or 'Mayfly'), but rather a part of the municipality's ongoing work. It is quite clear that many positive things came out of the project; among others one can mention:

1. The employees have a larger degree of awareness with respect to ethical dilemmas in their daily work and are more comfortable when mastering these dilemmas.
2. Cooperation across professions is in greater focus than before.
3. The need for guidance became clear in the Nursing and Care department and the department has commenced activities to increase its competency with respect to advising and communication with clients.
4. The employees have gained experience with comprehensive project and process work in a large organization.

In order to keep this alive in an organization, and particularly as this project deals with attitudes and ethical standards within Health and Social services, it is necessary to do a follow-up. It is our desire to perform an evaluation two or three years after project completion in order to check how the groups and departments have implemented the different initiatives into their daily work. It will also be important and interesting to get feedback on how the forums to discuss ethical dilemmas are used in practice. We also desire to have a client survey performed to get feedback from the municipal clients as to whether they are satisfied with our services and how they are treated by our employees.

## NOTES

1.  In order to have a common attitude and ownership of the project it was important for me, as leader of the municipality, to have my closest subordinates participate actively in the project.
2.  All of the municipality's employees participated in this work.

# 18. Moral competence: a non-relativistic, non-rationalistic definition

## Tomas Brytting

Moral problems are challenges to *the common good*, that is the flourishing and manifestation of each and everyone's potentials. I define and restrict – tentatively – moral competence to be the ability to handle these moral problems at work.[1] Starting from these broad and simple definitions, how could the concept 'moral competence' be elaborated in order to be of practical and theoretical value? Why is the concept needed in the first place?

Democratization of work implies a transformation of work in a way which means that *who* is doing the work will influence *what* will be done at work. If the range of choice opportunities increases, so will responsibility. An increasing number of people discover that their choices at work have a significant impact on other individuals' welfare, pride and power. In other words, they have to handle moral problems at work. At the same time pressure on performance, both quantitative and qualitative, increases and traditional sources for moral guidance like the church, the school or homogenous, shared norms on the societal level, have lost much of their influential power. Instead, each individual nowadays has to develop the skills necessary to deal with responsibility. Without these skills, that is without moral competence, not only the common good may suffer but also the actor himself. Morally induced stress or 'burn-out' may be the result.

## FROM TAYLORISM TO RELATIVISM

The development of organizational theory during this century is a good example of how the kind of rationalism, which spurred the economic development of the Western world from the Enlightenment onwards, has been abandoned. Slowly but steadily, it has been replaced by a less simple-minded yet still confident and authoritarian relativism. Allow me to be very brief in sketching this background, as far as organization theory is concerned.[2]

Fredrick W. Taylor's extreme rationalism at the turn of the century, built on the economic-man paradigm insisted on one simple solution to the organizing problem generally: scientific management, best illustrated by the pre-planned, closely supervised, hierarchical, conveyor-belt-based factory. The so-called Aston School in the 1960s and 1970s left this single-solution model. It suggested that organizational structures and processes should be studied as a kind of dependent variables determined by sets of independent variables like: organization size, technology, batch size, industry characteristics and so on. This deterministic perspective was in turn seriously challenged by the actor's view on organization, represented by David Silverman's book from 1970. Instead of focusing on an 'outer' logic, which determined the structure of organizations, he argued for the importance and possibilities of the 'inner' logic of individual actors. Companies had already discovered that efficient work organizations had to be flexible and open to individual's characteristics, so Silverman's and others' voluntaristic view came in handy. Democratization of the workplace was backed up by both industrial practice and scientific theory.

By then, an even more radical theoretical step had already been taken by sociologists, for example in the book by Peter Berger and Thomas Luckmann published in 1966. The cognitive, or social constructivistic school of organization theory, developed and had a landmark in the publication of the second edition of Karl Weick's book in 1979 (its first appearance in 1969 didn't catch much attention). In that book he argued that organizations do not exist. 'Organizing' exists and preferably in the minds of individual actors. He defined organizing as '... a consensually validated grammar for reducing equivocality by means of sensible interlocked behaviors'. Organizations thus became social constructions, conventions, as it were.

The concepts 'strategy' and 'organizational environment', were later dismantled by Linda Smircich and Gareth Morgan 'in favor of a largely socially-created symbolic world'. Strategic management, they say, is in essence 'the management of meaning' (Smircich and Morgan, 1982). Therefore, organizations have no environment in the classical sense. Instead, the environment as it is conceived within the organization, is being 'enacted' by the organization itself

To make a long story short, organization theory has developed with close contacts with organizational practice. To that extent, it has provided practitioners with useful tools and theorists with insightful concepts and models. Putting much of what we normally conceive of as given features of organizations inside our heads in this way was undeniably a theoretical step forward. Many puzzling organizational phenomena could thereby be better understood and managed, for example organizational inertia and communication disturbances.

But it is evident that somewhere along the line, the field's attraction to a sceptical, not to say relativistic epistemology, became infected with a relativistic ontology. The study of organizational structures and processes was then no longer only a question of trying to understand the way in which human beings made sense of, and put some order into everyday experiences; the reality was no longer studied as a kind of interpreted reality. Reality *became* a social construction in itself.

## INTRODUCING ETHICS

Too little attention has been paid to the ethical implications of this line of reasoning. Take the issue of 'environmental fit' for example. The basic idea behind this concept is that factors outside of the organization's control borders execute certain normative pressure on it. Normally this pressure is understood as customer demands, technological development, legal requirements and so on. In a way Smircich and Morgan may be right in saying that these factors do not activate pressure or restrictions directly on the organization. They are always mediated by individual actors and subject to internal political processes and to 'sense-making' within the organization.

But problems arise if nothing real at all is accepted. Take the term 'environmental fit' to mean: responding to moral claims stemming from stakeholders, for example the right of slave-like child-labourers to have their conditions improved. From the radical social-constructivistic viewpoint, we would be discussing this issue – their suffering – in terms of a 'socially created symbolic world'. Their suffering would exist only to the extent decision-makers in that organization decides it to be the case.

In addition, radical constructivism offers no theoretical tools with which we could confront the lack of moral competence inherent in statements like: 'It's only a matter of common sense', 'Just follow the law'; 'This is how we have always done it'; 'The boss said I had to'; 'This is what everybody else is doing' and so on. These statements all become expressions of a 'consensually validated grammar' and the constructivistic organizational theory has no basis for judging them on moral grounds. To make my point clear: radical constructivism treats all ethical issues as artefacts produced in a process of sense-making, and this puts a limit on ethics, reducing it to the conventional level.

## MORAL COMPETENCE – BETWEEN RATIONALISM AND RELATIVISM

Rationalism runs into difficulties when treating the significance of post-conventional thinking and actions. The English philosopher Raimond Gaita, exemplifies this in an interesting discussion of Martin Luther standing in front of his judges in Worms 1521, saying: *Here I stand, I can do no other. So help me God!* (Gaita, 1991). Is Luther here admitting feelings of incompetence (not being able to leave the place)? From a rational perspective we could support him, telling him that he hasn't got the facts right; that the door is still open; that no one will stop him if he tries, and that the escape is within reach – 'to give it a go' nonetheless! But that seems a totally absurd thing to say. What we really ask of him then would be to change his whole conception not only of the precarious situation in which he finds himself, but also to change his idea of who he is and of the task that he has set for himself All of these things are much more personal than the rationalistic perspective can capture. It is not able to capture the essence of the situation as it presents itself to Luther: its personal, here-and-now-for-me character, or what Gaita calls: the *sui generis* character of moral problems. It puts a strait-jacket on our reflections and therefore distances us from the moral issue we face. (Suggesting a utilitarian calculus would introduce exactly the same distance.) This undermines the relevance of the rationalistic perspective as such, since we no longer recognize the accounts it offers. Moral issues call for our presence, not for our distance.

The main target for Gaita's criticism is the rationalistic way in which ethicists dissect moral situations. But the example he brings forward – Luther – also illustrates the weaknesses with the radical constructivistic perspective. What the constructivistic perspective could do is to open up the possibility of reinterpreting the situation, to turn it into something else. From that perspective Luther's inability to escape is just the result of one out of a multitude of possible versions of a social situation. Growing a constructivistic eye would make it possible for him to reconstruct the scene in a way that would give him more leeway for action. Would that make him more morally competent? Of course not. The significance of the situation, for Luther, is that he 'can do no other', not that he *wants* to do something else. It would certainly not make sense for Luther to investigate his own moral reasoning in terms of social constructivism, eventually making him able to recreate or renegotiate the situation into one in which he can do whatever he wants. I'm not saying that it couldn't be done. The point is that the constructivistic perspective not only bridges the distance between issue and subject, a distance I accused rationalism of creating but instead, *it turns the moral issue into an image of the subject*. Such an 'ability' does not increase moral competence.

The Canadian philosopher Charles Taylor argues that if we want to live an authentic life, it is not enough to choose actions freely, or to follow our own unique life-path (Taylor, 1991). In order to make our choices, and through them also ourselves, meaningful and non-trivial, something significant must be at stake. The most significant choices are made in connections to *moral* claims originating from something more general and enduring than our own whims or feelings:

> Only if I exist in a world in which history, or the demands of nature, or the needs of my fellow human beings, or the duties of citizenship, or the call of God, or something else of this order *matters* crucially, can I define an identity for myself that is not trivial.

It is questionable whether the constructivistic view allows any demands at all to matter in this particular sense, since it is open to the possibility that not only 'something else' but *anything else* could be just as important.

The citation above also gives us a clue to understand Luther's position better. With his: 'I can do no other', he does not express feelings of incompetence – he expresses the *significance* of his action! *The 'realness' of the moral issue affects the image he has of himself.*

It is not freedom then, but restrictions – for example moral prohibitions – which render our actions significant. In that sense we exist, as Charles Taylor puts it, as authentic selves in a 'moral space' which reaches far beyond ourselves. And if we accept a constructivistic ontology, this moral space would lose its significance. In the words of Smircich and Stubbart, moral space – for example moral claims – would enter into organizational decision-making and action 'not by a process of *perceiving* the environment, but by a process of *making* the environment' (Smircich and Stubbart, 1985).

## A HERMENEUTIC PERSPECTIVE

In summary then, rationalism shows difficulties in grasping and accordingly also in helping out in personal moral situations, situations that are *sui generis*. Constructivism, on the other hand, denies that situations can contain absolute moral claims. They also represent theoretical developments increasingly distant from the reality of practitioners. Thus neither of them 'make sense' of moral problems as we face them and know them. A practically and theoretically relevant definition of moral competence must accept the personal character of moral issues and at the same time retain the reality – or 'order'– of moral claims. If not, it will not do its job. As Abraham Kaplan puts it (Kaplan, 1964):

> A theory is a way of making sense of a disturbing situation so as to allow us most effectively to bring to bear our repertoire of habits, and even more important, to modify habits or discard them altogether, replacing them by new ones as the situation demands.

This quote introduces a key word: 'theory'. I propose that in order to be morally competent, it is necessary to have a proper theory, that is 'a way to allow us to bring to bear, or modify, our habits as the situation demands'. (This should not be confused with a demand for ethical theories in the more scientific sense. These belong to philosophers.)

What I call for is a hermeneutic understanding of moral competence, which involves the whole person in his or her struggle to live meaningfully in a complex but real world. The interpretations we make of the reality we meet – the theories that we use – must be able to convey relevant aspects of it. And if we talk of moral (interpretive) competence, our interpretations must be able to convey the *moral* aspects of reality, that is the ways in which the common good is challenged.

The fact that our interpretations reflect our social history does not necessarily imply relativism. All it does is that it points out the relevance of other people, and of social structures, in the formation of our perceptions of reality. An example is the role of information in working life. Information is most often supplied to us by other people; filtered through organizational structures; supported, suppressed or manipulated for individual or ideological reasons; it deteriorates with time, and is tainted by our emotions. Moral competence is the ability to handle moral problems *given* these circumstances, not succumbing to, or embracing them like constructivism seems to recommend, or ignoring them like rationalism does.

## MORAL COMPETENCE DEFINED

Let me briefly define moral competence in the following way:[3]

- Moral competence is a capacity, which brings perception reflection and action together into a coherent whole.
- Moral competence is the ability to understand our choices and actions as non-trivial since they confront us with significant claims stemming from outside ourselves.
- Since the human person is a social being, moral competence is not a strictly individual characteristic. It is socially influenced and can even sometimes appear as a collective ability, especially in working life.
- At the same time, moral competence is the ability to understand the self as a personally responsible subject. However, this understanding is also socially influenced, something which makes the self intimately connected to the welfare of others. Others' claims on us make our own lives meaningful. Thus, how we relate to others influence our capacity to understand ourselves.

- Moral competence can be supported by more or less formalized structures.

## MORAL COMPETENCE IN PRACTICE – THE CASE OF LOSS ADJUSTERS

In order to further explore this theoretically derived conception of moral competence, especially its social and collective aspects, I interviewed loss adjusters working with people inflicted by severe physical damages. The rationale behind that choice was that I was looking for practitioners working in situations where the well-being of others was challenged, and where the practitioner's behaviour had a major impact.

The loss adjuster shall conduct an investigation assessing the direct costs related to the accident: hospital treatment; transport; necessary adjustments of living conditions caused by the disablement; loss of income and so on. Compensation is also paid for the suffering and the disablement itself. The challenges involved in this work is illustrated by this story told by one of the interviewees:

> It was this old couple who were out driving with their three grandchildren. Grandpa makes a mistake and crashes. Both grandparents die. One of the kids dies, one is severely hurt. One kid comes out reasonably well. The parents are newly divorced so the kids live with their mother. So the mother loses both her parents and a kid, one is severely hurt. How do you create a pleasant atmosphere when you meet such a person?

The task of the loss adjuster is to put a price-tag on accidents like this one, balancing the interest of the victim, the insurance company and its other customers (who want to keep the fees low), within the limits of the law and the terms of the insurance contract. What kind of competence is needed to solve this task?

Emotions and empathy are definitely needed but competent loss adjusters according to themselves – cannot rely on feelings:

> I mustn't get so empathic that I get stuck in the investigation process. That process has to be taken forward by me. I cannot just sit there crying in the phone, so to speak, together with the victim. I have to handle those questions that for me are of a non-emotional nature: establish former income-levels, assessing things etc… That this individual had had an accident which in this individual's life is unique and which have changed this individual's life more or less dramatically, that is for me a routine matter.

Instead, a lot of the assessments that have to be made are being done through a rather bureaucratic (in a non-pejorative sense) process or 'routine' which I will describe below.

Now, remember the definition of moral competence as being: the integration of perception, reflection and action in support of the common good. The two outcomes just mentioned – that is being paralysed by empathy or just following standardized routines – offer two extreme positions in terms of action. Somewhere in between lies morally competent behaviour. The loss adjuster must employ perception and reflection – that is make interpretations of individual circumstances – which leads to actions that support the common good. How do these interpretations look?

**Finding the 'Right' Level – Rationalistic Perception and Reflection**

Seeing the work from its bureaucratic side, the loss adjuster has to follow certain strict formal guidelines. For instance, there are standardized price-lists for lost limbs or different kinds of disablement. A formally competent physician, using standardized definitions, must establish the degree of disablement. Direct costs must be 'reasonable', which in most cases means that they have to be supported with receipts. Loss of income must be documented and is calculated according to a fairly strict model and so on. Simply by following these and similar guidelines, the loss adjuster can get a fairly good estimate of the compensation level without having to execute individual judgement. Moreover, it is not up to the loss adjuster to settle the matter finally. Based on the investigation, he or she puts forward a suggestion for decision to a special board. This board consists of representatives from involved parties: lawyers, patient associations and loss adjusters from other companies. It is this board that takes the final decision. It is also this board that authorizes or adjusts the different formal procedures and standards that is being used in the process.

Through this process the tragic accident is being translated into a figure which gets a kind of objectivity around it. And in the mind of many loss adjusters there are, accordingly, compensation levels, which are considered to be 'right' or 'correct', expressions that reflect this objectification. Thus, to be a competent loss adjuster is to be: knowledgeable; objective; thorough; and discrete. Added to this list is also suspicion, in order to be able to look through attempts by some victims to fool the system.

But is this really a listing of what it takes to be a *morally* competent loss adjuster? Is it not rather a description of the bureaucratic mind in general? Hesitations like these reflect the limitations of the rationalistic spirit, which permeates this version of the process. It leaves out feelings and individual circumstances. At the same time it leaves out people, and without people the moral issues seem to disappear altogether. However, let us not forget that bureaucratic structures often function as support structures, sometimes even as a manifestation of collective moral competence in the sense that they make it possible to handle moral problems at work. In that sense they may be necessary, but they are not sufficient.

No loss adjuster would accept the bureaucratic version of their work as being a complete description. There are aspects of their work which simply cannot be, and is not, treated this way. And even more important, the reduction of both loss adjuster and victim inherent in this kind of description is rejected on moral grounds by the ones involved.

## 'Like being God' – Rationalism Let Loose

Sometimes the idea of looking for the 'right' compensation becomes in itself meaningless. Take the following example: an eight-year-old girl has been hit by a car and suffers from serious and permanent brain damages. It is then up to the loss adjuster to calculate the 'right' figure for the loss of future income for this girl. What would she have been working with as an adult? What would she be earning in 20, 30, 40, 50 years time if the accident hadn't occurred? Needless to say, these are difficult questions, but nevertheless questions which the loss adjuster has to answer.

For the rational mind, this problem is simply unsolvable – there is no right or wrong answer – and the pragmatic way out would be to settle, more or less arbitrarily, for a standardized mean-salary (which in practice most often becomes the solution). But does the unsolvable character of these questions mean that the loss adjuster experiences *incompetence* in situations like this one, and if so, would they like to be more competent in the rational sense, meaning that they would like to be more knowledgeable, having insights into this girl's future?

During the interviews I confronted the interviewees with a hypothetical situation in which they had access to a gene test that could tell them, with some accuracy, something about the capacities of the little girl. If the genes could paint a picture of a bright intellect or an artistic genius, or of a dull mind for that matter, would that simplify the work of the loss adjuster? Wouldn't such a gene test improve the accuracy of their guesses concerning the future income of the girl, helping them to come closer to the 'right' level?

Everyone was shocked by this possibility: 'It would be very unethical', 'What an unpleasant question!' or 'It would be like being God!' as one put it, obviously trying to tell me how horrific it would be. They didn't want to be more competent in the rational sense. Why would it be so bad?

A first answer arises from the loss adjuster's tendency to use empathy as guidance in tricky situations:

I would react very strongly myself. Not only would I have to show what I had suffered, I would also have to reveal all the risks inside of me, which I carry with me as an inheritance. I may not want to know what future risks I may have to face. Maybe I live a good life in ignorance of what may strike me.

The second answer is that it would, literary speaking, put the life of this girl in the hands of the loss adjuster. Her secrets would be revealed to them and what would they do with that information? The question I asked focused on the heavy burden which responsibility implies. Being like God means being able to let your own judgements have a major impact on the life of others.

The loss adjusters are trapped in a dilemma. They have an impact on the life of the victims, a power which stimulates and scares them at the same time. But, on the other hand, their hands are tied by rules and through supervision from others, something which is taken with relief. This ambivalence between subjectivity as a burden and rules as a support was expressed in the following way:

> The big moral dilemma is whether I have made a correct judgement. Have I made the necessary investigation in order to reach a level of compensation which is as right as possible? Have I let myself be influenced by my own prejudices? When I investigate this, do I choose route based on my initial – unconscious? – impression of this individual? Do my investigations thereby cut off possible compensations? This is a moral dilemma... We all carry ideas about things, we like certain people more or less and that may affect our work. I often think about that. Is it right? Is it wrong? Have I 'read' this person correctly? Could this person have done what s/he says? There is a lot of economic power in my hands, that's for sure.

As a matter of fact, the loss adjusters saw no way in which increased knowledge in this sense would allow them to be more competent in their work because they saw their work as something much more than reaching an economic settlement.

> Our customers shall get what they are entitled to but more important is that they understand that they got what they were entitled to and that they are satisfied. Explain!... Tell the customer that you understand. You understand that they have lived through hell. Tell them, but tell them also what they can and cannot get compensated for. If you can explain this, the customer will say: Alright, I didn't get all what I wanted, but they understood that I had a hard time and I got what I was entitled to.
>
> I had this case a couple of years ago; I worked with it for several years. I visited him and his family. We found each other... He got no more or less than any other, but I made a thorough investigation and I listened to them. I got postcards from him years afterwards.

It is the interplay between the strictness and objectivity of the rules and the softness – ambivalence and uncertainty, if you like – of the individual case, which forms the arena on which the loss adjusters do their work.

## Constructivistic Perception and Reflection

If the work of the loss adjuster was studied from a radical constructivistic perspective, the process in which they take part would actually be the one in which the accident and its consequences were created. The only reasonable conclusion from such an account would be to close down the whole business!

The perspective could be taken in a slightly less radical way, saying that the moral challenges inherent in the loss adjuster's work could be studied as something 'socially constructed' and 'consensually validated'. Then no substantial criticism could be raised towards, for instance, the bureaucratic process just described. In fact *no process whatsoever* needs further justification. (In the case of the little girl, a constructivist mind would not be able to see a moral difference in settling for a mean salary or any other level as long as an agreement is reached.) Any described process simply illustrates how reality - that is the accident and its consequences - is socially constructed and validated within the insurance company - full stop!

It is hard to see what normative message may come out from the constructivistic perspective, apart from the idea, maybe, that the construction and validation process ought to support the goals of the organization. That, in turn, would imply that the definition of moral problems lay in the hands of the management! I saw no traces at all of such an idea in my interviews. Another normative conclusion could be that the construction and validation of 'reality' ought to support the common good. However, as far as the common good is seen as a social construction in itself, this line of reasoning runs in circles.

On a superficial level, the loss adjuster, the physicians, the victim and his or her legal counsellor, and the board, where involved in a process, a kind of negotiation, in which the social reality - that is the accident, its consequences and the size of the compensation - were constructed in a way that could be accepted as a consensus view among the ones concerned. In that sense, the work of the loss adjuster is to take part in a social construction of reality reflecting the interests of all parties involved, in that sense supporting the common good.

I have three objections to this way of using the perspective. First of all, the result of this kind of negotiation is hardly a consensus view but rather a compromise in which power has had a strong influence. Thus, the result might reflect the common good but then just by accident. Second, the issue which is 'constructed' in this process is definitely not the moral challenge as such. That challenge, which is about the right of individual persons to be treated with dignity and not to be abused because they lack power in a particular situation, that challenge is never an issue itself. What is not the object of construction is whether the loss adjuster should respect the dignity of the victim or not! Third, the negotiations described by the loss adjusters are about events (What happened exactly? How has the life of the victim changed after the accident?) and about the application of legal and bureaucratic rules. Reality is taken for granted and what is discussed is whether different accounts of that reality are in correspondence with it or not.

In summary, the constructivistic theory does not make sense to the loss adjusters themselves, and from a researcher's point of view, it doesn't seem to convey what they actually do when they face moral problems at work.

## 'As if it Never had Happened' – Hermeneutics in Practice

The hermeneutic perspective is theory in between. It implies a loosening-up of the rationalistic perspective without falling into radical (ontological) constructivism. If this perspective is used to describe and analyse the work of the loss adjuster, it will no longer be a question of finding the 'right' level of compensation but rather to draw a line between 'reasonable' and 'unreasonable' levels of compensation. For instance, when is it correct to take a taxi to the hospital and when should one go by public transport? Does the victim have the right to be compensated for household work – if there are teenagers at home? If the victim was forced to work part time after the accident, is this only because of the accident? In all these cases there is no longer a clear line between right and wrong. A zone of ambivalence appears in which the loss adjuster has considerable degrees of freedom, and responsibility, in terms of perception, reflection and action.

When the individuality of persons and situations came up during the interviews, many interviewees stopped talking about 'correct' compensation. Instead they shift to another expression: they said that they seek compensation levels which can recreate – adjust – the situation to what it was before: 'as if the accident had never happened'. This reinterpretation allows for the loss adjuster to use much more of his or her competences than just the rational mind. By meeting with the victim and with the family, by visiting their house or apartment; learning more about their daily lives both before and after the accident, the loss adjuster involves much more of him or herself into the investigation. Note however that it is not the kind of limitless empathy which paralysed the loss adjuster in the example above. It has more to do with using one's whole personality as a tool to solve a professional problem: to investigate the changes that the accident has caused in the victim's life. Together they develop an interpretation of the situation, which reflects and respects the personality of both parties.

> *Researcher*   But if you have to deal with seriously disabled people, whose life and property is being ruined; is it possible to create a comfortable situation?

> *Loss adjuster*   Yes, but on condition that you do not take it lightly. You have to

understand them, but you cannot let it get to you too much. You cannot go home to people and cry.

*Researcher*   It is a thin line between empathy and 'go home to people and cry'. How do you know where to draw that line?

*Loss adjuster*   It is nothing you can learn. It's just something you notice when you do it right, and you notice it when it's possible to continue. You have a dialogue.

*Researcher*   The dialogue proves that you have taken in enough but not too deep?

*Loss adjuster*   Right!

The interesting thing here is to notice how dialogue appears as a result when the other is being treated as a subject and not simply as the object of a bureaucratic routine process. The mechanism works both ways:

> I find it very difficult when I speak with somebody and I realize that here we have certain expectations on the compensation level, or that certain things must be paid for, and I notice that this person doesn't understand... 'You don't want to give me...'; 'You come from a big company and you step on me'. 'You use your strength against me'. They don't believe my good intentions to do this as well as possible, as right as possible. My starting point is that I'm not earning money for my company when I'm on this job. I'm very clear on that. We have the right to pay compensation... But I can't make them understand...

The loss adjusters, on their part, also experience frustration; they even call it a moral problem, when they are not being treated as subjects in themselves but as representatives of a large anonymous company. This also destroys the dialogue.

## The 'Good' Bureaucracy

After having rejected the constructivistic perspective, there is obviously a risk of falling back into the rationalistic fallacy, that is that moral challenges can be described and solved through a disciplined, systematic analysis. For instance, the rationality that is reflected in the bureaucratic way of organizing work clearly has to face this risk. Bureaucracy filters information, thus influencing the perceptions and reflections of the people working in it. It is part of its nature to specify in considerable detail how people should act in certain situations. In other words it influences, or sometimes even controls the perception, reflection and action of individuals.

Nevertheless, I would argue that a certain amount of bureaucracy is necessary. First of all, it solves a lot of practical probems by offering solutions once and for all. Solving each new problem as if it was unique, as if no experience could be drawn upon, would be unrealistic. No party would benefit from a process in which the loss adjusters were totally free from bureaucratic control – then they would 'be like God'. The individual responsibility that a totally unregulated work situation would create would be unbearable. Such a process would relieve neither the victim nor the loss adjuster from emotional problems. On the contrary, both parties gain from having a professional relationship. Even within the present situation problems of 'burn-out' are common.

> We had a meeting with young people in wheelchairs. They didn't care too much about this thing with loss adjustment. Practical matters had taken over and in a way that felt good. When it comes down to it, we play a rather limited part in their lives.

How long would a loss adjuster be able to function if it was up to him or her personally to fix the price-tag of a destroyed human life?

My conclusion is that bureaucracy could be an important thing allowing the loss adjusters to execute moral competence. It makes up a kind of moral space (albeit in a fairly soft sense compared to other 'horizons of significance' in Charles Taylor's words). Following bureaucratic rules and procedures may therefore be a kind of execution of collective moral competence, under the condition, of course, that these rules and procedures support the common good! Going against them and acting in a contrary, individual way, on the other hand, intensifies the significance of the individual action.

## NOTES

1. These definitions may raise more questions than they answer but that is a risk that has to be taken considering the limited space available here. A more elaborate discussion can be found in Brytting (2001).
2. A slightly more detailed account of this process can be found in Brytting (2000).
3. Apart from Charles Taylor (1989, 1991), Martin Buber (1987) and a pragmatic view on ethics has inspired this definition. For a much more elaborate treatment of the two concepts: 'competence' and 'moral competence' along these lines, see Brytting (2001).

## REFERENCES

Berger, Peter and Thomas Luckmann (1966), *The Social Construction of Reality - A Treatise in the Sociology of Knowledge*, London, Penguin Books.
Brytting, Tomas (2000), 'The Preconditions for Moral Competence: Contemporary Rationalization and the Creation of Moral Space' in Verstraeten, Johan (ed.), *Business Ethics - Broadening the Perspectives*, Leuven, Peeters, pp. 81–95
Brytting, Tomas (2001), *Att vara som Gud - moralisk kompetens i arbetslivet*: Malmö, Liber Ekonomi.
Buber, Martin (1925, 1987), *I and Thou*, T. & T. Clark.
Gaita, Raimond (1991), *Good and Evil - An Absolute Conception*, London, Macmillan Press.

Kaplan, Abraham (1964), *The Conduct of Inquiry - Methodology for Behavioural Science*, Chandler Publishing Company.

Silverman, David (1970), *The Theory of Organizations*, London, Heinemann.

Smircich, Linda and Gareth Morgan (1982), 'Leadership - The Management of Meaning', *Journal of Applied Behavioural Science*, **18**(3), pp. 257-273.

Smircich, Linda and Charles Stubbart (1985), 'Strategic Management in an Enacted World', *Academy of Management Review*, **10**(4), pp. 724-736.

Taylor, Charles (1989), *Sources of the Self - The Making of the Modern Identity*, Cambridge, Mass., Harvard University Press.

Taylor, Charles (1991), *The Ethics of Authenticity*, Cambridge, Mass., Harvard University Press.

Weick, Karl (1979), *The Social Psychology of Organizing*, Reading, Mass, Addison-Wesley.

# 19.  Habits of the heart: arguments for an ineffable, social grammar

## Verner C. Petersen

---

Kohlhaas, der du dich gesandt zu sein vorgibst, das Schwert der Gerechtigkeit zu handhaben, was unterfängst du dich, Vermessener, im Wahnsinn stockblinder Leidenschaft, du, den Ungerechtigkeit selbst vom Wirbel bis zur Sohle erfüllt? Weil der Landesherr dir, dem du untertan bist, dein Recht verweigert hat, dein Recht in dem Streit um ein nichtiges Gut, erhebst du dich, Heilloser, mit Feuer und Schwert und brichst wie der Wolf der Wüste in die friedliche Gemeinheit, die er beschirmt.
(Dr Martin Luther's handbill in Heinrich von Kleist's *Michael Kohlhaas*)

## REACTIONS TO INJUSTICE

In Michael Kohlhaas, Heinrich von Kleist (Kleist, 1808) tells the grim story of how a relatively small injustice escalates almost into civic insurrection. It is the story of the wealthy horse trader Michael Kohlhaas.

The strange and unhappy story of this man takes it beginning one day when he is travelling to Saxony with a couple of well-fed young horses. Crossing the border he is asked to show his travel permit. Michael Kohlhaas has never heard that such permit is necessary, and does not have money available to pay for one. Instead he leaves behind as security two black horses together with a boy who is told to care well for them. They are all placed in the care of the castle bailiff, Junker Wenzel von Tronka.

When Michael Kohlhaas later arrives in Dresden he finds out that a travel permit was not necessary. He succeeds in selling the rest of his horses and returns to collect his two black horses and the boy. He finds the horses in miserable condition in a stable, while the boy has been chased away for disobedience.

Kohlhaas is incensed and refuses to accept the horses as they are. Instead he carries his case to the court, but his complaint is turned down, apparently because the bailiff, Junker Tronka, is related to the officials of the court. His wife goes to Berlin to deliver a petition in person. Guards hinder her in delivering the petition and by accident one of them wounds her fatally.

Kohlhaas swears revenge. He rides to the castle of Junker Wenzel von

Tronka, and burns down everything. The Junker has already fled to Wittenberg. Kohlhaas follows him, torches part of the town, and threatens to continue until the Junker is delivered to him. The Junker flees to Leipzig with Kohlhaas at his heels. A growing number of people is following Kohlhaas. What began as a personal vendetta has grown into a small, but dangerous insurrection.

At this point Dr Martin Luther enters the story. As a result of Luther's intervention the case is reopened, while Kohlhaas receives some kind of amnesty. Later another incident involving Kohlhaas leads to his arrest and a trial against him. In this trial he is condemned to death. On the day he is being led to his execution, his lawyer presents him with the sentence in the new process relating to his two black horses. The original sentence has been overturned, and Kohlhaas receives the justice that he had sought with the original complaint. His demand for compensation has been met, all lost property given back and Junker Wenzel has been sentenced to two years in jail. Overwhelmed Kohlhaas kneels and declares that 'his highest wish on earth has been fulfilled', with this he turns to the scaffold, 'wo sein Haupt unter dem Beil des Scharfrichters fiel' (Kleist, 1808, p. 148).

How do we see the story of Michael Kohlhaas? Most people would presumably agree that he was unjustly treated, but after that agreement might dissolve. Some might see the injustice done to him as nothing more than a slight, something like this happens, he might have taken his horses and tried to forget that he was slighted. The death of his wife was a result of an accident. Others may follow him part of the way, but perhaps not in setting his enemy's castle on fire and burning down the towns. They may understand his fight for justice, but not the means he employs.

Still the story may have many parallels with individuals fighting what looks like a hopeless fight against injustice and despotic regimes. From the fictional, but vivid pictures of lone rangers and individual avengers of American Western movies, to what is seen as terrorist or freedom fighters fighting for a new social order. On a smaller scale we may know our own Michael Kohlhaas replicas, as individuals fighting against what they regard as lies and injustice in organizations, often alone and often in a losing battle, making the fight seem pointless and difficult to understand for the more passive bystanders.

## JUDGEMENT

How do we judge Michael Kohlhaas? I suppose that many would answer by saying that it was evident that he was treated unjustly: when asked for a travel permit; when attempting to collect the horses; and when he was turned down by the court. But what standards are we using when perhaps implicitly judging like this?

Do we change our opinion later, when we hear what he does to get his revenge? Is he now acting unjust and unfair? In the end he seems to accept that he gives his life to get justice. How much of his efforts do we condone and how much do we condemn? How right or wrong are Michael Kohlhaas' actions in the light of what we know?

One of the aspects that probably trouble us today is his almost total disregard for the consequences of his actions; nothing seems important to him; neither his horses, the boy taking care of them, his home, his wife, nor all the others touched by his revenge. In a way they are important of course, but principle seems even more important.

When judging Michael Kohlhaas there are many different and overlapping ethical principles to choose from. What then makes us choose a certain version? Internal consistency? A feeling that one's version is the right one?

Perhaps our question is wrong, perhaps we do not have to choose, because every principle may be incomplete and represent a biased single-sided view. Perhaps our judgements of ethical dilemmas contain aspects from all these theories.

In Hume's view (Hume, 1740) moral judgements are based on feelings. They do not and cannot represent any objective principles. What these feelings are and how they have evolved is not really answered, and this leads to serious problems with the approach of Hume. The feeling may be strictly personal and not shared by others, and one may question the morality of separate and different individual moralities.

In *Grundlegung zur Metaphysik der Sitten* (Kant, 1785) Kant argued against basing morality on emotions and feelings. He could not warn strongly enough against smuggling empirical motives and feelings into moral judgements. Instead he maintained that all moral commands must take the form of categorical moral imperatives, meaning that moral commands must be independent of individual wishes and goals, of the consequences, and individual feelings and wants. Kant himself though castigated certain sexual practices, 'on the ground that they are contrary to nature and especially because they "degrade" a person to the level of animals and make him "unworthy of his humanity. He no longer deserves to be a person"' (Brandt, 1997, p. 137).

Here trouble brews. Where did Kant get his condemnation from, if not from something apart from his own principles, from culture, religious conviction or whatever? Another problem inherent in any attempt to use Kantian principles in practice is immediately evident. The principles may lead to insolvable conflicts, and what principle ought to guide us then?

Turning to consequentialism one might think that here at least we would have a universal principle that would be as applicable today as when the first utilitarians formulated it. According to Bentham and Mill, what increased happiness or pleasure was right and what decreased it wrong. 'The creed which accepts as the foundation of morals, Utility or the Greatest Happiness Principle, holds that actions are right in proportion as they tend to promote happiness, wrong as they tend to produce the reverse of happiness. By happiness is intended pleasure, and the absence of pain; by unhappiness, pain, and the privation of pleasure' (Mill, 1859–65, p. 6).

The trouble starts with the question of what should count. What about the pains of animals compared to the pleasures of watching a bull fight?

Mill's solution was to leave judgement of what pleasures are to count as pleasures to competent judges, meaning people with experiences of both higher and lower pleasures. Would we accept that kind of judgement today?

All the theories that we have referred to contain important elements that are somehow irreducible and outside the theory. Where do emotions and sentiments originate? What are pleasures and pains, why are some pleasures qualitatively better than others, and why do certain pleasures carry intrinsic value? In the Kantian theory we saw the problem with judgements like 'unworthy of his humanity. He no longer deserves to be a person'.

It seems reasonable to presume that Kant's judgements like everyone else's in this exposition are coloured by a preconceived conception of what is right, just and ethical, that cannot be explained by the theories they are expounding, but must originate somewhere else – nature, intuition, culture, ineffable inclinations, conditioned reflexes, or something else.

It is as if these colorations belong not to reason, but to habits we do not question or think about, perhaps we may call them habits of the heart.

## HABITS OF THE HEART

Suppose for a moment that making a moral judgement is in some way analogous to recognizing a face. It may seem strange, but please humour me for a moment. It is rather difficult to get to know the particulars of what makes us recognize a face that we have never seen in exactly this shape before, in the sense that it is 20 years ago that we saw that person last. Here we are of course presuming that the person in question does not have some very recognizable feature, like a large mole on the tip of his nose. That would give the game away. We are also able to recognize a whole range of facial expressions, although we may not be able to state the particulars of this process. We just do it (Russell and Fernandez-Dols, 1997).

If routine moral judgements are made in the same way, we may not be able to give a lot of reasons for our judgements; we may just be able to state that we feel that this would be the right or the wrong thing to do. When asked why this would be right or wrong, we are unable to appeal either to universality, utility or any other criterion. To us it might be evident almost in the same way that it would be evident that *this* is the face of someone we know.

A simpler example might involve discerning between a genuine smile and a faked smile. I suppose that almost everyone would know immediately what I mean by a genuine and a faked smile. Not that most people know anything about the muscles of face; we just say that a faked smile would be revealed by the eyes. Damasio has the story of the particulars (Damasio, 1994). A smile of real joy requires the combined involuntary contraction of two muscles, the zygotic major, and the orbicularis oculi. We can wilfully control the first while the orbicularis oculi is beyond wilful control. Normally we would not be able to explain that, but we recognize the effect. We see the smile of joy. 'These reasoning instincts are powerful inference engines, whose automatic, non-conscious operation creates our seamless experience of the world' (Cosmides and Toby, 1994, p. 66).

These reasoning and judging instincts enable us to recognize faces, genuine smiles, faked smiles, chairs, sexual harassment, almost pathological justice-seeking avengers, and judgements on strange sentences violating our moral sense.

Before we can draw such a conclusion we have to find some convincing arguments. In doing this we shall have to show the plausibility and importance of a tacit and ineffable foundation of our value judgements. We begin with the tentative model outlined in Table 19.1

*Table 19.1   The tacit foundation of value judgements*

| | |
|---|---|
| The internal cautioner | Locating judgements in ourselves |
| | Individual responsibility |
| | Somatic markers |
| The social and ethical grammar | The social foundations of our judgements |
| | The collective unconscious |
| *'Großvaters Zopf'* | The importance of evolution and heritage |
| | for our social grammar |

## THE INTERNAL CAUTIONER

A bright sun is shining through my window for the first time this spring, and suddenly I become aware of an almost irresistible urge to leave the computer. Some inside cautioner warns me to stay in my place in spite of the urge I feel. Written rules and explicit threats of external sanctions prohibiting or limiting a certain kind of behaviour would never be able to equal the internal tacit cautioner saying 'No' to me. Is this perhaps the only place where we can locate our much sought after individual sense of responsibility? We shall see.

Perhaps we may glean some insight on this internal cautioner by employing Damasio's concept of somatic markers (Damasio, 1994). Damasio sets out by raising almost the same sort of objections that we have raised against the reasoned approaches to explanation of our judgements. To him this is the 'high reason view'.

In a way a somatic marker represents a more sophisticated version of what we may call gut feeling. The unpleasant feeling that shows when we may not be comfortable with a certain decision or action. This also seems to be the reason for the name somatic marker. Soma for body, or bodily reactions and marker because it marks the sketches of the mind. A somatic marker may act more subtly than that, no queasy feeling in stomach is necessary, the uneasiness may show itself in a bias that we are unaware of. It may reveal itself in no more than the expression: 'I feel it would be right'.

A similar argument can be found in Richardson's attempt to analyse practical reasoning about final ends. '... some judgements cannot adequately be expressed except when accompanied by the appropriate emotion, this emotional layer is essential to full self-awareness. We can be left groping for words adequate to express our judgements, and forced consequently to rely upon tone of voice to add the difference. 'It was horrible! for example, is said in many ways' (Richardson 1994, p. 186).

We may see a somatic marker as a biasing device; it does not put us on a kind of autopilot, but it subtly guides and restricts us in our judgements as well as in our actions. Somatic markers may be felt when we talk about a certain action giving us a bad taste, or a queasy feeling in the stomach. In ways we cannot individually understand and explain they signify a bias of our feelings, and there is not much we can consciously do about that.

We are not quite back with Hume; it is not just any emotion that is allowed to pass through and influence actions. We are talking about conditioned feelings, feelings like embarrassment, shame and remorse. Feelings 'acquired by experience, under the control of an internal preference system and under the influence of an external set of circumstances which include not only entities and events with which the organism must interact, but also social conventions and ethical rules' (Damasio, 1994, p. 179).

Perhaps these feelings and markers are also what compel us to act, making us feel that we have to, almost without thinking. We just feel that it is the right thing to do. The internal cautioner may in some cases urge us to act, in other cases put up a warning sign saying 'No way!' As we have argued before, any reference to Kantian principles or any calculation of pros and cons will not be enough to compel us to act.

We may have the mistaken belief that we reason according to the principles of Mill, Kant, or Rawls, but like them we are biased by the lumps of ineffable feelings that we can never hope to explain. In a sense this may turn out to have both positive and negative effects. On the one hand it limits our reasoning and acts as invisible barriers to arbitrary changes in values, on the other hand this may be of decisive importance for our most basic ethical stance. If we cannot touch this stance with the cerebrum, or the part of the brain where conscious thought is found, then we cannot change it to suit what might seem to be advantageous to us in a given moment. We are stuck with our bias.

This may bring us an accusation of subjectivism. We might all have different forms of bias and our somatic markers may make our pulse throb or our face blush red in widely different situations. We hope to avoid this accusation by showing that there might in fact exist a non-subjective foundation for the biases and somatic markers that we possess, without being able to state explicitly what these biases are.

## THE SOCIAL AND ETHICAL GRAMMAR

We presume that the moral judgements are made according to what might be seen as a social and ethical grammar. We prefer to use the terms social and ethical, because we want to underline the social part of this grammar, realizing of course that certain parts of the grammar may be social, but not necessarily have anything to do with ethics. Table manners, dress codes, and so on come to mind as something that may belong to a social grammar, but have little relevance for ethics and morals.

Perhaps our concept of grammar may have something in common with Wittgenstein's 'Sprachspiele'. In '*Philosophische Untersuchungen*' he writes 'Grammatik sagt nicht, wie die Sprache gebaut sein muß, um ihre Zwecke zu erfüllen, um so und so auf die Menschen zu wirken. Sie beschreibt nur, aber erklärt in keiner Weise, den Gebrauch der Zeichen' (Wittgenstein quoted in Haller, 1981, p. 59).

A small example found in Cosmides and Toby (Cosmides and Toby, 1994, p. 67) may demonstrate how a social grammar might work. We have to consider two sentence samples:

1. If he's the victim of an unlucky tragedy, then we should pitch in to help him out.
2. If he spends his time loafing and living off others, then he doesn't deserve our help.

Contrast this with:

3. If he's the victim of an unlucky tragedy, then he doesn't deserve our help.
4. If he spends his time loafing and living off others, then we should pitch in to help him out.

I suspect that most readers would find nothing wrong with sentences 1 and 2, while sentences 3 and 4 may seem rather odd or disturbing. Why should anyone want to say something like that? Sentences 3 and 4 state something that seems unjust to our moral senses, perhaps leading to us to blurt out: 'This wouldn't be fair would it?'

Presumably most people intuitively see these sentences as stating something that would be unjust. It would be seen as evident, not as something that had to or could be explained. What is happening may be analogous to what is happening, when we recognize a face. We cannot tell what particulars were involved, we just recognize it. It may be in this sense that the two sentences violate an ineffable grammar of moral and social reasoning.

Social in the sense that Cawell is talking about. 'We learn and teach words in certain contexts, and then we are expected, and expect others, to be able to project them into further contexts. Nothing ensures that this projection will take place (in particular, not the grasping of universals, nor the grasping of books of rules), just as nothing ensures that we will make, and understand, the same projections. That on the whole we do is a matter of our sharing routes of interest and feeling, modes of response, senses of humour and of significance and of fulfilment, of what is outrageous, of what is similar to what else, what a rebuke, what forgiveness, of when an utterance is an assertion, when an appeal, when an explanation – all the whirl of the organism Wittgenstein call, 'forms of life'. Human speech and activity, sanity and community, rest upon nothing more, but nothing less, than this. It is a vision as simple as it is difficult' (Cawell, 1976, p. 52).

The social grammar that consists of partly covert rules and examples and partly covert norms and predispositions[2] makes us able to judge and act in relation to specific cases, almost in the same sense that we are able to construct sentences, without looking up explicit rules or making prolonged calculations. 'In the study of reasoning, a grammar is a finite set of rules that can generate all appropriate inferences while not simultaneously generating inappropriate ones. If it is a grammar of social reasoning, then these inferences are about the domain of social motivation and behaviour; an 'inappropriate' inference is defined as one that members of a social community would judge as incomprehensible or nonsensical' (Cosmides and Toby 1994, p. 68-69).

We assume that a social grammar would be characterized by being:

- layered, and contingent, not derivable from simple principles;
- shared as a collective conscience, internalized by individuals;
- generative and non-determinative.

*Layered*   We have discussed the layers of ethical reasoning elsewhere (Petersen, 1998). On the basis of this discussion we presume that parts of the social grammar may be found in the explicit rules regulating and limiting the behaviour of people in a community. All the way from The Declaration of Human Rights, parts of national constitutions, via specific laws against corruption or sexual harassment, to family and personnel policies. These rules would seem to represent a surface layer of explicit ethical norms that either have or can be given a written expression.

Making ethical judgements apparently involves much more than following written ethical codes and laws regulating behaviour though, it involves as we have seen an internalized ethical grammar, or a set of tacit norms, and a certain level of knowledge. At this intermediate level judgements seem to relate to some vaguely defined norms, which we can only talk about in a roundabout way. They are not usually written down, but are expressible in a general way, for instance when we talk about fairness or justice. They may also be likened to the tacit rules of a moderately skilful chess player, who according to Black is 'guided by memories of his own previous successes and failures and, still more importantly, by the sifted experience of whole generations of masters' (Black, 1990, p. 108).

We can think consciously about the norms and values, and they seem to be part of our common sense. Maybe this is the level where we can locate the philosophical discussions of ethics and instances of ethical appeal. Maybe this is the level where we can find expressions like: 'It is in the interest of all ... that this kind of behaviour is not condoned'. At this level we are still able to give some kind of reason for judgements we make, although the arguments may be rather philosophical.

An even deeper level would represent the really unconscious layers of the mind, containing ineffable ethical norms and feelings, inclinations and emotions that belong to the collective unconscious. This is the layer where the somatic markers originate.

Our layer concept may even help us avoid a problem troubling Sidgwick (Sidgwick, 1907) in a discussion of practical reasoning in the case where two practical principles overlap and in doing so give conflicting advice. Sidgwick's solution was to devise a kind of practical rationality involving explicit reasoning. In the end he is taking the hedonistic road like others before him, concluding: 'If we are not to systematise human activities by taking Universal Happiness as their common end, on what other principle are we to systematise them?' (Quoted in Richardson, 1994, p. 130).[3]

Others have proposed different solutions to the same problem. McIntyre (McIntyre, 1981) for instance prefers to invoke a kind of narrative unity.

In our conception we see no need for complete hierarchical consistency, only an overall coherence, anchored in a decentralized way in the collective unconscious. There is no single overriding principle. Only a tacit consistency between a multitude of possible practical judgements on the surface and the deeper layers. Like a linguistic grammar a social grammar is in no need of a single overriding principle.[4] What we have instead are mutually supporting decentral elements.

*Shared and silent*   Angell argues that every group of people has to share something in the nature of moral order. 'People cannot work together without overt or tacit standards of conduct corresponding to their common values' (Angell, 1958, p. 9).

These shared and tacit standards may be anchored in the collective unconscious. We may even use part of Jung's vocabulary and definition. 'The collective unconscious ... represents a psyche that ... cannot be directly perceived or "represented", in contrast to the perceptible psychic phenomena, and on account of its "irrepresentable" nature I have called it "psychoid"' (Jung, 1968, p. 436).

The unconscious part of this consists in 'everything of which I know, but of which I am not at the moment thinking; everything of which I was once conscious, but have now forgotten; everything perceived by my senses, but not noted by my conscious mind; everything which, involuntarily and without paying attention to it, I feel, think, remember, want, and do; all the future things that are taking shape in me and will sometime come to consciousness: all this is the content of the unconscious' (Jung, 1968, p. 185).

Members of a community would expect that the grammar they are using would be shared by everyone else in the community, so that when they act according to the grammar, they can count upon the other members of the community. We must have this implicit faith in the judgements and actions of our fellow human beings or we would have no community.

'A social organism of any sort whatever, large or small, is what it is because each member proceeds to his own duty with a trust that the other members will simultaneously do theirs' (James quoted in Moser and Nat, 1987, p. 211). In fact it is the tacit belief that others will do their part that will help create the fact that will be desired by all.

To use a grammar is to observe and follow a certain social habit, usage or 'rule'. 'Einer Regel folgen, eine Mitteilung machen, einen Befehl geben, eine Schachpartie spielen sind *Gepflogenheiten* (Gebrauche, Institutionen)' (Wittgenstein quoted in Morscher, 1981, p. 121).

This does not mean that every member of a community has to hold the same values, one of the more or less tacitly held values may after all be tolerance towards others, or magnanimity. It means though that there are social limits to the values that can be held by individuals and groups if the community in question has to survive as a community. This is a problem of coherence.

*Generativity*  We do not have to learn a preconceived set of sentences by heart; we form our own sentences. As long they are formed according to more or less tacit demands of the grammar, they may be regarded as instances of well formed sentences. We can form sentences never heard before, and still they would be recognized as applications of the grammar. In a way it may be like playing according to well-understood general rules of a game. They define the game, but they do not define the individual actions. We are not forced to learn a fixed set of sentences by heart. This shows the general generativity of a linguistic grammar. A generative grammar is thus a set of explicit and tacit rules that can be used to create new sentences, which would be regarded as well formed and grammatical in a given language. A generative grammar will not allow the generation of sentences that are ungrammatical, meaning that they would be regarded as ill formed in a given language.[5]

Might not the social grammar allow a similar generativity? In the sense that the ineffable norms and feelings of the deeper layers of this grammar will allow many different concrete moral judgements to be generated, all in some way compatible with the shared, but ineffable grammar. As long it is recognized that our judgements and actions conform to the tacitly shared social grammar, there is space for individual conceptions of the more concrete expressions of morality and ethics.

An attempt to describe, say in a set of detailed written rules, all permissible ethical judgements, would limit this possibility and at the same time move responsibility away from the individual. This may indicate that the space and possibility for individual responsibility depend on the generativity of the shared, but ineffable, social grammar.

The ineffability of the grammar means that it cannot be changed at will, subjectively. It is way beyond our reach, we can only listen to it. This may also be important for individual responsibility. We cannot easily avoid tell-tale signs of the work of the somatic markers. If we could, then our judgements might become arbitrary. As Jung once said: 'The conscious mind allows itself to be trained like a parrot, but the unconscious does not – which is why St. Augustine thanked God for not making him responsible for his dreams. The unconscious is an autonomous psychic entity; any efforts to drill it are only apparently successful, and moreover harmful to consciousness. It is and remains beyond the reach of subjective arbitrary control, a realm where nature and her secrets can be neither improved upon nor perverted, where we can listen, but may not meddle' (Jung, 1970, p. 51).

Still we want to emphasize that 'listening' does not mean that our judgements and actions would just be involuntary expressions of the collective unconscious, the deep inaccessible layers. Grammar does not determine specific judgements and actions.

We see ourselves neither as unreasoning expressions of a hidden and incomprehensible grammar buried deep inside us, nor as Capekian Robots just carrying out a program encoded in explicit rules belonging to the upper layers. We are reasoning individuals, or reflective practitioners in Schön's sense.

In our reasoning process we rely on a grammar that neither determines the outcome of our reasoning, nor 'allows' arbitrary or subjective outcomes. We may use the arguments of Deacon: 'Ideologies, religions, and just good explanations or stories thus exert a sort of inferential compulsion on us that is hard to resist because of their mutually reinforcing deductive and inductive links. Our end-directed behaviors are in this way often derived from such "compulsions" as are implicit in the form that underlies the flow of inferences' (Deacon, 1997, p. 435).[6]

## '*GROßVATER'S ZOPF*'

Writing about our virtues, Nietzsche looks to their origin. He asks both 'What does it mean to believe in one's virtue?', and whether this 'nicht im Grunde dasselbe, was man ehedem sein "gutes Gewissen" nannte, jener ehrwürdige langschwänzige Begriffs-Zopf, den sich unsre Großväter hinter ihren Kopf, oft genug auch hinter ihren Verstand hängten?' (Nietzsche, 1886, p. 110).

He believes that we, the last Europeans, still carry our grandfather's pigtail of virtue on and especially in our heads. Although he talked about the back of our heads one may wonder whether Nietzsche already had a notion about the importance of amygdala for emotions that we cannot explain and now perhaps even virtues.

We are looking for the origin of the social grammar. Perhaps this pigtail of history shows where the social grammar originates. In the history of man's development, in the evolution of man and of community. Parts of our social grammar may be remnants of values that evolved in periods of evolution of communities that we have either no evidence, or only very circumstantial evidence of.

Our purpose is to bring forward the theses that the deepest and most durable elements of our social grammar may very well be a result of this evolution, all of it. If our theses are right, then some of our fundamental notions of and feelings about morality will have origins hidden so deep in our evolution that we can only transmit them from generation to generation as habits and inclinations we are not even aware of, and if we are, then we cannot give any explanation for them. We may of course guess as to their possible purpose and function, but in fact it might be even more difficult to explain why we should have certain moral dispositions, than it would be to explain why we have the morphology that most human beings have today. Why this relation among the different parts of our bodies and not another? Why this number of fingers, the placement of the eyes, the larynx, and so on. Such questions might even sound curious, but similar questions with regard to our basic moral dispositions would sound even more curious.

Might we not be fairly confident though in assuming that although many other configurations might have been possible, the configuration that we have is consistent and important to a degree that we may only begin to comprehend. It is not arbitrary, there is a 'reason', but we may never be able to comprehend it. The 'reason' has been produced and reproduced during man's evolution, transmitted from generation to generation, leaving an echo in somatic markers, deeply held convictions and in cultural habits.

This reason is not transcendental, is not given *a priori*, it does not represent a decree from God. It is located on the earth, in man. This reason has been produced by man, but we can have no recollection of the process; we may only carry the faint imprints in our feelings and reactions. This does not mean that this reason is innate, it may be imprinted in other ways, and if it is hardwired in any sense it might be in the neural network of our brain. This reason acts as the field of an invisible magnet on iron particles, orienting us into patterns or into grooves that we cannot comprehend.

These patterns, grooves or imprints are ineffable and tacit, in the same way that a part of our knowledge is. We only experience the feelings, not the reasons, not the explanations. These imprints may be so much part of what it means to be human that we cannot really think about them or question them, they make themselves felt in the way they influence our thoughts. The elements of the grammar we become aware of may likewise be regarded as 'natural' intuitions. Natural in the sense that we suppose they are shared by other human beings.

Richardson's view is that 'Tacit exemplars resist rational deliberation because it is difficult to become fully aware of them. Their influence in giving life to terms we use and the views we hold is so pervasive that it is very difficult to bring them at all to consciousness, let alone to obtain a critical perspective on them' (Richardson, 1994, p. 292).

'Very difficult' would certainly be an understatement; in our view it would be impossible at least when we talk about the most deeply seated 'natural' intuitions. In a way they define natural, and there is not much we can do about that, at least as long we have not met extraterrestrials, with different imprints. In which case we may realize that our world is not the only natural.

It is in these 'natural' imprints we locate the roots of those intuitions that philosophers have grappled with and attempted to anchor in first principles; attempts that we have to regard as rather futile in the light of our theses.

If the imprints are not a result of transcendental *a priori* categories, or God-given commands, or innate dispositions, they have to stem from somewhere else. The imprints we are talking about seem to exist independent of any specific individual; after all we have been talking about the collective unconscious. Where do they originate, what has kept them alive during the evolution, if they are not located in the genes?

The answer is of course '*Großvater's Zopf*', the values instilled and transmitted from grandfathers to fathers, to sons and to their sons. The values instilled by a community of grandfathers – and grandmothers.

This would mean that repetition of rituals, the meaning of which might elude us, would by the sheer repetition lead an individual subject to these repetitions to somehow distil some of the general aspects of the social grammar, without being able to explain what they are. This represents once again a parallel to the first acquisition of linguistic grammar. In a sense it can be said that we learn the grammar by repetitive use of a language based upon this grammar. We seem able to generalize from this repetition, but we may never have understood explicitly any of the fundamental rules underlying our use of the language. We do not learn the grammar directly by being taught social grammatical rules, we learn it indirectly from people who use it, by imitating, by approval, and disapproval, expectations, praise, and so on.

The tacit layers show up in social habits, habitus, rituals, and so on that are all part of *Großvater's Zopf*, or the imprints left in us of the evolution of man and community.

## NOTES

1. A more extensive discussion of these ideas can be found in some of my recent working papers (Petersen 1999a, 1999b, 1999c).
2. Rules are here understood to mean ethical norms that have an explicit expression in laws, guidelines, and so on, while norms following Richardson, are principles – with propositional content which has at least potential normative significance.
3. Somehow the intuitions that could be derived would seem to fit England at that time. This is also the view of Singer in his *The Expanding Circle – Ethics and Sociobiology* (Singer, 1983, p. 30).
4. See also Richardson's attempts to find a decentralized alternative to Sidgwick's first principles (Richardson, 1994).
5. Discussions on generativity in general can be found in Hofstadter's *Gödel, Escher, Bach: An Eternal Golden Braid* (Hofstadter, 1987). It is this general generativity we are using, not the special generativity that for instance Chomsky has been advocating.
6. Actually this leads Deacon to conclude that 'thinking in symbols is a means whereby formal causes can determine final causes. The abstract nature of this source makes for a top-down causality, even if implemented on a bottom-up biological machine' (Deacon, 1997, p. 435).

## REFERENCES

Angell, R.C. (1958), *Free Society and Moral Crisis*, Ann Arbor: University of Michigan Press.

Black, M. (1990), *Perplexities – Rational Choice, the Prisoners Dilemma, Metaphor, Poetic Ambiguity, and other Puzzles*, Ithaca, NY: Cornell University Press.

Brandt, R.B. (1997), *Facts, Values, and Morality*, Cambridge: Cambridge University Press.
Cawell, S. (1976), *Must We Mean What We Say?*, Cambridge: Cambridge University Press.
Cosmides, L., and Toby, J. (1994), Beyond Intuition and Instinct Blindness: Toward an Evolutionary Rigorous Cognitive Science, *Cognition*, (**50**), 41–77.
Damasio, A.R. (1994), *Descartes' Error*. New York: Grosset/Putnam.
Deacon, T.W. (1997), *The Symbolic Species – The Co-evolution of Language and the Brain*, New York: W.W. Norton.
Haller, R. (1981), *Sprache und Erkenntnis als Soziale Tatsache*, Wien: Hölder-Pichler-Tempsky.
Hofstadter, D.R. (1987). *Gödel, Escher, Bach: An Eternal Golden Braid*, Harmondsworth: Penguin.
Hume, D. (1740), *A Treatise of Human Nature* (1969 ed.), Harmondsworth: Penguin.
Jung, C.G. (1968), *Psychology and Alchemy, Collected Works 12*, Princeton, NJ: Princeton University Press.
Jung, C.G. (1970), *The Structure and Dynamics of the Psyche, Collected Works 8*, Princeton, NJ: Princeton University Press.
Kant, I. (1785), *Grundlegung zur Metaphysik der Sitten* (1962 ed.), Hamburg: Verlag von Felix Meiner.
Kleist, H. v. (1808),. *Michael Kohlhaas – Aus einer alten Chronik* (1976 ed.), Weimar: Greifenverlag zu Rudolstadt.
McIntyre, A.C. (1981), *After Virtue: A Study in Moral Theory*, Notre Dame, IN: University of Notre Dame Press.
Mill, J.S. (1859–1865), *Utilitarianism, On Liberty, and Considerations on Representative Government* (1977 ed.), London: J.M. Dent & Sons.
Morscher, E. (1981), Inwiefern ist die Sprache ein Soziales Phänomen? In R. Haller (ed.), *Sprache und Erkenntnis als Soziale Tatsache*, Wien: Hölder-Pichler-Tempsky.
Moser, P.K., and Nat, A.v.d. (1987), *Human Knowledge: Classical and Contemporary Approaches*, New York: Oxford University Press.
Nietzsche, F. (1886), *Jenseits von Gut und Böse* (1989 ed.), Berlin: Der Goldmann Verlag.
Petersen, V.C. (1998), *Tacit Ethics – Creation and Change*, Aarhus: CREDO working paper, Department of Organization and Management, Aarhus School of Business.
Petersen, V.C. (1999a), *Judging with Our Guts – The Importance of an Ineffable, Social Grammar*, Aarhus: CREDO working paper, Department of Organization and Management, Aarhus School of Business.
Petersen, V.C. (1999b), *Thinking with Our Hands – The Importance of Tacit, Non-Algorithmic Knowledge*, Aarhus: CREDO working paper, Department of Organisation and Management, Aarhus School of Business.
Petersen, V.C. (1999c), *Weaving the Moral Fabric – Emergence, Transmission and Change of Social Values and Norms*, Aarhus: CREDO working paper, Department of Organisation and Management, Aarhus School of Business.
Richardson, H.S. (1994), *Practical Reasoning about Final Ends*, Cambridge: Cambridge University Press.
Russell, J.A. and Fernández-Dols, J.-M. (1997), *The Psychology of Facial Expression*, Cambridge: Cambridge University Press.
Sidgwick, H. (1907), *The Methods of Ethics* (1962 ed.), London: Methuen.
Singer, P. (1983). *The Expanding Circle – Ethics and Sociobiology*, Oxford: Oxford University Press.

# 20. Ethical competence training for individuals and organizations

## Iordanis Kavathatzopoulos

Competence to handle ethical problems in a satisfying way is a very important aspect of business leadership. Unfortunately in concrete situations business people, just as other people, are often lacking knowledge about what is the right thing to do; they neither know how to acquire that knowledge. Consequently one of the main aims of business ethics research and practice should be to find ways to evaluate and promote ethical competence.

There is great pressure today to find the right answers and actions in business. Ethical problems may have very serious consequences. They can inhibit and obstruct normal business activities. On the other hand, it is beyond any doubt that anticipation of ethical problem situations and their proper solution can facilitate the attainment of business goals.

We live in a world that changes rapidly. Society is open, global, more unpredictable and complex than before. Old moral authorities, leadership styles, codes and guidelines are not very useful. General principles are of course still valid and accepted, but their application under the conditions of today has changed radically. We cannot find easily any more the right answers to concrete real life moral problems in old ways, habits, conventions and traditions.

Organizations, groups and societies abandon the hierarchical structure and try to be more decentralized and flexible in order to adapt to the new conditions. They delegate responsibilities to lower echelons often without the corresponding power. Those changes, accompanied by an intense public and media interest about every action or inaction, forces people and organizations to seek desperately ethical guiding. However, acquisition of functioning moral knowledge and creation of working ethical rules demands stable conditions, and this is not what we have today. Furthermore, it is often very difficult to decide what the right principle would be in a certain ethical situation because of the nature of moral knowledge, which is very controversial with a lot of emotions involved.

Therefore, what we are looking for in business ethics research (see for example Stark, 1993), or what we should be looking for, are answers to these questions: How do we know that an ethics situation is present or imminent? How can we anticipate it? How can the level of ethical awareness be raised and decision-makers made more alert to ethical issues? How can we make a decision that resolves an ethical conflict satisfactorily? Which method is best for handling problems of ethics? How can we make a decision and live with it? How can ethical rules be constructed that can help us in your professions? How can an organization formulate and continuously develop its ethical rules? How can we explain our decision and convince others that it was the right one?

It is important, however, to be clear about how we attempt to seek the answers. The common-sense picture of ethics education is that knowledge about what is right is drawn from philosophical theories and subsequently transmitted to decision-makers through different training programmes. Indeed, this idea is very strong and pervasive, but, still, it is easy to understand the ineffectiveness of this approach (Jackson, 1994). Another method which does not have a positive impact on ethics education (Weber, 1990, see also Anderson, 1997), but which is generally practised, is the training of philosophical argumentation about abstract and hypothetical moral issues. However, if we really want to help decision-makers to make the right decisions we have to find other ways. For it would be impossible to transfer moral principles to other people, particularly to people in responsible positions, and convince them what is right and what is wrong, according to the opinion of the educator. Responsible people already have a clear picture of what is generally right or wrong. They do not need someone else to tell them.

On the other hand, it is not so easy to handle moral problems in real life. Decision-makers may not always be able to foresee the appearance of ethical dilemmas and conflicts. They may also have great difficulty solving such problems and formulating ethical rules. They may not know how to explain, argue, and defend their decisions convincingly. It is in these areas that we can help them. Any attempt to transmit moral principles is deemed to fail. It is not fruitful. If an educator, despite that, tries to tell decision-makers in business what is right, they are not going to listen. One strong reason is that if they accept an educator's authority in this matter, they feel a corresponding loss of their own responsibility, and they do not want this.

Secondly, even if they internalize the normative content transmitted to them, and we assume that this is the right one, or even if they become skilful in discussing abstract moral-philosophical issues, still it is reality they are going to confront and to which the principles must be applied. And in reality they are still going to meet the same problem of how to anticipate and solve concrete dilemmas. Knowing what is generally right is not the problem, but rather how to handle a real life situation where any solution is both right and wrong and where a real choice has to be made.

Therefore, one of the things educators can do is to help decision-makers in heightening ethical awareness so they can be better prepared. This implies helping decision-makers to see when and where an ethical issue may arise. Educators can point to the fact that public, customers, employees, and so on, usually have certain opinions and moral feelings about different issues that affect them. Educators can also inform decision-makers about what issues are important for various groups or individuals.

By doing this, educators do not transmit moral principles. Rather, they are highlighting the effect certain actions and decisions have on values and interests involved in any concrete situation. Yet, this is of great significance since decision-makers become more aware of, and more informed about the ethical aspects of their decisions. It is then easier to anticipate ethical conflicts. This capacity provides better preparation to deal with such issues and to make better decisions.

Anticipation of ethical issues is, however, not enough for optimal decisions. It is also necessary to know how to cope with ethical conflicts. Indeed, knowing how to handle ethical issues makes anticipation much easier. Anticipation of ethical issues, construction and development of ethical principles and guidelines together with other people in an organization, and the ability to argue convincingly for a decision that has been made are closely related to the way a decision-maker handles ethical issues. Furthermore people need the confidence to handle and implement their decisions (see Table 20.1). Ethical competence is very significant in this area where the problems used to be very controversial and often involve strong emotions.

Ethical competence cannot be achieved without the use of an effective method. We know that people have the capability to reason and act very successfully in solving problems they confront in their lives. But for different reasons, for example conservation of energy, fixation to previously functional problem solving methods, avoidance of responsibility, emotions and motivation, authority dependence, and so on, people do not use this ability (Eysenck

*Table 20.1    The five components of ethical competence* (Kavathatzopoulos, 2000)

| Ethical competence |
| --- |
| High ethical awareness |
| Individual skills to handle ethical issues |
| Organizational processes to handle ethical issues and for continuous development of ethical rules |
| Argumentation skills to explain and motivate |
| Confidence in own skills and emotional strength |

and Keane, 1995). This happens very often when people try to solve technical problems. In confronting moral problems, however, these obstructions to rational handling grow stronger. Emotions are much stronger, avoidance of responsibility is more tempting, and fixation to old solutions is more reassuring.

Therefore, what seems to be the most significant issue in business ethics education is to change focus from moral content to non-normative psychological processes. That means to find ways to make people use better skills when they have to, for example when old moral knowledge is not working. This ability, that is critical thinking, is at the core of Western civilization and has always been at the focus of Western philosophy, science, and religion. So there is nothing strange about this. It is almost trivial. But, the study of this phenomenon, its scientific description, and especially its application in assessment and education, are surprisingly much more difficult (see for example Holt et al., 1997/1998; Vitell and Ho, 1997).

Nevertheless, the ability to handle ethical issues in a functional way can be described, assessed and trained. A lot of research has been done to study how people reason about and solve ethical problems, and how the different methods they adopt for that purpose can help or hinder them in reaching the solutions and the goals they strive for. For example, we know now that, faced with an ethical problem, people often confuse their own moral goals, values, feelings and emotions, and those of others, with the decision-making and problem-solving strategies adopted in order to reach these same goals. Usually, they do not clearly see the context of the problem and it is difficult for them to analyse ethical problems critically. In psychological theory (Piaget, 1932) this is described as the moral phase of heteronomy, which means that people do not use functional problem-solving strategies, in contrast to autonomy which is systematic, independent and critical thinking.

It is possible then to describe people's different ways of solving ethical problems, and train them in using the better ways. Such description and training do not follow the normative dimension of moral right and wrong or the discovery and adoption process of a certain principle (such as the early work of Kohlberg, 1981, 1984 or the work of Gilligan, 1982; Brown, Tappan and Gilligan, 1995). Assessment methods and education programmes based on the psychological theory of autonomy are focused on the functional value of ethical problem-solving strategies.

## ASSESSING ETHICAL COMPETENCE IN BUSINESS

The different ways people handle ethical problems are described by means of an assessment method based on this view (Kavathatzopoulos, 1993, 1994a;

Kavathatzopoulos and Rigas, 1998). This consists of a questionnaire, Ethical Autonomy Questionnaire-Working Life and Business (EAQ-WLB), containing business ethics dilemmas constructed so as to be very close to real and common ethical problems in business.

Business people who answer the questionnaire are instructed to accept the dilemmas as their own and try to identify themselves with the main actor in the dilemma. Then, four alternatives are presented to them concerning what to consider in making a decision. These alternatives represent different ways of thinking according to the heteronomy–autonomy dimension. Two alternatives represent an uncritical, automatic, reflexive, emotional, authoritarian way of thinking. The other two imply starting the process of critical examination of the concrete dilemma context, that is reflection, suspension of judgement, generation and weighing of alternatives, consideration of important relationships, and so on. There are two alternatives in every group in order to make the subject's choice independent of his or her preferred solution to the dilemma, that is, to bribe or not, as in the following dilemma sample:

> You are CEO of a company that has a good chance to obtain a big order from a foreign country. This order is vely important for your company since you are going to be able to pay for the further development of your products. The problem is that you have to pay bribes to politicians in that country. This is not only usual but also necessary in such countries. Besides, the bribes are going to be paid as consulting fees so that everything is done according to the law.
>
> Which of the following alternatives are, in your opinion, the most and second most important for your decision? (Mark with 1 and 2, respectively.)

> The profit is very important for the company.
> Bribes imply help to corrupted politicians.
> A bribe scandal would cost too much.
> Bribes are accepted in that country.

EAQ-WLB contains six such items and has been tested on 1234 decision-makers in different business organizations and organization levels. The reliability coefficients of EAQ-WLB were satisfying. Cronbach's alpha coefficient was .61, which indicates that the scale has sufficient homogeneity, and the stability coefficient was .72. A confirmatory factor analysis has also shown that EAQ-WLB measures autonomy as a way to cope with ethical problems (Kavathatzopoulos, 2000).

The results have also shown that decision-makers on higher levels of organizations score higher than employees on lower levels (see Figure 20.1). This means that people in higher positions are more autonomous in handling ethical issues and conflicts compared to people in lower positions. People in higher positions use a more functional method to anticipate ethical issues, to

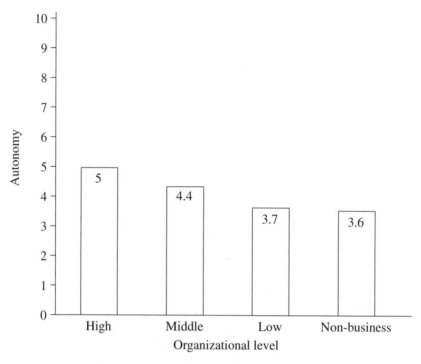

*Figure 20.1   People on higher business organizational levels score higher on
autonomy and business people score higher than non-business
people* (Kavathatzopoulos, 2000)

solve ethical problems and to argue for their decisions. Business people are,
however, much better at this compared to people with no business experience.

Despite its limitations, common to all paper and pen questionnaires, the
standardization of EAQ-WLB allows us to use it for different purposes: for
example, evaluation of training programmes, mapping of ethical skill needs,
as well as for recruitment and selection. The strength of this test is that it is
free of normative aspects and, therefore, applicable and acceptable in many
different business organizations.

## TRAINING FOR ETHICAL COMPETENCE

As we have seen previously, the needs of business decision-makers regarding
ethics include the ability to anticipate ethical issues, the ability to handle moral
problems and formulate ethical rules at individual and organizational levels,
the ability to explain, and the confidence to handle ethical issues and to

implement decisions made (see Table 20.1). Consequently the goal of an education programme in business ethics is to promote the use of a more functional method in handling all these ethical issues.

The training programme suggested is a two-day workshop with a follow-up at least a month later (see Table 20.2). It focuses on the use of autonomy method in moral problem solving. The training of this skill renders the participants aware of ethical conflicts. They learn an optimal way to copy with such conflicts and to reach their moral goals. Together with other persons in the same organization they acquire a method to discuss ethical issues and to formulate, futher develop and continuously revise and adapt their ethics codex.

*Table 20.2   Focus and structure of education for ethical competence* (Kavathatzopoulos, 2000)

| Training programme | |
|---|---|
| Focus | Structure |
| • Real problems | • Two-day workshop |
| • Psychological processes/autonomy | • Small groups |
| • Associated values | • Follow-up |
| • Respect | • Evaluation |

Workshop participants work together in small groups with real problems from their professional life, which they experience as significant and about which they are deeply concerned. Adoption of real ethical problems in the training programme is very important for learning to use autonomy. Research on this issue has clearly shown that training on hypothetical problems and general discussions about moral principles do not result in the application in professional life of what has been learned in training (Weber, 1990; Adams, Harris and Carley, 1998). In this case, working with real issues enables participants to feel immediately the value of autonomy skill by applying it directly on serious problems they know are hard to deal with. Feeling and seeing clearly the worth of what is offered by the training programme are the most important factors for learning the skill and applying it in reality (see also LeChair and Ferell, 2000). Working with real problems is one of the two bases of the training programme.

The other basis of the programme is participants' own moral values. No transmission whatsoever of moral principles is attempted. On the contrary, during training participants learn how to make their own moral goals clear and how to use the autonomy method to reach those goals. Their personal values and duties, as well as the goals of their organization are respected. Satisfaction of personal moral feelings, facilitating duties, and attainment of moral goals are the criteria for the evaluation of the training programme and, of course, learning and applying autonomy. Even in the case of constructing an ethics codex the aim is to make personal and organizational principles clear and concrete in everyday activities, and not just to make a list of what is generally and abstractly right and wrong.

The two-day training programme provides participants with a method, that is a cognitive tool, to use in solving ethical conflicts. The focus, therefore, is not on normative aspects, or on moral philosophical argumentation, or on general moral discussion, but on psychological processes, that is, the individual's – and the group's – way of reasoning, deciding and acting when confronted with real life moral problems (Piaget, 1932; Kohlberg, 1985; Higgins, 1995). Training improves decision-makers' ability to copy with such conflicts, personal as well as situational, and to solve these problems in an optimal way. By using autonomy in group discussions it is also easier to construct suitable ethical principles for the profession or the organization. The whole organization learns how to handle ethical issues effectively.

Workshop participants are trained to use the autonomy method, which implies analysis of concrete situations and adoption of critical reasoning in order to find optimal solutions. The autonomous critical method in decision making and solving business ethics problems means that decision-makers focus their attention on the concrete problem: they identify it, they make it explicit, and they formulate it in order to be able to work with it. They define their own position, duties, commitments, feelings, and values. They also take into consideration the interests, needs and values of all other relevant parties. They generate alternative solutions to the problem, they weigh them against all values involved, and at the end, as a result of this process, they make a decision and choose a course of action. Reflection upon decisions made and evaluation of actual consequences have to follow.

What participants learn to do is to analyse systematically own real moral problems. By doing this they become aware of all alternatives and the effect each of them has on all values and interests involved in the concrete moral problem situation. Thus they are fully informed before they make a decision, knowing as long as it is possible the implications of a decision. However, such knowledge is difficult to produce and hard to have because one is fully aware of his or her own responsibility. It is easy then to understand why people mostly prefer heteronomy to autonomy. Nevertheless training promotes higher confidence in own ability to cope with moral problems and makes it easier to take responsibility. Furthermore, explanation of decisions made is facilitated since one has better knowledge of all positions involved in the situation.

Decision-makers from private corporations and public sector organizations in Sweden have been trained to use this method. The results are very positive (see Figure 20.2). By responding to different versions of the Ethical Autonomy Questionnaire, the participants showed that they had acquired and used autonomy in their real professional life as an effect of the training, a gain that was also stable over time (Kavathatzopoulos, 1994a, 1994b, 2000).

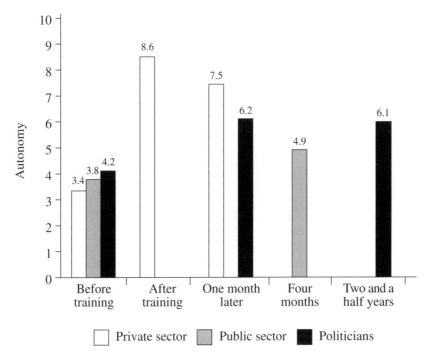

*Figure 20.2  Training promotes the acquisition of autonomy in different professions* (Kavathatzopoulos, 2000)

In addition to this assessment and in order to balance results by EAQ-WLB, participants received a special questionnaire where they reported their own experience of the effect of training on their ethical competence (see Figure 20.3). They reported that after training they had higher ethical awareness, it was easier for them to handle ethical problems, they were more effective in discussing ethical issues, and felt more confident. On the other hand, many of them were not satisfied with the way their organizations functioned regarding ethical issues. That depended on the orientation of the present education programme, which was focused on the training of individual and small group

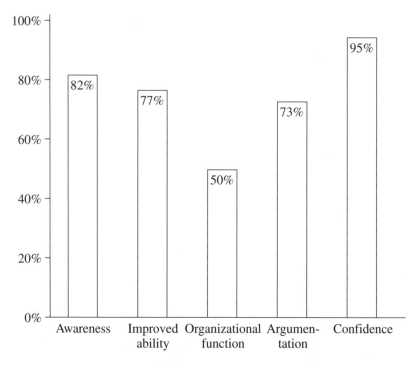

*Figure 20.3 Participants experience of the positive effect of training on ethical awareness, own skill to solve ethical problems, organizational function, argumentation skills, and ethical confidence (Kavathatzopoulos, 2000)*

skills. In order to achieve a full-scale effect on ethical competence it is necessary to train all individuals in an organization as well as to carry through proper organizational changes (see for example von Welzien Høivik, 2000).

## REFERENCES

Adams, J.S., Harris, C. and Carley, S.S. (1998), 'Challenges in teaching business ethics: Using role set analysis of early career dilemmas', *Journal of Business Ethics*, **17**, 1325–1335.

Anderson, J. (1997), 'What cognitive science tells us about ethics and the teaching of ethics', *Journal of Business Ethics*, **16**, 279–291.

Brown, L.M., Tappan, M.B. and Gilligan, C. (1995), 'Listening to different voices', in W.M. Kurtines and J.L. Gewirtz (eds), *Moral Development*, Boston: Allyn and Bacon, pp. 311–35.

Eysenck, M.W. and Keane, M.T. (1995), *Cognitive Psychology*, Hove, East Sussex, UK: Erlbaum (UK) Taylor & Francis.

Gilligan, C. (1982), *In a Different Voice: Psychological Theory and Women's Development*, Cambridge: Harvard University Press.

Higgins, A. (1995), 'Educating for justice and community: Lawrence Kohlberg's vision of moral education', in W.M. Kurtines and J.L. Gewirtz (eds), *Moral Development*, Boston: Allyn and Bacon, pp. 49–81.

Holt, D., Heischmidt, K., Hammer Hill, H., Robinson, B. and Wiles, J. (1997/1998), 'When philosophy and business professors talk: Assessment of ethical reasoning in a cross disciplinary business ethics course', *Teaching Business Ethics*, **3**, 253–268.

Jackson, J. (1994), 'Coping with scepticism: About the philosopher's role in teaching ethical business', *Business Ethics: A European Review*, **3**, 171–173.

Kavathatzopoulos, I. (1993), 'Development of a cognitive skill in solving business ethics problems: The effect of instruction', *Journal of Business Ethics*, 12, 379–386.

Kavathatzopoulos, I. (1994a), 'Training professional managers in decision-making about real life business ethics problems: The acquisition of the autonomous problem-solving skill', *Journal of Business Ethics*, **13**, 379–386.

Kavathatzopoulos, I. (1994b), 'Politics and ethics: Training and assessment of decision-making and problem-solving competency', *Uppsala Psychological Reports*, No. 436.

Kavathatzopoulos, I. (2000), *Autonomi och etisk kompetensutveckling: Utbildnings- och utvärderingsverktyg för personer och organisationer* [Autonomy and the development of ethical competence: Education and evaluation tools for individuals and organizations], Uppsala: Arktéon.

Kavathatzopoulos, I. and Rigas, G. (1998), 'A Piagetian scale for the measurement of ethical competence in politics', *Educational and Psychological Measurement*, **58**, 791–803.

Kohlberg, L. (1981), *Essays on Moral Development, Vol. I*: The philosophy of moral development, San Francisco, CA: Harper & Row.

Kohlberg, L. (1984), *Essays on Moral Development, Vol. II*: The psychology of moral development, San Francisco, CA: Harper & Row.

Kohlberg, L. (1985), 'The just community: Approach to moral education in theory and practice', in M. Berkowitz and F. Oser (eds), *Moral Education: Theory and Application*, Hillsdale, NJ: Lawrence Erlbaum Associates, pp. 27–87.

LeChair, D.T. and Ferell, L. (2000), 'Innovation in experiential business ethics training', *Journal of Business Ethics*, **23**, 313–322.

Piaget, J. (1932), *The Moral Judgment of the Child*, London: Routledge & Kegan Paul.

Stark, A. (1993), 'What's the matter with business ethics?', *Harvard Business Review* (May–June), 38–48.

Vitell, S.J. and Ho, F.N. (1997), 'Ethical decision making in marketing: A synthesis and evaluation of scales measuring the various components of decision making in ethical situations', *Journal of Business Ethics*, **16**, 699–717.

Weber, J. (1990), 'Measuring the impact of teaching ethics to future managers: A review, assessment, and recommendations', *Journal of Business Ethics*, **9**, 183–190.

von Welzien Høivik, H. (2000), 'Developing, managing and sustained moral values in organizations: A case study', paper presented at the 2nd World Congress of Business, Economics, and Ethics, Sao Paulo, Brazil.

# 21. The hard questions of international business: some guidelines from the ethics of war*

## Gregory M. Reichberg

### ETHICAL LEADERSHIP, IN WAR AND IN BUSINESS

For Thomas Aquinas and his successors in the just war tradition, decision-making about the use of armed force was viewed as having an inherently ethical dimension. The question faced by political leaders was therefore not only 'how can we succeed in war?', but also, 'under what conditions are we morally justified in using force to achieve our political ends'? Generals, like-wise, were expected to exercise moral leadership on the battlefield, avoiding tactics that would likely result in unnecessarily high casualty rates to their own troops, the needless slaughter of enemy troops, grave harm to non-combatants, and the violation of sworn truces or treaties. War, on this conception, was not deemed a free-for-all whose only measure was victory. On the contrary, war was considered justified only when used as a last resort, for a legitimate moral purpose and when undertaken with due restraint on the battlefield. Military strategy, on this account, was thus taken to be something more than the application of a science or art; it was also thought to involve a form of moral reasoning.[1] Hence the general was expected to cultivate a special moral virtue named *prudentia militaris* (military prudence) (see *Summa Theologiae* IIa IIae, q. 50, a. 4; in Thomas Aquinas, 1981, p. 1402).

To say that strategizing about war is a form of *prudentia*, highlights the inseparability of military planning and morality. The strategist who brackets out ethics entirely, and who thinks solely in terms of efficacy (victory), fails to exercise his craft as he should. 'Too many lives are at stake under too many varying circumstances for anyone to suppose that the connection between military tactics and strategy, on the one side, and morality, on the other, is not a very close one' (Fotion, 1988, p. 15).

In what follows, I show how a similar line of reasoning holds for business strategizing as well. In particular, I emphasize how Chief Executive Officers (CEOs) have a moral obligation to take into account the side-effects of trading in (and with) countries where human rights abuses are widespread, in much the same way as generals must weigh the collateral impact of military action on civilian lives and infrastructure. Decisions taken in each of these two areas can have far-reaching consequences for human lives. It is the mark of a good leader to investigate diligently what those consequences are likely to be.

## SOME HARD QUESTIONS

Much effort has gone into articulating an ethical vocabulary adequate to the complexities of modern business life – a vocabulary that can assist practitioners in sorting out the moral demands that arise within commercial transactions. Especially challenging has been the task of formulating norms that can guide business people in their dealings abroad. Identifying the path of right conduct can be especially vexing in situations where one's national legislation does not apply, where international regulations are few, and where the laws of the host nation are manifestly unjust or, when legitimate, go unobserved by civil authorities and others in positions of power.

What moral stance should a transnational firm adopt in trading with a repressive regime? What responsibility does it bear toward the local population if, for example, the firm knows that the immediate beneficiary of the business transaction is the central government, which may use its profits to purchase arms for a civil war, rather than to benefit the citizenry? Such appears to apply today in Angola, where several transnational oil companies operate. What should firms do when cognizant of the fact that the revenues they help produce for the host government enable it to perpetuate a repressive hold over its citizens, perhaps wasting valuable natural resources and despoiling the environment in the process? Allegations such as these have been levelled against the present government in Burma. Ethical problems have likewise arisen for firms that operate under the special protection of military units. In some cases these units have been implicated in the deaths of demonstrators who, for one reason or another, oppose the continued presence of such firms. This, apparently, has been the case in Colombia and in Nigeria. Does a firm bear responsibility for excesses committed on its behalf by a state-run security apparatus?

In these examples we are confronted with a special category of moral situation, one that goes under the heading of 'complicity'. Unlike bribery, fraud, or insider trading, where direct wrongdoing is at issue, in complicity the transgressions are carried out by one's partners, not by oneself The wrongdoing in question is indirect. Managers responsible for overseeing a firm's Angolan operations may know, with a high level of certainty, that the government uses its share of the oil revenues to finance the civil war. If the firm's management neither intends nor wishes that the revenues be put to this use, but merely ascertains that such is the case, does this count as complicity? The problem takes on special dimensions when the partners in question are in fact government officials, acting in their official capacity. Do corporate managers bear any responsibility whatsoever for the actions of the state partner? By helping the state earn revenues that are subsequently appropriated for a harmful purpose, these managers exercise a causal role in the wrongdoing. In such situations, what should persons and firms that place a high value on moral character do?

In ethics the challenge may reside not so much in figuring out what is right, but in doing the right thing, since occasions do arise when the exigencies of right and wrong seem clearly delineated. In other situations, however, it can be highly problematical even for upright moral agents to determine what should be done. Permissive decisions are often of this kind, especially when they involve calculations of the lesser evil. Should I allow *x* to happen, if preventing it may incur an even greater evil? Should I continue an activity – one unblameworthy in itself – when I can foresee the bad use to which it will be put by someone with whom I am associated?

Reaching ethically sound decisions in such situations requires a skill akin to what Aristotle terms 'phronesis' ('*prudentia*' in the Latin of Thomas Aquinas): a form of moral insight that incorporates reflection on basic moral principles, consideration of the relevant laws (national and international), consultation with informed and interested parties, recollection of similar cases in the past, and diligent study of the facts of the situation. To deliberate well about hard cases, we must take care to raise the most pertinent questions. In business transactions that involve foreign jurisdictions, in settings where fundamental human rights are systematically violated, and where one's business partner is a state entity, several layers of complexity accrue to the normal process of moral questioning. Here formulating the relevant questions presents in itself a special challenge.

## SOME PARALLELS BETWEEN ETHICS IN BUSINESS AND IN ETHICS IN WAR

And now, a perhaps unusual suggestion: in approaching the hard cases of international business, we can learn much from work that has been done on the ethics of war. When is recourse to arms morally justifiable? What moral constraints should apply to military conduct? Over the past two and a half millennia a substantive body of ethical reflection has emerged in response to these two questions. Under the rubric of 'just war' ('*justum bellum*'), this tradition of moral discourse has sought to provide a coherent and developed vocabulary for discussing war in ethical terms, a vocabulary useful for distinguishing between uses of lethal force which are morally acceptable and those which are not. Properly transposed, this just-war vocabulary can also help bring clarity to the hard cases of international business, particularly with regard to conducting business amidst political repression. There are in fact some relevant parallels between business and war:

1. A cloud of moral disapproval hangs over business, just as it does over soldiering. The promotion of consumerism, the institutionalization of greed, mean-spiritedness towards competitors, commerce with regimes that violate human rights, the unmerited wealth of corporate executives, and the destruction of cultural and environmental diversity – these are just a few of the many ills attributed to commerce. In some quarters, business continues to bear the stigma of a disreputable occupation, one that lacks the noble spirit of service to others which attaches to professions like teaching and health care. Similarly, the military profession has long borne the stigma of aggressiveness, and even cruelty.

2. Soldiering and business have often been viewed as standing in need of justification, in order that they may be deemed morally legitimate undertakings. Other professions, by contrast, seem unquestionably good – health care, for example. Engaging in them would require little or no prior justification. Here we may note that the first systematizer of just-war doctrine – the thirteenth-century philosopher-theologian St Thomas Aquinas – opens his treatment of both warfare and business with questions that reflect a presumption against the two occupations. Thus in *Summa Theologiae* IIa IIae, q. 40, within the section entitled 'De bello', the opening line asks 'whether it is always sinful to wage war?' (Thomas Aquinas, 1981: p. 1353). Likewise, when discussing profit (that is obtaining a monetary benefit above cost) in the same work, Aquinas begins by asking 'whether it is ever licit in trading to sell a thing for a higher price than was paid for it?' (IIa IIae, q. 77, a. 4; ibid., p. 1510).

   Taken as a kind of moral act, the use of military force was, in Aquinas's view, neither inherently bad (like theft, fraud, or adultery) nor inherently good (like the search for wisdom, caring for the sick, and so on) but ethically neutral: its goodness or badness would derive from additional criteria. He mentions three such criteria: just cause (resist unwarranted aggression), legitimate authority (not just anyone has the right to declare and wage war, but only specially designated civil authorities) and third, an upright intention (preserve or establish a just peace, not the pursuit of national aggrandizement). If any one of these three conditions be absent, the ensuing use of military force will lack ethical justification and hence will be morally defective. We return to these criteria shortly.

Similarly, Aquinas held that if we consider business for profit as a species of moral action, it is intrinsically neither good nor bad. Taken concretely, however, engagement in profit-seeking will be good or bad, due to additional moral conditions: chiefly the agent's intention (to what end does he or she seek to earn a profit?), on the one hand, and the specific circumstances in which the action is carried out (with whom, for whom, when, where, and so on) on the other. It is worth noting that Aquinas's moral evaluation of profit differs significantly from his treatment of usury (the practice of charging interest on loans). Usury he places in the category of acts bad in kind – a practice that could never be put to a morally good use, no matter how noble the agent's intended goal. In this manner, Aquinas departs from the position of Aristotle, who lumped profit-seeking and usury together in the category of disreputable acts. Aquinas's insight consists in distinguishing the ethics of profit from that of usury. Unlike usury, the pursuit of profit may be deemed justifiable when it is subordinated to the higher end of service to society. Severed from the goal of service, taken as an end wholly sufficient in itself, profit-seeking cannot but be morally bad, a source of injustice within the social fabric, and a cause of spiritual harm to those pursuing such activity. Thus, just as the intention of peace serves to legitimize the use of lethal force, likewise the goal of service to society is the condition *sine qua non* that legitimizes trading for profit.

Even so, Aquinas suggests that both waging war and business, despite their formal moral neutrality, exhibit a propensity to harmful misuse. Business (here understood as trading for profit) awakens the appetite for gain, which, if sought for its own sake, leads ineluctably to avarice and greed. Likewise, participation in war, even when undertaken on behalf of a justified cause, sets in motion a dialectic of violence that all too readily tends to excess. There is a pleasure to be taken in power (and in violence), just as there is in wealth. Each requires the cultivation of restraint.

3.  Both business and soldiering involve, not separate individuals alone, but groups structured according to a channel of authority: armies on the one hand, corporations on the other. In each case, authority 'secures coordinated behavior in a group by subordinating the decisions of the individual to the communicated decisions of others' (Simon, 1976, p. 134). When decisionmaking is hierarchically ordered in this way it invariably conveys a set of moral instructions. The organizational environment can do much to foster or hinder ethical thinking on the part of the group members. Indeed, the rightness of a decision may hinge upon the due observance of role responsibility.

4. Wars and business alike are conducted across national jurisdictions where cultural expectations and laws vary. The just-war tradition has grappled with the problem of cultural diversity; for this reason, its conceptual resources may prove useful within the international business setting as well.

5. In both warfare and business the pressure to engage in wrongdoing can be intense: wrongdoing is frequently justified as being 'part of the game'. Until the enactment of the Geneva Conventions and other such laws of war, atrocities were often accepted with a shrug: 'war is ugly, that's just how it is'. Similarly, vast networks of bribery and other forms of corruption have until recently enjoyed widespread acceptance as undesirable yet normal aspects of business practice. To challenge this sort of 'group-think' requires courage, so maintaining integrity within military and business life will often demand a special sort of moral heroism.

6. Finally, the just-war tradition that issues from Aquinas situates itself as a middle way between the outright condemnation of lethal force (pacifism) and the unrestricted acceptance of it (*realpolitik*); similarly, a business ethic based on the subordination of profit to societal service, constitutes a *via media* between, on the one hand, those who consider the profit motive morally disreputable – Aristotle, Marxist-inspired views, the implicit assumption of many university academics and numerous journalists – and, on the other hand, free-market libertarians such as Ayn Rand and Milton Freidman, for whom the pursuit of profit is naturally conducive to the good and hence requires no justification. According to this second view, it is when restrictions are placed on the pursuit of profit that justification is needed. Ethics is seen as having a merely extrinsic relation to business.

Thus far we have explored parallels between ethics in war and business. There are several additional points of actual convergence, about which a host of ethical questions could be raised. For instance, one form of commerce earns large profits from the sale of weaponry: the arms trade. Similarly, commerce can be used as a weapon of war: embargoes, boycotts, and the like. Inversely, economic assets can be the target of war, as when military strikes are used to destroy the economic basis of an enemy's war-making capacity or to weaken the enemy's resolve. Moreover, wars have on occasion been initiated with the express purpose of promoting or safeguarding a nation's business interests. And finally, on the peace side of the war–peace equation, business relations can play an important role in the resolution (or reduction) of international conflicts. Trade has long been viewed as a vehicle for promoting contact between peoples, and a condition that fosters peace. Only recently, however, has its potential been deliberately harnessed as a tool of conflict resolution and peace-building. Kofi Annan, Secretary General of the United Nations, has been promoting a UN alliance with the private sector. This initiative has provoked lively debate (see Bellamy, 1999).

## DEFINING COMPLICITY

When transnational firms operate under circumstances of political repression they risk becoming a party to the offences of the host regime – a charge that has been levelled against numerous corporations. Such accusations have pointed to offences of two different sorts:

1.  Direct wrongdoing, committed with the tacit or express approval of state authorities, as when a firm (or its subsidiaries) makes use of child or forced labour, maintains unsafe work conditions, or causes widespread environmental damage.
2.  Indirect wrongdoing, as when a firm's operation makes substantial revenues available to a repressive regime, revenues that solidify the regime's hold on power. Or, to mention another example, the presence of well-known foreign firms can lend an air of legitimacy to dictatorial regimes: such regimes will find it useful to publicize foreign investment in their country, as a ploy to win international approval. Complicity is another name for *indirect* wrongdoing. It obtains when one party's action (or inaction) enables another party to carry out some act of deliberate wrongdoing. 'All forms of behavior having the potential to either encourage or influence the perpetrator or help him carry out the offense can form the basis of complicity' (Smith, 1991; p. 33). Providing materials destined for future use in an offence, giving advice to perpetrators, egging them on, or withholding words of disapproval when it is known that this silence will embolden them further, all represent manifestations of complicitous behaviour.

    Agreement or common purpose between perpetrators and accessories is *not* an ingredient essential to complicity. One individual can be complicit in the transgressions of another, without in the least endorsing his immoral or criminal behaviour: it may be enough that cooperation be knowingly given, or that hindering action be deliberately withheld. Laws on criminal complicity reflect this point. '[T]he predominant attitude manifested in modern case law is against assent based liability, favoring instead responsibility based on foresight alone' (Smith, 1991, p. 150). In English law, for example, 'dispensation with any need for accessorial approval of, or stake in, the principal's actions throws the emphasis on the extent of an accessory's foresight; beyond the initial intention to act, it has become the only necessary source of mental culpability' (ibid., p. 194). In other words, one can bear complicity for another's malfeasance even while disapproving of his or her wrongdoing: knowingly providing the perpetrator with assistance can be a sufficient basis for complicity.

Complicity may now be defined as follows:

a.   a form of *derivative* responsibility for wrongdoing;
b.   due to some kind of facilitory action (or inaction);
c.   knowingly given (with foresight);
d.   and that *should* have been withheld.

Thus defined, complicity can be understood as a species of 'double-effect'. The double-effect principle states that from a single course of action two different sets of effects can follow: intended effects, which include both the goal sought and the means chosen for achieving it, and unintended effects. Of the latter, some are foreseeable and others not. Only foreseeable side-effects have moral significance: I can have no control over an event wholly unknown to me, even if it should happen that I am its cause. By contrast, if I know that some harmful event will occur as a result of my actions (or my inaction), I can be held accountable for it: for, had I abstained from carrying out my own directly intended action, I would have prevented the emergence of the negative side-effect. Thus, even if I in no way wished it to come about, I nevertheless can be said to will the negative side-effect indirectly, insofar as I allow or permit it to happen. In the case of complicity, the permitted side-effect is another person's immoral or criminal action. My action (or inaction) makes it possible for the other to carry out his or her misdeeds, hence I am indirectly (derivatively) responsible for his or her transgressions.

In the context of double-effect, however, responsibility should not be automatically equated with culpability: I can have good reason for allowing the malfeasance to occur, if the actions I could take to prevent it would result in an even greater evil. This brings to light a major difference between the two kinds of responsibility, direct and indirect. Calculations of lesser evil are valid with respect to the allowance of misdeeds committed by others. The converse, however, does not hold: there can be no justification for my own direct engagement in wrongdoing, even to prevent a grave evil.

Hence, what double-effect requires in the way of responsibility is that agents deliberate carefully about the likely side-effects of their actions. Culpability arises when agents permit harmful events that they could and should have prevented – either because they failed to exercise due diligence, or because they acted from faulty moral judgement.

## APPLYING THE JUST WAR CRITERIA

Knowingly engaging in actions that indirectly facilitate wrongdoing (either positively, by extending some form of assistance, or, negatively, by inaction, as when one deliberately refrains from preventing the malfeasance), is not of itself wrongful. There can be valid moral reasons which warrant such a course of action. Medical doctors who save the life of a hardened criminal can be said to contribute indirectly to the continuance of his unlawful behaviour, yet they are not themselves criminally or morally liable for his or her future misdeeds. On the other hand, there are times when such cooperation does in fact count as complicity: recent allegations over the role of Swiss banks in processing gold looted by the Nazis point in that direction.

Transnational firms have typically advanced two arguments to justify their involvement with dictatorial regimes: (1) it provides the local population with much-needed jobs; and (2) refusing to do business with such regimes will lack any beneficial effect, since less scrupulous firms will quickly step into the breach. The first argument entirely sidesteps the problem of indirect responsibility for wrongdoing. True, some good may result from the firm's presence in country $x$, but of itself this cannot justify the indirect harm done to the people of that nation. Only if it can be shown that the good in question significantly outweighs the harm would the argument hold water. But to reach this conclusion the firm would first have to conduct a careful study of the likely side-effects of its operation, both good and bad. Merely invoking the supposed good effects is not enough.

The second argument is even less valid, as it overlooks the issue of moral integrity in favour of a crass consequentialism. If it has been determined that a firm's presence in country $x$ indirectly causes significant harm to the local population, a harm not outweighed by a counterbalancing good, then to continue operations there would itself be wrongful. Complicity in malfeasance is in no way lessened by the fact that another firm might be willing to engage in the same behaviour. Any firm that values the integrity of its employees could never countenance such reasoning. Moreover, even if other firms take up the space left vacant, one should not thereby conclude that no good would be accomplished by disengagement: voluntary economic sanctions should not be measured solely by economic effects (see Baldwin, 1985, pp. 61–65). By refusing to cooperate with state-sponsored wrongdoing a firm will signal its moral opprobrium, and this can have a powerful impact in the order of public opinion.

Hardly any attention would be paid to fallacious arguments such as these were it not for the fact that calculations of lesser evil do indeed have ethical relevance when it comes to deliberations about indirect participation in wrongdoing. True, history is littered with abusive appeals to the principle of lesser evil: during the Second World War representatives of the Vichy regime made ample reference to this principle to justify their collaboration with Nazi rule. This alone does not show that the principle is invalid: it does indicate, however, that moral insight – and courage – is needed to apply it rightly.

Deciding when cooperation should be given or withheld is never easy. Where moral reasoning proceeds without the guidance of fixed rules (of the sort provided by law, for instance), it is vitally important to ask the most relevant questions. Let us now try to formulate a set of questions that corporate managers can ask themselves when deliberating about their firm's involvement in indirect wrongdoing. These questions are patterned after the list of criteria laid out within the just-war tradition.

For political leaders, resort to military force is one of several ways of influencing other nations. Its use should always be considered in comparison with other options, which typically include the threat of reprisals, public shaming in the international arena, forming hostile alliances, embargoes, boycotts, tariff increases, and so on. Likewise, corporate leaders can select from among a menu of responses to political repression: withdrawal, threats of withdrawal, public criticism, lobbying one's own government to apply pressure on the regime, constructive engagement, inaction, and so on. The purpose of the just-war criteria is to assist political leaders in considering the moral aspects of recourse to coercive force. In each case we will indicate how these criteria might be applied within the context of international business.

## Competent Authority

The decision to use lethal force is not a matter for private citizens, nor just anyone walking the corridors of power. Only specially designated public officials have the authority to engage the nation on a course of armed conflict. Such decisions should not be made in a moral vacuum: at the very least they should take account of the relevant international laws.

Applied within the business setting, the criterion of competent authority can serve as a reminder that one of the central tasks of the corporate manager, the CEO in particular, is to oversee the social impacts of the enterprise, a task that should be carried out with due attention to national and international law. Peter Drucker puts this nicely: 'Managing the enterprise's social impacts has importance because no organ can survive the body which it serves; and the enterprise is an organ of society and the community' (Drucker, 1974, p. 43). Managers have a responsibility for identifying and anticipating the harmful side-effects of their firm's operations. Attention to these adverse side-effects should be equated not with philanthropy – helping society alleviate ills not of the firm's making – but with an obligation of strict justice.

When negative impacts are the result of an exercise of authority, even if purely incidental and unintended, the authority has a responsibility to take measures to eliminate or mitigate them. This holds true for human rights abuses, which represent a particularly pernicious variety of side-effect. 'Competent authority' tells us that corporate decisions with a bearing on human rights should be made at the highest levels of the corporate hierarchy. Flat management structures are no excuse for ignoring the undesirable consequences of the organization's operations. Delegation of authority to local managers should not be used as a convenient strategy for turning a blind eye to human rights abuses. Firms need to establish definite procedures for handling these sorts of issues. Decisions involving direct investment in countries with widespread human rights violations should be made through the proper channels, and not merely on an *ad hoc* basis.

**Right Intention**

In just-war parlance, this criterion signifies that those waging war should aim at a worthy goal: neither revenge, nor domination, but an equitable concord between nations. Those who make the decision to engage in military action should think hard about what they hope to achieve once victory is achieved, as victory is never sufficient unto itself. The ultimate goal of waging war ought to be the restoration of civic friendship. Have we thought sufficiently about the shape of the peace to come? Are our military efforts likely to bring it about? This criterion makes note of the fact that an agent may have a just cause but nevertheless act from a wrongful intention – for example, the intent to dominate the other party instead of striving to achieve conditions to promote an equitable peace.

Applied within the commercial setting, this criterion focuses attention on the intention that ought to undergird participation in business. Just as victory cannot rightly be taken as the ultimate goal of war, likewise profit cannot be rightly taken as the ultimate goal of business.

We often talk about moral action in terms of restraint, of not doing what is bad. Yet, in adopting the language of restraint, we too easily forget that only the attraction of some good motivates a person to action. I avoid doing this or that out of love of the good that would be harmed were I to perform the wrongful action in question. It is the attainment (or preservation) of some hoped-for good that motivates me. What then is the good for the sake of which right-minded business people avoid doing wrong? Often this is described in terms of narrow self-interest: we might get caught, our reputations might be damaged, thus impairing our ability to maintain and augment our customer base, and so on. Yet, to construe motivation solely this way seems demeaning to business as a practice, as though it were ordered uniquely to the narrow self-interest of its practitioners. We would be loath to describe the purpose of medicine in terms of what's good for the physician. Rather, we define it by reference to the good internal to the activity itself, the restoration of health in the patient. What is business for? What is the goal internal to this practice? Does it aim to bring benefit to its practitioners – or is it ordered outside of this self-referential circle to something else, to the customer, and ultimately to the well-being of the community of which the customer is a member? Can the goal of business, the good positively aspired to, have something to do with love of the community, its well-being: in a word, service to the community? Is there a special nobility in the business profession insofar as it, like the military profession, has an ordination to the good of society, with each practice aiming, in its own way, to promote the common good?

This being said, we should beware of setting social responsibility and profits in opposition, as though what you give to one subtracts from the other. In reality, clever profit-making solutions often represent the optimal solution to social responsibility problems. The mistaken opposition between profit and service is but an application of a broader, more philosophical error: the oft-assumed dichotomy between self-interest and altruism, such that the most moral behaviour must needs be self-sacrificing (see Solomon, 1993; p. 106). Actually, attempts at harmonizing ethics and profits can prove a good strategy – morally speaking – challenging us to ponder how considerations of ethics can help create a more ethically minded work-place and business setting. Fostering an environment of honesty and integrity within a company certainly facilitates both the efficiency and the overall reputation of that company. Furthermore, paying heed to the ethically oriented customer can prove an important way to generate trust and customer loyalty. Here, ethics and (long-term) profits may go hand in hand.

There are times, however, when ethics and profit do not coincide. Perhaps the customer does not care about the moral message; or dishonest methods within an organization seem to generate considerable revenue. In such cases, and especially when matters of human rights and dignity are at stake, responsibility to one's fellow human beings must outweigh profit. We should beware of some contemporary strategies that subordinate ethics to profit: 'act ethically because the customer wants it'. Fine within its order, this never-theless cannot be the chief reason for acting ethically; otherwise, ethics would be held hostage to the vacillating beliefs of the customer.

In soldiering, too, there are times when immorality is highly expedient: the use of rape in ethnic cleansing, for example, can be a very effective way to 'persuade' an ethnic group to flee its home area. Thus it would be implausible to urge ethical behaviour on soldiers merely in the name of practical expediency. True, in war it sometimes happens that expediency speaks in favour of adherence to certain ethical norms. Observance of the Geneva Convention may be motivated by an expectation that the other side will reciprocate. Yet if the motivation to act morally is based solely on a *quid pro quo* of this sort, it will prove wholly inoperative the moment the other side decides to violate the terms of the bargain. Only reference to a higher interest, an interest that transcends the narrow circle of utility, can secure morality its proper due. By 'higher interest' we mean something like the role that integrity plays in classical virtue ethics, wherein happiness is so construed as to include moral uprightness as its main constitutive element.

Like military operations, business dealings are nested within a larger social and political context. In articulating our corporate objectives, have we reflected upon our moral obligation to contribute to the well-being of the local and national communities in which we operate?

**Open Declaration**

Before resorting to force, efforts should be made towards publicly airing one's grievances against the other side. Transposed to the business setting, 'open declaration' signifies that companies wishing to do business in places where human rights are systematically violated should publicly announce their intention beforehand. This will afford all interested parties the opportunity to express their views on the likely impact of the proposed business operation. Since the legitimacy of the foreign regime is in question, corporate decision-makers must take care to listen to opposition leaders, aid organizations, representatives of labour unions, local committees, and others with intimate knowledge of the country's political environment.

**Reasonable Hope of Success**

A nation should not go to war unless it thereby stands a realistic chance of achieving its goals. Similarly, transnational corporations that opt for constructive engagement with repressive regimes should do so only after having diligently investigated whether such action is likely to yield the intended result. The claim that political conditions will improve as a result of the constructive engagement will have moral worth only to the degree that it is backed up by an objective study of the facts of the situation. In business, as in war, good intentions alone are never enough. Have we taken the trouble to conduct a human rights impact assessment on our (proposed) activities in country $x$?

**Discrimination**

Attacks should target only the military capability of the enemy. It is *never* permissible intentionally to kill or maim non-combatants on the other side, even when highly expedient – say, to break down the enemy's morale. Thus, military operations with indiscriminate effects – for example the use of anti-personnel land mines – should be avoided. Likewise, in evaluating the probable impact of business strategies, careful thought must be given to the question: Who will benefit? Who will suffer? Members of the ruling élite or ordinary people? Discrimination should be taken into account when evaluating methods of constructive engagement, as well as when opting for withdrawal.

## Proportionality

The destructive impact of particular military operations must be proportional to the intended benefits. Causing great harm – including significant collateral damage – for the sake of a strategic goal of minor importance is unethical. The principle of double-effect must not be used to eschew responsibility for indirect harm done to non-combatants. Not only should non-combatants never be intentionally harmed (discrimination): they should be shielded, so far as possible, from the harmful side-effects of military action (see Walzer, 1992, pp. 151–159). Even though these side-effects are conditions in spite of which one acts, they must be brought into the moral deliberation over the act in question. In applying the double-effect principle, we must scrutinize what these effects are likely to be, take them into consideration as part of the description of our action, and then weigh them against the state of affairs we intend to bring about. This is not about ends justifying means: the question is whether some unintended effects can be justified because the intended effect of an action is so important to our overall end – peace.

Similarly, in business, we must give hard thought to the connection between the end we deliberately aim at, and the damaging side-effects that arise as a consequence of pursuing that end. Right intention is crucial here. If profit is seen as the self-enclosed end of business, then the adverse social side-effects will be inevitably viewed as an extraneous element in corporate decision-making, or they will be deemed relevant only to the degree that they impact on profits. It is sometimes claimed, for instance, that, because free trade is a good of such magnitude, firms should not be held accountable for the misuse of their products or services by unscrupulous state clients. This is a variant on the argument that 'sellers should not be their buyers' keepers'.

Let us instead apply the principle of proportionality as follows: 'the more serious the likely resulting social harm, the greater the individual's moral responsibility to ensure that assistance is not rendered; further, a certain level of personal and commercial convenience is overborne by the larger social interest of preventing serious criminal behavior' (Smith, 1991; p. 157). Efforts to prevent the violation of fundamental human rights must outweigh profit concerns. The inherent goal of business requires this of its practitioners.

## CONCLUSION

This chapter began with what may have seemed an improbable proposition: that the ethics of war can serve as a paradigm for thinking about the hard issues of international business. I have sought to show that the connection between these two spheres of activity is not merely coincidental. The war analogy has played a prominent role in the training of business managers in recent decades. And historically, the field of corporate strategy is an offshoot of the ancient art of military strategy, which in Greek (*stratêgema*) signified 'the act of a general'. If we can be persuaded that all is not fair in war, perhaps we can more easily admit this of business as well.

## NOTES

* In preparing this chapter I received much valuable input from my colleague Henrik Syse, with whom I have written several articles on points covered in this essay.
1. Proponents of the just-war tradition would accordingly not concede that 'strategy as such is neutral with respect to morality' ('la stratagie en tant que telle échappe à la morale' de Montbrial, 2000, p. 527), as writers on the topic so often assume. This neutrality is certainly not the case for military strategy and, I would add, for business strategy as well. See Fotion (1988), for arguments showing why military planning (tactics and strategy) necessarily falls within the domain of morality.

## REFERENCES

Baldwin, D.A. (1985), *Economic Statecraft*, Princeton: Princeton University Press.
Bellamy, C. (1999), 'Public, Private and Civil Society', statement to the Harvard International Development Conference on 'sharing responsibilities: public, private and civil society', Cambridge, Mass., 16 April 1999. UNICEFF Executive Speeches: www.unicef.org/exspeeches/99esp5.htm
Drucker, P.F. (1974), *Management*, New York: Harper & Row.
Fotion, N. (1988), 'Military Tactics and Strategy: In the Moral Realm', in *Moral Obligation and the Military*, Washington, DC: National Defense University Press, pp. 5–19.
de Montbrial, T. (2000), 'Stratégie' in *Dictionnaire de stratégie*, T. de Montbrial & J. Klein (eds), Paris: PUF, pp. 527–542.
Simon, H.A. (1976), *Administrative Behavior*, New York: The Free Press.
Smith, K.J.M. (1991), *A Modern Treatise on the Law of Criminal Complicity*, Oxford: Clarendon Press.
Solomon, R.C. (1993), *Ethics and Excellence*, Oxford: Oxford University Press.
Thomas Aquinas (1981), *Summa Theologica*, vols 1–5, trans. Fathers of the English Dominican Province, Westminster (Maryland): Christian Classics [written circa 1268, variously referred to *Summa Theologiae* and *Summa Theologica*].
Walzer, M. (1992), *Just and Unjust Wars*, 2nd edn, New York: Basic Books.

# Index